Pro Football and the Proliferation of Protest

Lexington Studies in Political Communication

Series Editor: Robert E. Denton, Jr., Virginia Tech University

This series encourages focused work examining the role and function of communication in the realm of politics including campaigns and elections, media, and political institutions.

Titles in the Series

Political Humor in a Changing Media Landscape: A New Generation of Research, edited by Jody C. Baumgartner and Amy Becker

The Influence of Polls on Television News Coverage of Presidential Campaigns, by Vincent M. Fitzgerald

Political Conversion: Personal Transformation as Strategic Public Communication, by Don Waisanen

The 2016 American Presidential Campaign and the News: Implications for the American Republic and Democracy, edited by Jim A. Kuypers

A Rhetoric of Divisive Partisanship: The 2016 American Presidential Campaign Discourse of Bernie Sanders and Donald Trump, by Colleen Elizabeth Kelley

A Newsman in the Nixon White House: Herbert Klein and the Enduring Conflict Between Journalistic Truth and Presidential Image, by Wafa Unus

Pro Football and the Proliferation of Protest: Anthem Posture in a Divided America, edited by Stephen D. Perry

Pro Football and the Proliferation of Protest

Anthem Posture in a Divided America

Edited by Stephen D. Perry

LEXINGTON BOOKS
Lanham • Boulder • New York • London

Published by Lexington Books
An imprint of The Rowman & Littlefield Publishing Group, Inc.
4501 Forbes Boulevard, Suite 200, Lanham, Maryland 20706
www.rowman.com

6 Tinworth Street, London SE11 5AL

Copyright © 2019 by The Rowman & Littlefield Publishing Group, Inc.

All rights reserved. No part of this book may be reproduced in any form or by any electronic or mechanical means, including information storage and retrieval systems, without written permission from the publisher, except by a reviewer who may quote passages in a review.

British Library Cataloguing in Publication Information Available

Library of Congress Cataloging-in-Publication Data Available

ISBN 978-1-4985-8917-8 (cloth)
ISBN 978-1-4985-8918-5 (electronic)

Contents

Acknowledgments   vii

1   Division and Hermeneutical Ignorance in America: Reasons to Examine the Anthem Kneeling Controversy   1
Stephen D. Perry

2   The More Things Change . . . : A History of National Anthem Protests   15
Varaidzo Nyamandi and Andrew Bolin

3   Government versus Protesters: A Historical Look at How the Media Chooses a Winner   31
Haley Higgs and Dara Phillips

4   America's Greatness Compromised: The "Star-Spangled Banner" as a Symbol of Nationalism, Identity, and Division   45
Pauline A. Andrea and Elizabeth Sheffield-Hayes

5   Influencing America: Sports and Conservative Radio   59
Kelvin King and Eric Frederick

6   Kaepernick Portrayals: A Content Analysis of Six Media Outlets   73
Kimberly Feld, Deborah Sacra, and Steve Butler

7   How Social Media Activists and Their Hashtags Have Encouraged and Informed Their Followers on the Take-a-Knee Movement   85
Nadine Barnett Cosby

8   The Memes of Take-a-Knee: A Case Study of Power Structures in Social Media Use   101
Brooke Dunbar

9   NFL National Anthem Protests: A Cluster Analysis of President Trump's Tweets   115
Kalah Kemp

10   Celebrity Response to Take-a-Knee, Kaepernick, and NFL Protests   129
Candace Moore

11	The Role of Race in the Perceptions of and Response to the Protests *Nadine Barnett Cosby*	145
12	Rights and Respect: How Politicians and Their Followers View Anthem Protests *Michael Rhett and Joshua Weiss*	159
13	Together We Tweet: A Cloud Protest Exploratory Study Examining the Evolution of #TakeAKnee *Jana Duckett and Deborah Sacra*	175
14	A Great American Race: Visual Rhetoric in NASCAR's National Anthem Ceremonies *Christina Bullock*	193
15	Articulating Christianity and Patriotism: Identifying a Hermeneutical Impasse through Emerging Meanings *Brian Mattson and Andrew Phillips*	209
16	Pigskins and Protests: An Examination of the NFL Boycotts in Response to the Take-a-Knee Movement *Megan Westhoff and Jennifer Saint Louis*	225
17	Female Athletes in Media: Participating in the Take-a-Knee Movement *Colleen Kappeler and Nancy Flory*	241
18	Sitting to Take a Stand: Take-a-Knee and Student Protesting *Michelle Tabbanor*	253
19	Solutions to the Fallout: Invitational Rhetoric and Differing Viewpoint Political Conversations *Katie Clarke and Chris Connelly*	269
20	Reflections in Overtime *Stephen D. Perry and Shreya Shukla*	283

Index	291
About the Editor	299
About the Contributors	301

Acknowledgments

Thanks to Nadine Barnett Cosby, whose dissertation proposal gave me the idea for this book. Congratulations on completing the dissertation and thanks for contributing from it for this volume. Special thanks to Kalah Kemp and Shreya Shukla for their help in serving as editorial assistants at various points during the process of creating this edited volume to which both have contributed greatly. Their incredible knowledge and attention to detail have enhanced this work and made the process of editing this volume a joy instead of a drudgery.

Also special thanks to my wife, Kay Lynn Perry, for the sacrifice of time and for listening to my long-winded one-sided discussion about this project on too many occasions. You are a patient and wonderful woman whom I cherish and love.

Dedicated to my wonderful children, Alex, Grace, and Myles, who make me so proud!

ONE

Division and Hermeneutical Ignorance in America

Reasons to Examine the Anthem Kneeling Controversy

Stephen D. Perry

America is a divided country today as much as at any time since the Vietnam War (Hechtman, 2017). A policy proposed by a president or congressperson with a (D) party designation is immediately opposed by those with the (R) designation and vice versa. Even when one side had previously staked out a position, if that position is taken up by the opposing party it suddenly is no longer palatable to the initiating party. These differences are evident in the public sphere and are emphasized by the media's coverage of politicians. When one group starts a social movement, there is another group that opposes it. No one seems to strive toward a goal of a unified American voice emanating from mutually satisfactory resolutions anymore, if they ever did. Instead, there are several Americas divided by everything from race to immigration status to religion. And of course there are political divisions. Recent research shows that over half of Democrats and almost half of Republicans say the other party scares them (Doherty, Kiley, & Jameson, 2016).

How do we alleviate the inclination to heighten division? Division has always been a part of America with the Loyalists opposing the American Revolution in 1776 and the Separatists supporting it. Then there was the Southern States vs. the Northern States starting with ratifying the constitution and going through the Civil War and through the civil rights movement of the 1960s. Today we've had the Black Lives Matter movement, women's marches, gun control protests, #MeToo, and the current

Take-a-Knee conflict. Perhaps the most peaceful of them all is taking a knee during the playing of the national anthem, primarily at American football games. Yet the verbal and mediated rancor it has caused may provide the best place for scholars to step in and review both the rhetorical devices and the articulated issues that each side brings to the table.

Anderson (2017) refers to the early actions of Colin Kaepernick's kneeling for the national anthem and the response to it as an example of a hermeneutical impasse. He notes four types of such impasses, but three revolve around not understanding the complexity or vernacular in one's speech. The fourth deals with prejudices held by all groups that influence their interpretation of the other's meaning in the phrases they utter. It is this type of prejudice that forces a Democrat to find issue with a Republican who utters the same phrase that the Democrat uttered last year or vice versa. The argument is not with the phrase, but it is an underlying suspicion of the other, a suspicion egged on, it seems, by various components of the media.

Prejudice is connotatively negative in society, though prejudice, by some definitions at least, can suggest positive bias. If you love your neighborhood or your state or your alma mater you are prejudiced toward them. I am prejudiced toward my own children, my nieces, and my pet. I would hope that you are just as prejudiced toward your own pet, child, school, or whatever. But prejudice, of course, is more often thought to have negative valence. A definition of prejudice that will serve us well in this book would be that they are judgments, positive or negative, that are resistant to counter-evidence because of held emotional attachments on the part of the subject (Fricker 2009). This definition allows for people's judgments of events, objects, and other people to be classified as a prejudice. Thus, someone's view of the flag, a national anthem, a sport such as football, a team like the 49ers, a uniform like the blue of a police officer or the fatigues of a soldier, or a race involving darker or lighter skin can be the focus of one's prejudice.

Note here that the prejudice of a San Francisco 49ers fan can be favorable toward the person wearing the uniform and against anyone not wearing the uniform. Similarly, an Oakland Raiders fan may oppose anyone wearing a 49ers uniform simply because they come from the city across the bay. Of course, people with darker skin may be prejudiced in favor of anyone with darker skin just like they could be prejudiced against someone with lighter skin or with darker skin still (Blair, Judd, Sadler, & Jenkins, 2002). And the reverse is true for someone with light skin. So, as Anderson (2017) notes, when African Americans say "black lives matter," if this is positive bias toward their own race that phrase doesn't mean that white lives don't matter. When a parent says, "Go Jessie, kick that ball" it doesn't mean that the parent down the row should get offended thinking, "What about Natasha? Why won't you cheer for her to kick the ball?" But similarly, when the second parent hollers out, "Go Natasha" in response to the first parent's cheer, that equalizing of the playing field doesn't get the same hearing when the chant is "all lives matter" or even "blue lives matter," though an occupational designation is certainly on a different scale from race. In each case the unwillingness of one group to hear the other group's chant as a "Go Natasha" or "Go Jessie" moment is what Anderson calls "hermeneutical ignorance" (p. 6). Such ignorance is a willful ignorance when the break is caused by someone's refusal to engage with the other side's concerns.

In this book, several authors will look at the hermeneutics of various sides in the debate over whether athletes and football players should protest during the national anthem at sporting events. The goal is to do the opposite of picking a side. Instead, authors in this volume have been asked to engage with the hearing of voices on both (or perhaps several) sides of the issues involved. In fact, we may call this an attempt to stamp out hermeneutical ignorance by providing a venue through which the reader may engage with each and every sides' concerns, realizing that prejudices exist positively and probably negatively on all sides. In a couple of chapters, the communication content to be observed failed to reveal perspectives on all sides (e.g., analyzing President Trump's tweets), but in such cases the goal is still to provide the reader a sense of a specific segment in society and how it understands and speaks to the issues in question. Perhaps in so doing we will begin the path to healing the division in America, because ultimately a house divided against itself cannot stand (Mark 3: 25; as used by Lincoln, 1858).

THE KNEELING PROTEST

The *New York Times* wrote about Colin Kaepernick's kneeling during a pre-season NFL contest's national anthem in September 2016. Kaepernick had knelt with fellow San Francisco 49er Eric Reid to bring attention to issues of racial injustice and police brutality. He had stated that this did not indicate an anti-American attitude, but that instead he loved America and was fighting to make it better. Many fans clearly sided with him and thanked him for his actions. He took pictures with them and signed autographs freely. However, photos of him wearing socks adorned with pigs in police hats surfaced, raising questions about his actions in the minds of some (Witz, 2016).

Kaepernick continued his kneeling position into the 2017 season even though it violated the NFL's Game Operations Manual which specifically said, "all players must be on the sideline for the National Anthem. During the National Anthem, players on the field and bench area should stand at attention, face the flag, hold helmets in their left hand, and refrain from talking." It goes on to note players can be fined or suspended for violations (Tillison, 2017).

But Kaepernick's protest was allowed to continue by the NFL and he was joined by many others across the league. Though Kaepernick did not retain a roster spot in the 2017 season, perhaps both because of opposition by some fans as well as his lack of stellar productivity, other players continued what he started. As the protests grew at the start of the 2017 season, coaches of the Steelers, Titans, and Seahawks tried to keep their teams in the locker room until after the anthem had played to quell backlash to the protest from fans. Steeler player Alejandro Villanueva, a military veteran, was captured on camera in the entrance to the locker room tunnel with his hand over his heart during the anthem, making him a celebrity with those on the anti-kneeling side (Fowler, 2017).

President Donald Trump weighed in on the practice that had raised increasing controversy starting on September 23, 2017, and continuing for at least a month. His participation carried weight to change the conversation, suggesting that not standing was anti-military and anti-American and leading many to respond for or against him. This took the focus of continued discussion away from the original concern of police brutality and racial injustice. In response to the changing conversation, NFL coaches began to encourage or even insist that players stand since the message that was being delivered was not the one that players said they intended (Madani, 2017). Author Kalah Kemp looks at Trump's tweets—over 30 of them—later in this book. The tweets raised the level of discord even higher with Congresswoman Sheila Jackson Lee kneeling on the floor of the House of Representatives to support Kaepernick's social action stance and to oppose the President for even getting involved in the protest, not to mention the controversial nature of his remarks that she deemed racist (Lang, 2017).

By the Fall of 2018, Kaepernick had inked a marketing deal to be a Nike endorser. The ad campaign featuring him with the slogan, "Believe in something, even if it means sacrificing everything." Demonstrating that strong feelings about the kneeling still persisted into the 2018 season, initial and immediate reaction to the Nike campaign resulted in a 3% decline in value for Nike's stock (Ellefson, 2018; Zail, 2018), though analysts didn't think that was going to affect the company long term (Bary, 2018). Many fans contacted their college alma maters noting their refusal to buy team apparel made by Nike due to the Kaepernick ad (Wolken, 2018). And College of the Ozarks in Missouri announced its intention to drop the use of any apparel with the Nike symbol, as the Christian college emphasized the importance of patriotism for their students and even went so far as to create a mandatory course called "patriotic education and fitness" (Ellefson, 2018).

The NFL passed a new policy in May 2018 requiring players to either stand or remain in the locker room during the anthem. But they delayed implementation of the policy or enforcing penalties early in the season as they engaged in talks with the NFL Players Association concerning the controversy and the league's approach to social justice issues (Darrah, 2018). Thus, a smattering of players continued to kneel, sit, or raise fists in support of the social justice concerns raised by Kaepernick as the season started (Chaitin, 2018) and Trump continued to express his displeasure (Dopp, 2018).

ATHLETE PROTESTS OVER INJUSTICE

Kaepernick's action of kneeling, regardless of the effectiveness of the protest vehicle, follows other types of protests by athletes who were trying to promote social change in society. Tennis great Arthur Ashe refused to play in a championship tennis match in South Africa unless the stands were integrated, while Billie Jean King insisted on playing former male number one Bobby Riggs, whom she beat in a match dubbed the "Battle of the Sexes," to prove that women should be able to earn equal pay on the court (Tignor, 2015). Curt Flood challenged the Major League Baseball reserve clause by filing suit against the league, ending the league's control over players. A group of African American athletes participated in a boycott of representing the United States at the 1968 Olympics, but only one of those—Lew Alcindor, later known as Kareem Abdul-Jabbar—was prominent enough to receive much attention. Internationally, in 1970 fans were encouraged to whistle in protest at dictator Francisco Franco during a soccer match in Spain. As a result, the government filled stadiums in the future with supporters who would enthusiastically applaud Franco (Claret & Subirana, 2015).

More recent protests have included NBA players donning t-shirts with slogans responding to the deaths of black men at the hands of police as well as having a group of St. Louis Rams football players exit the locker room tunnel with their hands up in reference to the claims that Michael Brown's hands were raised and he was saying, "don't shoot" when he was fired upon and killed in Ferguson, Missouri (Gill, 2016; Hall, Marach, & Reynolds, 2017), claims that took on legendary status despite the absence of factual evidence, earning the story four Pinocchios by the *Washington Post* (Lee, 2015). Still, the overarching concern for an inordinate number of deaths by black men is real, not to mention the police who have been gunned down in retaliation.

Scholars have asked whether sports can be unpolitical, claiming that denying athletes the chance to speak out is a political decision in and of itself, even if the choice of speaking on the field or court may be an example of "wrong place, wrong time, wrong means" (Thiel et al., 2016, p. 253). Wasserman (2006) argues that fans cheering and supporting a particular team is a free speech act and that the singing of the national anthem, which began in the 1918 World Series, as well as the playing of "God Bless America" during the seventh inning stretch after the terrorist attacks of September 11, 2001, make the notion of political speech a clearly accepted aspect of sporting events. McGinty (2017) looks at the issue from a legal perspective and concludes that Kaepernick should be applauded for his intent but that the way he chose to protest may violate labor and contract law. He suggests finding another way to protest "that does not create further divide" (p. 77).

The phenomenon of sports figures using the national anthem as an opportunity to protest racial inequality or tension in America became especially prominent in 2017 with various media outlets giving extensive coverage to these acts. Social media fostered collective support and opposition for the idea of taking a knee during the national anthem rather than standing in honor of the U.S. flag. Talk radio outlets spent hours discussing the pros and cons of sports icons choosing to kneel and how the audience should or was likely to respond to such displays that some considered unpatriotic.

The symbolism of taking a knee, facilitated through social media hashtags as #TakeAKnee or #KneelNFL among others, is not the first example of athletes protesting the anthem. Olympians Tommie Smith and John Carlos raised their fists during their gold medal ceremony in 1968 while the American national anthem was being played and were stripped of their medals as a result (as covered by Nyamandi & Bolin in chapter 2). Mahmoud Abdul-Rauf refused to stand for the anthem twenty years ago and was suspended by the NBA for two games (Witz, 2016). Thus, the take a knee movement is a new demonstration of an idea that's been tried before, but it has gained more momentum and more public outcry this time than in the past.

Various subjects in this book were discussed with, suggested by, and assigned to doctoral students who worked under the supervision of the book editor to conduct original research on each of the topics covering a range of questions regarding the anthem kneeling controversy. Studies include looking at the protest (1) historically, (2) based on the media coverage it received, (3) through impact on public behaviors and attitudes, and (4) from racial, religious, gendered, and political identification perspectives.

MEDIA AS A MOBILIZER OF SOCIAL MOVEMENTS

Social movements need symbols to reinforce their goals. Those symbols may take the form of individuals such as how Jesse Owens was used as a symbol against Hitler's claims of Arian race superiority (Milford, 2012). Or other artifacts may be deemed important including social media hashtags (Bennett & Segerberg, 2013). Scholars have tried to assess whether citizen engagement in social movements is enhanced through social media mobilization where activism in that realm might encourage people to rally, to vote, to write letters, to boycott, or any number of other behaviors related to the cause in question. Some think that social media enhance such citizen action, while others think that the social media activism makes people feel like they have already participated, and thus they don't carry their activism further (Vissers, Hooghe, Stolle, & Maheo, 2012).

Social media enable users to form relationships across time and space with selected others with whom them may desire to form and share connections. In some media those connections can be kept private or shared broadly. In other services the posts are more generally visible. This allows users to search for key terms that become synonymous with a cause, subject area, or movement. The use of hashtags allows those key words to be made unique and searchable more easily (Boyd & Ellison, 2007). Because of this, certain social media hashtags have become symbols used by groups who speak out on certain issues. One of those issues is the concern by many that there is unequal treatment of primarily African American males in their interactions with police. The social media symbols have included multiple iterations of hashtags such as #BlackLivesMatter, #BLM, and the versions specific to the current kneeling practice, #TakeAKnee or #KneelNFL (See chapters 7 and 13). Memes have provided other sources of symbols in the anthem kneeling discussion (see chapter 8).

For both the practice of burning the flag and the practice of kneeling, many segments of society object to the continued claim that America is racist. This includes, for example, some members of the military who have fought for the country directly and other citizens who reject the notion that a post-civil-rights era America in which a black man has been elected president can still be stereotyped as limiting the opportunities for blacks. Political talk radio hosts, for example, question how police can be criticized as universally racist any time a black individual is shot, when black on black crime in cities like Chicago is rampant and it's the police who are keeping more such crime at bay (Hannity, 2017; and see chapter 5). But in the realm of sports talk, Kaepernick's concern is supported (chapter 5).

Mainstream media may likewise lean toward support of one side or the other on this issue. The rhetoric employed by various media outlets that cater to predominantly African American, Hispanic, or mainstream audiences can be compared to the search for variations in coverage as Feld, Sacra, and Butler do in chapter 6. Historically, the media's approach to framing protests and protesters has also varied. In order to put this particular controversy in perspective for how those who kneel have been treated in the media, Higgs and Phillips in chapter 3 examine coverage of a few past protests.

THE INPUT OF CHRISTIAN RELIGIOUS SPOKESPEOPLE

Christians have sometimes embraced the movement to "take a knee" for racial injustice including a Columbus Day event on the National Mall in Washington, DC. Thousands agreed to kneel in prayer to repent for past racial injustices and to ask for healing and reconciliation. But added to the concern of youth who are shot in the streets was the concern of babies of any race who had been aborted. Speakers prayed and called on God for forgiveness for that sin, clearly indicating that the relatively few black youth killed by comparison with the number of abortions made only praying for the former and not the latter problematic (Smith, 2017). But Christianity and patriotism have also been linked by many representatives of the Christian faith, such as those at the College of the Ozarks mentioned earlier, leading many to question kneeling (see chapter 15). Of these some have spoken against the kneeling during the anthem, pointing out that it is not the country but the sinful heart of man that is the problem. They have emphasized early American presidents and founding fathers who spoke against the evils of slavery and racism based on scripture, leading toward the eventual eradication of slavery and the vast improvements in the social conditions of the African American (Idleman, 2017).

Others have claimed that making Christianity equal to nationalism by opposing the right of some to take a knee on the grounds that America is Christian is the equivalent of idolizing the country and claim that Christians must acknowledge that the pains of the black or brown skinned brothers and sisters among them are real (Villodas, 2017). But perhaps pro-standing Christians and others can avoid idolatry while still thinking that kneeling and refusing to salute may be akin to spitting in the face of those who fought for improvements. Instead of honoring the idea that the American experiment has provided the way for overturning racism, those who support kneeling either believe that the American experience is not overturning racism quickly enough or can't acknowledge that the experiment may be working. Stand-for-the-anthem supporters would claim that the progress for civil rights shows that the democratic American way should be saluted instead of being bashed. This leaves the perception that those on the kneeling side refuse to appreciate anything short of perfection, a standard that Christians teach is not possible in a fallen world. Such refusal of course again reflects hermeneutical ignorance.

RESPONSES FROM THE PUBLIC

The rancor of the debate has led to efforts to boycott the NFL from both those who are upset at the kneeling and from those upset that Kaepernick failed to obtain a roster spot that supportive fans and his attorney argue is retaliation for his social protest. Copeland (2014) analyzed the use of political consumerism and suggests that changing citizenship norms led some to feel it is their duty to boycott or to buycott, the practice of going out of one's way to support the company that behaves in accordance with one's values. Boycotting is more common among members of marginalized groups, especially when businesses or groups become organized targets (Gardberg & Newburry, 2009). Chapter 16 analyzes the specific motivations for boycotting in this context.

Since this issue has risen within the National Football League, that league may suffer financially while others may be seen as a cultural alternative such as NASCAR. Perhaps those who would reject the NFL brand, at least from those who do so because they believe in patriotically standing for the anthem, would choose to support a sport that revels in patriotic symbolism. Chapter 14 in this book looks at how that sport has chosen to display love of country with little occurring in the way of protest.

Participants in other sports, including female athletes, have joined in the kneeling. Women have played an important role in other social movements (Boler, Macdonald, Nitsou, & Harris, 2014), so U.S. Soccer player Megan Rapinoe got into the act during an international friendly against Thailand. U.S. Soccer as an organization spoke out against her individual action while representing her country, which might make her action slightly more challenging for public acceptance than Kaepernick's (Hays, 2016). Kappeler and Flory, in chapter 17, examine how women have been part of the protest and examine how the media have covered their part in the Take-a-Knee movement.

PROTESTING DURING THE ANTHEM

But why has the anthem become the magnet for protests in the United States in this case? Perhaps there is something in the song itself that merits review. Obviously any national anthem evokes strong feelings from the nation's citizens. National identity is often wrapped up in that symbol regardless of age, race, gender, etc. (Gillboa & Bodner, 2009). Perhaps using "The Star-Spangled Banner" as the nation's anthem falls short of representing the broad spectrum of Americans. The song is about battle though many Americans abhor war. Verses in the song, while interpreted differently by critics, are perceived by some as a reminder, if not as being supportive, of slavery (chapter 4 examines this).

Perhaps a different song that did what Gillboa and Bodner (2009) suggest by providing a more unifying identity would help redirect protests. Certainly other kinds of marches and protests have been seen more broadly as acceptable ways to express opposition to political policies and many times have not received the backlash that anthem protesting has.

Thus, understanding the perceptions of the anthem is attempted in the pages of this book.

CROSSING THE PROVERBIAL AISLE

Whatever side one falls on in this debate, the question is, "Can you hear the other side?" The protest itself was started out of respect for the rights and fair treatment of people of color. The backlash revolves around respect for those who have defended rights under the flag. Do people have the right to have different opinions on this issue? No matter which side people are on, they know some on the other side. Perhaps they have not been able to avoid discussion of this issue when football games are turned on or when reciting the pledge or hearing the anthem in school (see chapter 18). And of course those on different political sides may feel obliged to recite the party (or anti-other party) line when in front of the media or a town hall whether they are politicians (see chapter 12) or celebrities (see chapter 10).

This book peaks with an investigation of what strategies people have used to protect and preserve relationships with others while disagreeing on the anthem kneeling controversy. Invitational rhetoric has been promoted as a tool that emphasizes understanding rather than persuasion. It urges that people enter a dialogue with each other to share perspectives. In so doing, people may at least see the complexity of the issue about which the parties disagree (Bone, Griffin, & Scholz, 2008). Some criticize this theory in that it might serve to silence or calm the impassioned voice of those who believe they are disadvantaged and even challenge the goal of this book—one of seeking unity in an imperfect society (Lozano-Reich & Cloud, 2009). Clark and Connelly examine the methods through which people have preserved relationships, often significant ones, with those who disagree. Similarly, they look at where relationships have failed and compare these findings with an invitational rhetoric approach (see chapter 19).

Ultimately, this book seeks to promote listening to each other. Some communication scholars have investigated the actual police-civilian interactions and have found that lack of communication accommodation contributes to uncertainty, stigmatizing the other, and ultimately altercations (Dixon, Schell, Giles, & Drogos, 2008). This book is likewise concerned with how communication issues may contribute to dissension and partisanship, as well as how communication may be employed to bring some national healing. May you read the findings of these chapters in that spirit.

REFERENCES

Anderson, L. (2017). Hermeneutical Impasses. *Philosophical Topics, 45*(2), 1-19.
Bary, E. (2018, October 3). Nike Stock could be out of catalysts. *Barrons.* Available at https://www.barrons.com/articles/nike-stock-could-be-out-of-catalysts-1538582048?mod=GzkaFOctjg5ZP8jMJQZLXNtccmQ82CEY.
Bennett, L. & Segerberg, A. (2013). *The Logic of Connective Action: Digital Media and thePersonalization of Contentious Politics.* Cambridge: Cambridge University Press.
Blair, I.V., Judd, C.M., Sadler, M.S., & Jenkins, C. (2002). The role of Afrocentric features in person perception: Judging by features and categories. *Journal of Personality and Social Psychology, 83,* 5–25.
Boler, M., Macdonald, A., Nitsou, C., and Harris, A. (2014). Connective labor and social media: Women's roles in the 'leaderless' Occupy movement. *Convergence: The International Journal of Research into New Media Technologies,* 20(4). 438-460. DOI: 10.1177/1354856514541353.
Bone, J. E., Griffin, C. L., & Scholz, T. M. (2008). Beyond Traditional Conceptualizations of Rhetoric: Invitational Rhetoric and a Move Toward Civility. *Western Journal of Communication,72*(4), 434-462. doi:10.1080/10570310802446098.
Boyd, D. M., & Ellison, N. B. (2007). Social Network Sites: Definition, History, and Scholarship. *Journal of Computer-Mediated Communication, 13,* 210-230.
Chaitin, D. (2018, September 11). Marshawn Lynch sits, only two players kneel for anthem in first week of 2018 season. *Washington Examiner Magazine.* Available at https://www.washingtonexaminer.com/news/marshawn-lynch-sits-only-two-players-kneel-for-anthem-in-first-week-of-2018-nfl-season.
Claret, J., & Subirana, J. (2015). 1970, 1925, 2009: Whistling in the stadium as a form of protest. *Journal of Iberian & Latin American Studies, 21*(1), 75-88.
Copeland, L. (2014). Conceptualizing political consumerism: How citizenship norms differentiate boycotting from buycotting. *Political Studies, 62*(S1), 172-186.
Darrah, N. (2018, August 10). NFL preseason sees kneeling, raised fists, during national anthem. *Fox News.* Available at https://www.foxnews.com/us/nfl-preseason-sees-kneeling-raised-fists-during-national-anthem.
Dixon, T. L., Schell, T. L., Giles, H., & Drogos, K. L. (2008). The influence of race in police-civilian interactions: A content analysis of videotaped interactions taken during Cincinnati police traffic stops. *Journal of Communication, 58*(3), 530-549. https://doi.org/10.1111/j.1460-2466.2008.00398.x
Doherty, C., Kiley, J., & Jameson, B. (2016). Partisanship and Political Animosity in 2016. Washington, DC: Pew Research Center.
Dopp, T. (2018, August 10). Trump chides NFL players "at it again" in kneeling during anthem. *Bloomberg.* Available at https://www.bloomberg.com/news/articles/2018-08-10/trump-chides-nfl-players-at-it-again-in-kneeling-during-anthem.
Ellefson, L. (2018, September 7). Missouri college drops Nike over Kaepernick ad. *CNN.* Available at https://www.cnn.com/2018/09/07/us/college-of-the-ozarks-drops-nike-colin-kaepernick-trnd/index.html.
Fowler, J. (2017, September 25). Steelers, Seahawks, Titans remain in locker room during national anthem. *ESPN.com.* Accessed March 16, 2018, at http://www.espn.com/nfl/story/_/id/20801902/pittsburgh-steelers-remain-locker-room-national-anthem.
Fricker, M. (2009). *Epistemic injustice: Power and the ethics of knowing.* New York: Continuum.
Gardberg, N. A., & Newburry, W. (2009). Who boycotts whom? Marginalization, company knowledge, and strategic issues. *Business & Society, 52*(2), 318-357.
Gill, E. (2016). "Hands up, don't shoot" or shut up and play ball? Fan-generated media views of the Ferguson Five. *Journal of Human Behavior in the Social Environment 26*(3/4), 400-412.
Gillboa, A., & Bodner, E. (2009). What are your thoughts when the national anthem is playing? An empirical exploration. *Psychology of Music, 37*(4), 459-484.

Hall, E., Marach, R., & Reynolds, J. (2017). Policy point-counterpoint: Do African American athletes have an obligation to fight against racial injustice? *International Social Science Review, 93*(2), 1-9.

Hays, G. (2016, September 16). U.S. Soccer: We expect our players, coaches, to stand for anthem. *ESPN.com*. Accessed 4-6-2018 at http://www.espn.com/espnw/sports/article/17558219/us-soccer-midfielder-megan-rapinoe-kneels-again-national-anthem-friendly

Hechtman, M. (2017, October 28). America is most divided since Vietnam War: poll. *New York Post*. Accessed 4-12-2018 at https://nypost.com/2017/10/28/america-is-most-divided-since-vietnam-war-poll/.

Idleman, S. (2017, September 25). Should Christians take a knee during the national anthem? *Charisma Caucus*. Accessed November 17, 2017, at https://www.charismanews.com/politics/issues/67425-should-christians-take-a-knee-during-the-national-anthem.

Lang, H. (2017, September 26). Congresswoman kneels on house floor to protest Trump's criticism of NFL. Accessed March 16, 2018, at http://www.cnn.com/2017/09/26/politics/sheila-jackson-lee-nfl-protest/index.html

Lee, M. Y. H. (2015, March 19). "Hands up, don't shoot" did not happen in Ferguson. *Washington Post*. Accessed March 16, 2018, at https://www.washingtonpost.com/news/fact-checker/wp/2015/03/19/hands-up-dont-shoot-did-not-happen-in-ferguson/?utm_term=.a538bb4bb112.

Lincoln, A. (1858, June 16). *Republican Principles*. Speech given to the Illinois Republican State Convention.

Lozano-Reich, N. M., & Cloud, D. L. (2009). The Uncivil Tongue: Invitational Rhetoric and the Problem of Inequality. *Western Journal of Communication, 73*(2), 220-226. doi:10.1080/10570310902856105

Madani, D. (2017, November 5). 3 Miami Dolphins players kneel during anthem, reversing team policy. *Huffington Post*. Accessed March 16, 2018, at https://sports.yahoo.com/three-miami-dolphins-players-kneel-043541507.html.

McGinty, R. J. (2017). Forth & inches: Marking the line of athletes' free speech (a Colin Kaepernick inspired discussion). *Pace Intellectual Property, Sports, & Entertainment Law Forum, 8*(1), 39-78.

Milford, M. (2012). The Olympics, Jesse Owens, Burke, and the implications of media framing in symbolic boasting. In K. Bissell & S. D. Perry (Eds.) *The Olympics, Media, and Society* (pp. 5-25). London: Routledge.

Smith, S. (2017, October 10). Thousands of Christians 'take a knee' on national mall to repent for racial injustice. *Christian Post*. Accessed November 17, 2017 at https://www.christianpost.com/news/thousands-of-christians-take-a-knee-on-national-mall-to-repent-for-racial-injustice-202234/.

Thiel, A., Soler, A. V., Toms, M., Thing, L.F., & Dolan, P. (2016). Can sports be 'unpolitical'? *EJSS. European Journal for Sport and Society, 13*(4), 253-255.

Tignor, S. (2015, April 9). 1973: Arthur Ashe breaks sporting color barrier in South Africa. *Tennis*. Accessed April 12, 2018, at http://www.tennis.com/pro-game/2015/04/1973-arthur-ashe-breaks-sporting-color-barrier-south-africa/54575/.

Tillison, T. (2017, September 26). Has anyone checked the actual rule about the anthem? NFL's Game Operations Manual is very specific. *Bizpac Review*. Accessed March 16, 2018, at http://www.bizpacreview.com/2017/09/26/anyone-checked-actual-rule-anthem-nfls-game-operations-manual-specific-540864#.

Villodas, R. (2017, September 25). What does Jesus say to the #TakeAKnee issue? *Missio Alliance*. Accessed November 17, 2017, at http://www.missioalliance.org/jesus-say-takeaknee-issue/.

Vissers, S., Hooghe, M., Stolle, D., & Maheo, V. (2012). The Impact of Mobilization Media on Off-Line and Online Participation: Are mobilization effects medium-specific? *Social Science Computer Review, 30*(2), 152-169.

Wasserman, H. M. (2006). If you build it, they will speak: Public stadiums, public forums, and free speech. *Nine, 14*(2), 15-26, 191.

Witz, B. (2016, September 1). This time Colin Kaepernick takes a stand by kneeling. *New York Times*. Accessed March 16, 2018, at https://www.nytimes.com/2016/09/02/sports/football/colin-kaepernick-kneels-national-anthem-protest.html.

Wolken, D. (2018, October 4). What fans told their college programs after Nike launched Colin Kaepernick ad campaign. *USA Today*. Available at https://www.usatoday.com/story/sports/ncaaf/2018/10/04/how-fans-reacted-college-sports-nike-colin-kaepernick-ad/1498729002/.

Zail, C. P. (2018, September 13). Nike boycott proves patriotism's still in style. *AMAC Daily Newsletter*. Available at https://amac.us/nike-boycott-proves-patriotisms-still-in-style/?utm_source=fox-news&utm_medium=triplelift&utm_campaign=nike-boycott&campaign=FOX:%20Article-Nike-Boycott.

TWO

The More Things Change . . .

A History of National Anthem Protests

Varaidzo Nyamandi and Andrew Bolin

INTRODUCTION

Understanding the relationship between the media and protesters in past prominent national anthem protests can provide valuable insights into the media's role in contemporary ones. Symbolic and silent protests during the national anthem are not a revolution of this generation (Bunch & Skorton, 2017). Examples of such political and societal expressions can be found both in the United States and globally. This chapter analyzes two national anthem protests in sports from a global perspective using James Carey's ritual view of communication. Focus will be on using the 1968 Olympic protest in Mexico and the protests during the period leading to the World Rugby Cup in South Africa.

The Take-a-Knee protests have led to a renewed interest in what some scholars view as an expression of symbolic forms. James Carey's perspective centers on the creation and recreation of symbolic forms such as feelings, moral ideas, and beliefs in which communication generates culture (Subtil, 2014). Through the Careyan perspective, communication is a means of interaction and exchange of collectively produced meanings through symbolism (Subtil, 2014). While acknowledging the utilitarian view of communication, society requires means of communication through which experiences are described, shared, modified, or preserved (Subtil, 2014). Taken in this light, the Take-a-Knee protest has made a specific statement about the national anthem, similar to protests witnessed during the 1968 Olympics and the South Africa national anthem controversy. Consequently, the need to consider examples from the past, which offer both negative and hopeful outcomes drives the impetus for this study. By exploring the history of national anthem protests, this chapter serves as a backdrop to current demonstrations in the NFL and other professional sports in the United States.

COMMUNICATION AS RITUAL

The relationship between communication and the concept of the ritual in modern societies involves sports, events, religious civic festivities, and celebrations that incorporate symbolic interactions, interpretations, and partition (Subtil, 2014). To understand how communication and culture co-create societal norms, it is important to show the role of communication in discovering new models of interaction (Subtil, 2014). It is also important to interpret the dynamics and diversity of the many forms of expression which are involved in the co-creation of a culture. Scholars highlight the undeniable involvement of the media in national anthem protests (Tamir & Bernstein, 2015). Following Carey's (1992) postulation of communication as ritual, the interaction between the national anthem protesters and the authorities as highlighted by the media needs to be understood as a creation of culture. Because of the power that the media wields during protests, sport administrators have sought to influence the media into maintaining the status quo, control, and power. For protesters using communicative opportunities to shape the national dialogue and culture, having their voice heard often leads to the success of the protests and sometimes, the successful resolutions of their concerns (Hanska-Ahy & Shapour, 2012). To place the experiences of the protesters in perspective, it is important to retrace events of the national anthem protests and highlight the gaps created by the unequal voice given to the protesters.

This study examines news stories written about national anthem protests, and thereby seeks to answer the following research questions:

> RQ1: How have national anthem protests historically been covered by the media?
>
> RQ 2: What implications might national anthem protests of the past provide for understanding contemporary national anthem protests such as the Take-a-Knee movement?

METHODOLOGY

To understand the history of national anthem protests, we examine events chronologically in order to step back and look at how the events in a given country influenced each other.

Chronological narrative is often used in media criticism in other areas. For instance, Silverstein (2012) used the method to explore the Jewish Holocaust history within Jewish high school classrooms. The author analyzed curricula and interviewed teachers in Melbourne, Australia, and New York, United States, which provided insight into ways in which the Holocaust was being understood (Silverstein, 2012). This paper seeks to accomplish similar goals. Through the Lexis/Nexis database, the researchers selected news articles for the 1968 Olympics story from 1967–1968 reports. On the South African anthem protests, articles were mostly from 1991 to 1995. A few news articles published after these periods were also used. Additional protest examples are then briefly explored.

A RAISED FIST ... A SILENT STATEMENT

Perhaps one of the most recognized and powerful images of the 1968 Summer Olympics in Mexico City was that of United States champions Tommie Smith and John Carlos. The pair of 200-meter runners won gold and bronze medals respectively. When the medal ceremony began, Smith and Carlos shifted the dialogue of the 1968 Olympics for years to come. While attending San Jose State College (SJSC) in California, Carlos and Smith were fierce competitors on the track. However, racial tensions were brewing not only within the California college campus but across the United States as a whole, including threats of a boycott of the 1968 Summer Olympics by black athletes (C.W., 1967).

On December 14, 1967, in New York City, Dr. Harry Edwards, an associate professor of sociology at SJSC announced a boycott of the 1968 Summer Olympics by all black athletes because he viewed the chairman of the International Olympic Committee (IOC) as "a devout anti-Semitic and anti-Negro personality" (United Press International, 1967, p. 14). News of this announcement quickly spread across the country. Newspapers such as the *Arizona Republic*, the *Pensacola News*, and the *Waco News-Tribune* displayed the support of national civil rights leaders such as Dr. King with headlines such as "Negro Olympic boycott supported by Dr. King" and "Rights leaders support proposed Olympics boycott" (Associated Press, 1967a; Associated Press, 1967b; Associated Press, 1967c).

Still, other newspapers framed the International Olympic Committee as "targets" of the boycott (Associated Press, 1967d). In fact, many stories in the days following the announcement allowed for IOC chairman Avery Brundage to rebut the claims of racism and bigotry. In an article by the Associated Press (1967e) in the *Green Bay Press-Gazette,* Brundage stated, "I have opposed racial and religious discrimination all my life." (p. 14). The *Chicago Tribune* ran a similar story by the Associated Press (1967f) in which Brundage said "it is a monstrous lie" to call him anti-Semitic or anti-Negro (p. 42).

Journalists from across the country began writing their own opinions on the boycott and the possible consequences. Many journalists wrote about the potential negative outcomes for black athletes. "Negro athletes will be making a mistake if they boycott the Olympic games. . . . The Olympic races provide the ideal stage for dramatizing the situation they deplore." (Baker, 1968, p. 21). Dave Hicks of the *Arizona Republic* wrote "But who, realistically, will be robbed? . . . Existing prejudice won't be eradicated by a boycott. What would be erased is an opportunity for deserving Negro athletes to compete under the U.S. banner" (p. 66).

Even famed African-American athletes such as Jackie Robinson struggled with the overall cause of the boycott. "My first reaction was this: I was opposed to it. Later in the day, however. . . . I was not so certain the proposed boycott was a bad idea. I decided it is something that the American public ought to at least—look at" (Robinson, 1967, p. 7). Thoughts about the Olympic boycott resulted in some opposition from students at SJSC. But Lee Evans, another 1968 Olympic athlete from SJSC supported the idea while admitting "he would probably run if only three of the original five demands [of the boycott] are met" (Jordan, 1968, p. 1).

The call to boycott the Olympics had ripple effects in other major events (Litsky, 1968). However, despite all this momentum at the beginning of 1968, by September, both John Carlos and Tommie Smith said "the black boycott of the Olympics is dead. . . . 'We're going all out for America in Mexico City, but we're going to show in some way we're also representing the black people'" ("Carlos, Smith confirm," 1968, p. 76).

October 16, 1968, four days after ABC's opening ceremony coverage of the Mexico City Olympics, Carlos and Smith lined up for the medal round of the men's 200 meter race ("SJS Track," 1968). Smith broke his own 200-meter world record and won gold; Carlos clinched bronze (Grimsley, 1968). At the medal ceremony, Smith and Carlos could be seen walking up to the podium shoes off and wearing black jackets and gloves. However, the true moment of protest occurred with the playing of the United States anthem. As the flags were raised and the anthem played, Smith and Carlos raised their clenched fists as a symbol of the black power movement taking place across the United States (Battsek, 2008). This nonverbal moment of protest would produce one of the most iconic images in Olympic history.

As described by Smith (1999), overall national news coverage of the event was "the same, largely due to their dependency on wire services"

(p. 238). However more can be discovered in the various "columns, editorials, and letters to the editor" in many of the major newspapers of that time (Smith, 1999, p. 238). Grimsley (1968) of the *Sheboygan Press* wrote about the mixed reactions to the protest, "'I think it's a shame and a disgrace,' said Bill Toomey, America's decathlon champion. . . . 'We all thought it was a bloody good show,' commented John Wetton, Great Britain's 1,500-meter hope" (p. 25). However, Grimsley (1968) calls Carlos "a militant spokesman in the Negro athlete's civil rights movement" (p. 25) revealing his bias. Other news articles lend a sense of credence to Smith and Carlos's gesture, "Smith represented 'black America'" wrote the Associated Press (1968). The *Los Angeles Times*, headline "'Black power' on victory stand" also seemed favorable (Povich, 1968, p. 61).

Some differences in the coverage of the protest come in the form of how the event was written about by white journalists versus African American. Mainstream national newspapers such as the *San Francisco Chronicle* ran the story of the protest with a picture of Smith and Carlos captioned as "American Negro runners" ("Olympic racial protest," 1968). In the predominately African-American focused *Chicago Defender*, Smith called out coverage of the Olympics and the vocabulary used by journalists, specifically the use of the term "negro." "We are black and we're proud to be black . . . but if I did something bad, they'd say a Negro" ("Carlos, Smith feel," 1968, p. 38).

The fallout of the protest continued in the weeks following the closure of the Olympics, especially on the heels of Carlos and Smith being expelled from the United States Olympic team. Bill Hurschmann (1968) from the SJSC newspaper, *Spartan Daily*, wrote that Smith and Carlos "were given 48 hours to get out of Mexico following their expulsion . . . for 'untypical exhibitionism'" (p. 1). The headline on the lower half of the front page of the *New York Times* read, "2 black power advocates ousted from Olympics" (Sheehan, 1968, p. 1). Within the text of the article, Smith and Carlos are referred to as "Negro" or "Negro American" multiple times (Sheehan, 1968). In an article in Great Britain's *The Economist* (1968), the author describes how the "Negro militants" were "indoctrinated" . . . at SJSC on black power and how "Americans can be thankful that black militance . . . did not take the form of a boycott . . . there would be far fewer gold medals to America's credit" ("Olympic Power," p. 50).

Upon his return to SJSC, Smith called the Olympics "too exciting" and stated the Olympic Committee's decision to expel the runners was simply because "they're a bunch of racists" (Amon, 1968, p. 1). In a later edition of the *Spartan Daily*, Carlos stated, "We'd do it again tomorrow" (Amon, 1968, p. 1).

The 1968 Olympic protest proves a pivotal point in the history of anthem protests. As noted by Smith (1999) one of the major issues in media coverage of the protest was how journalists described the event as either "pride" or "defiance," drawing stark differences in reports across the nation (p. 258). Smith notes "the press misrepresented [Smith and Carlos's] intentions and others dismissed the objectives of the incident solely because the event occurred in a setting many deemed inappropriate" (p. 258). Reports stated, "There is no place for personal spleen or politics in the Olympic Games" (Grimsley, 1968, p. 25).

Media representation of the 1968 Olympic protest, including the influences and underpinnings beginning at SJSC in 1967, through the expulsion of Smith and Carlos and the weeks of reactions, illustrates the positive and negative perceptions of the protest. It also illustrates the power of symbolic imagery, such as the national anthem and the black power fist.

SOUTH AFRICAN RUGBY AND ANTHEM PROTESTS

A protracted political conflict characterized South Africa from the beginning of the nineteenth century to the early 1990s. The conflict was over the unequal treatment of black people and other nonwhites on one side against white people on the other side. The apartheid system, ended in 1991, leveled social, economic, and political injustice against nonwhites (Gade, 2011). After apartheid ended, the Springboks, the South African rugby team, were allowed to compete internationally and started preparation for the World Rugby Cup Championships, held in 1995. National anthem protesters spoke out against "Die Stem" (The Call) as an anthem insensitive to the injustices of apartheid. Instead the protesters preferred "Nkosi Sikelel' iAfrika" (God bless Africa), which they considered to be an expression of the black majority's struggle for freedom (Jones, 1992). The song later came to symbolize political and spiritual mobilization for freedom and it was sung at most liberation struggle gatherings in South Africa, and neighboring countries; Zambia, Namibia, Tanzania and Zimbabwe (Jules-Rosette & Coplan, 2004). Generally, in South Africa, the news about the protests initially supported maintenance of the status quo. During the impasse between the white Afrikaner government and the black African National Congress (ANC) over the words to the anthem, media articles reflected more awareness of the concerns of the government. Proposals by the National Olympic Committee of South Africa to replace "Die Stem" were met with resistance from the status quo. This is in part explained by the acknowledgment of uneven power relations in society, where class, status, or power form a ritual (Carey, 1992). The relationship between the media and the national anthem protesters was in part shaped by the polarized relationship between the protesters, mostly members of the ANC, and the media, which tended to align itself on the side of the sport dominated by the status quo. Consequently, the initial news coverage of the national anthem protests gave a human-interest angle to the experiences of the senior government officials, such as the then president, F.W. de Klerk. While the news covered the South African Olympic Committee's decision to ban the national anthem, the stories clearly lacked any input from protesters. Government reaction was described in the *Guardian* as "a roar of patriotic protest" (Beresford, 1991, para. 6). Phrases such as "whose anger," "bellicose threats," "lambasted," (Beresford, 1991, para. 8), describing how President de Klerk reacted to the ban lent a voice to the government official. Not only was the media aware of the concerns of the government but also alluded to the legitimacy of the government in its indignation over the ban. President de Klerk is reported to have "underlined his personal allegiance to the symbols of the state," while South Africans of "every persuasion furiously debated" (Beresford, 1991, para. 9).

Nine months after the ban on "Die Stem" at any Olympics-related events in South Africa, the newspapers expressed a variety of views. During that time, issues pertaining to the concerns of the black protesters were not prominent in some of the newspapers. Four news articles by the *Toronto Star* (Canada), the *Gazette* (South Africa), the *Guardian* (United Kingdom), and the *Globe and Mail* (South Africa) highlighted how games between the Australian rugby team and the South African team could be canceled after the ANC's protest against the singing of the national anthem. While the focus of the articles was on the fate of the rugby games, there was a sense that the ANC was responsible for ensuring or preventing the success of the games. The *Toronto Star* wrote that the Australian Rugby Union awaited "what action the ANC would take" ("S.A Rugby Uproar," 1992, p. 39). The articles showed the willingness of the Australian rugby team to comply with the decision of the ANC, further alluding to the responsibility of the match on the ANC. The four newspapers quoted Joe French, president of the Australian Rugby Football Union, saying "we will pack our bags and quietly go home" ("Aussies May Leave," 1992, p. B5). The newspapers highlighted the ANC as posing a threat to rugby in South Africa with phrases like: "The ANC said it would decide the future of the tour at a meeting today, warning the future of such tours was in the balance" (Jones, 1992, p. 68).

Another view, though not prominent in the news articles, was the sense that the ANC was not quite justified in protesting the singing of the national anthem. They reported that "organizers ignored agreements to substitute a minute of silence for victims of political violence for the anthems" (p. 68) as the reasons for the protest. During that period "Die Stem" was the national anthem, but negotiations were underway to replace it with "Nkosi Sikelel' iAfrika." The protesters complained "after white fans sang the South African national anthem" (p. 68). However, the concerns of the protesters were not given media attention, thereby suggesting that they were insignificant.

Although the consensus among the media at the time was that politics generally disrupted sport, outside the country the *Sydney Morning Herald*, expressed the culpability of the sports fraternity and their fans in the social and political concerns of the ANC (Growden, 1993). It reported, "the disgraceful behavior of the virtually whites-only crowd," and the fact that "the only blacks sighted were serving the white" were indications "that something was amiss in this country" (p. 46). Although words such as racial inequalities were not explicitly mentioned, Growden (1993) pointed out that the inequality between the black and white South Africans should not be trivialized.

Eventually the media sought to understand their middle ground over the impasse. There was a sense that the ANC had come to accept the rugby games happening, on the condition that "Die Stem" was not played. On August 19, 1992, the *Sydney Morning Herald* published an article by Nick Farr-Jones, a prominent player on the Australian rugby team. The article focused on the meeting between the ANC president Nelson Mandela and officials of the Australian rugby team including the author. The meeting discussed the impasse over the national anthem protests and the looming cancellation of the games. The author highlighted Mandela as a sincere leader advocating for fair consideration about the social concerns of black people and genuinely seeking a positive outcome to the impasse. Farr-Jones "wanted to personally thank [Mandela] for his support," mentioning the "presence that Mr. Mandela has in abundance" (Farr-Jones, 1992, p. 13). The author also drew attention to the abject poverty among black people. This supported the concerns of social and political injustice that underscored the ANC protests. Expressing his "full sympathy to the ANC position," (p. 13), the author described how the white sports organizers played "Die Stem" just hours after the meeting, in bad faith against their earlier commitment not to.

On the same day, the *Herald Sun* focused the bulk of an article on the political implications of gaining the ANC's full support for the games. The focus of the story seemed to support the ANC, against the white fans, saying anthem treatment "can make rugby a reconciler of people or they can use it as a ritual that celebrates conquest and domination of black people" ("ANC backing for," 1992, para. 6). When the paper reported that the sports administrators waited to "react to provocation from white fans at Saturday's Test" (para. 10), it seemed to place more accountability for the protest on the white fans. Similarly, Chairborne (1992) of the *Washington Post* discussed a risk the ANC was placing itself in over its decision to support the rugby games. These tensions between the black protesters and the ANC on one hand and the white fans, supported by the government, caught the attention of the international sports bodies.

Subsequently, the International Rugby Association and the International Olympics Committee banned "Die Stem" at all international tournaments. On November 12, 1992, during a match between South Africa and England, Jones (1992) of the *Evening Standard* painted a picture of complication describing how playing the national anthems of rugby teams competing against South Africa was banned at the tournaments, although teams such as the French had ignored the ban. The author said, "talks are being held at the highest level between the two unions" (Jones, 1992, p. 68), called the issue "politically sensitive" (p. 68), and categorically stated there was "still no question of "Die Stem" being played" (p. 68). The paper also quoted South Africa's ambassador to England as saying that "we have closed the book on apartheid." It seems that by this point, the attention of the media was more on the political implications of the reactions to the ban and its implications for the political events taking place in South Africa.

By 1993, the media was evaluating the national anthem protests and placing the responsibility on the South African rugby officials. For example, the *Sydney Morning Herald* questioned a South African rugby official responsible for the national anthem protest a year earlier, saying that he "still believes his actions were correct" (Growden, 1993, p. 48).

After the 1994 government change, the media focused on President Nelson Mandela's government and its relationship with the South African rugby team to prepare for the 1995 World Cup. The *Charleston Gazette* evaluated how rugby was central in the coming together of black South Africans, white South African rugby fans, and the Springboks. The article spoke of how the "courage of black South Africans, and their white allies, sparked that change" (Nyden, 2008, p. 1E), and noted "Mandela's growing friendship with members and fans of the nation's rugby team—for decades a powerful symbol of the all-white apartheid Afrikaner government" (Nyden, 2008, p. 1E).

During the 1995 World Cup a former South African rugby official said the fans, players, politicians, and the media: "were all on the same side" (Nyden, 2008, p. 1E), after a revised "Nkosi Sikelel'iAfrika," was chosen as the national anthem, amalgamated with some parts of "Die Stem." Related events could have also contributed to the fans' transition from the old national anthem to the new one. The *Independent* narrates how the Australian team threatened to walk away from the game if the minute of silence was not observed and if "Die Stem" was sung (Carlin, 1995). The *Independent* narrates how the white fans somehow realized that "a stubborn adherence to apartheid, was not after all in their best interest," (Carlin, 1995, para.12).

During the game against Australia, the minute was so silent that "you could have heard a pin drop" (Carlin, 1995, para. 12). The new rugby team captain Francoise Pienaar championed "Nkosi Sikelil'iAfrika." Following his meeting with Mandela, Pienaar "declared that he would instruct the Springboks to learn and sing the new national anthem" (Carlin, 1995, para. 16). In 2017, *The Economist* would vote "Nkosi Sikelil'iAfrika" as the best national anthem in the world ("*The Economist*'s playlist," 2017, para.1). *The Herald* mentions how both anthems were amalgamated for the new national anthem to be acceptable to both blacks and whites.

While words such as compromise or conciliation were not mentioned at the time, in retrospect, the amalgamation was a compromise for acceptability.

On November 18, 2009, *Cape Times* reported that black and white South African rugby players, administrators, politicians, and fans all expressed anger when "Nkosi Sikelil'iAfrika" was not sung well during a rugby game in France. This showed that in the decade and a half since the anthems were combined the people had come to own the new song as their anthem. Rugby player Victor Matfield said, "Every time (we) go out on the field and sing the national anthem . . . that really fires you up because you know you are playing for your country" ("The Springboks were," 2009, p.24).

This historical examination shows the national anthem's role as a collective national symbol, with media gatekeepers in the forefront of choosing which group's concerns found a voice. Also, the sports personalities themselves, those who are in the center of a protest, can collaborate in finding a peaceful resolution. The South African example shows the journalists were initially tentative in their reference to the national anthem protesters. However, over time they brought the political and social concerns surrounding the protests into perspective. Overall the media highlighted the opinions, frustrations, and anxieties that fans, sports authorities, and politicians expressed through the national anthem protests.

UNKNOWN TO FRONT PAGE

Of course there have been other small-scale protests. In the small college town of Purchase, NY, a relatively unknown Division III college basketball team at Manhattanville College got caught up in a social movement of silent protest. In 2003, female senior forward Toni Smith, although standing, refused to face the American flag during the singing/playing of the United States anthem before home basketball games. Press reports said Smith, "creates ill will by turning [her] back on the flag" (Sheridan, 2003, p. 4).

"A Vietnam veteran came onto the court . . . and held an American flag in front of [her] after the Division III player again refused to face the flag during the national anthem" wrote *The Orlando Sentinel* ("Vietnam vet disrupts game," 2003, p. D8). The veteran stated, "she disgraced herself and she disgraced the flag" (Sheridan, 2003, p. 4).

In a statement, Smith detailed why she protested as, "the inequalities that are embedded in the American system . . . which allows the rich to get richer, the poor to get poorer" ("Anthem Protest Is," 2003, p. 5). The protest drew ire from other coaches though. Coaches "say they wouldn't tolerate similar behavior from their own players, and they don't seem too concerned about whether that behavior is legal" (Bagnato, 2003, p. 2-3).

The protest, however small, rallied the small town. Ford (2003) tells how Smith's turning of her back paved the way to "flag-waving frenzy" (p. D01). "When the Manhattanville team played a conference semifinal game at home last night, its little gym was sold out again, protesters waving flags were at the college's main gate, and network television cameramen elbowed each other again for the best vantage from which to film Smith's personal protest" (Ford, 2003, p. D01). The events that unfolded at Manhattanville College highlight how even small protests can gain coverage when a story is pitting antagonist against protagonist.

Spanish vs. English

What seemed like a simple gesture to celebrate the "millions of immigrants seeking a better life" turned out to be yet another cry of anthem protest (Wides-Munoz, 2006, p. 3). British music producer Adam Kidron came up with the idea of the Spanish version of the United States Anthem in the early 2000's. Kidron was even successful in getting hip-hop star Pitbull to record a version, *Nuestro Himmo*, or *Our Anthem*, which debuted April 28, 2006 ("Spanish anthem triggers," 2006, p. 9).

The fight against the Spanish version quickly took to the internet where "bloggers and others are infuriated" ("Spanish anthem," 2006, p. 1). The protest even found its way to the White House where then-president George W. Bush advocated for the English version (Silva, 2006). The fight over the anthem triggered "pro-immigration protests around the country . . . and the record label [urged] Hispanic radio stations to play the cut at 7 p.m. in a sign of solidarity" (Wides-Munoz, 2006, p. 3).

NATIONAL ANTHEM AND GENDER

Recent national anthem controversies in Canada involved concerns over gender bias. In 2010, following a great showing of female athletes at the Olympics, a member of the Canadian parliament opened her speech asking the House "to consider changing the phrase 'in all thy sons command' . . . to more gender-neutral wording" ("Canada not to," 2010, p. 1).

The effort fell on deaf ears. "The proposal came under attack from all quarters, including the media, talk shows, women and leaders of the ruling party" ("Canada not to," 2010, p. 1). Commentators in the *Hindustan Times* said, "my guess . . . some feminist got to [the prime minister] and said, 'We ought to revise the national anthem'" ("Canada not to," 2010, p. 1).

A PROTEST IN AUSTRALIA

Since 2013, Australian boxer Anthony Mundine continues to stir controversy over his protests of the Australian national anthem. In an article in *The New Daily*, Mundine stated he was "simply trying to educate people that [the anthem] is a theme song for the divisive White Australia policy" ("We're not young," 2017). Mundine referred to Australian legislation which prevented "large-scale Asian immigration" and other non-European immigrants from coming into Australia in the early 1900s (Atkinson, 2015, p. 204). Mundine, an Aboriginal activist, has made it difficult for fight organizers to make plans and deal with security. *The Daily Telegraph* reported security would be on heightened alert when the anthem began (Paul, 2013). In previous boxing matches, judges had been abused, which was one of the reasons for added security (Paul, 2013).

DISCUSSION

The news archives show how groups of people representing different races and perspectives participated in protesting national anthem rituals. The shared meanings of the national anthems result from a transformative process involving the media, fans, political parties, and sportspeople, in which the media is an active participant. Through the cultural studies lens, the study explored the intrinsic relationship between communication and important ritual. This includes the incorporation of symbolic interactions, interpretations, and participation (Subtil, 2014). In turn, these shared meanings across groups facilitate common ritual practices during one's national anthem. The interaction between the national anthem protesters, the authorities, the fans, and the media needs to be understood as a creation of culture. In this study the media play the dual role of being a participant and a conduit for communicating the actions of the other participants. The literature review highlights how a collective self-image is complicated by the fact that collective images themselves are vulnerable to the ever-changing interpretations of groups (Daughtry, 2003). The interpretation of the protesters' concerns through the media can be considered as facilitating understanding of the protesters' group by the public and the sporting fraternity. Increasing awareness over time facilitated the media becoming more perceptive of the complexities of the political and social implications of the national anthem of concern, resulting in coverage of issues expressed by both protesters and those in the status quo.

IMPLICATIONS FOR THE TAKE-A-KNEE PROTESTS

The study has important implications for developing an understanding regarding how people of diverse racial backgrounds can perceive national symbols. Andrea and Sheffield-Hayes (2019, this volume) found race played a role in participants' perspectives about whether the Take-a-Knee protest had adversely affected American football. This study shows possibilities for the portrayal of collective images, with the media in the forefront of seeking to understand each group's concerns. The sports personalities themselves can help facilitate understanding of the issues. A nation's ability to reconcile its practices with its democratic image (Robb, 2016) is only possible where individuals are willing to explore new perceptual territories, assume new roles, and dare to venture outside of social comfort zones. News articles on national anthem protests initially focused more on the sport and less on the protests. However, as they focused more on the issues, they also assumed the roles of social and political reporters in ways that brought the political and social concerns surrounding the protests into perspective. With unique perspectives on both sides of Take-a-Knee, perhaps concerns over the sports venue will succumb eventually to concerns for the issues.

CONCLUSION

This chapter examined past examples of anthem protests and the media representations of such events in an effort to provide a better understanding of the Take-a-Knee controversy. We argue that national anthems are an important symbol of a nation's image that holds both positive and negative meanings, beliefs, and values for individuals and cultural subgroups within a country. Media representation of such occurrences are important to study in order to understand how media contribute to shaping individual and group ideologies on social issues.

Social issues such as inequality of race and gender are strong motives in anthem protests. However, it is important to note that in many cases, it is not the anthem itself that is being protested, but what (and whom) the anthem represents. In the instance of the 1968 Olympics, Smith and Carlos's raised fists were in protest against the strong racial ideologies of the IOC chairman. In the case of the South African protest, it was political unrest and the rise of new political power realities. Again in 2003, the protest by the Manhattanville College student was for economic inequality. Thoughts that the American national anthem should be sung in English and that changing the language was changing the overall meaning provoked a protest in 2006. In 2010, the fight was for gender inclusion in the Canadian anthem, which some felt was too patriarchal. These protests highlight deeper social issues where the anthem was used to make a stand for or against these causes.

The role played by the media is significant in shaping societal response to not only the protests but also to acceptance or rejection of the underlying causes. Media representation of Carlos and Smith after the 1968 Olympics depicted the athletes as "prideful" or "defiant" (Smith, 1999). These descriptions hold two very stark differences. Indeed, reports out of SJSC showed support for Carlos and Smith while other newspapers chose to denounce Smith and Carlos's political move as a "shame and disgrace" (Grimsley, 1968, p. 25). Nevertheless, it is important not to downplay the significance such writing and reporting have in framing and creating meaning of these events. As anthem protests such as Take-a-Knee are covered by the media, how such events are framed and reported can and will add to the overall interpretation and consequently national support of or opposition to these events as seen in past examples of anthem protests.

REFERENCES

Amon, S. (1968a, October 22). Smith, Carlos back in San Jose after 'too exciting' time. *Spartan Daily*, p. 1.
Amon, S. (1968b, October 23). We'd do it again tomorrow, John Carlos tells SJS crowd. *Spartan Daily*, p. 1.
ANC backing for Wallabies. (1992, August 20). *Herald Sun*.
Andrea, P.A., & Sheffield-Hayes, E. (2019). America's Greatness Compromised: The Star-Spangled Banner as a Symbol of Nationalism, Identity, and Division. In S. D. Perry (Ed). *Pro-football and the proliferation of protest: Anthem posture in a divided America*. Lanham, MD: Lexington.
Anthem protest is free speech. (2003, March 3). *Green Bay Press-Gazette*, p. 5.
Associated Press. (1967a, December 15). Negro Olympic boycott supported by Dr. King. *Arizona Republic*, p. 47.
Associated Press. (1967b, December 15). Rights leaders support proposed Olympics boycott. *Pensacola News*, p. 4.
Associated Press. (1967c, December 15). King, McKissick back Negro Olympic boycott. *Waco News-Tribune*, p. 7.
Associated Press. (1967d, December 15). Olympic director target. *Sedalia Democrat*, p. 4.
Associated Press. (1967e, December 16). Brundage answers boycott charge: No Negro-Jew bias. *Green Bay Press-Gazette*, p. 14.
Associated Press. (1967f, December 16). Brundage says bigotry talk is lie. *Chicago Tribune*, p. 42.
Associated Press. (1968, October, 18). Smith represented 'black America.' *Tampa Tribune*, p. 51.
Associated Press. (2006, April 28). Spanish anthem triggers protest. *Florida Today*, p. 1.
Atkinson, D. C. (2015). The White Australia Policy, the British Empire, and the World. *Britain & the World*, 8(2), 204-224.
Bagnato, A. (2003, March 3). Protest irritates coaches. *Chicago Tribune*, pp. 2-3.
Baker, R. (1968, January 1). Gradualism at the Olympics. *Atlanta Constitution*, p. 21.
Battsek, J. (Producer). (2008, July 9). *Black Power Salute* [Television Broadcast]. London, England: BBC4
Beresford, D. (1991, November 12). De Klerk leads the fifth to keep the old flag flying. The *Guardian*.

Boks miffed at botched anthem. (2009, November 18). *Cape Times*, p. 1
Canada not to change national anthem. (2010, March 6). The *Hindustan Times*, p. 1.
Carey, J. W. (1992). *Communication as Culture: Essays on Media and Society*. New York: Routledge, Chapman and Hall, Inc.
Carlin, J. (1995, May 24). South Africa plays in harmony. *Independent*.
Carlos, Smith confirm that boycott's off. (1968, September 12). *Los Angeles Times*, p. 76.
Carlos, Smith feel beautiful. (1968, October 24). *Chicago Defender*, p. 38.
Chairborne, W. (1992, August, 19). ANC drops its objections to S. African Rugby Game: white fans admonished not to sing the anthem. *Washington Post*.
C. W. (1967, December 1). Sacrifice in vain? *Spartan Daily*, p. 2.
Daughtry, J. M. (2003). Russia's new anthem and the negotiation of national identity. *Ethnomusicology*, 47 (1), 42-67.
Ford, B. (2003, February 28). A small gesture, a big deal. *Philadelphia Inquirer*, p. D01.
Grimsley, W. (1968, October 17). Reaction varied in Carlos-Smith black-gloved protest at games. The *Sheboygan Press*, p. 25.
Growden, G. (1993, May 2). Luyt stands by anthem decision: rugby. *Sydney Morning Herald*.
Hicks, D. (1967, December 16). Negro will lose most in boycott. *Arizona Republic*, p. 66.
Hurschmann, B. (1968, October 21). Smith, Carlos ousted from Olympic Games. *Spartan Daily*, p. 1.
Jones, C. (1992, November 12). Anthem talks: fans fury could force a U-turn. *Evening Standard*.
Jones, N. Farr- (1992, August 19). In the hands of the ANC. *Sydney Morning Herald*.
Jordan, K. (1968, January 16). Evans still supports the Olympic boycott. *Spartan Daily*, p. 1.
Jules-Rosette, B., & Coplan, D. (2004). "Nkosi Sikelel' iAfrika": From Independent Spirit to Political Mobilization ("Nkosi Sikelel' iAfrika." De l'esprit indépendant à la mobilsation politique). *Cahiers D'Études Africaines*, 44 (173/174), 343-367.
Nyden, PJ. (2008, December 28). Redeemed. *Charleston Gazette*, p. 1E.
Olympics. (2014, July 18). *Full Olympic Film—Mexico City 1968 Olympic Games*. [YouTube] www.youtube.com/watch?v=pVsQYRZgb10.
Olympic power. (1968, October 26). *The Economist*, p. 50.
Olympic racial protest. (1968, October 16). *San Francisco Chronicle*
Paul. (2013, January 29). Anthony Mundine speaks about a plan to boycott Australian anthem. *Daily Telegraph*. Retrieved from https://www.dailytelegraph.com.au/sport/boxing-mma/anthony-mundine-speaks-about-australian-anthem-boycott/news-story/92114e772d3f95b23e2dabb14284246c?sv=3214bb33994279b9c623636b32d1d5f3
Povich, S. (1968, October 17). 'Black power' on victory stand. *Los Angeles Times*, p. 61.
Robb, D. (2016). The mobilizing of the German 1848 protest song tradition in the context of international twentieth-century folk revivals. *Popular Music*, 35 (3), 338-359.
Robinson, J. (1967, December 16). Mixed emotions over boycott of Olympics. *Pittsburgh Courier*, p. 7.
Sheehan, J. (1968, October 18). 2 Black power advocates ousted from Olympics, *New York Times*, p. 1.
Sheridan, C. (2003, February 23). Manhattanville athlete creates ill will by turning back on flag. *Star-Gazette*, p. 4.
Silva, Mr. (2006, April 29). Not the same old song for bush. *Chicago Tribune*, pp. 1-3.
Silverstein, J. (2012). Jewish Holocaust histories and the work of chronological narratives. *Journal of Jewish Education*, 78, 58-83.
SJS track team represented. (1968, October 10). *Spartan Daily*, p. 3.
Smith, M. (1999). Identity and citizenship: African American athletes, sport, and the freedom struggles of the 1960s. (Doctoral Dissertation). Retrieved from ProQuest. 9951727
Spangled mangled in other language. (2006, April 28). *Tampa Bay Times*, p. 9.

Subtil, F. (2014). Carey's cultural approach of communication. *Intercom: Revista Brasilira de Cienncios da Comunicado, 37*(1), 1-17.
The Economist's playlist of national anthems. (2017, December 17). *The Economist.* Retrieved from https://www.economist.com/essay/2017/12/19/the-economists-playlist-of-national-anthems
United Press International. (1967, December 16). College professor raps Avery Brundage. *Bennington Banner,* p. 14.
Vietnam vet disrupts game. (2003, February 23). *Orlando Sentinel,* p. D8.
We're not young and free. (2017, January 30). *The New Daily.* Retrieved from https://thenewdaily.com.au/sport/boxing/2017/01/30/mundine-national-anthem/.
Wides-Munoz, L. (2006, April 28). Spanish version of US anthem raises protests. *Albuquerque Journal,* p. 3.

THREE

Government versus Protesters

A Historical Look at How the Media Chooses a Winner

Haley Higgs and Dara Phillips

The media has long been examined for their influence on the public's thought process producing various theories to explain the phenomena. The media's influence has the potential to impact the views of the public regarding controversial issues raised by often overlooked groups. In general, the media has been thought to side with the status quo and to marginalize protesters who were considered to be in direct opposition to the norm. As a result, the public may form an opinion about a particular protest and take on the opinion of the media. Questions arise as to why media take a position rather than report news as it happens or who is influencing the media's message concerning protests? The assumption is the government sets the tone toward the sudden and unexpected protests and the media abides by those tones.

A historical examination of major protests in the United States can hopefully explicate the aforementioned questions as well as shed light on the media's reporting on the recent Take-a-Knee protest in the National Football League (NFL). More than studying famous protests, the focus will be on the media's portrayal of the protesters and their causes. Specifically, the women's suffrage movement, the Vietnam War, and Occupy Wall Street will be examined to provide a basis of understanding for the current controversy.

LITERATURE REVIEW

Women's Suffrage Movement

The women's suffrage movement shines significant light upon the media's stand on protests. Hoffert (1993) examined the early stages of the women's movement that officially began in the 1800s. Prior to the Civil War, little coverage of women's rights was mentioned in newspapers. Papers were "frequently controlled by political interests" and were designed to serve the needs of politicians and businessmen (p. 657). The 1830s saw the rise of the "penny press" which allowed for papers to be printed quickly and sold at low cost. However, the papers did little to move the women's agenda along. Hoffert examined the news stories surrounding the women's rights conventions in New York in three of the leading newspapers (*New York Daily Herald*, *New York Daily Times*, and *New York Daily Tribune*) during the antebellum period. She discovered that the conventions drew much attention and the newspapers did give news and editorial coverage. All three papers tended to sensationalize the women's activities. While initial support for women's rights were presented and even supported by one paper, interest waned and it joined the other papers in putting down women's efforts, ridiculing them, and not discussing the point of their protests.

Fast forwarding from pre-Civil War to the 1960s, Ashley and Olson (1998) conducted a content analysis of the *The New York Times*, *Time*, and *Newsweek* coverage of the women's movement over a twenty-year period from 1966 to 1986. Based on their research, the women's movement was considered a fringe movement receiving little attention from the media, causing female protesters to make dramatic gestures to attract the attention of the media. Using framing theory, Ashley and Olson discovered that the women's movement was marginalized by the media but unlike the framing of women in Hoffert's study the women were not painted in a humorous light. The feminists were delegitimized but the anti-feminists were legitimized (Ashley & Olson, 1998, p. 272). The researchers did find that news coverage did not paint either group as deviant and suggest future research should edit the operational definition of "deviant" as they seem to think it limited their results.

Vietnam War

The Vietnam War protests occurred during major upheaval in the United States. Colleges experienced protests on campuses and others like Kent State in Ohio saw shootings as a result of the anti-war protests. Researchers have subsequently been interested in examining how the media treated the protests and the protesters.

Boyle, McCluskey, McLeod, and Stein (2005) conducted a longitudinal study of protest coverage in five Wisconsin newspapers over a forty-year period. Their interest was in noting if protests challenged the status quo as well as the degree of support or criticism received. In comparing the civil rights, Vietnam War, and other social protests, the war protests were covered more critically than other social protests. The Vietnam War protests followed on the heels of the civil rights protest and the authors noted the country was in great social turbulence. However, over time the degree of criticism in the newspapers declined. The drop in criticism was theorized to be due to the reduction of protests and the deviance level of war protests (p. 654).

Occupy Wall Street

Occupy Wall Street took place in 2011 and primary sources are readily available in simple Google searches. This protest is unique from the other protests in that it was essentially the first one to be started with a tweet: #occupywallstreet (Sharlet, 2011). This more modern protest affords us the opportunity to examine how legacy media framed the protests. Not only how they framed the protest across traditional formats but how their own social media accounts influenced their stance on the protest.

In addition, researchers have been studying the media's view on this protest. For example, Cissel (2012) analyzed articles written by mainstream and alternative media sources and found discrepancies in reporting. Interestingly, Occupy Wall Street highlights the differences between these two media sources. On the one hand, the mainstream media portrayed Occupy as a directionless and confused gathering of "hippies"; on the other, alternative media focused on how the police, corporations, government, and mass media were preventing them from having a voice by prohibiting their free speech through legalities and logistics. Even as recently as this protest, legacy media tended to side with the status quo and was critical of protesters and their cause.

Based on the literature, there are still unanswered questions and uncertainties as to what the media will or will not do. Therefore, the following research questions were developed:

RQ1: How does the media tend to side with the government versus protesters historically?

RQ2: What trends do the media follow when reporting protest coverage?

THEORETICAL FRAMEWORK

The assumption is that the media frames news articles in such a fashion as to give their audiences a particular lens through which to approach an issue. Volkmer (2009) writes that frames help reduce complex information but also aid in interpreting and reconstructing reality (p. 407). Framing is "helpful to analyze the imbalances and underlying power structures" and can detect differences in how news stories are set across news outlets (p. 408). In de Vreese's (2005) study, he mentions that framing consists of distinct stages: frame-building, frame-setting, and individual and societal level consequences (p. 52). Frame building refers to internal and external factors that affect the structural qualities of news frames (p. 52). Specifically, de Vreese states that "the frame building process takes place in continuous interaction between journalists and elites and social movements" (p. 52). Frame-setting looks at the "interaction between media frames and individuals' prior knowledge and predispositions" (p. 52). This theory is prominent in journalistic research and therefore an obvious choice for this study.

In this research study, framing theory applies through the way the media told the stories of each protest. According to Ward and Ostrom (2006), the media has great power in influencing the attitudes and opinions of the masses when it comes to protests. The authors go on to say how the changing of one word can completely change the tone and view the masses receive from the article. This can be seen when looking at this study and the clusters of words that appeared. These terms, coined by the media, give great power to the articles. This is the framing technique of protests. When it is all said and done, the media starts the conversation for how the protest will go (Ward & Ostrom, 2006).

When it comes to framing theory, the media not only holds the power to tell the masses what to think about but also what to think about what they think about (Scheufele, 1999). By utilizing this theory in the present study, the researchers made the assumption that the media controlled the conversations around each protest and, therefore, selected cluster analysis as the method to assess this control.

METHODOLOGY

A cluster analysis looks to cluster language that centers around one symbol (Foss, 2009). By tracking down specific words used, the reference behind the words, and the reputation of those works, the cluster analysis drew rhetorical conclusions based on the intentional use of varying terminology. In order to determine if and how the media sides with the government instead of protest groups, the researchers decided to examine newspaper articles covering the women's suffrage movement, Vietnam War protests, Occupy Wall Street, and the NFL Take-a-Knee protests. The newspapers chosen were: *The New York Times, The Washington Post,* the *Los Angeles Times,* the *Denver Post,* and the *Atlanta Journal-Constitution.* These recognizable newspapers were selected since they represented five regions of the country and potentially offered a variety of perspectives regarding each protest. The researchers then selected two articles per event per newspaper to conduct the analysis.

Kenneth Burke (1969) developed cluster analysis to uncover the meaning, attitudes, or actions undergirding a rhetorical text (p. 41). A cluster forms around key terms that either repeat or appear to be significant. Ideas develop from the clusters and provide information for the critic to use to assess the rhetor's actual feelings or worldviews (Foss, 2009). Burke (1969) suggests that individuals form identities through various properties that enable them to share commonalities with others by using the other's speech and imagery. This is known as consubstantiality. In contrast, individuals may be disassociated from others simply by being physically separated from them. In this case, individuals communicate in an attempt to rid the division through expressions of unity.

Messages communicated by rhetors provide their audience with terms and emotions to interpret a situation as the rhetor sees it. As Foss (2009) writes, "the terms we select to describe the world constitute a kind of screen that directs attention to particular aspects of reality rather than others" (p. 64). Analyzing clusters in these various newspapers will demonstrate the intensity with which the media sides with and perpetuates the message of the government or the protesters.

The following results reflect the terms identified in the articles from the above mentioned newspapers as they pertain to women's suffrage, the Vietnam War, Occupy Wall Street, and the NFL Take-a-Knee protests. Specific criteria for the articles included a minimum of 150 words and that they had to be from the time period of the protest. The articles were selected via mainstream newspapers' websites and/or via newspapers.com. Search terms included words such as: protest, movement, war, kneeling, etc. to identify potential articles, and then a purposive sample was chosen. We analyzed positive versus negative terminology when it came to how the media viewed protesters.

RESULTS

Women's Suffrage

The suffrage movement spanned several decades beginning roughly around 1848. However, the nineteenth amendment giving women the right to vote was not ratified until 1920. National women's organizations spent many hours educating and lobbying for change and as a result taking part in protests. As this was an extensive time period, the dates of the articles analyzed ranged between 1915 and 1920, leading up to national ratification. The newspapers reviewed were *The Atlanta [Journal] Constitution*, the *LA Times*, *The New York Times*, the *Washington Post*, and *The Salt Lake Tribune*. Results of the analysis showed that "suffrage," "women," "suffragists," "National Woman's Party" and "amendment," appeared approximately three to four times per article across the selection of newspapers.

The term "suffrage" was depicted as a human right and necessary for the war effort. World War I was in full force during the push for nationwide ratification and war articles shared a similar amount of space with suffrage articles in newspapers. Women were insisting that since they were actively involved in the war effort, they should be recognized as full citizens permitted to vote. Women insisted that having equal suffrage was the "first step to equal responsibility and equal power" ("The Nineteenth Amendment," 1920). Based on the results, newspapers showed that suffragists were leveraging their help in the war for the basic right to participate in politics.

The next term "women" did not appear as often as "suffrage," however, the descriptive terms surrounding this cluster word were more extensive. *The New York Times*, *Atlanta [Journal] Constitution*, and the *LA Times* provided a positive outlook on the women participating in the suffrage movement. Women were said to be much like men but to possess more honor than men, be very patriotic, highly democratic, and just as competent as men. Specifically, *The New York Times* offered a more complete demographic description of female participants: rich, poor, all political faiths and religions, and nearly every class and race ("New Suffrage Drive," 1917). This shows that all women were working together for one common cause with no concern for basic differences between them. Unification and determination were therefore implied.

Interestingly, the term "suffragists" received its own recognition in the papers and was treated negatively compared to "suffrage" and "women." Those individuals included in this category were said to be militant and even antagonized their own supporters ("Suffrage Outlook Dark," 1917). They were described as "sentinels" but were also "prisoners." These suffragists were charged with obstructing traffic and unlawful assembly while protesting outside the White House. *The Washington Post* theorized that hot weather had warped the suffragists' judgment as they denounced President Wilson for being the reason the Senate had not ratified the amendment that year ("Suffrage Militant," 1918).

"National Woman's Party" received more critical treatment. According to both *Washington Post* articles, the party wanted to be acknowledged publicly for its effort to move suffrage into ratification and have its turn in the "limelight." The *LA Times* said the party contained the radical suffragists who were responsible for the White House pickets and were the ones who introduced their "insidious" card catalogue system for profiling congressmen. Still, the newspapers said the National Woman's Party worked untiringly and that several Democratic congressmen viewed the formation of the party as "a fact of serious political significance" (Small, 1916).

The final key term, "amendment," was handled in more neutral language than the prior terms. Researchers assumed there would have been stronger remarks made about this term. Newspapers stated that the amendment had no expiration unlike the prohibition amendment. Moreover, the likelihood of passing the federal suffrage amendment was excellent. Only in a *New York Times* article was socialism and radicalism associated with the amendment ("New Suffrage Drive," 1917). The article pointed out that "enormous amounts of money" had been applied to the cause in passing New York State's suffrage amendment.

Vietnam War

The Vietnam War protest began slowly, rooted mainly in the Cold War scare. Protesters believed the war was wrong and they thought that the United States shouldn't be involved, said one *New York Times* article. They were countered by those who supported the war and saw the protesters as unruly and disruptive, according to media reports. It goes without saying that to understand the protest movement in the United States, one must understand the events of the war.

The articles reviewed for this analysis were accessed via newspapers.com. The predominant four newspapers represented in this analysis are *The Atlanta [Journal] Constitution, The LA Times, The New York Times,* and *The Salt Lake Tribune*. The dates of the articles analyzed span from 1967 to 1971.

When looking at various newspapers on the Vietnam protests, it was clear that the media has a very positive viewpoint on the movement and protesters. It was clear from the accessed articles that the media did not support the war either. The top word clusters in the examined articles were "war," "protesters," "campus," "Cold War," and "reaction." These words appeared the most often, on an average of three to four times in each news article.

The *Atlanta [Journal] Constitution, The LA Times, The New York Times* and *The Salt Lake Tribune* all maintained the theme that the "protesters" were in the right. One article stated "protesters" were "speaking out" and having a reaction to "an unjust war." The articles in these papers mainly focused on the destruction that the war was causing and not the protesters. While the media relayed that the government's position did not change, it also communicated how the protesters were "in the right" for their speaking out against the war.

A common theme in *The Salt Lake Tribune* was the slight angle supporting college students speaking out against the war. They highlighted three on-campus protests within the articles and called one a "barricade" on campus. This paper also cited the "Cold War" on multiple accounts, taking into account that this was a "joint protest" and Vietnam was the start of the Cold War.

Media also focused more on the protest, rather than the political. The *LA Times* highlighted the reasons America should not be in Vietnam, while most focused mainly on the protests stateside. The *LA Times* went on to say America didn't "belong" in Vietnam and many articles said that America should get "out."

Occupy Wall Street

Although the Occupy Wall Street movement began in July 2011, the media did not begin full coverage of the protests until the following October. The time frame for the protest expanded from 2011 into early 2016. This matched the time frame of the articles analyzed.

Though the protest spread across the country, #OccupyLA became its own branch of the protest by early October 2011. When looking at various newspapers on the Occupy Wall Street protests, it is clear that the media had a very negative viewpoint on the movement and protesters. The top word clusters in the examined articles were "protest," "protesters," "arrests," and "movement." They appeared the most often on an average of three to four times each news article, excluding "arrests," which only appeared in half of the articles.

The word "protesters" garnered a mainly negative connotation. For instance, when discussed during the Occupy Wall Street movement, protesters were described in the *New York Times* as "rebels" and "rioters." When looking at the *Los Angeles Times*, with its own branch of the protest, "protesters" were often written about as being arrested or breaking laws. The *Washington Post*, looking back on the movement, described "protesters" as violent and having a disregard for authority.

The *Atlanta Journal-Constitution* and *The Washington Post* continued using the key words "protest" and "protesters." The articles in these papers mainly focused on the destruction the protest and protesters were causing. They also focused more on the political response, rather than the protest, itself. These papers highlighted the response of politicians over giving more press to the protesters.

In contrast, the *Denver Post* was most positive toward protesters in calling Occupy Wall Street a "movement" rather than a "protest." This was the only paper to do so. The normalized term "protesters" was often replaced in the paper with "revolutionists" and "the heart of America." This media slant gave more favor to the protesters for their actions.

Take-a-Knee Protest

Take-a-Knee protests began in August 2016 but did not receive full-scale attention until 2017.The articles used for this study covered September 2016 to March 2018. The results of the analysis on the Take-a-Knee protests determined that the focus of attention rested on "players" and "protest." These two key terms occurred six times out of the ten articles selected. Two other top key terms, "Trump" and "NFL," appeared four times each.

The first notable key term "players" received more positive representation for their choice to kneel during the playing of the national anthem. They were characterized as loving their country, brave, courageous, not disrespectful, and outspoken. However, a few articles classified "players" in a negative light, especially when President Donald Trump was quoted as saying the players ought to be fired and one team owner referred to players as "inmates" (Newberry, 2018). Furthermore, the players were said to be engaged in a "disgraceful protest" and were disrespectful of the flag and the sacrifice of those Americans who gave their lives to allow these players to "play a kid's game" (Thiessen, 2017). Finally, one *Washington Post* article declared that the NFL players struggled to connect with Colin Kaepernick's protest and preferred to indirectly support Kaepernick's NFL lock out by doing nothing.

"Protests" received favorable attributes from the newspapers. *The New York Times* and *Washington Post* surrounded the key terms with clustering words like "compelling," "heartfelt," "peaceful," an ongoing movement or even more poetically depicted as an "interpretive dance." Newspapers clearly explained that the protest represented social injustice but they did suggest the protest would die down if players missed a few paychecks.

The president was portrayed as divisive, incendiary, and attacking the players in several of the papers. Interesting to the context of the protests, Trump was "obsessed with Obama." Still, in one *Denver Post* article it was noted that Trump did not start the fight and that he was not the first president to get involved in a social protest.

While the previous key terms received a mixed review, "NFL" received the most negative treatment from the media. The *LA Times* and *Atlanta Journal-Constitution* declared it was supposed to be a "symbol of harmony" and "represent much that is good in America" but instead was described as "self-serving," and "hypocritical." The negativity did not end there referring to (a) questionable links to the U.S. military, (b) Congress considering removal of the NFL's antitrust exemption due to rampant domestic violence allegations, and (c) how the NFL could stand to learn from the National Hockey League (NHL).

DISCUSSION

At the start of this research, the authors endeavored to discover if the media historically tended to side with the government over protesters. The assumption based on previous literature mentioned was that newspapers would frame all protests as fringe movements and depict protesters as troublemakers fighting against commonly held social values. However, the results of the cluster analysis show the media historically waffles in its framing of protesters. For example, when reporting events during the suffrage movement, the articles positively framed the suffrage protests as making progress toward equal voting rights and that women in general were very capable of participating politically. Still, suffragists and the National Woman's Party were cast as the rebellious type. They were the ones who picketed the White House and were most likely to do what they could to attract media attention for the sake of being recognized rather than obtaining equal voting rights.

In contrast, the results show the media completely upheld and defended the Vietnam protests. Newspapers remained in staunch opposition to the government, especially when stating America needed to leave Vietnam, and suggested that the protesters were correct in their sentiments. Occupy Wall Street was the only example of the media siding with the government. The protest and protesters were determined to be socially disruptive and the media pushed for governmental input. Thus, the results suggest that the media may tend to side with protesters rather than the status quo more than past research would suggest (Ashley & Olson, 1998).

In regard to the Take-a-Knee protests, the analysis shows that media outlets are still deciding how to frame the protest. Newspapers wrote from both sides of the argument mentioning that the president was causing division but was not the cause of the upheaval. In fact, the players were both commended and condemned for their behavior. Instead, the NFL was cast as the true culprit for the turmoil. With that in mind, it can be surmised that the media has collectively decided to not be biased for or against protesters or the government but to find a third party, the NFL, to show bias against. Perhaps, this action will be a new twist in the ongoing history of protests. Journalists have been likely to select one side over another when framing their reports, but now they may look to a scapegoat to avoid being called biased, a role the NFL itself seems to be serving. The Take-a-Knee protest is not over. Until that time, we can only theorize and watch what unfolds before committing it to history. Perhaps, the media will settle in to a particular frame to report or maybe they will continue with this third-party option.

In regard to media trends when reporting protest coverage, the authors determined that political climate and social temperament had an effect. Historically, women have remained in the background of both political and social platforms. When they began their quest for voting rights and equal treatment, the marches disrupted social reality causing the media to frame protesters in a negative light. The Vietnam War took place during a time of political and social unrest and likely led newspapers to editorialize and set the agenda for the public. The media's handling of Occupy Wall Street indicates that the protesters were disturbing a relatively stable political and social environment and were more a menace than a means to enlighten the public to economic inequality. Similar to the women's suffrage movement and Vietnam, the Take-a-Knee protests have occurred during political and social unrest spurring comments both for and against the protest. Moreover, had Trump not gotten involved, the protest may have lost momentum and the media could have determined which side to back. Therefore, the conclusion can be made that the media will frame events, influenced by what is happening in the country, and will select words that create positive or negative impressions when framing their news stories; remaining solely objective as a reporter is difficult as observed in this study.

Focusing on positive and negative terminology, the researchers found the media held the power to show protests in a positive or negative light. By clustering chosen descriptors around various key terms, the researchers were able to show framing in action and that framing theory explains how the media elicits a positive or negative attitude from the audience.

LIMITATIONS

Specific limitations to the research include difficulty accessing archived material and limited access to newspaper websites for non-subscribers. As a result, the researchers were restricted to newspapers.com for archival information. This site allowed researchers to access articles from several papers, although not all major papers were included on newspapers.com. Specifically, the researchers had to use a different newspaper, the *Salt Lake Tribune,* for women's suffrage and the Vietnam War for a mid-country sampling as the *Denver Post* was unavailable on newspapers.com for either protest. These two newspapers are certainly not representing the same viewpoint even though they both serve cities in the Mountain west. Further, many of the newspaper sources used in this study were internet only sources and are likely to have published articles the researchers could not access.

For future studies pertaining to this subject, the authors would suggest more current protests. This will allow for more information to be obtained and evaluated. In addition, future researchers could analyze whether journalist's gender affects the framing of protests. A final suggestion would be to take a quantitative approach to allow for comparison of specific frames presented by reporters.

CONCLUSION

This study sheds new light, yet creates more questions, in the ongoing study of the media's handling of protests. As discussed, the media does not necessarily side with the government in all protests but does not always uphold protesters and their cause. Furthermore, the media has a tendency to flow with the political and social climate of the times. In light of framing theory, this study demonstrates how the media can manipulate how protests are to be viewed via the masses using positive and negative terms. Presently, the media appear to be ambivalent to the Take-a-Knee protests. With the league owners' decision to fine any player who does not stand during the national anthem in the 2018 season, it remains to be seen how long the Take-a-Knee protest will last (Maske, 2018). The ruling is not a guarantee that the protest will end; it may just be a deterrent.

REFERENCES

Ashley, L., & Olson, B. (1998). Constructing reality: Print media's framing of the women's movement, 1966 to 1986. *Journalism and Mass Communication Quarterly, 75*(2), 263-277.

Boyle, M. P., McCluskey, M. R., McLeod, D. M., & Stein, S. E. (2005). Newspapers and protest: An examination of protest coverage from 1960 to 1999. *Journalism and Mass Communication Quarterly, 82*(3), 638-653.

De Vreese, C. H. (2005). News framing: Theory and typology. *Information Design Journal + Document Design, 13*(1), 51-62. Retrieved from https://s3.amazonaws.com/academia.edu.documents/32324999/Framing.pdf?AWSAccessKeyId=AKIAIWOWYYGZ2Y53UL3A&Expires=1524426337&Signature=X0cKKt%2B0vAxrN%2B99u635ucWLTiA%3D&response-content-disposition=inline%3B%20filename%3D51_News_framing_Theory_and_typology.pdf

Hoffert, S. D. (1993). New York City's penny press and the issue of woman's rights, 1848-1860. *Journalism Quarterly, 70*(3), 656-665.

Maske, M. (2018, May 23). NFL owners approve new national anthem policy with hope of ending protests. *The Washington Post*. Retrieved from https://www.washingtonpost.com/news/sports/wp/2018/05/23/nfl-owners-leaning-towards-requiring-players-to-stand-for-national-anthem-or-remain-in-locker-room/?utm_term=.aba7fbae6683

Newberry, P. (2018, March 16). Colin Kaepernick, you're still not wanted. *The Denver Post*. Retrieved from https://www.denverpost.com/2018/03/16/colin-kaepernick-youre-still-not-wanted/

New suffrage drive planned by women. (1917, November 7). *The New York Times*. Retrieved from https://www.newspapers.com/image/20661955/?fcfToken=4b7456743543416d35532f65325257715862647639 4c2b6f6e524f5234443733327a7165466e644132717a634764762f2b524d4b6f516138634f585866673 7149

Scheufele, D. A. (1999). Framing as a theory of media effects. *Journal of Communication, 49*(1), 103-122.

Sharlet, J. (2011, November 10). Inside occupy wall street. *Rolling Stone*. Retrieved from https://www.rollingstone.com/politics/news/occupy-wall-street-welcome-to-the-occupation-20111110

Small, Jr., S. W. (1916, June 14). Sees suffrage as main issue at convention. *The Salt Lake Tribune*. Retrieved from https://www.newspapers.com/image/289617888/?terms=suffrage

Suffrage Militant. (1918, August 8). *The Washington Post*. Retrieved from https://www.newspapers.com/image/31574458/?terms=suffrage

Suffrage outlook dark up the state. (1917, November 4). *The New York Times*. Retrieved from https://www.newspapers.com/image/20659512/?terms=suffrage

The nineteenth amendment. (1920, August 20). *The Los Angeles Times*. Retrieved from https://www.newspapers.com/image/380542616/?fcfToken=5035446c626a4f2f616c514d5771752f4946436c75366a73727a476936327162384d797071785534363030304d4e5258487845484a686854355a7451644130367457476b656b5a473743436b3d

Thiessen, M. A. (2017, September 26). Disrespecting the flag is a disgraceful way to protest Trump. *The Washington Post*. Retrieved from https://www.washingtonpost.com/opinions/disrespecting-the-flag-is-a-disgraceful-way-to-protest-trump/2017/09/25/506a1d4c-a228-11e7-b14f-f41773cd5a14_story.html?utm_term=.1c724e4f2148

Volkmer, I. (2009). Framing theory. In S. W. Littlejohn & K. A. Foss (Eds.), *Encyclopedia of Communication Theory* (407-409). Los Angeles, CA: Sage.

Ward, J. C., & Ostrom, A. L. (2006). Complaining to the masses: The role of protest framing in customer-created complaint web sites. *Journal of Consumer Research, 33*(2), 220-230.

FOUR

America's Greatness Compromised

The "Star-Spangled Banner" as a Symbol of Nationalism, Identity, and Division

Pauline A. Andrea and Elizabeth Sheffield-Hayes

Establishing the relationship between perceptions of American national symbols and the social environments from which they emerge provides valuable insight into American national identity. According to Barth (1969), "What makes American identity an ethnic identity is that it is established and maintained in the transactional process of social identification between the boundaries of 'us' and 'them'" (p. 24). Jenkins (1997) qualifies Barth's (1969) identity narrative by arguing that there is always a sense of American community when "there is a 'them' or 'others' against whom to identify" (p. 56). This sense of community reflects a multifaceted concept that simultaneously harbors senses of differences and similarities. Grant (2006) asserts that individuals' lives are structured by class, race, and other socially imposed categories, a perspective that is seemingly pervasive in American culture. The diverse interpretation of American symbols and ideals establishes a sense of collective in-group identity that can be effectively explored through the theory of identification.

In this chapter, the authors explore public discourse surrounding the "Star-Spangled Banner" as a symbol of American pride and patriotism, as well as protest. Beginning with original interpretations of the anthem, the authors move on to examine twenty-first-century interpretations of the anthem's music and lyrics. The anthem carries opinions and references, including the support of slavery, patriotism, racial injustice, and the power of music.

THE EXAMPLE HEARD AROUND THE WORLD—COLIN KAEPERNICK'S TAKE-A-KNEE PROTEST

The Take-a-Knee controversy, an expression of protest against racial inequality, places Colin Kaepernick at the core of what some view as a microcosm of a contemporary experience for African-Americans. Historically, the anthem "represents the ideas and values of the nation and state," giving traction to Kaepernick's platform (Gilboa & Bodner, 2009, p. 46). Some interpret this controversy as challenging what others have branded as America's greatness. The assertion that American society was founded on social discord, disobedience, and protest gives greater credence to the existence of Barth's (1969) "us" and "them" narrative within American culture. Kaepernick's kneeling gesture and its subsequent defense seemingly integrate patriotism and social activism, fitting well within what can be viewed as a patriotic tradition paradigm. This narrative on protesting racial inequality as a sign of patriotism provides a viable platform for advancing public discourse on several timeless social issues, such as individual rights, patriotic rituals, social injustice, racial inequity, free will, and liberty.

Kaepernick's approach has introduced an additional dimension to the anthem's role of representing a 200-year-old time in American history. But there are questions about the anthem's historical symbolism that are sometimes characterized as having far-reaching, socially deviant elements, such as supporting slavery and racial injustice, as well as strong feelings of patriotism (Jenkins, 1997).

EVOLUTION OF THE "STAR-SPANGLED BANNER"—A MIGRATION TOWARD POLITICAL CORRECTNESS

Historical and contemporary social activism calls for respect within anthems for all cultures and demographics. Scholars caution against the popular trend of compromising the symbolism of patriotic gestures, such as standing during the anthem, and replacing them with unpatriotic and politically correct engagements that diminish the core of American cultural symbolism and identity (Leepson, 2014). Patriotic pride, anxieties, memories of past glories and humiliations, and promises of future greatness are some of the sentiments condensed into a symbolic item like the anthem. Scholars agree that the anthem is one of the purest forms of political symbolism today (Jenkins, 1997). In light of this, exploring the roots of the "Star-Spangled Banner" can provide insight into its evolution and varying forms of symbolism.

National Anthems Universally Defined

Gilboa and Bodner (2009) believe that "When exposed to the anthem of their native country, people react with feelings of pride and patriotism," and that "the anthem has the power to unite people around similar associations" (p. 459). Jahoda (1963) discusses the social identification process that establishes the connectedness between an anthem's symbolism and a sense of community, and Kolsto (2006) argues that anthems, along with other national symbols, facilitate either unification or division based on ethnic and political orientations. While these studies explore themes tied to anthems, they don't analyze the musical component of the anthems. These analyses tie anthems to community, connectedness, and identity.

According to Schatz and Lavine (2007), strong sources of symbolism, such as anthems, should also be viewed through a psychological lens, the symbolic involvement paradigm, and associated ritualistic tendencies. Similarly, but from a more psychological perspective, establishing a relationship between anthems and nations can be branded "instrumental involvement," which Schatz and Lavine (2007) purport reflect "some utilitarian concern for the functionality of the nation's social, political, and economic institutions, and the perceived capability of those institutions to provide instrumental benefits to citizens" (p. 331).

"Instrumental involvement" shifts the view "from a pronounced cultural understanding to an instrumental-rational relationship with a nation" (Schatz and Lavine, 2007, p. 332). This perspective allows "national institutions to provide their citizens with an opportunity for instrumental involvement" (Schatz & Lavine, 2007, p. 332), establishing a platform for connectedness between the anthem as a national symbol and the nation's citizens.

The element of national memberships and revealing the distinct motivational concerns related to one's identity expression are at the core of the symbolic and instrumental involvement of citizens with their country's anthem (Jenkins, 1997). Schatz and Lavine (2007) are proponents of national symbolism, recommending that anthems promote messaging of psychological attachments to the respective nation. Through the positive symbolism that countries' flags and anthems represent, patriotism and identity can experience a renewal and revival. From compromised national security to an erosion of national identity, the anthem can be the source of a compelling narrative on the need to shape the global conversation regarding who we are (Butz, 2009).

Key, the Innovator—Social and Political Symbolism for the American Nation

With patriotic fervor and memories of the War of 1812 at the core of his motivation for writing what is now the "Star-Spangled Banner," Francis Scott Key penned a poem that was later set to music, and subsequently introduced as the song that today serves as the premise for a controversy. Discussion on the meaning of the "Star-Spangled Banner" has taken a renewed significance in light of the Kaepernick controversy. Research supports the contention that battling over the song's meaning is today an important element of the song's tradition, although not necessarily an integral component of Key's intended symbolism (Butz, 2009).

During the late eighteenth century, participation in chattel slavery was commonplace. Key's parents, members of the upper echelon of society, were proponents of slavery, and benefitted from it considerably. Key's academic career led to a successful professional career in the legal field, where he was branded one of the most prominent attorneys in Washington, D.C., in the early 1800s. One of Key's first and most critical assignments was being dispatched by President Madison during the Battle of Baltimore in 1814, with the intent to negotiate the release of prominent surgeon Dr. William Beanes. This experience, along with the existing political and social climate, partially served as the impetus for Key's penning of the anthem (Leepson, 2014). A critical element of his overall war experience was witnessing twenty-five hours of combat, which served as the premise for the lyrics "And the rocket's red glare, the bombs bursting in air." Key's assumption was that America had lost the battle, but he was later "elated" to realize that the Stars and Stripes were still flying the next morning at Fort McHenry, reflected in the lyrics "Gave proof through the night, that our flag was still there, Oh say does that star-spangled banner yet wave."

Key's experience with racial issues was not significant, and he is viewed as not having a "complicated or complex history with race" (Butz, 2009). However, research shows that he was a proponent of the repatriation of blacks in the United States to what he viewed as their point of origin, Africa (Gelb, 2004). Butz (2009) noted Key's pro-slavery, anti-black, and anti-abolitionist stance that reflected the prevalent perspective of his day. Artifacts and other records show that Key owned slaves during the time he wrote the anthem, and comments such as blacks being a distinct and inferior race have been attributed to him (Jackson, 2015). Smithsonian records (Gelb, 2004) reveal that he used his office as the district attorney for the city of Washington from 1833 to 1840 to defend slavery, attacking the abolitionist movement in several high-profile cases. His efforts to keep slavery intact include his unsuccessful attempt to have a New York doctor hung for his abolitionist mentality. While scholars have expressed dismay at Key's passionate anti-black stance, they have also credited him with successfully litigating several legal cases on behalf of slaves (Jenner, 2013).

Many researchers have explored and analyzed Key's contribution to American culture through his authorship of the anthem. Throughout a biography of Key, Leepson (2014) brands him a "self-proclaimed, self-righteous and opinionated man," whose perspectives reflected the convictions and contradictions of his time (p. 13). While Leepson (2014) views Key as a patriot and decent and respectable human being, he was appalled by Key's strong support for the repatriation of slaves to Africa. Leepson (2014) viewed Key as having an intellectual struggle between the reality of slavery and social injustice, and the Christian religion he devoutly espoused, resulting in his branding of Key as a "mediated racist" (p. 22). Leepson's (2014) perspective is instrumental in analyzing how Key's mindset and philosophies shaped his lyrics for the anthem.

The basis for the War of 1812 between the United States and the United Kingdom was the U.K.'s attempt to restrict U.S. trade, coupled with the latter's desire to extend its northern territory. Research shows that in 1810, over 15 percent of the U.S. population was enslaved, and the British engaged in the active recruitment of escaped slaves to ensure freedom for themselves through joining the British war effort (Butz, 2009). The U.K.'s Colonial Marines unit spearheaded this effort, culminating in the battle in Washington, D.C., in 1814. This battle led to activities such as setting fire to the White House. However, many troops in the Colonial Marines unit were killed in battle, leading to Key's lyrics "foul footsteps" of the "hireling and slave," for whom there was no recourse, and "No refuge could save" from "the gloom of the grave" (Gelb, 2004). Bond and Wilson (2001) assert that while the anthem is viewed by many as a patriotic song, it simultaneously reflects the dismissal of African-American fervor as they displayed the audacity to fight for their freedom.

The U.S. Anthem Defined Across Cultures

Having a long-standing affiliation with sports, the anthem has become a source of symbolism in American culture. This has established the basic premise for honoring and showing reverence for the anthem across cultures. As various themes and symbolic meanings of the anthem are explored, particular focus is placed on which of these meanings are elevated or silenced within cultures. While not commonplace, occasional elements of societal deviance due to pro-slavery and pro-war perspectives can be found in some cultures. In other cultures, prevailing social issues create a renewed sense of symbolic relevance within the anthem's symbolism narrative. Sherman (1993) explores the role repetitive play of the "Star-Spangled Banner" has on his family of Native American descent, and reveals the symbolism the anthem has for his family, including thoughts of war, family relationship preservation, and the power of music. Sherman (1993) also highlights concerns about the inability of families of Native American descent to conquer the prevailing issues of racial inequality for minorities.

Public policies have oftentimes been viewed as giving symbolism the green light to display support for political correctness. Freedom of expression is often eclipsed by the need for political correctness (Gill, 2016). Scholars, such as Butz (2009), recommend that society's exposure to national symbolism be explored through social and psychological lenses. The resulting narrative is that national symbols, such as the anthem, are not passive fixtures of people's environment. Advocates against assertions that the anthem is a source of division can claim that the anthem serves to enhance individual identity, and promotes group unity at a subconscious level. Heightened national identification and the propensity to automatically integrate concepts, principles, and philosophies associated with nationhood can be instrumental in intergroup relations. The anthem has historically facilitated a critical need for identification and connectedness across cultures.

The U.S. National Anthem—Historical Symbolism during Sporting Events

Establishing a close association with sports since being chosen as the official anthem for the U.S., the "Star-Spangled Banner's" future relevance in American culture was obvious when it was played during the 1918 World Series Red Sox versus Cubs game (Brady, 2017). Remembering the 100,000 American deaths during World War I created a relational experience between fans and the anthem (Brady, 2017). Red Sox third baseman Fred Thomas, on furlough from the Navy, engaged in a salute when the anthem was played. Other players put their hands over their hearts. The crowd, already on their feet, sang along, and the final notes were met with "thunderous applause, and filled the air with cheer that marked the highest point of the day's enthusiasm" (Brady, 2017, p. 12).

Since this initiation through baseball, American sports of all kinds have followed suit, solidifying this anthem tradition into American history (Brady, 2017). At the time, the U.S. did not have an official anthem in spite of the public's quest to establish and integrate a national anthem into American tradition. With the introduction of the tradition of the "Star-Spangled Banner," Congress voted to make it the official anthem in 1931. Though the anthem has not historically been played and sung at every sporting event, many feature the song, along with "pregame festivities" and "the introduction of wounded soldiers" (Brady, 2017, p. 25). Today, the anthem ritual comprises standing, placing a hand over the heart, listening to, and possibly singing the song.

METHODOLOGY

A critical element of understanding today's perspectives on the anthem's symbolism is collecting data through qualitative and historical research to gain greater insight into the anthem's branding as a phenomenon. Historical research comprising primary and secondary sources from various on-site and online artifacts, manuscripts, and historical collections were thoroughly examined and analyzed. Reflections and opinions were also documented through qualitative research involving fifteen southern state interview participants of varying ages, races and genders, providing insight into how at least some of the country interpret the anthem.

The following fifteen participants were interviewed in April 2018 through individual face-to-face communication: Nancy Autry, high school teacher; Robbin Burris, executive assistant and grandmother to two teenage boys; Stacey Davis, avid football fan and recreational employee; Margaret Hatcher, high school counselor; Alexander Hawkins, university counselor; Shawn McGee, high school teacher and coach; Deena Newman, high school counselor; Terrie Patterson, baseball mom; Jeremiah Pitts, university counselor; Steven Preston, high school teacher; Anita Reed, high school librarian; Amy Sloan, high school teacher; Carol Taylor, high school counselor; Jonathan Watson, coach; and Monica Whitley, university athletic counselor. All names are changed to protect the participants from any repercussions. The interviews were recorded, transcribed, and analyzed for themes. The interview process explored, in detail, participants' personal views on the anthem's symbolism. Interviews primarily revealed the prevailing themes of slavery, patriotism, racial injustice, and the power of music. The historical and qualitative data were then organized into historical knowledge and themes surrounding the anthem's symbolism in light of recent anthem-based protests, and more specifically the Kaepernick protest.

DIVERGENT VIEWS ON THE ANTHEM'S SYMBOLISM—THE PUBLIC RESPONDS

Historical research aims to interpret both the original and current symbolism of the anthem, facilitating how past symbolism may have predicted current interpretations. The anthem's symbolism, at least theoretically, transcends time, place, and cultures within the U.S., and particular interpretations of the anthem can potentially shape individuals' ideals and values. For example, when interviewed Preston expressed that he grew up in a military home where flags and the anthem were an integral part of his young life, shaping how he now feels toward the anthem. Autry stated that watching baseball games with her father and playing softball, both of which had the anthem played at the beginning of each game, shaped how she now interprets the anthem. An exploration of interviewees' repetitive themes of slavery, patriotism, racial injustice, and the power of music provides insight into how at least some Americans, all from the South, viewed and valued the anthem.

Slavery and the Anthem

Bond and Wilson (2001) were dedicated to exploring the lyrics of *Lift Every Voice and Sing*, an attempt to pay homage to African Americans' desire to honor American culture, patriotism, and the history of racial and social equity struggles. Branded the African-American anthem and "Negro spiritual," the song's lyrics reflect optimism by "facing the rising sun of our new day has begun," and unity reflected in "let us march until victory is won" (Bond & Wilson, 2001, p. 4). This African-American perspective promotes the message of hope, peace, strength, and confidence that served as a worldview and source of inspiration, a clarion call to African Americans to "lift every voice and sing" (Bond & Wilson, 2001, p. 18). Though not proposed for nationwide adoption, this desire was an audacious idea that never gained traction and met with much resistance. This song exists in sharp contrast to the "Star-Spangled Banner." African Americans used this spiritual as their organizing element for paying a personal tribute to what they hoped would be the enduring power of this song, portraying American life from an African American's perspective.

Some historians purport that the legacy of black slavery is enshrined in the anthem, and that perceptions of a celebration of slavery are unequivocally laced in the fabric of the "Star-Spangled Banner" (Leepson, 2014). According to Grant (2006), an opponent of the divisive underpinnings of the anthem, this "hidden racism" suggests we need repudiation of the white supremacy mantra espoused by Key and others, and is necessary to eliminate the anthem's racial overtones (p. 23). Olson (2017) stated with conviction that the anthem "is an expression of racial hostility toward African Americans, and should be either retired or at least acknowledged as a subject of national embarrassment" (p. 2). Several interview participants agreed with Olson's (2017) assertion. For instance, Whitley stated, "It is discouraging that our country is still so divided that we keep a racist song as our anthem." In support, Hawkins espoused that "this song is a symbol of racial inequality. It is humiliating to me as a black man to have to listen to this song before all my favorite sports and hear my little sister sing it before a game, knowing that the song was not written for my freedom as an American citizen."

Slavery is undoubtedly a symbolism narrative surrounding the anthem today through "verses that seem to encourage slavery," which further encourages interpretations not reflecting African American or immigrant culture (Sloan). This perception is extended through the long-standing contention by scholars that the anthem is an "intellectual and moral atrocity" that perpetuates the historical elements of slavery and oppression of African Americans (Grant, 2006, p. 5). To support this claim, scholars point to the anthem's excerpt, "No refuge could save the hireling and slave, From the terror of flight or gloom of the grave" (Leepson, 2014, p. 9). Sloan's interview interpreted the perceived theme of slavery as "the writer is taking a hit at those who were slaves at the time and went over to the British." Whitley, an African-American interviewee, stated "I no longer sing this song because it was obviously not meant for my ancestors and their freedom." This sentiment has also been argued from opposing perspectives addressing slavery, or addressing the issue of the British who taxed and "enslaved" the colonist. Kaepernick supports the first view, claiming that the anthem does not express support and patriotism for "a country that oppresses black people and people of color" (Huntington, 2004, p. 15).

Racial Injustice and the Anthem

According to Sage (1998), sports-oriented social scientists agree that all sports make for a powerful political stage. In an article juxtaposing African American and Caucasian football fans, Sorek and White (2017) concluded that Caucasian fans viewed the Take-a-Knee protest as upending what "they see as the innocent, colorless patriotism of football," whereas African-American fans express "feelings of alienation toward the imposed patriotism in NFL games" (p. 3). Seventy-five polls administered by Sorek and White (2017) between 1981 and 2014 compared the relationship between national pride and Caucasian and African-American football fans, concluding that national pride has declined among Americans across all races, particularly within the African-American community.

Parallels with the aforementioned views were reflected in the responses of interview participants. Twelve of the fifteen participants classified themselves as white, and eight of the twelve participants agreed that the Take-a-Knee protest was a major source of disruption prior to a football game. The other seven participants, three of whom identified as African American, shared Watson's view that "The Kaepernick protest was well-placed, and a good way to make feelings known." Sentiments shared by interview participants ranged from thoughts of patriotism to expressing no identification with the anthem. Many participants referenced phrases in the anthem as having serious racial overtones. Other views expressed included the anthem being "unsympathetic to those who were not free during the writing of the song" (Hawkins); concerns of the anthem "being racist" (Sloan); and the anthem "not fitting my cultural heritage in America" (Whitley).

However, many interviewees integrated into their narrative Preston's positive themes of "love of country," "bravery and triumph over what is perceived as evil," and "respect and love for our country and each other as a melting pot of Americans"; and Newman's "respect for our military and what they do." Several interview participants also expressed a need for a balanced perspective through a song that "reflected my culture's history as well as white Americans' history" (Mcgee). As Patterson expressed, "The anthem is the American people standing up for their freedom, their personal heritage, their rights, and everything else that America currently stands for."

Kaepernick's racial injustice platform was viewed by Sloan as "The perfect setup of being in the spotlight for just long enough to call attention to an issue that was being passed by. If protesting during a national symbol where thousands are watching because it is football, and that is the way to get the attention on an issue like this, then so be it." Pitts saw it similarly saying, "The anthem represents America and its ideals. Coupled with the large sporting arena, this made for a perfect protest stage."

Patriotism and the Anthem

Anthem themes of patriotism, unity, and freedom were valued by many interview participants. Pitts remarked, "The anthem is not about one culture or another. It is about how a bunch of mismatched people came together to fight off oppressors; where we came this close to losing, but we didn't. We were the little guy who defied the odds and won the fight." Nevertheless, some may view one's choice to either kneel or stand during the anthem as a choice of patriotism reflecting individual expression, obedience, and love of country. Dissenting opinions state that kneeling or sitting during the anthem reflects a lack of patriotism. Newman expressed feelings about kneeling by stating, "Not standing for the anthem shows that you are against America as a whole. Not standing is inappropriate. Standing is a symbol of respect for the anthem, the flag, the country, and the fights we've been through since before our inception as a nation."

Notwithstanding its initial wave of popularity for many decades, the "Star-Spangled Banner" ranked third behind other anthem considerations *Hail Columbia* and *Yankee Doodle* as America's default musical expression of national and patriotic fervor (Sherwood, 2012). However, during the Reconstruction era, the "Star-Spangled Banner" emerged as the predominant American hymn that later served as the anthem (Grant, 2006). Huntington (2004) associated the anthem's patriotic flavor as "entrenched by its association with flag-raising ceremonies practiced during the war" (Huntington, 2004, p. 46). Other scholars assert that phrases such as "land of the free and home of the brave" elevate the anthem to American iconography, with a subtle reminder that partisanship is critical to democracy (Grant, 2006, p. 7). Interviewees agreed, with Taylor stating, "The flag is an important image in the anthem, because when you think of America, you think of the flag. To have the flag linked with the anthem is a powerful reminder of almost losing the battle, of knowing that the American fort was not taken, of emotions that are hard to explain at the relief, with a capital R, that Americans were saving themselves from British rule." Huntington (2004) espoused, "The song is a verb, and citizenship is a verb, and that these are part of the process of identity negotiation" (p. 45). The multifaceted and contentious development of America is also reflected in the song's origin, and facilitates the echoing of American history. In essence, the anthem is viewed as an all-encompassing human rights treatise of sorts.

The Power of Music and the Anthem

Interview participants responded in varying ways to the anthem's patriotism symbolism through the music. Most participants expressed a great deal of pride in the anthem, defining it as a symbol of freedom. Though it is a song, Hatcher commented that the anthem "may be intangible insofar as one cannot touch sounds, but the words and the score can be held in one's hands and/or touched; so perhaps it should also be considered a tangible symbol." Davis emphasized the anthem's potency as "It is sung so many different ways, each singer doing it a little differently. This also shows American's freedom of expression. It's not how you sing it, it's the message found in the way it is sung and the lyrics."

Most participants confirmed that they knew at least the first verse of the anthem, with Reed viewing it as "a victory celebration for an expression of national identity, unity, and pride." Many participants echoed Preston's sentiments that playing the anthem before sporting events is a "patriotic ritual" that Davis further qualified as showing pride "in those who are playing the sport, and having the potential to possibly represent our country through sports." Sporting events bring together people rooting for the same teams; however, the anthem being sung at the beginning "brings both teams and fans together to show their pride and love of country," allowing people to be united under an umbrella symbol, Burris said.

Patterson said the messages of patriotism and "a battle hard fought" are found not only in the music, but also in the text of the song, and how it is presented at most sporting events. Most interview participants were familiar with the idea of the anthem being introduced with an announcer stating, "We shall now sing our anthem" (Pitts), or a certain singer will "now lead us in singing our anthem" (Davis). Special focus on a call to action to eventgoers to also sing the anthem, as well as the use of the word "our" was appreciated by many participants, who viewed this invitation as creating unity throughout the venue where the anthem is being sung. According to Patterson, southern communities "love football and will fight over teams, but the anthem brings the opposing teams together for a moment to remind them that they are all under the same flag," as well as "those who live in the Bible belt believe in God, guns and fighting for what we believe in. The song includes all of this."

When individuals sing the anthem with conviction and passion, they give a voice to their own citizenship in a manner that informs their vision of the country (Schatz & Lavine, 2007). Performances of the anthem that do not fully embrace the ethos of national introspection warrant a resurrection of the song's original multifaceted meaning (Leepson, 2014). Some claim the anthem is less musically and lyrically powerful than other songs. But "America the Beautiful," for instance, which was once a viable anthem option, has an even more militaristic and nationalistic tone compared to the "Star-Spangled Banner," and some see it as having further allusion to slavery (Huntington, 2004).

With the original version of the anthem being four verses long, the potency of the themes in that version has been diminished. Many Americans, Preston noted, "do not know anything past the words of the first verse." For instance, while the first verse expresses the thoughts of a young man peering into a foggy and rain-soaked dawn to find out whether his country has been conquered in battle, another verse seemingly contradicts the "land of the free and the home of the brave" assertion. Themes of war, bloodshed, slavery, terror, graveyards, and gloomy environments pervade the lyrics, and triumphant words such as "The star-spangled banner in triumph doth wave" reflect a rich and eclectic mix of emotions and perspectives that only a few, including Key, experienced firsthand (Baptiste, 2018).

DISCUSSION

Engaging in a departure from current-day patriotic traditions is a critical element of the anthem protest narrative. Scholars recommend that individuals make the anthem uniquely theirs lyrically and psychologically by integrating their personal tone and dimension to the lyrics without compromising the intended symbolism. This is reflected, for instance, in the customization of the stately descent of "O say" at the beginning of the song for a profoundly changed and deeply moving rendition (Schatz & Lavine, 2007). According to Robin (2014), "Key really wouldn't recognize what we sing today" (p. 2). This disparity in symbolism perspectives justifies the claim of the anthem as a source of division. Kaepernick's Take-a-Knee protest has brought renewed attention and significance to long-standing contentions surrounding the anthem. Further, his narrative is viewed by some as compromising the anthem's intended symbolism, and by others as reflecting the anthem's original messaging. The prevailing sentiments from data collected through interviews and historical research align with the slavery, patriotism, racial injustice, and power music themes that have become pervasive in historical and current public discourse surrounding the anthem's symbolism.

Further, current-day southern Americans provided insight into the range of perceptions about the anthem. These had social and racial dimensions. These dimensions were often reflective of what scholars have argued about the anthem's origins and how people have historically felt about the anthem. The presence of these perceptions and themes both challenges current sentiments, and provides a source of patriotism in current-day Americans. The anthem, even after multiple attempts to reverse its adoption as the nation's patriotic song of choice, continues to enjoy staying power at most sporting events. The National Football League's most recent stance on not allowing players to kneel on the field, but allowing them to remain in the locker room during the anthem has propelled the conversation on diversity of thought.

CONCLUSION

Through the integration of the historical and qualitative research methods, various historical and current-day elements of the "Star-Spangled Banner"'s symbolism have been explored. The originally intended symbolism has not outlived its purpose, but prevailing contemporary social issues create a renewed sense of symbolic relevance within the nationalism narrative. Through the interview process, the exploration of how current-day southerners interpret, respond to, and feel about the anthem's intended (original) and perceived symbolism facilitates a mediated environment through which Kaepernick's stance can be perpetuated. Like other items with historical symbolism, society must decide if the anthem will be perceived as aligning with the patriotic and nationalistic symbolism in the more acceptable first verse, or being subject to the intended/original symbolism in the song as a whole. That symbolic meaning may influence the perception of whether the anthem provides an appropriate moment during which to demonstrate against racial inequality.

REFERENCES

Baptiste, L. (2018). Manuscript: The Star-Spangled Banner. Christie's Auction House: New York.

Barth, F. (1969). "Introduction" and "Pathan identity and its maintenance," in F. Barth (ed.) *Ethnic Groups and Boundaries: The Social Organization of Culture Difference*; London: Allen & Unwin, pp. 9-38, 117-134.

Bond, J., Wilson, S. K. (2001). *Lift every voice and sing: A celebration of the Negro national anthem; 100 years, 100 voices*. New York: Random House.

Brady, E. (2017) How the anthem became an essential part of sports. Retrieved from https://www.usatoday.com/story/sports/nfl/2017/09/26/how-national-anthem-become-essential-part-sports/706243001/

Butz, D. A. (2009). National symbols as agents of psychological and social change. London: Routledge.

Gelb, T. (2004). Manuscript: Where's the debate on Francis Scott Key's slave-holding legacy? Retrieved from: https://www.smithsonianmag.com/smithsonian-institution/wheres-debate-francis-scott-keys-slave-holding-legacy-180959550/

Gilboa, A., Bodner, E. (2009). What are your thoughts when the anthem is playing? An empirical exploration. *Psychology of Music Journal*, 37(4), pp. 459-484.

Gill, E. L. (2016). "Hands up, don't shoot" or shut up and play ball? Fan-generated media views of the Ferguson Five. *Journal of Human Behavior in the Social Environment*, 26 (3-4), pp. 400-412.

Grant, P. (2006). *Our anthem: American symbolism defined*. New York: Simon and Schuster.

Huntington, S. P. (2004). *Who are we? The challenges to America's national identity*. New York: Simon and Schuster.

Jackson, C. (2015). Star-Spangled Banner Manuscript, Spelman College Library.

Jahoda, G. (1963). The development of children's ideas about country and nationality: National symbols and themes. *British Journal of Educational Psychology*, 33(1), pp. 47-60.

Jenkins, R. (1997). *Rethinking ethnicity: Arguments and explorations*. London: Routledge.

Jenner, F. (2013). Manuscript: Francis Scott Key and Slavery, Clark Atlanta University Art Museum.

Karageorghis, C., Priest, D.L. (2008). Music in sport and exercise: An update on research and application. *The Sport Journal*, 48(2), pp. 19-22.

Kolsto, P. (2006). National symbols as signs of unity and division. *Ethnic and Racial Studies*, 29(4), pp. 676-701.

Leepson, (2014). *What so proudly we hailed: Francis Scott Key, a life*. New York: Simon and Schuster.

Olson, W. (2017). Is the Star-Spangled Banner racist? *National Review*, 34(2), pp. 1-3.

Robin, W. (2014). How the anthem has unfurled. Retrieved from https://www.nytimes.com/2014/06/29/arts/music/the-star-spangled-banner-has-changed-a-lot-in-200-years.html

Schatz, R. T., Lavine, H. (2007). Waving the flag: National symbolism, social identity and political engagement. *Political Psychology Journal*, 28(3), pp. 329-355.

Sherman, A. (1993). Because my father always said he was the only Indian who saw Jimi Hendrix play the Star-Spangled Banner at Woodstock. *Atlantic Monthly Press*, 403(2), pp. 24–36.

Sherwood, E. (2012). Manuscript: Anthem Considerations. Clark Atlanta University Art Museum.

Sorek, T., White, R. (2017). The difference between black football fans and white football fans. *The Conversation*, 23(3), pp. 6-14.

FIVE

Influencing America

Sports and Conservative Radio

Kelvin King and Eric Frederick

INTRODUCTION

Through radio broadcasting, celebrities and notable spokespersons have reached into people's homes for nearly one hundred years, starting in the 1920s. While many in today's internet generation prefer online blogs or internet chats to engage in social debates and discussions, others continue to cling to the radio as their medium of choice for ideological exchange. Given the rabid fan bases in competitive national sports, competing opinions are inevitable, and the combatants in such discussions are found on sports radio primarily, but sometimes even on conservative talk radio. In this study, we compare sports radio and conservative radio. Sports radio features dozens of personalities on stations such as ESPN, Fox Sports, NBC Sports Radio, and CBS Sports Radio. However, this study focuses on two popular urban sports-talk shows: *The Right Time with Bomani Jones* and *His & Hers* (the latter hosted by Michael Smith and Jemele Hill). The shows from the conservative talk show circuit also include a number of radio personalities, but this study features Rush Limbaugh and Glenn Beck. Using critical analysis, we examined the collective views of both the conservative and sports-based camps to identify shared narratives. Furthermore, we contrasted the two types of shows and explored the foundational issues they champion which could be political, racial, economic, social, generational, religious, historical, or traditional. It is important to note that this study is not exhaustive and that the aforementioned radio personalities may have addressed these issues in forums beyond their radio shows, such as on cable television or on other radio networks. But this research will at least sample the themes espoused by these sports and conservative radio programs since radio is a powerful medium that impacts the national consciousness and provides forums that perpetuate diverging views.

Talk Radio's Social Reality

The social construction of reality differs between social groups, institutions, and ideologies (Gamson, 1992). Constructing reality is a multilayered process, and the media's role is central to establishing public opinions and perceived realities (Hoffman, 1991; Squires, 2000). Berger and Luckmann (1966) postulated that people only worry about what are important considerations when a problem arises.

Within the talk radio community, hosts and receptive audiences are generally categorized as conservative or liberal. Since the 1990s, nationally syndicated talk show hosts such as Rush Limbaugh, Sean Hannity, and Glenn Beck have secured a superior space in the industry (Berry & Sobieraj, 2011). Historically, talk radio has remained conservative, middle-aged, and male especially in view of Air America Radio's 2004 launch and subsequent failure in January 2010 (Kovarik, 2016). Other nationally syndicated talk shows emerged in the form of sports radio, mainly ESPN Radio.

Talk radio is tribal in nature, constructing narratives that feature protagonists, antagonists, dramatic tension, rising and falling action, and denouements. The divisions penetrate the psychological and relational fabric of individuals and society at large. "Commercial systems create a heated, emotional, and devoted (to the host's opinions) public of passion" (Dori-Hacohen, 2012, p. 168).

Conservative Talk Radio

Conservative talk show host Rush Limbaugh is considered a freedom fighter for his loyal following, but reviled by opponents as a demagogue. He represents a large segment of the United States that embraces his ideology either in whole or in part. According to one critical scholar, "Limbaugh tells his listeners he will remain on radio until every American agrees with him" (Bennett, 2009, p. 80).

Conservative talk show host Glenn Beck is also a prominent national voice. According to Beck, public policy and politics seem to be the bedrock of the nation's conscience. One critical scholar writes, "Glenn Beck used his own version of critical pedagogy to teach his audience a defensive citizenship designed to help them resist the contemporary threats to American democracy" (Childers et al., 2013, p.49).

Sports Radio

Sports and talk radio hosts remained predominantly white males in the early 2000s. Nationally syndicated African American talk radio host Tom Joyner and the *Tom Joyner Morning Show* (TJMS) incorporated sports, music, politics, and other sociocultural topics to combat talk radio's conservative slant. Other nationally syndicated urban radio show programming resembled TJMS programming because African American listeners expected African American hosts to address perceived controversies that were covered by their white counterparts (Squires, 2000).

The literature examining the methods through which contemporary ESPN radio hosts construct social realities through sports is limited. Because sports is an inclusive, integrative social force, talk radio's ability to converge sociocultural symbols and meaning is amplified. For example, ESPN's Paul Finebaum in 2016 apologized for saying this country is not oppressing black people (Boren, 2016), while in 2014, African American host Stephen A. Smith offered an explanation for his views concerning women and domestic violence (Boren, 2014). Consequently, ESPN's sports radio coverage of anthem kneeling acts and understanding the protesters' social realities needs further exploration.

In summary, the literature clearly divides talk radio into camps often delineated by politics, race, social groups, and ideologies. Both forums include hosts, guests, and regular callers. Also, conservative talk often discusses sports, and sports talk often discusses politics. Therefore, our goal is to identify the differing positions, and then compare and contrast the distinctions in hopes that each side can learn from each other.

METHODS

This study is based on Bormann's (1972) rhetorical criticism of small-group communication, which is called fantasy theme analysis (FTA). We combined a critical, reflective approach, which is useful for investigating how participants on conservative- and sports-radio talk shows exchange ideas and how these ideas provide a framework through which the hosts and callers interact to make sense of their social world. A fantasy theme is an interpretive narrative that provides a coherent and artistic dramatization of an event.

Process

In this study, the first step involved coding the artifact for three components of FTA: setting, character, and action. The setting evaluates characteristics of where the action takes place. Character coding is significant because identifying how the characters are perceived requires focusing on how their attitudes and behaviors create a fantasy theme. The characters include the hosts and guests on conservative- and sports-radio talk shows such as *Rush Limbaugh, Glenn Beck, The Right Time with Bomani Jones,* and *His & Hers* with Smith and Hill. Actions, in FTA, refer to the ways in which drama affects people, including those who share realities.

The second step in FTA involves constructing a rhetorical vision. In an FTA, it is important to identify patterns within and among the themes of each artifact. The last step is to interpret the rhetorical vision through the symbolic aspects of social reality surrounding the National Football League (NFL) anthem protests including President Donald Trump's comments on September 22, 2017, in which he stated, "Wouldn't you love to see one of these NFL owners, when somebody disrespects our flag, say 'Get that son of a bitch off the field right now. Out! He's fired!'"

Transcripts

Transcripts were acquired from conservative- and sports-radio shows occurring after Trump's comments. The *Rush Limbaugh* transcripts were retrieved from the archives at RushLimbaugh.com. The *Rush Limbaugh* artifacts consisted of five episodes that were specific to the anthem-related take-a-knee movement. Episodes of *Glenn Beck* were retrieved from GlennBeck.com. In this study, the *Glenn Beck* artifacts consisted of seven episode transcripts. The episodes included monologues by Beck, interviews, and audience responses.

The other two shows are from ESPN. Two artifacts are from *The Right Time with Bomani Jones* and three artifacts from *His & Hers*, which stars Smith and Hill. These two shows' transcripts included discussions with other ESPN radio and television hosts, with callers, and debates among retired NFL players regarding the kneeling protest in the NFL.

SPORTS RADIO AND CONSERVATIVE RADIO ANALYSIS

Setting in Sports Radio

To understand a group of people one must study their sports-mediated reality (Nimmo & Combs, 1983). *The Right Time with Bomani Jones* and *His & Hers* each construct virtual spaces in which people express opposing perspectives (Botes & Langdon, 2006). The shows' hosts transport the audiences through language, fantasy, and imagination. For both shows the United States is a *fantasy theme* where audiences' imaginatively travel at the discretion of the host.

Jones transported the audience by discussing complaints from NFL advertiser Papa John's CEO Steve Richie regarding NFL commissioner Roger Goodell's lack of control over the protests. Jones stated, "Miami has much more of a delivery system setup, because it's more of a vertical place. But I feel like people in New York City don't understand that in the rest of the world, you just don't have people delivering to you all the time" (*Right Time*, 2017a). Jones's audience thus envisions several cultures within the United States that exist in bubbles regarding how the rest of the nation experiences pizza delivery on Sundays during NFL games. Nonetheless, the fantasy is that audiences and host will experience sports in America similarly.

His & Hers played a recording from the Dallas Cowboys' owner, Jerry Jones, which captured the essence of FTA setting, "We're trying to get peoples' minds away from the troubled times. We're trying to take them away from all other parts of the newspaper and we're trying to get them over to the sports page" (*His & Hers*, 2017c). NFL owners' desire is to focus the fans' fantasies on a certain game time and place. The intended setting refocuses fans' attention away from a United States and the social issues that are part of reality. The focus is still America but situated in an isolated setting. Such a setting supports Jerry Jones's, and other league owners' revenues. Sports radio establishes settings to guide listeners' fantasies. At this stage of FTA, sports radio presents fantasy-based visions of the United States. Various groups claim legitimacy and ownership of the nation's past, present, and future; therefore, sports radio's attempt to redirect its audience's vision is reasonable.

Setting in Conservative Radio

The settings from conservative talk radio emanate from several fronts. One aspect of setting, according to Limbaugh, revolves around the political arena where liberals work as opportunists to promote their left-wing agendas in every arena in life including sports. He said, "To leftists—wherever they are, media or elsewhere—this is a flawed country that is just soaking in injustice" (*Rush Limbaugh*, 2017a). In his view, the socialist left stirs up controversy regarding racism and white supremacy at every turn, even claiming that the white owners and the black players are in a master–slave relationship. The left, according to Limbaugh, does not like what the NFL stands for—strong, masculine, rugged individualism and patriotism.

A second setting, according to Limbaugh, is the Colin Kaepernick controversy, which originated with a poor contract decision that then conveniently descended into a racial discrimination issue. According to Limbaugh, Kaepernick's diminishing skills and imprudent business advice were the cause of his downfall. He emphasized the fact that the 49ers offered Kaepernick a contract that he walked out on. He contended that, "Kaepernick can't get hired 'cause he can't play" (*Rush Limbaugh*, 2017b).

Another setting perpetuated by Limbaugh is the consumer business relationship between the media and the public. He argued that the media caters to the progressives, but Middle America tends to be forgotten.

According to Limbaugh, the NFL had lost sight of who their fans were. They are not what he called white-wine-sipping, left-wing social justice warriors or college snowflakes; instead, they were people who bought Ford trucks and cases of beer (*Rush Limbaugh*, 2017c).

Beck offered a positive setting by singling out the Cowboys organization as a beacon of light when they decided to kneel and pray as a team and then stand for the national anthem. As other teams fumbled about with part-time kneelers or raised fists, the Cowboys found a way for both sides to, as Beck's saw it, feel respected.

Beck proposed a more antagonistic setting surrounding the NFL's commemoration of Veteran's Day. He stated, "You can't defecate all over the flag every other day leading up to Veteran's Day and then all of a sudden pretend, oh, no. You can't fix this with a parade or theatrics or camouflage clothing" (*Glenn Beck*, 2017c).

Within the FTA rubric the settings comparison provides a stark contrast between the two camps. Sports radio criticizes wealthy owners, domineering leaders, and out-of-touch old school patriarchs who turn a blind eye to cultural diversity, inequality, and variations in pizza delivery. Conversely, conservative talk radio hosts paint a different landscape, emphasizing strong leadership, tradition, bedrock principles, and capitalism that categorized Kaepernick's unemployment as an unfortunate reality of market forces.

What type of setting do these opponents share? The two sides care about family prosperity, opportunity, and a better future for the United States. While sports radio calls for grassroots leadership to be a guiding light, conservative talk radio elevates the bedrock foundations of a country built on patriotism, strong leaders, and core values.

CHARACTERS

Characters in Sports Radio

Groups' realities converge because they have similar fantasies regarding the dramatization of characters. Sports-radio personalities construct protagonists and antagonists for their listeners' consumption. For example, shaping Trump into a public enemy who threatens to propel the United States back to the antebellum South, or the civil rights era, is an attempt to play to the audience's fantasies. In short, periods that were synonymous with sociopolitical imbalances are opposed to the concepts of nationalism and patriotism. For example, Jones's guest host Pablo Torre stated, "What happened was the president of the United States decided that this is an advantageous bit of ground to wage a culture war" (*Right Time*, 2017b). One guest, Dominique Foxworth proposed, "It seems like the president is using this kind of modern-day Southern Strategy" (*His & Hers*, 2017c).

Jones identified, not a villain, but villainous acts of patriots that sought independence from British tyranny: "Never mind that whole American Revolution was rich dudes complaining. But, no, they are not trying to hear from the rich Black dudes saying what is wrong with the world" (*Right Time*, 2017a). Jones also attempted to merge the two sides of the anthem protest by focusing on villainous acts and ideologies as opposed to individuals. The idea of a character sustaining both the hero and villain identities appeared again when Jones indicated that fans did not actually like the players: "They like the athletic things that the players can ultimately do, but they are doing everything they can, where you do not actually pay attention to the players" (*Right Time*, 2017a). Trump, Jerry Jones, and the NFL commissioner were not necessarily the villains; rather, the nation's skewed political, racial, and economic ideologies have promoted division.

Hill revisited the identification of Trump as a public enemy because of the historical inequalities in the United States. For example, Hill commented, "This is a Gallup done in 1961 about the Freedom Riders, the Civil Rights activists that went throughout the South to protest against segregated bus terminals. Sixty-one percent of this country disapproved with what they were doing. Twenty-two percent approved. Eighteen percent had no opinions" (*His & Hers*, 2017a). Those who committed these acts are the enemy and Trump is a symbol of past atrocities. Hill pleaded to the country's collective morality by drawing parallels to past discriminatory ideologies—even though many in the United States may regard NFL players as the enemies instead of Trump. Furthermore, Jones inserted another layer to the perception that Trump was the villain when he suggested that Trump's capitalization of the word "flag" in his tweet subliminally raised the stakes in the anthem debate: "If you'll notice, there's a subtle attempt to make all these symbols into things that you capitalize" (*Right Time*, 2017a). For a moment, Smith applauded the president's performance because Trump "acknowledged that it [the anthem] bothers people" (*His & Hers*, 2017a). Thus, Smith and Jones each explained that the flag symbolizes both heroes and enemies.

Thus, the true hero in this dramatization is not the NFL players; it is actually the United States because of what it can offer. Therefore, one group holds onto fantasies regarding one group's interaction with the United States with the hope that these benefits would eventually reach them. Character dualism explains sports-radio character fantasies. The audience's appreciation for athletes and for the United States was both portrayed as ambiguous in sports radio. The sports-radio hosts attempted to bridge sociopolitical gaps through fantasies that communicated the dualistic meanings of U.S. symbols.

Characters in Conservative Radio

The characters that emerged from conservative radio included a few major protagonists and some unsung heroes. For Limbaugh, the true victims in this debacle are the fans. He lamented that the NFL disregarded the fans in favor of the owner's revenue and a potential boycott by the players. According to Limbaugh, longstanding fans are no longer attending games, are canceling their cable subscriptions, and are not watching games on television. He argued that the purpose of sporting events is entertainment and escape—not disrespecting the flag.

Another character that emerged was Green Bay Packers' quarterback Aaron Rodgers. Prior to a Thursday night game on September 28, 2017, Rodgers announced that the team would be locking arms as a sign of unity and invited the fans to join them. In response, the majority of the fans rejected the request and instead raised their voices and chanted "U-S-A!"

One conciliatory mediator was a CNN viewer who stepped out of his liberal box and complimented the conservative Beck. After Beck appeared on a left-leaning CNN Sunday night program to make a good-faith plea to U.S. citizens to stop quarreling, a twenty-three-year old named Maxwell penned a response letter to Beck thanking him for his willingness to try and bring the nation together. Beck responded by saying, "Maxwell, thank you. . . . Your letter actually really gives *me* hope. We have to resist the soundbite, knee-jerk reaction world and actually stand for principles" (*Glenn Beck*, 2018d).

Another character that emerged from the fray was former U.S. Army Ranger and current Pittsburgh Steeler Alejandro Villanueva. Prior to a game, he stood outside the locker room and saluted the flag while the rest of the team stood in the tunnel behind him. He later apologized to his teammates and coaches for not being a team player. Beck turned this apparent negative (Villanueva's apology) into a positive when he said that Villanueva stood outside the tunnel out of respect for a certain private who died in Afghanistan. He said, "Villanueva has something that the rest of America is sorely missing: honor, integrity, and real perspective" (*Glenn Beck*, 2017b).

Easily one of the most prominent and controversial characters in this saga is Trump. Many Americans identify with the president as was evidenced by the election. Beck was more critical of the president than other conservative voices, stating that the president was stupid for telling companies how to handle their employees, but in the same breath, condemned the players for disrespecting the flag. According to Beck, if the players truly wanted change, then they need to build bridges with law enforcement to bring about positive change.

Within the FTA, sports radio hosts decried the historical injustices of the past, and yet, ultimately nuanced their message by not vilifying

Trump, Jerry Jones, or the NFL. In their view, the true heroes are not the NFL players, but the United States which has an opportunity to lead with justice and equality. For the conservative camp, the victims are the fans, caught in a tug of war between profit driven owners and opportunistic player entertainers. Both sides have shown progress in reaching across the aisle, with sports radio tempering the blame, and conservatives willing to enter into dialogue. The fantasy created for listeners may yet lead to conversationalists who engage in respectful dialogue and open-minded civil discourse.

ACTIONS

Action in Sports Radio

Will Cain is an *ESPN* guest host on *His & Hers* who explained why the protests have been divisive, stating that, "I am insulted by the act of kneeling before the American flag" (*His & Hers*, 2017c). The dramatization of the scene is part of the action theme of FTA. In this drama, the action evolves because both sides develop the ability to have conversations without an actual conversation. This stage of FTA is grounded in the dualism of action and motion, which are analogous to the plotlines of a drama (Jackson, 2000).

Radio hosts and guests have discussed why real conversation fails to occur, theorizing that it is because powerful rich men gather to discuss what is best for the country. For Jones, the plot was initially manufactured through Trump's conversation with Dallas Cowboys owner Jerry Jones: "You know I didn't really think about that until talking to Donald Trump" (*Right Time*, 2017b). Through their power and media influence, the rich control society's perceptions, Bomani Jones argued. Smith suggested that "we're talking about him and still debating the flag and the anthem, so there's no conversation" (*His & Hers*, 2017c). The lack of communication and the reasons behind it are what Hill probed when she stated, "People don't want this protest and the reason they don't is because the genesis of why it even started, they don't want to acknowledge, deal with or be made uncomfortable" (*His & Hers*, 2017c). Those whom the protests have made uncomfortable sympathize with Trump's version of the United States. Unknowingly, Smith acknowledged the power of FTA and the confusion with Trump's appeal, as "people live vicariously through him. He's able to say things in a way that they would love to be able to say" (*Right Time*, 2017a). Trump provided a mechanism for facilitating conversation and for returning relevance to a group that had felt forgotten. However, others were unsympathetic, including the Packers' Rodgers, who commented, "This is about unity and love and growing together as a society and starting a conversation about something that might be a little uncomfortable for people" (*His & Hers*, 2017b). Unity, as Rodgers suggested, can only be implemented through meaningful conversation.

Sports-radio hosts attempt to unite both sides of the drama and to alter the conversation regarding the anthem controversy. Hosts and guests seem conflicted until they acknowledge that their only course of action to end this dramatic episode is to engage in legitimate conversation regarding the nation's past, present, and its future trajectory. Although Cain's dissatisfaction with the protest was apparent, he volunteered his presence so that he could have honest and uncomfortable conversations with his cohosts and "whoever wants to have them" (*His & Hers*, 2017c). A conversation is the first step toward any resolution. However, Hill's perspective solidified that the sports-radio hosts' version of real communication can only occur when: "Conversation does imply listening, and it does imply you bring a level of understanding and perspective and a great word I like to use, empathy" (*His & Hers*, 2017c).

Action in Conservative Radio

One of Limbaugh's methods for action is to set an agenda and mobilize the masses from a position of power. His talk show includes calls from listeners who offer questions or voice their opinions on daily topics. Limbaugh is not known for appearing on shows aligned with his political opponents; instead, he finds support from other conservative hosts such as Sean Hannity. Also, Limbaugh's goals include rallying conservatives to support a boycott of NFL games, to demand that players respect the flag, and to honor our service men and women.

Beck, who is a registered independent, tends to take a softer and more optimistic stance. He proved himself to be conciliatory when he appeared on a left-leaning CNN show. He said, "The interview was an opportunity to reach people who would never listen to me because of our different team jersey" (*Glenn Beck*, 2018d).

In one broadcast, Beck demonstrated his willingness to be proactive and venture outside the box. He sought to unite the NFL world by describing the history of the "Star-Spangled Banner." He detailed how the writer, Francis Scott Key, peered through a ship's porthole during the heat of battle, wondering if America would survive, if freedom would survive. Beck said, "If we don't . . . make peace with both the good and the bad, it will not be too long before we get up in the morning and we ask sincerely, 'Does the flag still wave? Is it still there? Are we still America?'" (*Glenn Beck*, 2017a).

Within the action theme of the FTA, there is an apparent commonality between sports and conservative radio, namely conversation. Sports radio identifies conflict and discomfort as the catalyst for reticent opposition, thus nullifying conversation. Therefore, the antidote is dialogue. In the conservative camp, Beck plays good cop to Limbaugh's bad cop by shedding a bullish hardline and instead leaping into the fray and wrestling through the arduous complexities. The action on both sides features a drive toward resolution, and therefore, increased conversation seems to be the remedy.

RHETORICAL VISION

Rhetoric in Sports Radio

The fantasies of sports-radio hosts communicate atrocities that those with wealth, power, and influence have systematically committed against other communities. Trump has outraged some communities, but others have excused his comments because they share the fantasy in which the United States as setting and a character has been threatened. U.S. history shows that divisive characters are not the enemies; rather, the abuse of power has been used to influence groups' collective imaginations and to benefit the wealthy.

Communication through sympathetic understanding is what the hosts of sports-radio attempted to achieve. The sports-radio hosts demonstrated the fragility of the controversy; at times, based on their liberal perspectives, they still attacked the conservative persons whom they deemed responsible for the protest disagreement. However, after accepting the others' perspectives, the perceived enemies shifted from individuals to ideologies.

These sports-radio hosts adjusted by legitimizing their villain fantasies. They agreed that the athletes were the losers and recognized the fans as bystanders in this conflict, which was actually between owners and players whose extreme differences exposed divisions in the NFL. Because Trump's fantasies are based in his identification with NFL owners and other groups, the sports-radio hosts adopt fantasies of race to connect and explain to their audiences.

Rhetoric in Conservative Radio

Within FTA, Limbaugh and Beck represent the conscience and worldviews of millions across the country. While sports radio's rhetorical vision emphasizes respect, equality, power, and control, by contrast, conservative radio upholds patriotism, traditional values, and the separation of politics and entertainment.

Conservative-radio hosts are not interested in silencing the opposition but instead seek to expose the corruption and inconsistencies in their views. Beck and Limbaugh's messages differ slightly, but their ideologies are unified against identity politics that are being played out in the sports arena.

CONCLUSION

Sports and conservative talk radio hosts have conflicting opinions regarding the anthem protests and Trump's comments in some instances, because of their different perceptions concerning the construction of fantasy themes. Limbaugh, Beck, Hill, Smith, and Jones's fantasies disregard whether the United States is a hero or villain, but rather consider how and why the character obtained the label. Considering the United States as heroic is challenging, because the nation's character has caused distress for some even as it has caused pleasure for others. Those who are negatively affected may enjoy fantasizing about the United States being heroic and may wish to experience those pleasures themselves. For both sports and conservative hosts, the United States' characterization and setting is important, but all collaborated to create the character and conspired in its development as a setting. In many instances, one radio group's fantasies and interpretations resemble a macro perspective, while the other's micro assessment dictates the host's rhetoric. Additionally, sports and conservative radio personalities suggest similar ideas—they just present them differently, and the two versions of talk radio reject their commonality and emphasize their differences.

Apparently, because fantasies emanate from a particular type of radio personality, they tend to frame Trump and kneeling fantasies more than the actual rhetoric. For example, both the conservative- and the sports-radio hosts emphasized patriotism, the separation of politics and entertainment, the opposition of the conservative and progressive agendas, and the need for a unified country. However, because past and present fantasies conveyed certain conservative or liberal agendas, the audiences' perception of the personalities shaped the fantasy themes. In turn, conservative- and sports-radio personalities fail to reveal where and how parallels exist with their fantasies. Instead, hosts challenge the others' fantasies, which bounce between the two versions of talk shows. If both forms of talk radio decided to merge their fantasies without labels restricting the rhetoric, audiences could recognize that more similarities than differences exist between the two. Conservative- and sports-radio fantasy themes need the opportunity to fully develop, and radio personalities need to possess the abilities to rhetorically and responsibly deconstruct those fantasies.

REFERENCES

Bennett, S. E. (2009). Who listens to Rush Limbaugh's radio program and the relationship between listening to Limbaugh and knowledge of public affairs, 1994-2006. *Journal of Radio & Audio Media, 16* (1), 66-82.

Berger, P. L., & Luckmann, T. (1966). *The social construction of reality: A treatise in the sociology of knowledge.* Garden City, NY: Doubleday.

Berry, J. M., & Sobieraj, S. (2011). Understanding the rise of talk radio. *Political Science & Politics, 44*(04), 762–767. doi:10.1017/s1049096511001223

Boren, C. (2014, July 28). This isn't the first time Stephen A. Smith has blamed women for domestic violence. *Washington Post.* Retrieved from http://eres.regent.edu: 2048/login?url=https://search.proquest.com/docview/15487 66488?account=13479

Boren, C. (2016, September 1). ESPN's Paul Finebaum apologizes for saying this country is not oppressing black people. *Washington Post.* Retrieved from http://eres.regent.edu:2048/login?url=https://search.proquest.com/docview1815919588?accountid=13479

Bormann, E. G. (1972). Fantasy and rhetorical vision: The rhetorical criticism of social reality. *Quarterly Journal of Speech, 58*(4), 396–407.doi:10.1080/00335637209383138

Botes, J., & Langdon, J. (2006). Public radio talk show hosts and social conflict: An analysis of self-reported roles during debates and discussion. *Journal of Radio Studies, 13*(2), 266-286. doi:10.1080/10955040701313446

Childers, J. P., & Meserko, V. M. (2013). Critical pedagogy as public modality: Glenn Beck's undemocratic defensive citizenship. *Western Journal Of Communication, 77*(1), 34-53.

Dori-Hacohen, G. (2012). The Commercial and the public "public spheres": Two types of political talk-radio and their constructed publics. *Journal of Radio & Audio Media, 19* (2), 152-171.

Gamson, W. (1992). *Frontiers in social movement theory* (C. M. Mueller & A. D. Morris, Eds.). New Haven, CT: Yale University Press.

Glenn Beck Program, The (a)[Transcripts, Radio broadcast]. (2017, August 24). *A Plea for Freedom: The History of the Star-Spangled Banner Should Keep Protestors on Their Feet.*

Glenn Beck Program, The (b)[Transcript, Radio broadcast]. (2017, September 26). *You've Seen Alejandro Villanueva in Headlines. Do You Know His Amazing Backstory?*

Glenn Beck Program, The (c)[Transcript, Radio broadcast]. (2017, November 13). *People Just Want to Watch Football Without All the Politics*

Glenn Beck Program, The (d)[Transcripts, Radio broadcast]. (2018, February 27). *Liberal Millennial Pens Powerful Message to Glenn Beck After CNN Interview*

His & Hers (a)[Transcript, Radio broadcast]. (2017, September 25). *LeBron speaks out.* Bristol, Connecticut: ESPN.

His & Hers (b)[Transcript, Radio broadcast]. (2017, September 26). *FBI probe reveals potentially deep-rooted scandal.* Bristol, Connecticut: ESPN.

His & Hers (c) [Transcript, Radio broadcast]. (2017, October 10). *Goodell and The National Anthem.* Bristol, Connecticut: ESPN.

Hoffman, G. (1991). Racial stereotyping in the news: Some general semantics alternatives. *ETC: A Review of General Semantics,* 22-30.

Jackson, B. G. (2000). A Fantasy theme analysis of Peter Senge's learning organization. *The Journal of Applied Behavioral Science, 36*(2), 193-209. doi:10.1177/0021886300362005

Kovarik, B. (2016). *Revolutions in communication: Media history from Gutenberg to the digital age* . New York ; London ; Oxford ; New Delhi ; Sydney: Bloomsbury.

Nimmo, D. D., & Combs, J. E. (1983). *Mediated political realities.* New York: Longman.

Right Time with Bomani Jones, The (a) [Transcript, Radio broadcast]. (2017, October 10). Bristol, Connecticut: ESPN.

Right Time with Bomani Jones, The (b)[Transcript, Radio broadcast]. (2017, November 1). *Papa John's Not happy* . Bristol, Connecticut: ESPN.

Rush Limbaugh Show, The (a)[Transcripts, Radio broadcast]. (2017, August 28). *From Banning Gone With the Wind to Calling NFL Fans Racists, Leftists Rip US Apart by Race.*

Rush Limbaugh Show, The (b)[Transcripts, Radio broadcast]. (2017, September 29). *Colin Kaepernick In His Own Words.*

Rush Limbaugh Show, The (c)[Transcripts, Radio broadcast]. (2017, September 28). *The NFL Doesn't Know its Audience.*

Squires, C. R. (2000). Black talk radio. *Harvard International Journal of Press/Politics, 5* (2), 73-95. doi:10.1177/1081180x00005002006

SIX

Kaepernick Portrayals

A Content Analysis of Six Media Outlets

Kimberly Feld, Deborah Sacra, and Steve Butler

In the beginning of the 2016 NFL season, San Francisco 49ers backup quarterback, Colin Kaepernick, sat on the bench while the American national anthem was played during the pre-game program. Kaepernick aimed to bring attention to the social injustice and racial inequality plaguing minorities in America, which was highlighted by the July 2016 incidents of African American males Alton Sterling and Philando Castile being killed by police officers (Funke & Susman, 2016). Kaepernick expressed his purpose: "I am not going to stand up to show pride in a flag for a country that oppresses black people and people of color. To me, this is bigger than football and it would be selfish on my part to look the other way. There are bodies in the street and people getting paid leave and getting away with murder" (as quoted in Wyche, 2016, para. 3).

A few weeks later, at the suggestion of a former player who was a military veteran, Kaepernick changed his protest to kneeling on one knee during the anthem to show greater respect to the military (Cosby, 2019; Denker, 2017). At the time, the NFL encouraged but did not require players to stand during the national anthem (Wyche, 2016).

Kaepernick's protest produced polarized opinions of him. Love (2017), a CNN contributor, explained, "For his political protests on the field, Colin Kaepernick has faced accusations he is un-American. Yet freedom of expression is quintessentially American, and fighting to make one's country match its rhetoric with its actions is an ultimate form of patriotism" (para. 20). When Kaepernick continued his protest into a second season, President Donald Trump said the player was disrespecting the flag, should find a new country to live in, and wanted NFL owners to, "Get that son of a bitch off the field right now" (Breech, 2017, para. 3). Kaepernick's actions instigated heated ideological debates about freedom of speech, patriotism, social protest, and sport. What fueled and framed many opinions was media coverage. Some media reports touted Kaepernick as a hero, whereas others villainized him. The purpose of this study is to discover which of these frames were portrayed and perpetuated in media that are regularly consumed by conservative, liberal, African American, or Hispanic populations. Applying framing and agenda setting theory, we discuss the impacts and implications of the patterns of framing on the outlets and audiences.

LITERATURE REVIEW

Professional athletes are paid to play a sport. Controversy ensues when athletes step out of their player shoes and assert their political opinions. African American athletes have protested politically in the past and incurred consequences. In 1992, when the Chicago Bulls were visiting the White House as NBA champions, player Craig Hodges handed a personal letter to President Bush expressing discontent with policies about the poor and minorities. Shortly after, Hodges was released from the Bulls and never received an offer or tryout from another team (Gill, 2016). Hodges joined other athlete-activists who had been suspended or released for expressing a controversial political opinion. After Tommie Smith and John Carlos, 1968 Olympic medal winners, each protested by raising a fist covered by a black glove and wearing black socks and no shoes, they were suspended and sent home by the U.S. and International Olympic officials (Davis, 2008). Smith, who was under contract with the Los Angeles Rams, had his contract terminated upon his return (Hall, Marach, & Reynolds, 2017). More recently, five Saint Louis Rams players protested the police shooting of a young black man in a nearby city in 2014 by raising their arms into the "hands up, don't shoot" gesture upon entering the football field before a game. They were not reprimanded by the NFL, although 22 percent of fans responding on social media called them derogatory names and 13 percent thought they should be punished (Gill, 2016).

The debate continues over athletes' right to protest. One side believes they do not have a right, arguing they are doing the job they are being paid for. Others believe protests are not only an appropriate form of social expression, but political activism is part of the history in American sports (Hall et al., 2017). Thiel and colleagues (2016) posit, "To deny them their right to protest is by no means a justified strategy to secure the neutrality and political autonomy of sport. In contrast, it serves the political agenda of those who want to prevent the discussion about social injustices receiving a larger forum and, consequently, more attention" (p. 2).

As the 2017–2018 NFL season began, news reporting of American sentiment toward Kaepernick and his protest reflected this debate. Contemplating the divide in a guest editorial in the *Washington Post*, sportswriter turned Lutheran minister Angela Denker (2017) offered background information about Kaepernick, a devout Christian, the biracial son of a poor mother, adopted by a white family, who had achieved a 4.0 grade point average in high school and All-State awards in football, basketball, and baseball. Yet, his stellar background aside, Kaepernick was seen by some as "The brash young athlete who doesn't understand politics, trying to make a political stand . . . who stupidly insulted the military and the country." Like those who came before him, Kaepernick was accused of not playing his role of positively supporting an American sports ritual, Sunday football games, an institution that has made him and other African American men millionaires. Denker added, "Is it possible that rather than disrespect, it is instead a deep respect for the principles of America and the God who granted this nation its freedom that causes Kaepernick to kneel?"

In March 2017, Kaepernick opted out of his contract with the San Francisco 49ers. He was not hired by any other team. He filed a lawsuit against the NFL for collusion (Belson, 2017). The possibility exists that Kaepernick could also sue President Trump for violating his constitutional right to free speech (Edelman, 2018).

In May 2018, the NFL owners created and approved a new policy governing player behavior during the national anthem. Under the new policy, an NFL team will be fined if a player on the sidelines is not standing during the anthem. The team can pass on the fine to the player or players. The new policy allows players to stay in the locker room if they don't want to stand (Knoblauch, 2018). The NFL Players Association filed a grievance against the league because of this policy, and negotiations are still ongoing between the two entities (Dwyer, 2018).

THEORETICAL FRAMEWORK

Agenda-setting and framing theories provide two different ways to evaluate media coverage of an issue. In agenda setting, media corporations convey how much attention they want the audience to pay to an issue, and in framing, how they want the audience to think about and judge the issue.

Agenda setting is a function of mass media gatekeepers, who allow some information to flow and other information to be restricted as they decide which stories they will cover through their outlet. Agenda setting is usually measured by the frequency with which a story is covered and the prominence it is given, signifying media attempts to keep an issue in the forefront of the public mind (Cacciatore, Scheufele & Iyengar, 2016; McCombs & Shaw, 1993). Though still strong in political issues, agenda setting power is not what it used to be, as media corporations monitor and attend to the public's agenda put forth on social media (Groshek & Groshek, 2013; Neuman et al., 2014). Partisan bloggers and emerging news websites also exercise influence over the agenda setting of larger media outlets (Meraz, 2011; Vargo & Guo, 2017).

Entman (1993) defines framing as making selected aspects of an issue "more salient in a communicating text, in such a way as to promote a particular problem definition, causal interpretation, moral evaluation, and/or treatment recommendation" (p. 52). Media frames are created by journalists to simplify and contextualize a news story for themselves and the audience, but audiences evaluate, adopt, and change frames according to their own categories, beliefs, and stereotypes as well (Edy & Meirick, 2007). In the past, to capture an audience, journalists were motivated to create frames that tapped into consensus values, beliefs, and perspectives. Because today's media environment is more fragmented and partisan, people choose media that aligns with their political views (Iyengar & Hahn, 2009). As a result, we can expect that media outlets will be likely to frame issues in ways that are consistent with the bias of their audience.

On the other hand, Chong and Druckman (2007) argue that competitive framing environments impact the development and effectiveness of opposing frames, and call for more research into these conditions. The strength and intensity of competing frames, the values they highlight, and the combination of frames in a given situation will be factors in the success or failure of a frame to gain support from the public and from those in power. For example, Aarøe (2011) demonstrated that emotional frames that take a narrow, episodic perspective are more persuasive than thematic, hypothetical frames in a competitive situation.

In the coverage of Kaepernick's protest, two frames emerged: Kaepernick as a hero of free speech, or as a villain who disrespects his country and the military. Arguably, more conservative outlets may tend to portray protest events in a negative manner, depicting them as threats to patriotism, the flag, or as inappropriate behavior incorrectly labeled as freedom of speech. Conversely, more liberal media outlets may tend to depict these same protest events as signs of patriotism and behavior appropriately labeled as freedom of speech. However, each of these frames had to contend with the competition of the other. Therefore, the relative occurrence of the two frames would be of interest, and would answer the call to examine the dynamics of competitive framing environments.

Based on prior research, the following research questions are proposed:

RQ #1: Do media outlets exhibit a preference in their choice of frame for Kaepernick and his protest?

RQ #2: What frames appear in mainstream media outlets?

RQ #3: Which frames do media with politically conservative, moderate, and liberal audiences prefer?

RQ #4: Which frames do media popular with minority audiences prefer?

METHODOLOGY

Media that focus their coverage for audiences with different political ideologies as well as those that reach specific minority audiences have covered the Kaepernick controversy. As indicated, framing and agenda setting theory asserts media outlets tend to report stories that influence and/or line up with viewers political ideologies or racial backgrounds (Iyengar & Hahn, 2009). Therefore, a content analysis of six online news sources was conducted using headlines and lead paragraphs as the units of analysis. Online news sources were chosen specifically since over 85 percent of the population reported to get news on a computer or mobile device (Barthel & Mitchell, 2017). Mainstream online news titles selected for analysis were CNN with 44 percent of the readers self-identified as liberal, with 19 percent identifying as consistently liberal and 25 percent identified as mostly liberal. Of the remaining 56 percent, 40 percent identified as mixed, 13 percent as mostly conservative, and 4 percent as consistently conservative. Of the *Wall Street Journal* readers, 41 percent percent of readers self-identified as liberal with 20 percent consistently liberal, and 21 percent mostly liberal. The remaining 59 percent identified as 24 percent mixed, 22 percent mostly conservative, and 13 percent consistently conservative. Fox News readers reported to self-identify as liberal 18 percent of the time, 14 percent mostly liberal, and 4 percent consistently liberal. Fox News readers self-identified as conservative 46 percent of the time, with 27 percent mostly conservative and 19 percent consistently conservative. The remaining 36 percent identified as mixed (Mitchell, Gottfried, Kiley, & Matsa, 2014).

In addition to mainstream news outlets, three other online news sources that served minority populations were chosen for analysis. The three largest ethnicities in the United States are White (60.7 percent), African American (13.4 percent), and Hispanic (18.1 percent) according to the United States Census Bureau (2018). Black Entertainment Television (BET) offers online news and is popular with African American audiences, and therefore was also chosen for analysis. Fifty percent of Hispanics get their news in both English and Spanish, and 82 percent of Hispanics get at least some of their news in English (Lopez & Gonzalez-Barrera, 2013). To include both English and Spanish speaking news consumed by Hispanic populations in the United States, two online outlets were chosen for analysis, *Los Angeles (LA) Times* and Univision. The Los Angeles metropolitan area has the largest Hispanic population in the United States (Brown & Lopez, 2013), and therefore the *LA Times* was chosen for analysis. Univision is the largest Spanish-language media company in the United States, (Matsa, 2015). Univision articles were translated by a bilingual expert author of Spanish language textbooks (Borrás, 2007). Forty-seven percent of the Hispanic population and 70 percent of African Americans identify with the Democratic Political Party and the media outlets that cater to them are considered to be more liberal than conservative (Pew Research Center, 2016, p.15).

The authors developed a coding scheme to determine frames of how Kaepernick and the protests were portrayed. Frames of positive, neutral, and negative portrayals were used. A positive frame indicated the majority of the text showed support for Kaepernick and the protest. Support for Kaepernick might include positive recognition of areas such as his character, awards, athletic ability, or philanthropic efforts. "Colin Kaepernick honored at ACLU Bill of Rights Dinner in Beverly Hills" is an example of a headline coded as positive (Tchekmedyian, 2017). A neutral frame indicated no clear leaning, either positive or negative, or a balance of positive and negative ideas about Kaepernick and his protest. An example of a neutral frame included, "Colin Kaepernick Takes a Stand (and Sits) During the Anthem" (Gordon, 2016). An example of a lead paragraph that contained both positive and negative comments was, "Former 49ers quarterback Colin Kaepernick has yet to find another NFL job, but he's donating some of his old suits in order to help others find work" (Associated Press, 2017). A negative frame contained criticism of any aspect of Kaepernick or expressing disrespect or dislike of his protest. A negative frame example included, "GQ should've named Colin Kaepernick its 'Coward of the Year'" (Starnes, 2017). After four practice rounds, a Krippendorf's Alpha score of .92 was obtained on the fifth round of coding sixty cases.

A systematic sampling method was used to obtain thirty headlines and thirty lead paragraphs from the same articles from each of five different online media titles. The date range for the articles was from August 25, 2016, to March 17, 2018. Articles were pulled from one mainstream liberal, one mainstream moderate, one mainstream conservative, one African American, and one English-speaking news source in the area with the largest Hispanic population. In addition, fifteen headlines and fifteen lead paragraphs were chosen for analysis from a Spanish-speaking Hispanic news title. This number is smaller because a smaller number of articles existed from which to choose. To gather a data set from each source, a search was conducted using the word "Kaepernick" in the search feature provided on the homepage of the news outlet. *Wall Street Journal* articles were obtained in the same manner after a subscription was secured. The *LA Times* did not have an adequate search method, so articles were obtained through a LexisNexis Academic search.

After the articles were gathered, the headlines and lead paragraphs were numbered and coded. The total number of cases was 330. The independent (news type) and dependent (frame) variables were labeled and input in the SPSS program. Chi square analyses were conducted to determine differences between the categories of data.

RESULTS

The research question predicting that media outlets will exhibit a preference in their choice of frame for Kaepernick and his protest was significant according to the Chi-Square statistic (χ^2) = 51.70, df = 10, $p < .01$. Next, our research questions about preferences for different media audiences will be discussed (see Appendix).

Three media outlets were chosen based on political preference as ranked by Mitchell et al. (2014) including CNN (liberal), *Wall Street Journal* (moderate), and Fox News (conservative). These three will be reported individually, as well as a group. The total number of articles available online between August 25, 2016, and March 17, 2018, using the key word "Kaepernick" varied between media outlets. The search in CNN netted 297 online articles; the *Wall Street Journal* posted 158 online articles; and Fox News published 665 online articles.

As mentioned earlier, the frame used to analyze how Kaepernick was portrayed in media outlets contained three levels: positive, neutral, and negative. CNN, a liberal leaning media outlet, presented Kaepernick in a positive manner 53 percent of the time. Twenty-seven percent of the time CNN's portrayals were neutral, and 20 percent of the time they were negative. *The Wall Street Journal* represented Kaepernick positively 45 percent of the time, neutrally 37 percent of the time, and negatively 18 percent of the time. Fox News, a favorite among conservatives, portrayed Colin Kaepernick in a positive manner 33 percent of the time, 18 percent were neutral portrayals, and 48 percent of the time he was portrayed negatively.

Because American culture suggests serious news consumers generally use certain mainstream outlets, the three mainstream media outlets analyzed (CNN, *Wall Street Journal*, and Fox News) are grouped for further analysis. The combined positive portrayals in all three were 44 percent. The neutral portrayals occurred 27 percent of the time, and negative portrayals occurred 29 percent of the time collectively.

Those who see themselves as outsiders or those with different interests in America may look to other outlets. Thus, media outlets that cater

Table 6.1. Frames by outlet, media type, and targeted audience's political leaning

	Positive	Neutral	Negative
CNN	53%	27%	20%
Fox News	33%	19%	48%
Wall Street Journal	45%	37%	18%
BET	47%	45%	8%
LA Times	53%	37%	10%
Univision	53%	47%	0%
Mainstream Media	44%	27%	29%
Minority Media	51%	42%	7%
Liberal	53%	27%	20%
Moderate	45%	37%	18%
Conservative	33%	19%	48%

Note: Chi-Square statistic ($\chi 2$) = 51.70, df = 10, p < .01 for differences across news outlets.

Source: Kimberly Feld, Deborah Sacra, and Steve A. Butler.

to African American and Hispanic audiences were also grouped for analysis. Black Entertainment Television, Univision, and the *Los Angeles Times* will be reported separately as well as in a group representing minority audiences. Black Entertainment Television online news tended to portray Kaepernick positively 47 percent of the time, neutrally 45 percent, and negatively only eight percent of the time. In Univision news, Kaepernick was portrayed positively 53 percent of the time and neutrally 47 percent of the time. In the articles selected from Univision, Kaepernick was not portrayed negatively at all. Finally, in the *Los Angeles Times*, frames for Kaepernick were positive 53 percent, neutral 37 percent, and negative 10 percent of the time. The combination of minority-oriented media portrayed Kaepernick positively 51 percent of the time, neutrally 42 percent of the time, and negatively 7 percent of the time.

DISCUSSION

In review, agenda setting includes telling the public which issues are most important by allowing or restricting information covered. Framing presents aspects or details of a story to show how an audience should think about an issue. This study suggested that the political preferences of media audiences impacted whether Kaepernick was portrayed positively, negatively, or neutrally. In addition, the study also suggested minority audiences will have a preferred frame for the Kaepernick controversy.

The conservative news outlet, Fox News, published over twice as many articles as CNN and four times as many articles as the *Wall Street Journal* during the same time frame. Because of this higher frequency, it seemed important for Fox News to keep the story in front of readers more than others, with a negative slant in almost half of the articles. Increased polarization of political parties has been fueled by more media choices and the revival of selective exposure. It is speculated that the media environment provided strong economic incentive to media outlets to serve news stories their viewers would find agreeable (Iyengar & Hahn, 2009). Using this argument, Fox News told their viewers stories that portrayed Kaepernick more negatively, and they possibly had political and economic reasons for doing so. Along the same lines, the combined minority media reported fewer negative portrayals of Kaepernick.

The frames for this issue were emotionally laden. Patriotism, equality, and free speech are highly regarded values and thematic issues. These issues were layered with the episodic issue of Kaepernick and his protest, offering a "face" to the debate, along with the episode of Trump's tweet calling for getting kneeling players off the field. Issues involving episodic frames tend to be more emotionalizing and personalizing than thematic, hypothetical ones (Aarøe, 2011). The initial episode was an African American professional athlete kneeling in protest during the national anthem over equality issues. Since audiences tend to choose media that favored certain frames based on their own categories, beliefs, and stereotypes, the conservatives supported the network that defended the national anthem and patriotism by judging and negatively framing Kaepernick and his protest (Edy & Meirick, 2007). Conversely, liberal and minority audiences were supporting and endorsing the media that switched between lauding and reporting neutrally on Kaepernick.

The predominant frame for liberal audiences and minority audiences was positive. CNN audiences were thus encouraged to be supportive of Kaepernick and his protest, because the protest began to bring awareness to racial injustice and the unfair treatment of African Americans by police officers. Logically, BET was also in favor of Kaepernick. A reporter from the *Washington Post* similarly argued for support of Kaepernick and against those who opposed him: "You want Kaepernick to go away, to stand up and salute the flag and shut up because we can tolerate abuse of other human beings but we cannot tolerate being disrupted when we want to pretend that everything is okay. Of course, to be black in America is to know that everything is not okay. Not when black Americans are arrested, incarcerated and killed at much higher rates than white Americans" (Denker, 2017, p. 3).

One interesting finding in this study was that Univision articles chosen for this study, representing the Spanish-speaking Hispanic audience, did not have any negative frames of Kaepernick. Admittedly, there were fewer Univision stories analyzed than from other media outlets because of available articles. Thus, insufficient examples could be a limitation of this finding.

The researchers believe that a lot of the media focus was on the kneeling debate itself which diverted energy and time away from analyzing the initial reasons behind the controversy. Future research could include analysis of the impact of social issue framing to either bring about change or reinforce existing attitudes.

Political polarization and ideological consistencies are greater now than 30 years ago (Mitchell et al., 2014, Iyengar & Hahn, 2009). The agenda setting and framing of the Kaepernick protest portrayed him as either more a hero or villain depending on the news outlet being examined. In light of the agenda setting argument presented above, it appears as if the weight of conservative media's negativity, as analyzed on Fox News, was the most influential. Kaepernick is without a team and the NFL now has policies to govern player behavior during the national anthem.

REFERENCES

Aarøe, L. (2011). Investigating Frame Strength: The Case of Episodic and Thematic Frames. *Political Communication, 28*(2), 207–226. https://doi.org/10.1080/10584609.2011.568041

Associated Press. (2017, May 2). Kaepernick hands out old suits outside parole office. *Wall Street Journal*, 7:49 a.m.

Barthel, M., & Mitchell, A. (2017, May 10). Americans' attitudes about the news media deeply divided along partisan lines. *Pew Research Center*. Retrieved from http://assets.pewresearch.org/wp-content/uploads/sites/13/2017/05/09144304/PJ_2017.05.10_Media-Attitudes_FINAL.pdf

Belson, K. (2017, December 8). Kaepernick vs. the N.F.L.: A primer on his collusion case. *The New York Times*. Retrieved from https://www.nytimes.com/2017/12/08/sports/kaepernick-collusion.html

Borrás, G. (2007). *Intercambios: Spanish for global communication*. Boston: Cengage.

Breech, J. (2017, September 23). Donald Trump rips NFL, says owners should cut any players who kneel during anthem. *CBS Sports*. Retrieved from https://www.cbssports.com/nfl/news/donald-trump-rips-nfl-says-owners-should-cut-any-players-who-kneel-during-anthem/

Brown, A., & Lopez, M. (2013). Ranking Latino populations in the nation's metropolitan areas. *Pew Research Center Hispanic Trends*. Retrieved from http://www.pewhispanic.org/2013/08/29/iv-ranking-latino-populations-in-the-nations-metropolitan-areas/

Cacciatore, M. A., Scheufele, D. A., & Iyengar, S. (2016). The end of framing as we know it . . . and the future of media effects. *Mass Communication and Society, 19*(1), 7–23. doi 10.1080/15205436.2015.1068811.

Chong, D., & Druckman, J. N. (2007). A theory of framing and opinion formation in competitive elite environments. *Journal of Communication, 57*(1), 99–118. https://doi.org/10.1111/j.1460-2466.2006.00331.x

Cosby, N. B. (2019). How Social Media Activists and Their Hashtags Have Encouraged and Informed Their Followers on the Take-A-Knee Movement. In S. D. Perry (Ed.) *Pro football and the proliferation of protest: Anthem posture in a divided America*. Lanham, MD: Lexington.

Davis, D. (2008). Olympic athletes who took a stand: For 40 years, Olympians Tommie Smith and John Carlos have lived with the consequences of their fateful protest. *Smithsonian Magazine*. Retrieved from https://www.smithsonianmag.com/articles/olympic-athletes-who-took-a-stand-593920/

Denker, A. (2017, September 24). Colin Kaepernick and the powerful, religious act of kneeling. *The Washington Post*. Retrieved from https://www.washingtonpost.com/news/acts-of-faith/wp/2017/09/24/colin-kaepernick-and-the-powerful-religious-act-of-kneeling/?noredirect=on&utm_term=.fe933df2ab03

Dwyer, C. (2018, July 10). NFL Players Union Files Grievance Over League's New National Anthem Policy. *National Public Radio*. Retrieved from https://www.npr.org/2018/07/10/627717067/nfl-players-union-files-grievance-over-leagues-new-national-anthem-policy

Edelman, M. (2018). Standing to kneel: Analyzing NFL players' freedom to protest during the playing of the U.S. national anthem. *Fordham Law Review Online, 86*, 1-15. Retrieved from https://ssrn.com/abstract=3122145

Edy, J. A., & Meirick, P. C. (2007). Wanted, dead or alive: Media frames, frame adoption, and support for the war in Afghanistan. *Journal of Communication, 57*(1), 119–141. doi 10.1111/j.1460-2466.2006.00332.x

Entman, R. M. (1993). Framing: Toward clarification of a fractured paradigm. *Journal of Communication, 43*(4), 51–58.

Funke, D., & Susman, T. (2016, July 12). From Ferguson to Baton Rouge: Deaths of black men and women at the hands of police. *Los Angeles Times*. Retrieved from http://www.latimes.com/nation/la-na-police-deaths-20160707-snap-htmlstory.html

Gill, E. L. (2016). "Hands up, don't shoot" or shut up and play ball? Fan-generated media views of the Ferguson Five. *Journal of Human Behavior in the Social Environment, 26*(3/4), 400-412. doi:10.1080/10911359.2016.1139990

Gordon, J. (2016, August 29). Colin Kaepernick Takes a Stand (and Sits) During the Anthem. *Wall Street Journal*. Retrieved from https://blogs.wsj.com/dailyfix/2016/08/29/colin-kaepernick-takes-a-stand-and-sits-during-the-anthem/.

Groshek, J., & Groshek, M. C. (2013). Agenda trending: Reciprocity and the predictive capacity of social networking sites in intermedia agenda setting across topics over time. *Media and Communication 1*(1), 15–27. http://dx.doi.org/10.17645/mac.v1i1.71

Hall, E., Marach, R., and Reynolds, J. (2017). Policy point-counterpoint: Do African American athletes have an obligation to fight against racial injustice? *International Social Science Review (Online), 93*(2), 0_1,1-9.

Iyengar, S., & Hahn, K. S. (2009). Red media, Blue media: Evidence of ideological selectivity in media use. *Journal of Communication, 59*(1), 19–39. doi 10.1111/j.1460-2466.2008.01402.x

Knoblauch, A. (2018, May 23). NFL owners approve national anthem policy for 2018. *National Football League*. Retrieved from http://www.nfl.com/news/story/0ap3000000933971/article/nfl-owners-approve-national-anthem-policy-for-2018

Lopez, M., & Gonzalez-Barrera, A. (2013, July 23). A growing share of Latinos get their news in English. *Pew Research Center*. Retrieved from http://www.pewhispanic.org/2013/07/23/a-growing-share-of-latinos-get-their-news-in-english/#

Love, D. (2017, August 22). Kaepernick protest is gaining support while he's still out of a job. *CNN*. Retrieved from https://www.cnn.com/2017/08/22/opinions/kaepernick-protest-gaining-support-opinion-love/index.html

Matsa, K. (2015, April). Hispanic media fact sheet. *State of the News Media 2015*. Pew Research Center.

McCombs, M., & Shaw, D. (1993). The evolution of agenda-setting research: Twenty-five years in the marketplace of ideas. *Journal of Communication, 43*(2), 58-67.

Meraz, S. (2011). The fight for 'how to think': Traditional media, social networks, and issue interpretation. *Journalism, 12*(1), 107–127. doi 10.1177/1464884910385193

Mitchell, A., Gottfried, J., Kiley, J., & Matsa, K. (2014, October 21). Political polarization and media habits. *Pew Research Center*. Retrieved from http://www.journalism.org/2014/10/21/political-polarization-media-habits/

Neuman, W. R., Guggenheim, L., Jang, S. M., & Bae, S. Y. (2014). The dynamics of public attention: Agenda-setting theory meets big data. *Journal of Communication, 64*(2), 193–214. doi: 10.1111/jcom.12088.

Pew Research Center. (2016, September). *The Parties on the eve of the 2016 election: Two coalitions, moving further apart*. Retrieved from http://assets.pewresearch.org/wp-content/uploads/sites/5/2016/09/09-13-2016-Party-ID-release-final.pdf

Starnes, T. (2017, November 13). GQ should've named Colin Kaepernick its 'Coward of the Year'. *Fox News*. Retrieved from http://www.foxnews.com/opinion/2017/11/13/gq-shouldve-named-colin-kapernick-its-coward-year.html

Tchekmedyian, A. (2017, December 4). Colin Kaepernick honored at ACLU Bill of Rights Dinner in Beverly Hills. *LA Times*. Retrieved from http://www.latimes.com/local/lanow/la-me-ln-colin-kaepernick-20171203-story.html

Thiel, A., Villanova, A., Toms, M., Thing, L.F., & Dolan, P. (2016). Can sport be 'un-political'? *European Journal for Sport and Society, 13*(4), 253-255. doi 10.1080/16138171.2016.1253322

United States Census Bureau (2018). *Quick Facts*. Retrieved from https://www.census.gov/quickfacts/fact/table/US/PST045217

Vargo, C.J., & Guo, L. (2017). Networks, big data, and intermedia agenda setting: An analysis of traditional, partisan, and emerging online U.S. news. *Journalism & Mass Communication Quarterly, 94*(4), 1031–1055. doi 10.1177/1077699016679976

Wyche, S. (2016, August 27). Colin Kaepernick explains why he sat during national anthem. *National Football League*. Retrieved fromhttp://www.nfl.com/news/story/0ap3000000691077/article/colin-kaepernick-explains-why-he-sat-during-national-anthem

SEVEN

How Social Media Activists and Their Hashtags Have Encouraged and Informed Their Followers on the Take-a-Knee Movement

Nadine Barnett Cosby

SOCIAL MEDIA PHENOMENON

Social media has garnered much attention and discussion from media and communication professionals, business leaders, and scholars, among others (Qualman, 2013). The social media phenomenon is the culmination of traditional interpersonal communication styles and converging mass communication technologies. Social networking services (SNS) continue to transform the way individuals engage and interact with others, and with organizations, groups, and corporations. Through SNS, previously passive audience members have effectively become active participants in mass media. Furthermore, social media allows for a collective construction of ideas and, subsequently, the organization and mobilization of groups, due to the ability of users to not only post initial ideas, but to also comment, respond to, provide supporting media for, or even engage in debate with others regardless of familiarity or location. The purpose of this study is to examine political and civic discourse, participation, mobilization, and/or activism regarding the Take-a-Knee movement, as performed through the social networking sites Facebook and Twitter. These protests were first spearheaded by National Football League (NFL) player Colin Kaepernick as a means of raising awareness of police violence and injustice against people of color, and later reemerged as a reaction to President Donald Trump's 2017 comments denigrating NFL players who participate in silent protest during game-opening national anthems.

LITERATURE REVIEW

Numerous academic and non-academic writers identify social media as a major influence on interpersonal and group communication today. Still, there is no definitive diagnosis of the types of content available on these once alternative, but now mainstream, platforms, how racial and cultural identifications and perceptions impact these digital artifacts, and how they are used to effectuate political engagement or activism. Vissers et al. (2012) posit that there exists a "lack of strong conclusions" on the effects of online mobilization on real-world activity. Furthermore, the authors contend that there has been a failure to distinguish between online and offline participation, behaviors, and outcomes.

Tapscott and Williams (2006) described the early emergence of this new tradition as a culture of mass collaboration, asserting, "Profound changes in the nature of technology, demographics, and the global economy are giving rise to powerful new models of production based on community, collaboration, and self-organization rather than on hierarchy or control" (p. 1). Such communication behaviors are described as typical of traditional mass communication and media platforms. The collaborative nature of social media expands beyond group advocacy and mobilization, as is evidenced in newsgathering and even entertainment content that is produced, at least in part, by pooled resources and participation via digital platforms. Also atypical of conventional media, SNSs provide for very little gatekeeping by the platform itself. As such, it allows for more candid and diverse messages.

Social media allows for the simplified discovery of like-minded individuals based on whichever element is a primary connector. In this way, various communities of a new generation are constantly taking shape. Social media has also contributed to the ability of movements to operate on a global scale. Lastly, the articulation of agreed upon demands and practices is significantly impacted by social media platforms. Shared digital discourse and artifacts are essential in a movement's effective communication of common praxis and stipulations. This, however, is an area in which the cons of social media activism are as apparent as many of the pros. The democratic positioning of social media platforms presents difficulty for movements in the digital sphere to protect their identities and messages from corruption or false representations. Therefore, social movements that operate in the digital sphere are challenged with creating spaces and opportunities for public discourse around a movement's message.

THEORETICAL PERSPECTIVE

Because the mass media play such an influential role in society, it is important to address and seek to understand and explain the psychological and social mechanisms through which mass communication influences our perceptions, actions, behaviors and discourse. Social cognitive theory posits that segments of an individual's knowledge acquisition can be directly related to the observation of others within the context of social interactions, experiences, and external media influences. When one observes a subject performing a behavior, and likewise observes the consequences of that behavior, the individual recalls the series of events and uses this information to guide his own behavior. Observing behavior can also motivate an individual to behave in previously learned, but not often executed, manners (Bandura, 1986). This was termed social cognitive theory, to emphasize the major role that cognition plays in observance, encoding, decoding, and performance (Bandura, 1986).

Bandura attributes four types of learning effects to behavioral outcomes in social cognitive theory. According to Green and Peil (2009), the four learning effects include:

1. Observational Learning Effect: acquiring new behavior from a model
2. Response Facilitation Effect: increased frequency of learned behavior after that same behavior is reinforced in a model
3. Response Inhibition Effect: decreased frequency of learned behavior after observing that same behavior in the model resulting in punishment
4. Response Disinhibition Effect: return of an inhibited response after observing positive consequences from that same behavior in a model

I used social cognitive theory as a theoretical perspective in this study to further understand the social processes that occur and unfold on Facebook and Twitter in discourse related to the Take-a-Knee movement. In light of previous studies investigating the influence of social media engagement on real-world participation, two research questions were developed as a guide for this study:

RQ1: How has social media played a role in awareness and perceptions of social movements?

RQ2: How do users' experiences in social media platforms influence their attitudes?

METHODOLOGY

For this study, qualitative content analysis was employed to investigate the phenomenon of participation in socio-political discourse and action, and/or engagement with social movements through social media interaction. Eight hundred Facebook and Twitter posts related to the Take-a-Knee movement representing 200 posts for each of four primary hashtags for Take-a-Knee were analyzed. After conducting the content analysis, I performed a hybridized netnographic study by observing the Facebook timelines and Twitter feeds of my personal network in order to observe and reflect on the ways in which these individuals interacted with the movements and/or their hashtags, and engaged members of their networks on related topics. Finally, in-depth interviews with activists were conducted to further elucidate on the influence of social media on perceptions of the movement. Using social cognitive theory to frame my analysis, I examine how our divergent positions within complex systems such as dominance and oppression, privileged and marginalized, affect how people perceive and interact with social movements via online and temporal spaces. The following hashtags were identified for the search query, as they were the most prominently and frequently used hashtags in online discourse about the movement:

- #TakeAKnee – the hashtag originating in support of Kaepernick's silent protest during the singing of the national anthem at NFL games
- #KneelNFL – a variation, also expressing support of the #TakeAKnee hashtag
- #StandForAnthem – an outcry in rebuke of the anthem protests
- #BoycottNFL – used to represent a call to action to boycott the NFL due to the anthem protest issue. Interestingly, #BoycottNFL has been used by parties on both sides of the argument as noted by Westhoff and Saint Louis (2019, chapter 17 in this book).

The specific dates identified in the advanced search query are 9/1/2017 to 2/5/2018, which represent the period between the reigniting of the Take-a-Knee movement after Trump's related comments, through the day after Super Bowl 2018. A multistep coding was applied to the identified tweets. A primary coding was applied by conducting a textual and visual analysis of each tweet, looking for a *type of engagement* category in which to place that post or tweet. The identified types of engagement are as follows: (a) persuasive/call to action, (b) debate/argumentation, and (c) informational. Next, a second coding was applied to analyze tweets once again (within their primary grouping) to identify which rhetorical themes emerged. The predominant rhetorical themes were (1) race/racial terminology, (2) hate speech, (3) justice/equality, (4) solidarity/unity, and (5) patriotism/pride/respect.

The "race/racial terminology" code was applied to those posts that included racially explicit rhetoric, or distinct references to the construct of race or members of a certain racial group. The coding for "hate speech" differed from that of racial terminology in that the hate speech posts used language intended to attack, threaten, or offend a person or group of people based on their race. The "justice/equality" code was applied to those posts that included these words or terminology related to these doctrines. This code encompassed a broad spectrum of feelings and attitudes toward the movement. For example, some posts in this code referred to the core ideology of the Take-a-Knee movement, in terms of highlighting justice and equitable treatment of people of color. At the same time, other posts that received the same code mentioned notions of the "rights represented by the flag." Coding for "unity/solidarity" included posts that suggested agreement, accord, or like-mindedness based on a common factor or interest—such as posts discussing support of players' freedom of speech. Lastly, the "patriotism/pride/respect" code was used to reflect posts that made references to generic conventions of American patriotism, such as rhetoric related to the significance of the American flag, gratitude toward the U.S. military, constitution rhetoric, etc., as well as posts that either directly referenced the words *respect* or *disrespect*, as well as posts that included discussions of respect or a lack thereof when discussing the Take-a-Knee efforts.

RESULTS

Behaviors

Discourse related to the Take-a-Knee movement included the following hashtags: #TakeAKnee, #KneelNFL, #StandForAnthem, #BoycottNFL. The #TakeAKnee and #KneelNFL hashtags were used interchangeably. However, #TakeAKnee was used to categorize the topic of the post or connect to discourse about the movement as much as it was used as a distinct hashtag statement. Interestingly, #BoycottNFL was used by divergent user groups. In some cases users incorporated the #BoycottNFL hashtag to express disagreement with the blacklisting of Kaepernick after his protests. In other instances, the same hashtag was used to express a disapproval of the league for allowing players to kneel without punishment by the league.

A Call to Action

Posts that included the use of the hashtag #TakeAKnee, as well as several other related hashtags, frequently also presented the rhetorical purpose of a *call to action*. Posts that were coded into this category typically included a direct enlisting of readers to perform a direct, suggested, or implied action. The call to action presented an interesting contradiction on social media in that the perceived *action* is peculiarly event-specific in nature. Participants would typically be expected to kneel, sit, or engage in another silent protest posture during sporting events. As such, the majority of calls to action on social media utilized one of the hashtags in conjunction with images and pleas for support—literal or figurative—of the movement. An example of this is a Facebook post in which the user recorded video of the New York City Council taking a knee during a press conference. The user wrote, "Members of the New York City Council #TakeAKnee in solidarity with Colin Kaepernick and other athletes who are taking a knee to stand (well, kneel) for racial justice." The user uses that hashtag to express support of the movement, and in doing so, encourages others to articulate support. In many cases the hashtags were used to make a plea for others to stop making certain inferences or associations. For this reason, the call to action code most often presented concurrently with the Informational engagement category, and primarily involved (5) patriotism/pride/respect rhetoric. A prime example of this is a post in which a white, female Facebook user writes:

> As a veteran I am asking my friends NOT to ignorantly associate military service with the PEACEFUL protests of the NFL players who will #TakeAKnee to raise awareness for the BLATANT INEQUALITY AND RACISM that is TOO PREVALENT and present in this country. This country is NOT offering liberty and justice for all as our pledge of allegiance states.

Debate/Argumentation

A relevant and significant pattern of using alternative hashtags to express resistance to or disagreement with the perceived sentiments of the movement occurred in this engagement category of Take-a-Knee posts. Posts that were coded in the Debate/Argumentation engagement category represented all five rhetorical purposes: (1) race/racial terminology, (2) hate speech, (3) justice/equality, (4) solidarity/unity, and (5) patriotism/pride/respect. Posts in this category employed the most diverse variety of hashtags in a number of different ways, both affirmative and negative, to communicate feelings toward the movement. The predominant use of the hashtags #StandForAnthem and #BoycottNFL was as a defense mechanism or reaction toward supporters of Take-a-Knee, or posts and articles that painted the movement in a positive light. Debate/Argumentation most frequently occurred in the following pattern: initial post expressing a sentiment; comment reacting to post and expressing an opposing sentiment; and responses in support of either side.

There were far fewer users that utilized the hashtag #StandForAnthem than #TakeAKnee. However, in the cases where this hashtag was used, the rhetoric and supporting artifacts consistently revealed the rhetorical purpose of patriotism/pride/respect. In these posts, users had clearly adopted the narrative about kneeling being a disrespectful act to the flag and the military, and also disloyalty to the country. In this regard, the users' issues with the movement were inextricably linked to a counter-narrative of the movement's purpose and disregarded suggestions to the contrary. In many cases, the use of this hashtag also revealed the race/racial terminology and hate speech rhetorical purposes, in which users perceived race, specifically black people, to be ungrateful, disloyal to the country, or in support of disrespecting the national anthem, flag, or the military. An example of this phenomenon is evident in a Facebook user's post in which she wrote, "Penalties for those #NFL players who do not #StandforAnthem #RespectTheFlag #BLM is a #DomesticTerroristGroup and #AntiAmerican Get rid of them. CALL THEM OUT! Denounce #BlackLivesMatter #HateGroup." In this instance, the user transcends an initial patriotism/pride/respect rhetorical purpose regarding taking a knee, extending it into an indictment of Black Lives Matter as a terrorist group. The use of the word "terrorist" evokes a message of not only antipatriotism but also an overt threat to the nation's well-being. Race did not always present as a direct consideration, as many users of this hashtag articulated negative perceptions of athletes in general instead, and specifically expressed a resentment of using sports as a platform to protest, given the amount of money that athletes make.

The #BoycottNFL hashtag was used by social media users on either side of the movement. Interestingly, the hashtag was initially used due to the blacklisting of Kaepernick. NFL fans who supported the Take-a-Knee movement utilized the hashtag as a call for action to other users to join in a boycott of NFL games until Kaepernick was allowed to join a team again. Following Trump's inciting speech in which he too called for viewers to boycott the NFL for allowing kneeling, the hashtag reemerged to express the polar opposite in sentiments as compared to its original use.

Informational

The use of the hashtag #TakeAKnee and other related hashtags consistently presented a primary engagement code of *Informational*. Users fundamentally sought to explain their positions for or against the action of kneeling during the national anthem, and cited examples, experiences, or quotes—and/or artifacts containing such—to validate or corroborate their stance. In one Facebook post, a user shared a previous post in which a young man, Brennan Gilmore, posted a photo of his grandfather kneeling in grass. Brennan captioned the photo, "My grandpa is a 97-year old WWII vet & Missouri farmer who wanted to join w/ those who #TakeAKnee: 'those kids have every right to protest.'" The user who shared Brennan's post wrote, "#TakeAKnee Because everyone deserves to be judged by the content of their character, not the color of their skin. #TakeAKnee in support of athletes using their platform to challenge oppression." Many posts within this engagement category also fell into several of the other rhetorical categories. In most cases, these posts showed a significant amount of redundancy in efforts to explain Kaepernick's impetus for taking a knee and what the symbolic stance meant and/or did not mean. They challenged readers to consider the hypocrisy of those that were upset by the act of kneeling. This is evident in a comment by a white, male Facebook user who responded to a post by CNN about the controversy. The official CNN Facebook page posted an article titled, *The #TakeAKnee protests have always been about race. Period.* The article received numerous comments on either side of the movement. One user profoundly highlights a perceived hypocrisy by writing, "This Sunday, people should take pictures of people all across the US [sic] at bars or at home to show what the average American usually does while the national anthem is being aired. My guess, it would mostly be photos of people drinking beer and eating chicken wings."

Perceptions

A significant part of this study involved looking at the interaction of Facebook and Twitter users participating in or engaging with the Take-a-Knee movement. The research conducted in this study was greatly assisted by the ability of the researcher to act as a participant observer. The discourse provided a wide range of interaction, both in favor of and in resistance to the movement. In some cases, the interactions were very informed and reflected a thorough understanding and knowledge of the core mission of the movement, and reflected users having made particular effort in educating themselves about the movement. In many of these cases, the users' social media interactions also reflected an effort to inform others. There were equally a variety of posts in opposition to the movement as well. In many cases, the users' posts presented a resistance to a perceived ideology, goal, or mission of the movement. Utilizing the two most prominent social media platforms for the content analysis provided a variety of demographic representations, as well as a diversity and assortment of online communication styles. The very nature of both social media platforms dictates that users participate and communicate their ideas in different ways, and using different artifacts.

Real-World Engagement

In addition to the content analysis of user posts, some social justice activists were selected to participate in-depth interviews to provide another perspective of social media use and its impact on the Take-a-Knee movement. This section includes components gathered from Michael, Chinisha, and Nate, who were selected for their engagement with social media and the movement.

Michael, a thirty-four-year old African-American male and associate chaplain, articulated a very keen sense of employing purposeful and deliberate strategies to communicate his ideas of movement-related issues via social media. So keen, in fact, that he has taken the time to learn about the algorithms on Facebook and Twitter in order to expand the potential reach of his posts. He shares that his primary intended audience when posting on Facebook and Twitter is students on campuses of higher education because that is the demographic he is serving daily in his professional capacity, and engaging in social media discourse with this population helps inform his duties as a chaplain in that he can come to understand more fluidly how they are thinking and how they like to engage. He concedes to having understood different points of view regarding both movements much more clearly after engaging in social media discourse. In these instances, he states, his perceptions of the movement did not change, but his understanding of others' perceptions sometimes did. Michael frequently posted and shared comments regarding his boycott of the NFL 2017–2018 season games in support of Kaepernick. He also was inspired to write and produce a short film entitled "A Message to Colin Kaepernick," in which he donned some of his favorite NFL gear, stood outside on campus on a cold Michigan night, addressed Kaepernick directly, and committed to supporting him by protesting the Super Bowl, all done over a catchy rhythmic beat playing in the background. Michael posted the video on Facebook along with the hashtag "SittingThisOneOut," which quickly accumulated hundreds of reactions. After identifying these real-world behaviors of participation in the Take-a-Knee movement, Michael also shared that he donated to Kaepernick's Million Dollar Pledge campaign, instituted by the Colin Kaepernick Foundation. In October 2016, Kaepernick announced, "I will donate one million dollars plus all the proceeds of my jersey sales from the 2016 season to organizations working in oppressed communities, 100k a month for 10 months." The campaign was a huge success, sparking an additional program in which Kaepernick called on ten celebrities to donate $10,000 each to one of the organizations on his list. Kaepernick then personally matched each celebrity's donation (kaepernick7.com/million-dollar-pledge-recap/). Michael specifically cited giving a monetary donation to the foundation and its campaign as an opportunity for real-world engagement with the movement.

Chinisha, a thirty-one-year-old biracial filmmaker in Brooklyn, New York, backed away from social media as a major part of her function as an activist. For her, participation in the movement was about education from the start. Her goal in sharing artifacts was to educate and hopefully encourage others to take action by joining some aspect of the movement. She states, "If I were posting on Facebook it was generally related to something in the lane of social justice, economic justice, or environmental justice . . . and making calls to action because my frustration had always been that a lot of the conversation had been mostly rhetorical." For Chinisha, it is the dialogue and education that are most important in activism work through social media. She expresses disappointment (and I perceive it as closer to disdain) for "social media activists" who like or retweet something and in doing so feel that they have done their part toward participating in a movement. However, she immediately tries to make it painstakingly clear that she does not mean to diminish the importance of SNS numbers, because quantity is what contributes to getting a topic *trending*. Chinisha first describes her frustration with the dissonance between the goal and purpose of Kaepernick and other athletes taking a knee to support black lives and the narrative about disrespecting the flag and/or military. She states that taking a knee is essentially Kaepernick's corporeal interpretation and manifestation of #BlackLivesMatter, and is the equivalent of an athlete raising a fist during the Olympics; however, the alternate narrative surfaced and proliferated enough to intentionally detach Kaepernick's actions from his intentions. Her frustrations include the fact that, to her, athletes who began to take a knee, lock arms, or protest in some way after President Trump dictated that players should not have the right to play if they took a knee, calling athletes who protest "sons of bitches" never tried to engage in Kaepernick's intentions to begin with. Yet, Chinisha insists, they crucified him for his choice to silently and symbolically protest. Ironically, they felt completely comfortable to use the very same symbolic stance as a direct response and reaction to the president's comments. In doing so, according to Chinisha, "they have diverted attention away from the real issue, changed the subject, while continuing to vilify [Kaepernick]," all this while also coopting his efforts. Because of this, Chinisha has not chosen to engage in the second wave of the Take-a-Knee movement in any way. She also points out that in her perception of the movement it is difficult to actively engage in real-world efforts, and because of this, expresses a heartfelt respect and appreciation for Kaepernick and the significant sacrifice he has made by putting his career on the line to take an action in support of a larger movement, one that resulted in the possible end of his NFL career.

Nate Boyer, a thirty-six-year-old white male, was perhaps the most insightful subject to converse with on the topic due to his direct engagement and participation in the genesis of the Take-a-Knee movement. In 2016, when Kaepernick first decided to silently protest during NFL games he did so by sitting on the team bench during the playing or singing of the national anthem. This protest largely went unnoticed. However, Boyer noticed Kaepernick sitting and, unknowingly, found himself at the center of the Take-a-Knee movement. A former NFL player—a long snapper who was signed by the Seattle Seahawks as an undrafted free agent—Boyer penned an open letter to Kaepernick, which was published in the *Army Times*. Prior to Boyer's football career, he was a United States Army Green Beret who had served six years and multiple tours in Iraq and Afghanistan. In his letter, Boyer expressed that he was upset by the sight of Kaepernick sitting on the bench during the national anthem, and said that he wished Kaepernick would stand during the anthem, but that he was willing to hear him out regarding his reason for sitting. The letter not only received a lot of attention, but sparked an opportunity for conversation. Kaepernick reached out to Boyer and subsequently flew him out to San Francisco to have a face-to-face meeting, which eventually led to Kaepernick making the decision, with Boyer's support, to kneel instead of sit. Boyer described the implications of kneeling, "Soldiers take a knee in front of a fallen brother's grave, you know, to show respect. When we're on a patrol, you know, and we go into a security halt, we take a knee, and we pull security." To Boyer, the idea of *taking a knee* presented an opportunity to respectfully engage in a call for awareness or action. He states that his purpose in writing to Kaepernick was "to calm the country down." He felt that everyone was so committed to their particular posturing as it related to the idea of injustice to blacks and protesting during the anthem that there was no room left for conversation. Nate wanted people to understand the need for open-mindedness and respect, and hopefully, limit the vast political divide that had become too prevalent in the nation. While Nate's letter was met with mixed feelings and perceptions from the public, he noted that he is particularly self-aware of the role his own privilege, as an Army vet and ex-football player, played in potentially shielding him, at least partially, from even more potential vitriolic responses due to the respect people had for his unique and personal involvement with both major groups at the heart of the national debate. Nate also conceded that through conversation during his meeting with Kaepernick, he concluded that the protests were not about disrespect to the military, the flag, or the anthem at all, and were in fact simply intended to utilize a high profile venue to bring awareness to a valid cause for concern. He is clear that everyone should be free to voice their opinion, but regrets that social media gives equal space and voice to brilliance and ignorance, making it a tool of both good and harm. Nate believes that social media has done more harm than good to the Take-a-Knee movement due to the overabundance of "not well-thought out discourse." For this reason, he prefers to avoid SNS discourse, but admits to occasionally participating out of frustration with something he has seen or read.

DISCUSSION

Online social activism is a relevant phenomenon that is ripe for further examination. The prevalence of social networking sites have attracted more people to participate in public discourse on different political and social issues. Furthermore, Segerberg and Bennett (2011) contend that social media is proliferating so rapidly in society that they have become part of the tools of political and social activism. One of the primary reasons is the opportunity for organization, mobilization, and free expression of a movement's people, purpose, and plans. As a result, social media have become a preferred medium giving voice to the marginalized. However, one of the pitfalls of social media used in this way is the potential to effectively drown out or subvert the narrative of a movement by those presenting counter-narratives. This study sought to identify the evident and emergent narratives that occurred in social media conversations about this protest movement, and how those narratives potentially impact real-world perceptions and participation behaviors.

Perceptions and Behaviors

The first research question asked whether social media created awareness and influenced perceptions of social movements. As it relates to the Take-a-Knee movement, social cognition does appear to have meaningful impact on users' online perceptions and attitudes. Those who perceive a positive consequence of or reception from posting on social media using artifacts related to a movement consistently report that they are more likely to also participate in the movement offline. In fact, the interview subjects that associated the Take-a-Knee movement with efforts toward positive changes in society not only showed a tendency to participate offline (in their own interpretations), but they were more concerned with engaging in productive offline participation and avoiding the perceived "noise" inherent in social media. In these cases, proliferating the movement through real-world participation behaviors was more important than was the process of sharing through social media. Those users who agreed with the root causes of the movement but perceived negative consequences of online engagement—negative feedback, argumentation, and so on— were still willing to participate in the movements in real space and time because they saw it as a just cause. However, the users' interpretations of movement participation varied. From the very onset the Take-a-Knee movement was initiated with specific actions—taking a knee—during the singing of the national anthem at professional football games. Despite this, self-described participants of the movement in this study found other methods of engagement that they perceived as constructive, such as boycotting watching NFL games on television or not wearing their NFL jerseys or paraphernalia. Still others sat during the anthem at other sporting events as a show of solidarity with the movement.

It can be argued that the majority of users who utilize movement hashtags or artifacts in reference to a movement are primarily voluntary supporters or participants, but not truly representatives or even agents of the movement in an organized way. Among the 800 samples of hashtag use related to the Take-a-Knee movement, very few were actual activists or members of organized chapters or movement groups. When these participants choose to align themselves with a movement via social media, even when their intentions are to promote the movement, there is a potential watering down (or drowning out) of the true voice of the movement in terms of its ideologies, principles, and goals. This speaks to one of the inherent drawbacks of social media engagement—the propensity for the individual to be perceived to represent the universal. In examining the posts and comments analyzed for this study, the researcher frequently observed interactions in which individuals on divergent sides of the movement would not only often exchange personal insults, but the volatile exchanges would evolve into sweeping judgments of the movement (and/or counter-movement) itself, and in some cases, all individuals who agreed with one side or another. The democratic nature of engagement via social media is on one hand a positive aspect, but also contributes to digital noise and confusion concerning the true impetus, purpose, and goals behind a social movement. Hashtags, used as intended to align a user or post with a particular ideology, also run the risk of potentially aligning the entire movement with the negative perceptions of the user and others. This was evidenced, for example, in cases in which a user would author a post speaking negatively about all members of a particular race and include a movement or counter-movement hashtag at the end. Whether intended or not, the user in this case not only purports to be associated with the movement, but also inadvertently affiliates the movement with that biased ideology in the eyes of some other users. Likewise, the pervasiveness of creating counter-hashtags in response to a movement attempt to subvert or discredit the points or claims made by use of the original hashtags. However, in consideration of the counter-hashtags representing counter-narratives formulated to disrupt a movement, the public must filter through an extensive collection of noise and alternative narratives in order to even scratch the surface of possible solutions. This phenomenon differs from debate about a particular movement. The process of public discourse and debate via social media platforms is healthy in that it facilitates the public's understanding of the nuances of a movement in general. However, the proliferation of false narratives designed to create a particular perception of a movement, regardless of whether or not that narrative is intended to support or subvert the movement, is detrimental to the public's understanding and the function of the movement itself. This is evident in the many posts and/or tweets that associated Take-a-Knee with antipatriotism. The very nature of a movement, as far as public perception is concerned, can be corrupted or even co-opted by the experience of users who come into their personal knowledge of a movement solely or primarily through online participation.

The second research question sought to understand how attitudes and participation in real-world protests were influenced by experiences in social media platforms. The insight gained about a movement through online interaction guides more than online behavior. It also guides users' offline behaviors and participation. This phenomenon, however, has been shown to function in a cyclical process, which is also counterintuitive at times. For example, users who actively engage in real-world, on the ground movement participation tend to show a hesitation or decline in online engagement as they become more active offline. According to some of the interview subjects, this happens as a result of seeing a significant, immediate, or sometimes quantifiable result in their offline engagement. More important is the satisfaction that comes from contributing to and participating in movement activities without having to filter through the noise that comes with online engagement from individuals on either side. This perceived noise includes a range from argumentation and trolling from movement opposition to overemphasis on imagery or media by those purporting support of a movement. In the instances in which offline participation generated a decrease in online engagement, the subjects agree that the work is solely about the work, and not subject to the inherent distractions and backlash that is prevalent in social media engagement with a movement.

The primary focus of Bandura's (1986) social cognitive theory is a triad model involving reciprocity among an individual's environment, personal factors, and behavior. This triad model is evident in social media environments as well. The triad functions in a bidirectional manner featuring reciprocal influences. This form and function set the foundation for Bandura's conception of *reciprocal determinism*, which posits that (a) personal factors (such as cognition, goals, and biological events), (b) behavior, and (c) environmental influences generate interactions that yield a triadic reciprocity (Pajares, 2002).

In the domain of social media, Bandura's theory, particularly as it relates to reciprocal determinism, holds true and could/should be extended to include the nuanced experiences of online discourse. As it relates to the Take-a-Knee movement, social cognition does appear to impact not only users' online perceptions and attitudes, but also their offline behaviors and participation. Those who perceived a positive impact or reception of posting on social media using artifacts related to a movement seemed to also be aware of and open to productive offline movement activities and, in some cases, were inclined to participate in the movement offline. However, those that perceived negative connotations of the movement on social media, did not participate offline and also articulated negativity regarding offline movement activities. Notably, interview subjects who considered themselves to be activists, or admittedly participated in offline movement activities, also perceived negative responses to the movement which eventually deterred them from frequent online engagement. In these cases, it was not negative connotations about the movements themselves, but the trolling, argumentation, and general volatility of the discourse that deterred the subjects from continued online engagement. Beyond the movements, recognition of racism or bias led to more empathic responses when users responded to reports of these phenomena or to the movements themselves.

Social media itself exemplifies the environmental influences referred to in Bandura's theory. The social and technological innovations create new pressures and needs for adaptation that alter our development in the public communication of various topics. As our communication evolves to meet these pressures, so then does the technology itself continue to adapt and transform. Users alter and adapt their articulation of unique perspectives based on the platform in which they are communicating. As referenced by several interview subjects, their social media posts are designed specifically based on not only their intended message, but the way the platform functions, both internally and externally.

REFERENCES

Bandura, A. (1986). *Social foundations of thought and action: a social cognitive theory.* Englewood Cliffs, NJ: Prentice-Hall.

Green, M. & Peil, J. A. (2009). *Theories of human development: A comparative approach* (second edition). New York: Prentice Hall.

Pajares, F. (2002). Gender and perceived self-efficacy in self-regulated learning. *Theory into Practice, 41,* 116-125.

Qualman, E. (2013). *Socialnomics: How social media transforms the way we live and do business* (second ed.). Hoboken, NJ: Wiley.

Tapscott, D. & Williams, A. D. (2006). *Wikinomics.* New York: Penguin Group.

Vissers, S., Hooghe, M., Stolle, D. & Maheo, V. (2012). The impact of mobilization media on off-line and online participation: Are mobilization effects medium-specific? *Social Science Computer Review,* 30(2), 152-169.

Westhoff, M. & Saint Louis, J. (2019). Pigskins and Protests: An Examination of NFL Boycotts Due to the "Take-a-Knee" Movement. In S. D. Perry (Ed.), *Pro football and the proliferation of protest: Anthem posture in a divided America.* Lanham, MD: Lexington.

EIGHT

The Memes of Take-a-Knee

A Case Study of Power Structures in Social Media Use

Brooke Dunbar

In her 1999 book, *The Meme Machine,* Susan Blackmore suggests that memes have the power to influence thought and society. She writes: "Memes do not exist in isolation. All memes, at least at some phases of their lives, are stored in human brains, and humans are complicated creatures who strive to maintain some kind of consistency to their ideas" (p. 164). Memes have taken on the role of "cultural capital" of the internet (Nissenbaum & Shifman, 2015), dominating social media and representing a variety of perspectives. Likewise, the use of political memes is on the rise. The one-liner format is often appealing as a means to voice opinions about hard-hitting issues. Yet the specifics of that influence remain a topic of discussion among scholars as they sift through the complexities of how memes impact those who encounter them. The question remains whether this format creates dialogue and meaningful conversation or rather does the opposite.

Notably, the use of memes is not a new idea, but rather a new vehicle for a form of one-sided political discourse that began with such mediums as the political cartoon. Medhurst and Desousa (1971) offer an analysis of early political cartoons that emphasizes the use of shared symbols and themes to create caricatures out of complex issues. They note how the authors of political cartoons must utilize symbols to tell a large story in a small amount of space. As a result, this medium cannot tell the entire story and often lacks meaningful interaction with the opposing perspective. According to the authors, the most notable difference between early political cartoons that appeared in newspapers and the memes that have evolved from this format is the attention to readership. The challenges faced by the authors of early political cartoons were that they were required to avoid polarization for risk of losing readership. Today's political cartoons, or memes, lack this quality. In fact, they seem to cater to the most extreme views.

With this kind of impact and historical revolution, it seems imperative to understand how memes are part of our conversations about politics, faith, culture, and society in contemporary media. This research will specifically consider the use of memes in the debate over the 2017 National Football League (NFL) Take-a-Knee protests.

LITERATURE REVIEW

The word "meme" comes from the Greek "mimeme" meaning "imitated thing." Heighligen (1996) was an early meme researcher whose work only dabbled with the idea of memes as an internet phenomenon. Heighligen pointed out how most information that is handed down has a memetic quality, being reproduced and passed from person to person. Heighligen also contributed the idea of memes contributing to a "global brain" (Russell, 1995). He shared how memes contribute to understanding, pointing out that repeated exposure can change perception and contribute to a groupthink mentality.

Likewise, Blackmore's controversial book, *The Meme Machine* (1999) is foundational to a current understanding of memes, but her earliest work predates the contemporary digital meme. Blackmore stressed the "virus-like" quality of memes and helped to solidify the idea of "viral content." Yet, her work has fallen under scrutiny namely for its harsh critiques of memetics as a field of study given the struggle to specifically define a meme and for her suggestion that memes are anti-evolutionary and therefore problematic. By this, she means that they are an oversimplification of complex ideas and the removal of nuance from the discourse is an act of deception.

While the field of memetics is not new, a study of the genre of images known as "memes" in relation to new media is still evolving. Wiggins and Bowers (2015) attempted to offer a categorization of this genre as participatory media and clarify it despite its complicated nature. The authors suggest that there is no set theoretical framework for memes, something that they believe needs to be determined, making every study of memes important. Shifman (2013) agreed with Wiggins and Bowers on this point, categorizing the meme as a "troublemaker" noting the many challenges in both studying and explaining where memes fit into the world of new media.

The use of memes for political commentary is one of the most popular areas of study for memetics scholars. Re (2014) explains: "Memes can condense a complex political fact in a brief, powerful and effective container that engages people." Martinez-Rolan and Piñerio-Otero (2016) looked at the use of memes on Twitter during the 2015 Spanish State of the Nation debate through the eyes of high profile political Twitter accounts. This study is notable because it addresses the places where many memes are disseminated before being reposted by users.

Xiao (2012) did a side by side comparison of the memes surrounding Trayvon Martin and Chen Guangcheng, an unarmed black American teenager who was shot in his neighborhood and a political prisoner whose name was banned from Chinese media. The author focused on the use of symbols in memes and noted how the creators of memes use them to sustain a story, continue a conversation, and keep the memory fresh about stories that might otherwise be forgotten. Likewise, symbols allow for shared understanding of ideas and make greater use of smaller media spaces.

A method that has proven effective for the analysis of political memes is critical discourse analysis (Batstone, 1995). Van Dijk (2001) explains that it offers explanation for "social problems, and especially the role of discourse in the production and reproduction of power abuse or domination" (p. 96). This method is most effectively used in naturally occurring language or artifacts. Also, it moves beyond what is actually said to consider context, based on the idea that language is a social practice and does not exist without a context. Moreover, this method considers perceptions of power and how they are expressed. In memetics, this can include symbols, words, icons, culture, context, or images. Given the emphasis on power dynamics and social and cultural contexts, this makes critical discourse analysis an excellent vehicle for studying the memes of the Take-a-Knee protests and dialogue surrounding them as will be done in this study.

RESEARCH QUESTIONS

This research will consider ways that memes were utilized as a means of discourse about the Take-a-Knee protests. Research questions are:

RQ1: What are some of the most prevalent themes among popular memes posted during the height of the Take-a-Knee movement?

RQ2: What do popular memes suggest about how those posting them perceived the power dynamics involved in the Take-a-Knee movement?

RESEARCH METHOD

Critical discourse analysis was conducted of the memes with the "Take a Knee" label on the me.me database. A challenge in any study of memes is locating them as memes are often mislabeled, labeled with a catchy hashtag instead of a categorical one, or not labeled at all. Finding a nonpartisan database aids anyone researching them as memes are often posted to social media pages and reflect the beliefs of that particular page. Me.me is a nonpartisan collection of memes and gifs taken from a variety of searchable databases. In this way, it reflects the viewpoints of a wide demographic.

This critical discourse analysis assesses the top 100 memes on March 23, 2018. This selection of 100 offered a purposeful sampling of the most popular memes and the most prevalent viewpoints on the topic among those who create memes. A critical discourse analysis method was used because of the emphasis both on the social and cultural context of the item being analyzed, but also for the dialogue it presents about power structures. Memes were analyzed using Fairclough's (1989, 1995) method for critical discourse analysis according to the following criteria:

1. Textual analysis. This analysis describes the item and looks at the specific text being stated.
2. Process. This aspect looks at how the meme was created and disseminated and if there is significance to that.
3. Social and contextual analysis. This aspect looks at what the symbols mean in the social and cultural context in which they were created.

Within this structure, the researcher performed a thematic analysis, considering specific word groups, rhetorical themes, cultural references, direct and indirect references, overt and covert language and symbols that illustrate dominance, power, and privilege structures.

Using the applicable criteria for these memes, the researcher offers an analysis of how memes are used to further the conversation surrounding the Take-a-Knee protest and what that conversation indicates about the greater dialogue of power and race relations in the United States.

ANALYSIS

Throughout this research, it became apparent that two divided conversations were taking place. Evidence emerged that each side was making assumptions about the position of the other side and avoiding the unpleasant task of trying to understand the opposing perspectives. One of the most problematic aspects of the use of memes in political commentary is the removal of discourse from communication. Memes present short and catchy one-sided arguments that are rarely designed to create dialogue but more often, to discourage it. Those sharing the memes get to direct the presentation of facts, while avoiding ones that run contrary to their argument or seep into the grey areas surrounding it. In this way, the lack of invitational quality often leads to viewpoints moving further apart rather than seeking shared understanding.

Evidence suggests that those who support the protests base their primary arguments on the lack of attention to incidents of police brutality and social injustice against the black community. Kaepernick told the NFL in 2016 that he chose not to stand for the national anthem because, "I am not going to stand up to show pride in a flag for a country that oppresses black people and people of color" (Wyche, 2016). This came after several incidents of police using deadly force against black citizens without apparent justification. Those who oppose the protest focus on the perception that protesters were showing disrespect to the flag, what it symbolizes, and those who fought and died for the freedom it represents. Yet, noted in the analysis that follows, none of these memes adequately address the concerns raised by their opponents in the discussion.

While it is natural to emphasize one's own perspective, doing so without illustrating understanding of the opposing arguments is ineffective for the purpose of persuasion. Instead, it offers divisive arguments to separate ideologies into a dialogue of "us" versus "them." As discussed in chapter 20 of this book (Clarke & Connelly, 2019), Aron and Aron's (1996) self-expansion model suggests that in order to achieve personal growth, we must be exposed to opposing viewpoints. We do this through interpersonal relationships and dialogue (Aron et al., 2000; 2009). However, memes are counterintuitive to this type of growth. Instead, this study illustrates that memes are primarily effective for gaining social media likes, upvotes, and other forms of validation from like-minded individuals but rarely for the purpose of seeking mutual understanding or furthering conversation about a topic.

The memes in this study seem to be focused on shutting down opposing ideas, specifically ones that are deemed to be a threat. The evidence presented here suggests that those posting memes at the height of the Take-a-Knee protests either did not understand the opposing perspectives or as a power play were actively choosing not to acknowledge them.

It is also notable that the majority of the memes in this study are critical of the Take-a-Knee protests. This is not surprising given the nature of the issue as those opposed were responding to arguments made by Kaepernick and the other protesters through their symbolic actions. This itself speaks to the power dynamics of the protests. The need for a response to the protests at all suggested that there was a perceived threat that must be addressed.

The Trump Influence

The most prominent conversation that took place through these memes surrounded President Donald Trump. Although his direct involvement in the situation itself was minimal, his influence impacted the events surrounding the protests. Kaepernick's protests had been ongoing for over a year when they began to dominate the political dialogue. One of the catalysts for this was Trump's attention to them.

Trump condemned the protests via Twitter on October 23, 2017, stating "Two dozen NFL players continue to kneel during the National Anthem showing disrespect to our Flag & Country. No leadership in the NFL!" (2017b). He also called for action to be taken against them. He tweeted: "Sports fans should never condone players that do not stand proud for their National Anthem or their Country. NFL should change policy!" (2017a). The Take-a-Knee protests occurred in the midst of an already divisive political climate in which Trump was a central figure. While he made himself part of the conversation, many political figures and celebrities did the same, none of which garnered the level of attention Trump did in this conversation. Whether his influence is felt in the form of memes depicting screen shots of his tweets, memes critiquing him, or memes that utilize his message, it is apparent that he is influential to the discussion by the amount of emphasis on him.

A popular meme that disseminated widely and appeared as a profile picture for many users is one that emphasizes these dividing lines and stresses a "Trump" versus "Kaepernick" narrative. It states, in front of a red and blue backdrop, "I'll Take a Knee with Colin Kaepernick before I ever stand with Donald Trump" ("Stand with Kaepernick," 2017). This is notable because Kaepernick has never offered a direct commentary on Donald Trump during his protests. His official stance is about opposition to police injustice, yet the meme suggests that the two are key players in the debate with divided ideologies. The lack of graphics simplifies the message. It also emphasizes the words being used rather than utilizing photos to depict the two men in a particular light. This is unusual for memes regarding the Take-a-Knee protests because the majority of them offer photos with nonverbal depictions of either weakness, confusion, or power illustrated through artifacts or kinesics. The names of these two men stand alone.

The suggestion here is that the power in the scenario rests with Trump. This meme and its wide distribution suggest that those reposting it feel that Trump's influence is an important piece in the conversation. It suggests that those reposting it condemn Trump for his inaction or criticism of the protests and how he has chosen to use the power that they affirm that he holds. Yet, it fails to address his message or the content of it, but rather focuses holistically on Trump, his presidency, or his character. Memes that discuss Trump in various ways outnumber those addressing Kaepernick who was central to the protests.

It is apparent that an "us versus them" mentality is central to the political landscape that informed this conversation. While there are memes representing the views of other political figures on both sides of the issue, predominantly reposts of tweets by popular conservatives, the quantity that address Trump from both sides far outnumber those addressing any other major political or celebrity figure. Both groups seem to give considerable weight to the opinions of the sitting president (see also Westhoff & Saint Louis, 2019, in chapter 17 of this volume).

The Power of Nationalism

A conversation that seemed to be taking place during the height of the Take-a-Knee protests was the importance of national pride for some of those opposed to the protests. In this instance, they treat this as a cultural norm. Fairclough explains, "One aspect of this ordering is dominance: some ways of making meaning are dominant or mainstream in a particular order of discourse, others are marginal, or oppositional, or 'alternative'" (2001). Nationalism is a dominant theme among those who oppose Kaepernick's protests..

Many of the memes simply emphasize the flag or national anthem in a basic, nondescript way. While many do not directly address the protests, given the political and social context, the images allude to Kaepernick's action and the players who joined him. The implication is that the players and those who support them lack patriotism and concern for their country in choosing the flag and national anthem as a medium for their protests.

Another theme utilized was military sacrifice. These memes often utilized pathos and attempted to evoke strong feelings of nationalism and pride or sympathy for military members. A popular one shows the silhouette of a service member on one knee holding a gun in front of an American flag with the caption "this is how Americans take a knee." The text is accompanied with stars and stripes ("American Flag Service Member," 2017). The use of a weapon could be symbolic of the combat aspect of service or could suggest threatening undertones. Meanwhile, the backdrop of the flag focuses attention to the patriotic aspect of the discussion. It does not address the concerns named by Kaepernick.

Another similar meme is set in divided panes of four images all depicting some aspect of military sacrifice. The first image is of a woman crying on top of a coffin with an American flag draped across it. The implication is that she has lost a friend or loved one in service. The caption reads "this is why you don't step on the flag." Beside it is a man in uniform in a wheelchair with the American flag displayed behind him. The caption reads "this is why you stand for the National Anthem." The next shows a military tombstone in the middle of a cemetery. The caption reads "this is why we don't erase history." The last image displays a rustic looking tattered flag with the caption around it: "You're not a black, white, yellow or brown. You're an American. Start acting like it" ("This Is Why You Don't," 2017).

This one utilizes pathos and shame to suggest that doing any of these things, regardless of the reason, signifies that one is not "acting like an American." The visuals and dialogue allude to respect for the sacrifices of military members. The discussion of race as the tagline adds meaning beyond the visuals. This suggests an interesting element of the power structures perceived by its author and, given its wide dissemination, by many others beyond that; it asserts that pride in one's ethnicity should come secondary to pride in one's country. The choice of wording that addresses race and ethnicity is one of the few patriotic memes that include a commentary on the motivation behind the protests. The majority focus only on national pride or the sacrifice of military members. This meme offers patriotic imagery suggesting that this is the theme, but ends with the concluding remarks that undermine the racial element of the protests.

A widely disseminated meme included a black soldier in uniform who was sitting in a chair and wearing two prosthetic legs, emphasizing that he is an amputee. Against an otherwise dark background, the caption reads, in all capital letters "When you decide to take a knee during the national anthem, maybe you should give it to this guy. He gave 2 for you" ("Amputee Soldier," 2017). The meme also utilizes pathos by garnering sympathy for the wounded veteran. It insinuates that participation in the protests nullifies appreciation for the sacrifice of this particular soldier. This is similar to the images used in the previously discussed meme but the choice of a black soldier ties race to the argument to counter Kaepernick's racial concerns in a subtle way. It is not the only meme that utilizes black soldiers to "cross borders" and shift the narrative from one of black victimization to one of black patriotism.

A meme comparing football player-turned-soldier Glen Coffee to Kaepernick was among the most popular of the time period that followed the media attention on the protests. The meme depicts side by side photos of Coffee, also a black football player, in military uniform with a bag slung over his shoulder and a plane in the background while sharing a look of confidence with a picture of a dejected looking Kaepernick in his football uniform. The comparisons are listed underneath in alternating blue and red patriotic lettering. Those statistics listed include that they were both born in 1987, played for the San Francisco 49ers, and were both drafted in the third round of the NFL draft. The list ends by comparing how Coffee "Gave up a lavish career to serve his country as an Army Ranger" while under Kaepernick's photo, the meme reads "Refused to stand for the National Anthem because the 'flag stands for oppression.'" Under this, captioning both photos, is the question, "Who's the Real Hero?" (2018). Under this caption and beside an American flag, is stated "big difference." Like the previous meme, the author of this meme emphasizes that Coffee is a black man who must not share Kaepernick's feelings that the "flag stands for oppression." Notably, Coffee has not gone on the record about the Take-a-Knee protests.

These memes attempt to humanize those impacted personally by Kaepernick's refusal to stand. Yet, the memes often do so by comparing the sacrifices of the military community and its members to Kaepernick himself rather than those for whom he protests. None of the memes in this category mentioned the lives lost to police violence which signify the core of Kaepernick's protests. Again, the meme creators and posters are talking past one another and failing to address the actual concerns raised by either side.

Kaepernick as a Threat

While all parties seem to agree, whether knowingly or not, that Trump holds the primary power in this debate, evidence would suggest that those who do not support the protests believe that Kaepernick is a threat. A considerable number of memes disseminated during the height of the Take-a-Knee protests and even the months following it attacked the character of Kaepernick, suggesting that he was someone who must be discredited.

The military themes extended beyond a discussion of nationalism to poke holes in the ethos of Kaepernick through comparisons such as the ones listed above. Others feature his mansion, suggesting that his own comfortable lifestyle indicates that he must not have experienced racism or that he cannot have empathy for what others have experienced.

Similar to the meme juxtaposing Kaepernick and Coffee was a comparison made between Kaepernick and Tim Tebow, to some another polarizing NFL figure. Tebow was also known for kneeling, but in prayer. His one-knee pose became a well-known symbol. One widely disseminated meme featured Tebow in his signature pose, complimented by the text "This man did not Take-a-Knee in protest, he took a knee in prayer and was called 'controversial.' LET THAT SINK IN" ("Tebow Take-a-Knee," 2017). Beneath Tebow is written "the world is becoming more and more backward by the day." It has a white background behind the single photo of Tebow on the field.

The meme indicates that the societal "norm" of Christianity is subverted by kneeling in protest. Moreover, it also implies that Kaepernick's actions are contradictory to the Christian faith. Other memes expanded on this, notable because Kaepernick also professes to be a Christian and often suggests that his faith is the core of his fight for social justice. He shared with the *Washington Post*, "My faith is the basis from where my game comes from. I've been very blessed to have the talent to play the game that I do and be successful at it. I think God guides me through every day and helps me take the right steps and has helped me to get to where I'm at. When I step on the field, I always say a prayer, say I am thankful to be able to wake up that morning and go out there and try to glorify the Lord with what I do on the field" (Frost, 2017).

The meme's authors clearly believe that Kaepernick and his actions are a threat to their particular view of Evangelical Christianity.

Several memes mocked the fact that he was ousted from the NFL and did not retain his spot on the 49ers roster. One joked about him as "The Waterboy," referencing the popular 1998 movie ("The Waterboy," 2017). Yet others mocked his appearance, one with a disheveled Kaepernick looking like the robber Marv from the 1990 movie, *Home Alone* ("Kaepernick as Marv," 2017). Many of the memes addressing the character of Kepernick came on the heels of him winning GQ's coveted "Citizen of the Year" award. All of these memes sought to discredit the ethos of Kaepernick, thereby discrediting the protests.

The number of memes attacking Kaepernick personally offered no dialogue about the issue, yet were some of the most popular memes in this study. This suggests that those posting them perceived that Kaepernick and the other protesters held some type of power that must be discredited. In this case, it appears that the concern is that Kaepernick was leading people away from ideals that are currently the dominant ideology: patriotism, faith, and order.

Pro-Kneeling Memes as a Response to Criticisms

It's notable that the majority of the memes in this study, a purposeful sample of the most popular memes during the time period, oppose the Take-a-Knee movement. This is likely because there was less to be said by those supporting the protests, given that they set the dialogue, as it was Kaepernick's actions that were being discussed. However, the majority of memes that take a pro-keeling position combat the inference that the debate was primarily about patriotism. Others look to defend Kaepernick's character. It is notable that the pro-protesting memes were often direct responses to the anti-protest memes rather than standalone ideas as illustrated by the examples that follow.

The pro-kneeling memes that focused on nationalism pointed out the contradictions in the opposing argument. In one example, the meme is divided in half with the top picture depicting two men, presumably sports fans by their attire and the football that one is holding, sitting in a relaxed position on a couch. The one below it is a photo of Marvel's Captain America. The caption of the top picture reads: "this is you every Sunday when the National Anthem is played." The caption below Captain America reads: "this is you on social media acting like you are the biggest patriot on planet Earth when some football players sit during the National Anthem to protest injustice" ("This is You," 2017). The symbolism of Captain America versus the indifferent football fans claims those who critiqued the protests were hypocrites. The inference is that if someone does not stand every time the national anthem is played, he or she does not have the right to be angry that NFL players kneel in their public venue.

Another meme in this category features a white singer who appears to be singing the national anthem at a sporting event. In the background, several white women are in a posture that matches the posture taken by Kaepernick and other players during their protests as the women hold the on-field American flag during some type of ceremony. The caption above it states "I guess it's OK to Take-a-Knee during the national anthem" and finishes below it "Unless you are a black football player" ("Flag Kneeling," 2018). The juxtaposition of Kaepernick to the white women, who were not the target of public outcry claims this represents hypocrisy. Yet, the women were clearly participating in a ceremony that was honoring the flag, so addressing their posture both fails to satisfy the concerns about Keapernick's symbolic protest being disrespectful and suggests opponents are racist.

A considerable portion of the memes that offer support for the protests are focused on defending Kaepernick or his viewpoint. Some do so by clarifying or reframing the debate in defense of Kaepernick and players involved in the protests, while others utilize historical examples to argue against the concerns raised by the other side. A popular one features white lettering on top of a maroon background. There are no other graphics or writing. It simply says, "Thinking NFL players are 'protesting the flag' is like thinking Rosa Parks was protesting public transportation" ("Thinking NFL Players," 2017). Another lists names like Philando Castile, Eric Garner, and Trayvon Martin along with 16 others with the words "no conviction" next to their names. The caption reads: "if you don't understand why Colin Kaepernick knelt for police accountability in this country this is why" ("Police Accountability," 2017). Another, one of many memes that featured screen captures of Twitter conversations, offered a picture of black NFL player Marcus Peters sitting on the bench with the first Twitter comment by user Ryan Saavadre: "Nearly 600 people were shot last night but Chiefs player Marcus Peters still thought it was appropriate to sit during the national anthem." Below it is a response by another user named Richie Loco that continues the dialogue with, "A white man shoots 600 people but you're mad at the black man who is sitting peacefully not harming anyone. That's why he's protesting" ("600 people," 2017). Loco's thought that all 600 were victims of whites again makes race central to the meme.

Almost all of the memes in this category attempted to address some misconception held by the opposing side as opposed to advancing the supporting argument. Much like the opposing viewpoint, very few did so in a dialogic way. Both sides present assumptions or choose to only acknowledge the part of arguments that support their perspective.

CONCLUSIONS, LIMITATIONS, AND SUGGESTIONS FOR FURTHER RESEARCH

Fairclough suggests that, "Critical Discourse Analysis . . . is based upon a view of semiosis as an irreducible element of all material social processes" (Fairclough, 2001). The dialogue that takes place via memes offers a bird's-eye view of complex social, moral, religious, and political ideologies. Learning more about these dialogues helps us to gain perspective on the conversations that are taking place and how those participating in them perceive the power and social context that surround them.

What seems to emerge when analyzing the power dynamics of the Take-a-Knee protests through memes are the inconsistencies in the conversation. The two sides seemed to be having different conversations about what issue was at the core of the protests or the backlash against them. While the pro-protests side fought to return to core arguments made by Kaepernick, they did so without addressing the perceived disrespect to the flag. If this side felt that the protests were worth the outcry, they did so without acknowledging the reasoning behind the outcry. Meanwhile, the anti-protests side used memes to discredit Kaepernick or reframe his perspective to be a discussion of his disregard of the military and nationalism. Yet, these memes often overlook the arguments made by Kaepernick for why he chose to protest.

Problematic to a full understanding of how these memes were being used is an understanding of the intentions of those who posted them. Meme reposting popularity could suggest agreement, but others may have reposted with commentary to suggest their disagreement. While the purposeful sampling used here offers an analysis of some of the most popular memes, this study cannot ascertain what led to their popularity.

A limitation to this study was that the majority of the memes were created and posted by those opposing the Take-a-Knee protests. Further research could include an analysis of how those on the other side of the political spectrum utilized memes differently. Qualitative interviews would also offer some insights into user motivation for posting them. Moreover, aside from the lack of dialogue, this research also suggested that there are several prevalent subcategories of memes that are all utilized in different ways including reposted tweets, photos, wording, and pop culture references, among others. More in-depth research could offer insights into how each of these is utilized differently.

REFERENCES

"600 people." (2017, October 6). Retrieved from https://me.me/i/ryan-saavedra-real-saavedra-nearly-600-people-were-shot-last-night-18903210.

"American Flag Service Member." (2017, November 16). Retrieved from https://me.me/i/this-is-how-americans-take-a-knee-exactly-19457936.

"Amputee Soldier." (2017, September 26). Retrieved from https://me.me/i/when-you-decihe-to-take-a-knee-during-the-national-18809233.

Aron, A., Norman, C. C., Aron, E. N., McKenna, C., & Heyman, R. E. (2000). Couples' shared participation in novel and arousing activities and experienced relationship quality. *Journal of Personality and Social Psychology*, 78(2), 273.

Aron, E. N., & Aron, A. (1996). Love and expansion of the self: The state of the model. *Personal Relationships*, 3(1), 45-58.

Batstone, R.(1995) "Grammar in Discourse: Attitude and Deniability." In G. Cook and B. Seidlhofer, eds. *Principle & Practice in Applied Linguistics*. Oxford: Oxford University Press, pp. 197-213.

Blackmore, S. (1999). *The Meme Machine*. Oxford: Oxford University Press.

Clark, K. & Connelly, C. (2019). Solutions to the Fallout: Invitational Rhetoric and Opposing Viewpoint Political Conversations. In S. D. Perry (Ed.). *Pro football and the proliferation of protest: Anthem posture in a divided America*. Lanham, MD: Lexington.

Fairclough, N. (1989) *Language and power*. London: Longman.

Fairclough, N. (1995) *Critical discourse analysis*. London: Longman.

Fairclough, N. (2001). The dialectics of discourse. *Textus*, XIV(2), 231-242.

"Flag Kneeling." (2018, February 9). Retrieved from https://me.me/i/i-guess-its-ok-to-take-a-knee-during-the-20577965.

Frost, M. (2017, September 27). Colin Kaepernick vs. Tim Tebow: A tale of two Christians on their knees. *Washington Post*.

Heighligen, F. (1996). Evolution of memes on the network: From chain-letters to the global brain. In G. Stocker & C. Schöpf (Eds.), Ars Electronica Festival 96. *Memesis: The future of evolution*. (pp. 48-57). Vienna: Springer.

Janis, I. L. (1972). *Victims of groupthink; a psychological study of foreign-policy decisions and fiascoes*. Boston: Houghton, Mifflin.

"Kaepernick as Marv." (2017, March 6). Retrieved from https://me.me/i/colin-kaepernick-out-here-looking-like-marv-getting-electrocuted-in-11313753.

Martínez-Rolán, X., & Piñeiro-Otero, T. (2016). The use of memes in the discourse of political parties on Twitter: Analysing the 2015 state of the nation debate. *Communication & Society*, 29(1), 145-159.

McGregor, S.L.T. (2010) *Critical discourse analysis: A primer*. Halifax. Mount Saint Vincent University.

Medhurst, M. J., & Desousa, M. A. (1981). Political cartoons as rhetorical form: A taxonomy of graphic discourse. *Communication Monographs*, 48(3), 197.

Mina, X. (2012). "A tale of two memes: The powerful connection between Trayvon Martin and Chen Guangcheng," *Atlantic*. Retrieved from http://www.theatlantic.com/technology/archive/2012/07/a-tale-of-two-memes-the-powerful-connection-between-trayvon-martin-and-chen-guangcheng/259604/.

Nissenbaum A., & Shifman, L. (2015). Internet memes as contested cultural capital: The case of 4chan's/b/board. *New Media & Society*, pp.1-19

"Police Accountability." (2017, July 12). Retrieved from https://me.me/i/if-you-dontunderstand-why-colin-kaepernick-knelt-down-for-police-16609441.

Re, F.A. (2014). La política transmediática: nuevas formas de participación ciudadana. *La Trama de la Comunicación*, 18(1), 33-51.

Russell, P. (1995). *The global brain awakens: Our next evolutionary leap*. Alexandria: Miles River Press.

Shifman, L. (2013). "Memes in a digital world: Reconciling with a conceptual troublemaker," *Journal of Computer–Mediated Communication*, 18 (3), pp. 362–377.

Shifman, L (2013) *Memes in digital culture*. Cambridge, MA: MIT Press.

"Stand with Kaepernick." (2017, September 24). Retrieved from https://me.me/i/ill-take-a-knee-with-colin-kaepernick-before-l-ever-18778820

"Tebow Take-a-Knee." (2017, September 29). Retrieved from https://me.me/i/this-man-did-not-take-a-knee-in-protest-he-18798543

"The Waterboy." (2017, September 16). Retrieved from https://me.me/i/colin-kaepernick-the-merica-america-usa-waterboy-kaepernick-18600236

"Thinking NFL Players." (2017, September 25). Retrieved from at https://me.me/i/18800147

"This is Why You Don't." (2017, September 18). Retrieved from https://me.me/i/18690158

"This is You." (2017, September 25). Retrieved from https://me.me/i/this-is-you-every-saturday-and-sunday-when-the-national-18793835

Trump, D [Realdonaldtrump]. (2017a, September 24). "Sports fans should never condone players that do not stand proud for their National Anthem or their Country. NFL should change policy!" [Tweet]. Retrieved from https://twitter.com/realDonaldTrump/status/912080538755846144.

Trump, D [Realdonaldtrump]. (2017b, October 23). "Two dozen NFL players continue to kneel during the National Anthem showing disrespect to our Flag & Country. No leadership in the NFL! [Tweet] Retrieved from https://twitter.com/realDonald-Trump/status/922430688703451136.

Van Dijk, T. A. (1988) *News as discourse*. Hillsdale, NJ: Lawrence Erlbaum.

Van Dijk, T.A. (2001) *Ideology: A Multidisciplinary Approach*. London: Sage.

Westhoff, M. & Saint Louis, J. (2019). Pigskins and Protests: An Examination of NFL Boycotts Due to the "Take-a-Knee" Movement. In S. D. Perry (Ed.). *Pro football and the proliferation of protest: Anthem posture in a divided America*. Lanham, MD: Lexington.

Wiggins, B. E., & Bowers, G. B. (2015). Memes as genre: A structurational analysis of the memescape. *New Media & Society, 17*(11), 1886-1906.

Wodak, R. & Meyer, M. (2001) *Methods of critical discourse analysis*. London: Sage.

NINE

NFL National Anthem Protests

A Cluster Analysis of President Trump's Tweets

Kalah Kemp

"The issue of kneeling has nothing to do with race. It is about respect for our Country, Flag, and National Anthem. NFL must respect this!" was tweeted by @realDonaldTrump on September 25th (2017d). Over a year after Colin Kaepernick, a National Football League (NFL) quarterback, protested during the national anthem, other NFL players joined in by kneeling, and President Donald Trump began tweeting in response to these protests. In fact, Trump tweeted thirty-two times about this topic in 2017, from September 23 to October 23, and many other times after this research was completed. Kaepernick protested police use of unreasonable force and unequal treatment of blacks, and stated, "I am not going to stand up to show pride in a flag for a country that oppresses black people and people of color" (as cited in Alberto, 2017). Despite Kaepernick's cause, Trump's tweet above is the only microblog post out of the thirty-two tweets that mentions race. Due to this, an analysis of Trump's tweets will enable us to understand his worldview and how it was enacted concerning the national anthem protests, especially as the protests took place in games that are viewed by millions. Though the NFL's TV ratings in the 2017 season fell by about 10 percent in comparison to the previous season, the games still "accounted for 37 of the 50 most-watched programs of the year, according to Nielsen" (Battaglio, 2018). A typical game was viewed by 14.9 million people (Rovell, 2018).

From Trump's Republican nomination to the national anthem protests, America is becoming increasingly divided (Anthony, 2017). In fact,

Hechtman (2017) reported that Americans perceive the country to be as divided as it was during the Vietnam War. Some historians argue that "the rise of social media, combined with the decline of the central institutions that once defined borders of political debate, have created a potentially dangerous moment in our public discourse" (Gershon, 2017, para. 3). Specifically, Twitter has become a direct source of news, with politicians circumventing the press and criticizing the mainstream news media (Enli, 2017). Additionally, selective exposure of Twitter followership (Messing & Westwood, 2014) and limited cross-ideology engagement has contributed to division within social networking sites (Himelboim, McCreery, & Smith, 2013), paralleling the division in America.

Not only are new media outflanking the social boundaries of political discussions, but politicians' Twitter engagement with one another and citizens is redefining public affairs. For example, when former president Barack Obama opened the @POTUS Twitter account in 2012, the director of online engagement, Alex Wall, managed the account. In 2016, Trump hired Dan Scavino to act as the social media manager for @POTUS, and Trump also tweets from his personally managed account, @realDonaldTrump. Due to his unprecedented use of Twitter to attract media attention (Fox News Insider, 2017) and increase followership, it is imperative that scholars examine his rhetoric to discern his underlying ideologies. As such, this cluster criticism contextualizes anthem protests and evaluates Trump's reaction to the recent NFL protests based on thirty-two tweets from @realDonaldTrump to analyze his worldview.

BACKGROUND

On August 26, 2016, the San Francisco's 49ers' Kaepernick sat during the national anthem (Timeline, 2017). After Nate Boyer, a former Seahawks player, wrote to Kaepernick and they discussed respecting the military personnel, Kaepernick's next protest, on September 1, was demonstrated through kneeling instead of sitting (Brinson, 2016, para. 4). Teammates and other NFL players joined Kaepernick to kneel in the following weeks and through the 2017 season.

These anthem protests recall many others including the 1968 Olympic Games protests by medalists Tommie Smith and John Carlos (See Nyamandi & Bolin, 2019, chapter 2 in this book). Other anthem protests at sporting events continued through the 1990s. In 1972, Vince Matthews and Wayne Collett, both African Americans, were barred from the Olympics after they turned away from the American flag, rested their hands on their hips, fidgeted, and wore unzipped jackets (Johnk, 2017). President Nixon politicized football to gain "partisan and ideological advantage" (Freedman, 2017, para. 9). According to Ferris (2014), President Nixon and then NFL commissioner Pete Rozelle, "expected athletes to give up some of their civil liberties on the playing field," and not criticize America (p. 222). In 1973, an Eastern Michigan track athlete stretched during the anthem, and at Madison Square Garden, the anthem was not played before the Olympic Invitational track event due to the controversy of protests. More recently, in 1996, Mahmoud Abdul-Rauf was suspended from the National Basketball Association (NBA) because he would not stand during the anthem due to religious beliefs (Johnk, 2017). Then president Clinton did not publically respond to Abdul-Rauf's protests.

In all of these cases, black athletes protested the national anthem and flag. They sat, kneeled, lifted a fist, or engaged in some other peaceful demonstration to draw attention to systematic racism, oppression, or religious freedom. Historically, presidents have chosen to not respond or to respond indirectly by praising traditional acts of patriotism. In all of these cases, the protesters lacked verbal support from presidents, experienced backlash, and renewed the controversy of both racial inequality and forced patriotism within a democracy.

TRUMP RESPONDS

In light of the NFL protests, on September 22, 2017, Trump provided his perspective on the NFL protests at a rally for Luther Strange, an Alabama Republican senate candidate. He contended that if fans left the stadium, the protests would stop, and in response to a protesting player, the NFL owners should respond: "Get that son of a bitch off the field right now, he's fired. He's fired!" (Trump, as cited by Tatum, 2017). A few days later, Congresswoman Sheila Jackson Lee of Texas took a knee on the House floor because she perceived Trump's criticism as unwarranted due to first amendment rights, and also argued, "You tell me which of those children's mothers are a son of a B. That is racism" (as cited by Lang, 2017). According to Lang (2017), the president's comments and tweets have "escalated a nationwide controversy that has significant racial and cultural undertones" (para. 5).

As for Kaepernick, while he was voted as one of the most disliked players in the NFL, his jersey remains a top seller (Timeline, 2017). Kaepernick has acted as a free agent since March 2017, and was not signed to play for another NFL team. Despite his absence, more NFL teams, fans, owners, college sports teams, and even little leagues have participated in protests. In addition to his remarks at the rally, on September 22 Trump tweeted to criticize NFL owners for not penalizing athletes who refused to stand during the anthem. Since athletes representative of diverse ages, races, and sports continue to kneel regardless of Trump's criticism, the protests have become less about racial inequality, and more about the freedom of expression (Alberto, 2017).

After October 2017, when Vice President Pence left a Colts game in which players knelt during the anthem, some team owners responded by requiring athletes to stand, and Kaepernick has filed a grievance with the NFL, asserting that he was not signed to play due to collusion between team owners. Michael Bennett and other athletes called on the NFL to sign Kaepernick because "no one should be denied employment for having the courage to follow their convictions and take action for equality and social justice" (Bennett, as cited by Bieler, 2017, para. 1).

METHOD

In order to analyze Trump's unconventional response to the NFL protests, Burke's cluster criticism will be used. Kenneth Burke developed this method of analysis to identify rhetors' worldviews. Burke (1969) asserted the "basic function of rhetoric" is "the use of words by human agents to form attitudes or to induce actions in other human agents" (p. 41). When words induce actions, identification, also known as consubstantiality, takes place because an audience is successfully persuaded to unite with the rhetor on ideas, attitudes, objects, or other factors (Burke, 1969). Burke believed that consubstantiality is needed due to the natural disassociation individuals have with one another caused by separate physical bodies. Therefore, the role of communication is to increase identification and decrease disassociation. (Foss, 2009)

In addition to Burke's contentions of consubstantiality and disassociation, he asserted that rhetorical artifacts reveal a "vocabulary of thoughts, actions, emotions, and attitudes for codifying and thus interpreting a situation" (Foss, 2009, p. 64). Due to this, Burke argues that through the analysis of frequent or intense key symbols and their contexts, the worldview of the rhetor can be uncovered—of which the rhetor might not be conscious (p. 65). Burke refers to worldviews as terministic screens, and purports that rhetors' vocabularies reveal a "reflection," "selection," and "deflection of reality" (Burke, 1966, p. 45). By identifying the key terms in Trump's tweets and words clustered around those terms, I will uncover the terministic screens of the president as they are revealed through Twitter.

Further, Burke distinguished the difference between semantic and poetic meanings, congruent with denotations and connotations. According to Burke (1973), ideal semantics "get a description by the elimination of attitude" while ideal poetic language "attains a full moral act by attaining a perspective atop all the conflicts of attitude" (pp. 147-148). This analysis will be enriched by the implications of semantic and poetic uses of key terms.

Cluster Analyses

Recent studies have used Burkean philosophy including cluster analysis to examine the worldview behind adoption rhetoric and considerations of Twitter as a global forum. First, Potter (2013) used cluster analysis to examine the legal rhetoric of *adoption*. She found the differences between semantic and poetic meaning of the word *adoption* construct a variety of meanings. While the semantic term "adopt" refers to a legal process, the poetic meaning refers to choosing a child. The clusters around *adopt* include *economy* and *selection*, implying a "commodification" of adoption (p. 116). Second, Bates and Kalita (2016) asserted that clustering tweets is challenging due to the brevity of the content and colloquial language used to fit a message into 140 characters (p. 2). However, Saito, Hirata, Sasahara, and Suzuki (2015) argue that due to the real-time Twitter environment, the platform provides rich insights into "human social behavior" (p. 17). Finally, Ingram (2002) cautions against the use of cultural and political hegemonic frames in global forums because they imposes on others' norms and institutions. In this analysis, Ingram analyzes how Burke's identification in a globalized society will grow universality while stifling individual communities.

Twitter and Trump

Several studies have also been conducted to better understand the shift toward Twitter in political discourse. When Kaye and Johnson (2011) applied the uses and gratifications model to blogs, they discovered the popularity of blogs was increasing, in part, due to a distrust of the mainstream media (p. 239). Since blogs can satisfy the need for information and communication (p. 241), the shift toward Twitter follows as it satisfies these psychological needs. Trump's tweets including the hashtag #FakeNews reveal his distrust of media, inviting citizens with shared distrust to receive news about his administration from his @realDonaldTrump Twitter account. In his words, tweeting "is working," and "I can go bing bing bing . . . and they put it on and . . . as soon as I tweet it out," referring to the news reporting of his tweets (Report, 2017, para. 4). This trend was supported by Bode, Hanna, Yang, and Shah's study. They analyzed hashtags to discern political communication trends on Twitter and found that politicians employed tactics including hashjacking and using the "opposition's keywords" in an effort to "proselytize and agitate" those on the opposite side of the political spectrum (p. 7). The study also found that among political subgroups, the Tea Party movement used hashjacking more than any other group in 2010.

Other studies have explored Trump and Clinton's use of Twitter in their 2016 presidential campaigns to explain how tweets shaped individuals' perceptions of the candidates. In 2016, Lee and Lim found that

Trump's "high level of impulsive or uncivil tweets" imply that instead of using traditional public relations strategies, Trump used a high engagement level and user generated content to increase perceived credibility (p. 853). Enli (2017) further notes that Trump's amateur-style communication is a counter-trend to professionalism in politics, and is attracting both news media and social media participants to Twitter.

ANALYSIS

In addition to the cluster analysis, several trends were identified within Trump's tweets. These trends help to contextualize the tweets by describing the president's communication patterns through Twitter. By understanding Trump's use of handles, mention of people's names, and hashtags, one may gain deeper insights into this cluster analysis. Based on the frequency and intensity of *NFL*, *NFL fans*, and *respect*, these key terms shed light on Trump's worldview.

@Handles

First, Trump's lack of inclusion of Twitter handles in his tweets provides insight into his perspective on engagement. Even though Kaepernick and other athletes tweeted about the race-centered protests, Trump's tweets excluded the players' handles and instead focused on the NFL's *policies* and *ratings*. Interestingly, only two of Trump's tweets included handles, directly mentioning @NFL and @CNN; the @NFL handle was included to criticize the organization for "Too much talk, not enough action" (Trump, 2017f), and @CNN was disparaged for reporting "#FakeNews" and a " . . . Total lie!" (Trump, 2017c). This trend indicates that Trump seeks minimal Twitter engagement from the entities he is criticizing. Further, the President includes organizations' handles but omits personal handles. This implies that Trump prefers professional communication on behalf of organizations rather than from personal Twitter accounts, which is in stark contrast to his use of @realDonaldTrump versus @POTUS, the professionally managed account.

Names

Secondly, Trump's inclusion of people's and organization's names in tweets reveals his perception of their roles regarding the protests. The president did not include the names of Kaepernick, protesting players, NFL commissioner Roger Goodell, owners of teams with protesters, or organizations seeking to improve race relations in America. This, along with a lack of Twitter handles, reveals Trump's preference for one-way communication, and by ignoring Kaepernick's cause for the protests in thirty-two out of thirty-three tweets, some might conclude that he devalues race relations. General John Kelly, Jerry Jones, the Dallas Cowboy's owner, courageous patriots, and NASCAR were mentioned by Trump as supporting his stance on the NFL protests, but their handles were not included in tweets. In this case, the president includes the names of people and organizations he supports, while omitting the names of those individuals whose actions he opposes.

#Hashtags

Finally, Trump's promotion of campaign hashtags exposes whether he intends to stimulate a social movement. Hashtags also reveal ideological differences among Twitter users (Bode, Hanna, Yang, & Shah, 2015). In this case, Trump included #FakeNews in one tweet and #StandForOurAnthem in three tweets. Trump has criticized the news media for years, and the #FakeNews hashtag was formed to shed light on misleading news stories or publications with controversial interpretive journalism. Therefore, Trump's use of this hashtag discloses his attitude toward fake news reporting. The hashtag #StandForOurAnthem was developed to promote respect for the *National Anthem, American flag*, and the *country*. This hashtag shows that Trump believes that standing during the national anthem represents *respect* and *solidarity*. Trump values a public display of *solidarity* at sporting events in spite of America's current division. Ironically, kneeling in protest requests a public display of solidarity as well among Americans seeking to acknowledge racial injustice or police brutality. Due to the fact that only four of his tweets included a hashtag, Trump contributed to the anti-#FakeNews movement, and did not seek to stimulate a #StandForOurAnthem movement. In light of these trends, to better understand Trump's objectives for the NFL twitterstorm, three clusters, *NFL, NFL fans,* and *respect* were identified.

Key Terms and Clusters

The president expresses his disapproval of the NFL in twenty-nine out of his thirty-two tweets pertaining to the protests. The words surrounding NFL include *disrespect, force to stand, fire, suspend, change rule, change tax law, backlash,* and *boring games*. Trump (2017a) describes playing sports as "the privilege of making millions of dollars," and as such, players "should not be allowed to disrespect" the *American flag, National Anthem,* or the *Country,* echoing Nixon's sentiment. He argues that the NFL should *change* their *rules* to require and *force* athletes *to stand* during the *National Anthem*. If a player chooses to kneel, Trump calls on the NFL owners to *fire or suspend* that player. Additionally, Trump notes that while the NFL is granted *tax breaks*, the *players are disrespecting* the *national anthem*. As such, Trump states that the *tax law* should be *changed*, implying that he is not supportive of providing a tax break to an organization that does not respect the American flag. Finally, Trump asserts that the NFL has experienced *backlash* due to the protests, and that fans do not desire to view *boring games*. In this instance, Trump focuses on the NFL's ratings and game actions to demean the organization.

The next cluster pertains to *NFL fans*, and words around this term include *stay away, refuse, anger, never condone, demand respect, booed,* and *ratings are WAY DOWN*. Trump famously encouraged participants to boycott the NFL if the protests continue (BBC News, 2017). Supporting this message, Trump's tweets rally fans to *stay away* from the NFL and *refuse* to watch players who disrespect the national anthem. Trump also encourages fans to *never condone* anthem protests and *demand respect* of the national anthem from players. In one of his tweets, the president (2017e) typed, "The booing at the NFL football game last night, when the entire Dallas team dropped to its knees, was loudest I have ever heard. Great anger." In this tweet, Trump uses hyperbole to commemorate *booing* toward kneeling players. His use of *anger* assigns the audience an emotion to be felt when watching players protest the national anthem.

The final cluster to examine is *respect*. Trump aligns *respect* with the following terms: *flag, National Anthem, honor, #StandForOurAnthem, Country, courageous patriots, must stand,* and *Make America Great Again*. In three of the thirty-two tweets pertaining to the anthem protests, Trump uses a positive appeal to explain why individuals should stand. In one tweet, he (2017b) stated, "Courageous Patriots have fought and died for our great American Flag—we MUST honor and respect it! MAKE AMERICA GREAT AGAIN!" This is the only tweet pertaining to the military through the use of *courageous patriots*. The rhetoric in this tweet employs pathos to evoke pride among Americans. In several tweets, Trump uses *flag, National Anthem,* and *Country* synonymously as representations of America. The use of *stand* is also used synonymously with *respect*, showing Trump's value of standing to respect *America*. Finally, Trump included his 2016 presidential campaign slogan, *MAKE AMERICA GREAT AGAIN* in his tweet to reiterate that the country improved when Trump was elected, and will be made greater through *standing* during the *National Anthem*.

Poetic Rhetoric

Similar to Potter's (2013) study regarding Burke's assertion of semantic and poetic terms, it is also imperative to explore Trump's rhetoric within these tweets. The use of *respect, demand, anger,* and *solidarity* unearth further implications of Trump's worldview. First, in Trump's tweets, he assigns the act of standing as the only way to *respect* the anthem; however, kneeling is also a cultural act of showing high or special regard to something. While it is customary to stand for the anthem, the president infers that it is the sole method to show respect. Contrastingly, when Kaepernick shifted from sitting to kneeling, he attempted to show respect. Secondly, in one tweet, Trump recommends the NFL change its policy to require athletes to stand. However, his use of demand also reveals a poetic meaning of "command" as he proposed to change tax laws in response to the NFL's decision to not force players to stand. Trump's tweets are not directed toward the protesters, so he does not ask them to stand "with authority." Instead, he asks the NFL to change their policy and threatens to change tax law if they do not oblige.

Unlike Trump's poetic uses of *respect* and *demand*, his use of *anger* assigns an attitude to be felt about the protests. Trump tweeted for fans to feel *great anger*. In this case, he is using semantic rhetoric to enrage NFL fans. Moreover, Trump's use of solidarity denotes his understanding of unity as including only those who agree with his perspective on the protests. In this case, Kaepernick and other players kneeled to reveal a lack of unity regarding racial equality. As Trump's tweets containing *solidarity* are surrounded by other tweets including demands, a threat, and insults, the president does not seek to acknowledge or rectify racial inequality. Instead, the president seeks unity based on his "interests, objectives, and standards" pertaining to the anthem protests.

INTERPRETATION OF TRENDS AND CLUSTERS

Regardless of the president's consciousness of his own terministic screens, implications of his worldview were portrayed through these thirty-three tweets. Trump constructed reality through reflecting on respect, selecting to focus on the NFL protests, and deflecting issues of racism. While Bates and Kalita (2016) described the challenges of clustering tweets, Trump's tweets revealed thoughts, actions, emotions, and attitudes. Trump's limited use of handles suggests that he does not want to engage with NFL owners or protesters. Instead, the President seeks to post his opinions to increase identification among his followers; in turn, those who disagree with his stance on the protests are further disassociated from Trump.

Next, the president's exclusion of protester's names suggests that he does not value racial discourse or share the goal of improving race relations. For example, Trump did not request protesters to respond or speak with him about their cause because he did not approve of their form of protest. Instead, he criticized their teams' owners and the NFL establishment for the players' actions. Trump did, however, include the names of organizations and people that support his perspective on the protests. Therefore, he uses Twitter to criticize entities with which he disagrees, and specifically acknowledges those who agree with his ideology, increasing consubstantiality.

The final trend regarding hashtags suggests Trump values keeping news organizations accountable along with the importance of standing for the national anthem. Since he only used hashtags in four tweets, Trump was not seeking to stimulate a Twitter movement, but rather, media attention for these occurrences. Based on his use of handles, Trump's worldview values minimal engagement from those organizations with which he disagrees. Regarding names and hashtags, Trump seeks identification through acknowledging those with whom he agrees while disrespecting kneeling players because the protest vehicle disrespects the national anthem. Parallel to Bode, Hanna, Yang, and Shah's (2015) study, Trump used #FakeNews and *MAKE AMERICA GREAT AGAIN* to agitate the news media and those who did not support his candidacy. This rhetoric deepens the chasm between his critics and supporters.

Clusters

The NFL cluster used by Trump uncovered his *anger* for the NFL protests. He spoke negatively of the NFL, and perceives his call to action to the NFL fans and *boring games* as the causes for the NFL's decreased ratings. By bringing attention to the NFL's ratings, Trump denotes the organization as a loser, while promoting NASCAR and standing individuals as *winners*. This divisive rhetoric drives a wedge between himself and the NFL, himself and those seeking racial equality, and Americans standing with those who kneel during the anthem. Since most of his tweets pertained to the NFL cluster, the emphasis of his campaign was to divide those who identify with his perceptions from those who support the anthem protests.

Based on Trump's personal reaction to the NFL protests, he calls NFL fans to action within the second cluster. Trump seeks to negatively impact the NFL by encouraging fans to boycott the organization, boo, and demand respect from the players. Additionally, he argues that the owners should fire or suspend players, and change their policy to include the requirement to stand during the national anthem. The NFL and NFL fan clusters reveal Trump's terministic screens as valuing the division of "us" versus "them." Some interpret "us" to mean those opposing the NFL protests, while others interpret "us" as white Americans. According to LeBron James, an NBA all-star player, Trump "used the sports platform to try to divide us" (as cited in Carissimo, 2017, para. 2). Trump also pitted NASCAR against the NFL to spark debates between leagues, fans, athletes, and races. Klein (2017) asserts that "Trump is both a symptom and accelerant" of the nation's divide (para. 4). Therefore, it seems likely that Trump's rhetoric is exacerbating the division among Americans.

The last cluster regarding respect reveals that Trump values standing as a public display of respect for the national anthem. Trump's "us" versus "them" terministic screen achieves solidarity when the "us" is united. In this case, he uses positive appeals to encourage Americans to feel patriotic and demonstrate their respect for the flag. However, if marginalized or disenfranchised Americans want to resolve inequality before standing in solidarity with the "us," then they will endure criticism from the president of the United States on a public, global forum. Trump's limited rhetoric pertaining to race and the military demonstrates that he does not strongly correlate racial inequality or supporting the troops with the anthem protests. Since he does not address the first amendment, the president's reality deflects constitutional rights.

Poetic Meanings

Overall, Trump's rhetoric in these thirty-three tweets compares to his "uncivil" and "amateurish" candidate tweets (Lee & Lim, 2016; Enli, 2017). His understanding of *respect* is based on a culturally constructed act of standing, while his poetic use of the word suggests that he is not open to other forms of respect such as kneeling. Trump's use of *demand* is represented differently based on the tweets' contexts. In some cases, he uses the word semantically to request policy changes, while in another tweet, he commands tax legislation change as a threat to the NFL. In all of these cases, it is evident that Trump is angered by the protests and requests fans to have the same reaction. Even though some fans support the protests, Trump uses Twitter to proselytize fans to be angry with the protests. Further, Trump's divisive, poetic use of *solidarity* pits groups against one another, and leaves the audience to speculate whether he intends to increase the racial divide in America.

CONCLUSION

As the president averages six tweets per day and is ranked the 21st worldwide Twitter user (Donald J. Trump Twitter stats, 2017), it is imperative that scholars examine the rhetoric of Trump's tweets to better understand his worldview. Trump had over 43 million followers, and only followed 45 other Twitter users at the time of this writing, reiterating his preference of one-way communication. At the same time, his audience attentiveness score is high at 71 percent, which is evinced by his NFL tweets ranging from 17,000 to 208,000 favorites, 14,000 to 74,000 retweets, and 14,000 to 66,000 comments. This level of engagement satisfies the communication needs of microbloggers, driving more attention to the twittersphere (Kaye & Johnson, 2011). To understand the impact of his tweets, a cluster analysis of the comments should be conducted to reveal those who identify with Trump versus those who disassociate from him.

Based on this cluster criticism of Trump's thirty-three tweets pertaining to the NFL's protest, Trump's terministic screens were uncovered. This study is significant to scholarship not only to better understand politicians' rhetoric through Twitter, but also the worldviews shaping political discourse in America. Unlike former presidents, Trump has selected to use a global forum to criticize national anthem protests at professional sporting events. In light of this, his rhetoric also has global repercussions, which violates communal political discourse and seeks identification with a global audience (Ingram, 2002). Regardless of the president's awareness of his worldview portrayed through Twitter, some perceive Trump's presidency as valuing division instead of unity (Cillizza, 2017, para.6). These insights are important because they reveal the authentic, social behavior (Saito, Hirata, Sasahara, & Suzuki, 2015) of the president. Further research should also compare Trump's tweets with his other communication to verify his terministic screens. By better understanding Trump's behavior and underlying values, Americans may better navigate the implications of his communication. As a result, productive debates may occur to resolve the NFL protests, racial inequality, and cultivate solidarity among all Americans.

REFERENCES

Alberto, E. (2017, November 9). Divided we sit: Colin Kaepernick's protest. In *Los Angeles Times*. Retrieved from http://highschool.latimes.com/augustus-f-hawkins-high-school/divide-we-sit-colin-kaepernicks-protest/

Anthony, M. (2017, November 18). What the first Thanksgiving can teach a divided America. In *Fox News*. Retrieved from http://www.foxnews.com/opinion/2017/11/18/what-first-thanksgiving-can-teach-divided-america.html

Arnold, G. C. (2017, October 25). Colin Kaepernick signs $1 million book deal: Report. In *The Oregonian*. Retrieved from http://www.oregonlive.com/nfl/index.ssf/2017/10/colin_kaepernick_signs_1_milli.html

Bass, A. (1998). Race and nation in Olympic proportions: Televising black power at the Mexico City games. *The Spectator, 19*, 9-23.

Bates, A., & Kalita, J. (2016, March). *Counting clusters in twitter posts*. Paper presented at Information and Communication Technology for Intelligent Systems: Udaipur, India. doi: 10.1145/2905055.2905295

Battaglio, S. (2018, January 4). NFL ratings finish regular season down about 10% from last year. Retrieved from latimes.com.

BBC News. (2017, September 25). Trump NFL row: Defiance after US president urges boycott. Retrieved from http://www.bbc.com/news/world-us-canada-41379374

Bieler, D. (2017, November 16). Michael Bennett and other athletes call on NFL to sign Colin Kaepernick. In *Chicago Tribune*. Retrieved from http://www.chicagotribune.com/sports/football/ct-athletes-call-on-nfl-to-sign-colin-kaepernick-20171116-story.html

Bode, L., Hanna, A., Yang, J., & Shah, D. V. (2015, May). Mapping online clusters and networks: Candidate networks, citizen clusters, and political expression: Strategic hashtag use in the 2010 midterms. *The Annuals of the American Academy of Political and Social Science*, 1-11.

Brinson, W. (2016, September 27). Here's how Nate Boyer got Colin Kaepernick to go from sitting to kneeling. In *CBS Sports*. Retrieved from https://www.cbssports.com/

nfl/news/heres-how-nate-boyer-got-colin-kaepernick-to-go-from-sitting-to-kneeling/
Burke, K. (1966). *Language as symbolic action: Essays on life, literature and method*. Oakland: University of California Press.
Burke, K. (1969). *A rhetoric of motives*. Oakland: University of California Press.
Burke, K. (1973). *The philosophy of literary form*. Oakland: University of California Press.
Carissimo, J. (2017, Sepember 25). LeBron James says Trump "used the sports platform to try to divide us." In *CBS News*. Retrieved from https://www.cbsnews.com/news/lebron-james-donald-trump-nba-nfl-comments-sports-platform-divide-us/
Cillizza, C. (2017, September 26). Trump's NFL and Puerto Rico tweets prove his goal to divide, not unite the country. In *CNN*. Retrieved from http://www.cnn.com/2017/09/26/politics/trump-nfl-tweets/index.html
Davis, D. (2008, August). For 40 years, Olympians Tommie Smith and John Carlos have lived with the consequences of their fateful protest. In *Smithsonian Magazine*. Retrieved from https://www.smithsonianmag.com/articles/olympic-athletes-who-took-a-stand-593920/
Donald J. Trump twitter stats. (2017). In *Twitter Counter*. Retrieved from https://twittercounter.com/realDonaldTrump
Enli, G. (2017). Twitter as arena for the authentic outsider: Exploring the social media campaigns of Trump and Clinton in the 2016 US presidential election. *European Journal of Communication, 32*(1), 50-61.
Ferris, M. (2014). *Star-spangled banner: The unlikely story of America's National Anthem*. Baltimore, MD: Johns Hopkins University Press.
Foss, S. K. (2009). *Rhetorical criticism: Exploration and practice* (4th ed.). Long Grove, IL: Waveland Press, Inc.
Fox News Insider (2017, January 16). Report: Donald Trump to continue using @RealDonaldTrump twitter account as president. In *Fox News*. Retrieved from http://insider.foxnews.com/2017/01/16/trump-continue-using-personal-twitter-account-realdonaldtrump-president-not-potus
Freedman, S. G. (2017, September 10). Football and politics. In *The New Yorker*. Retrieved from https://www.newyorker.com/culture/culture-desk/football-and-politics
Gershon, L. (2017, November 8). Just how divided are Americans since Trump's election? In *History*. Retrieved from http://www.history.com/news/just-how-divided-are-americans-since-trumps-election
Glanton, D. (2017, September 26). Trump, the master manipulator, using anthem controversy to divide Americans. In *Chicago Tribune*. Retrieved from http://www.chicagotribune.com/news/columnists/glanton/ct-trump-nfl-racism-dahleen-glanton-met-20170925-column.html
Hechtman, M. (2017, October 28). America is most divided since Vietnam War: Poll. In *New York Post*. Retrieved from https://nypost.com/2017/10/28/merica-is-most-divided-since-vietnam-war-poll/
Himelboim, I., McCreery, S., & Smith, M. (2013). Birds of a feather tweet together: Integrating network and content analysis to examine cross-ideology exposure on twitter. *Journal of Computer-Mediated Communication, 18*, 154-174.
Ingram, J. (2002). Hegemony and globalism: Kenneth Burke and paradoxes of representation. *Communication Studies, 53*(1), 4-24.
Johnk, Z. (2017, September 25). National Anthem protests by black athletes have a long history. In *New York Times*. Retrieved from https://www.nytimes.com/2017/09/25/sports/national-anthem-protests-black-athletes.html
Kaye, B. K., & Johnson, T. J. (2011). Hot diggity blog: A cluster analysis examining motivations and other factors for why people judge different types of blogs as credible. *Mass Communication and Society, 14*, 236-263.
Klein, R. (2017, September 25). Analysis: The NFL kneeling controversy is about race, and that's what Donald Trump wants. In *ABC News*. Retrieved from http://abcnews.go.com/Politics/analysis-trump-race-sports-divide-inflame/story?id=50075367

Lang, H. (2017, September 26). Congresswoman kneels on house floor to protest Trump's criticism of NFL. In *CNN*. Retrieved from http://www.cnn.com/2017/09/26/politics/sheila-jackson-lee-nfl-protest/index.html

Lee, J., & Lim, Y. S. (2016). Gendered campaign tweets: The cases of Hillary Clinton and Donald Trump. *Public Relations Review, 42,* 849-855. doi: 10.1016/j.pubrev.2016.07.004

Messing, S., & Westwood, S. J. (2014). Selective exposure in the age of social media: Endorsements Trump partisan source affiliation when selecting news online. *Communication Research, 41*(8), 1042-1063.

Olympic protestors stripped of their medals. (2017). In *History*. Retrieved from http://www.history.com/this-day-in-history/olympic-protestors-stripped-of-their-medals

Potter, J. (2013). Adopting commodities: A Burkean cluster analysis of adoption rhetoric. *Adoption Quarterly, 16,* 108-127.

Report: Donald Trump to continue using @RealDonaldTrump twitter account as president. (2017, January 16). In *Fox News*. Retrieved from http://insider.foxnews.com/2017/01/16/trump-continue-using-personal-twitter-account-realdonaldtrump-president-not-potus

Rovell, D. (2018, January 4). NFL television ratings down 9.7 percent during 2017 regular season. Retrieved from espn.com.

Saito, S., Hirata, Y., Sasahara, K., & Suzuki, H. (2015). Tracking time evolution of collective attention clusters in twitter: Time evolving nonnegative matrix factorization. *PLoS One, 10* (9), 1-17. doi: 10.1371/journal.pone.0139085

Tatum, S. (2017, September 23). Trump: NFL owners should fire players who protest the national anthem. In *CNN*. Retrieved from http://www.cnn.com/2017/09/22/politics/donald-trump-alabama-nfl/index.html

Timeline: How anthem protests have evolved over past 15 months. (2017, November 13). In *ABC 7 News*. Retrieved from http://abc7news.com/sports/timeline-how-anthem-protests-have-evolved-over-past-15-months/2643163/

Trump, D. J. [realDonaldTrump]. (2017a, September 23). If a player wants the privilege of making millions of dollars in the NFL, or other leagues, he or she should not be allowed to disrespect . . . [Tweet].

Trump, D. J. [realDonaldTrump]. (2017b, September 24). Courageous Patriots have fought and died for our great American Flag—we MUST honor and respect it! MAKE AMERICA GREAT AGAIN! [Tweet].

Trump, D. J. [realDonaldTrump]. (2017c, September 25). @CNN is #FakeNews. Just reported COS (John Kelly) was opposed to my stance on NFL players diresepecting FLAG, ANTHEM, COUNTRY. Total lie! [Tweet].

Trump, D. J. [realDonaldTrump]. (2017d, September 25). The issue of kneeling has nothing to do with race. It is about respect for our Country, Flag, and National Anthem. NFL must respect this! [Tweet].

Trump, D. J. [realDonaldTrump]. (2017e, September 26). The booing at the NFL football game last night, when the entire Dallas team dropped to its knees, was loudest I have ever heard. Great anger [Tweet].

Trump, D. J. [realDonaldTrump]. (2017f, October 18). @NFL: Too much talk, not enough action. Stand for the National Anthem. [Tweet].

TEN

Celebrity Response to Take-a-Knee, Kaepernick, and NFL Protests

Candace Moore

In December 2017, Beyoncé—a Grammy Award-winning artist, actress, entrepreneur, and multimillionaire—presented Colin Kaepernick with the *Sports Illustrated* Muhammad Ali Legacy Award. The honor is bestowed on athletes at the "Sportsperson of the Year" awards show who directly or indirectly dedicate their platforms and personal beliefs to foster social impact (*Sports Illustrated*, 2018). Kaepernick—a former quarterback for the San Francisco 49ers—remained seated or knelt during the national anthem starting in 2016 to raise awareness of racial injustice, police brutality, and systemic oppression of black Americans and people of color. His actions initiated a wave of demonstrations by National Football League (NFL) players, teams, and athletic organizations across the nation. During Beyoncé's awards recognition speech, she thanked Kaepernick for his "selfless heart," "conviction," and "personal sacrifice" to "change the world for better," particularly for people of color (Nyren, 2017).

Time Magazine acknowledged Beyoncé as one of the most influential people in the world (Luhrmann, 2013). Alongside her husband, rapper and business mogul Shawn "Jay-Z" Carter, they are deemed pop culture icons and one of the most powerful celebrity couples in this generation (Forbes, 2017; Lurhmann, 2013). The entertainer's appearance at the *Sports Illustrated* awards show and involvement with Kaepernick's recognition was concealed from the public prior to the event yet covered by multiple news outlets following the presentation, including FOX, ABC, NBC, CBS, and CNN (Fox News, 2017; Gretzky, 2017; NBC News, 2017;

Respers France, 2017; Skiver, 2017). The prolific coverage emphasizes the importance of this chapter's inquiry about the convergence of communication, media, celebrity, and activism.

Several celebrities communicated in support of or in opposition to the national anthem protests spawned by Kaepernick and his stated social justice issues. They also reacted to the effects of these actions and the presidential remarks in response to the protest. This chapter is an examination of celebrities' responses to Kaepernick's Take-a-Knee actions and the NFL boycott dichotomy. Entertainers and professional athletes beyond football players are the celebrity focus. The purpose of this analysis is to investigate celebrities' communicative approaches to share their beliefs about a polarizing social justice issue. The timing of the messages will be assessed as well as strategies that celebrities used to construct their brand identity through discursive and non-discursive communicative messages. A critical analysis of their techniques will provide relevant strategic communication insight about influential figures' key message conveyances in this divisive situation.

LITERATURE REVIEW

Celebrity Influence

Celebrities have been shown to influence culture, trends, and public opinion. This includes athletes and their persuasive effects on audiences (Andrews & Jackson, 2001; Basil and Brown, 2004; Bush et al., 2004; Presnell, 2008). Nownes (2012) explained that celebrities' political endorsements impact public perceptions of candidates. The researcher suggests that their association with political "brands" affects people's perceptions and attitudes about the politician as well as the public's view of their individual persona (p. 497).

Social Identification

Burke's theory of identification (1969) provides the contextual schema of rhetorical messages that convey unification or division. Consequently, the rhetor produces terministic screens using images, terms, and discourse to guide attention to underlying meanings and influence audience opinion. These screens define human intent and further dialogic messages beyond the immediate proposition. Ultimately, the identification theory socially deconstructs the communicator's dialogue and conveys their worldview. Fraser and Brown (2002) associate celebrity values and media influence with Burke's theoretical construct of identification. Basil and Brown (2004) further apply the theory of identification to reveal notable sports figures' ability to influence audience behaviors and emotions with their actions. Brown (2015) examined specific areas of audience involvement with media personae including identification, transportation, parasocial interaction, and worship. He defined identification as the process of temporarily assuming a celebrity's identity. Brown suggests that celebrities' social influence is a significant area of study due to people's intense psychological connections with their persona. Consequently, he advanced previous research on the attitudes, values, and beliefs audiences adopt due to their infatuation with celebrity culture (Brown, 2010; Kelman 1961).

Identity and Social Identification

Values are essential in identity construction and communicative identification based on one's beliefs. Rokeach (1973) contends that moral messages express personal or social perceptions that significantly influence behavior. Polletta and Jasper (2001) define collective identity in social movements as a shared perception or relational status with a community. This mutual affiliation conveys positive feelings toward others in the identified group through cultural objects including names, narratives, symbols, verbal styles, rituals, and clothing. Accordingly, apparel is an expressive form of nonverbal discourse that visually represents group membership and identity (Campbell, 2012; González & Bovone, 2012; Lurie, 1981). Winge (2008) explains that socially conscious celebrities may wear garments to reveal their social, cultural, and political values; however, this expression is subject to vacillating trends in the fashion industry and individuals' identified preferences.

Racial Identification and Activism

The role of racial identification is a critical factor in celebrity activism. Jackson (2010) conducted a historical examination of black athletes and entertainers involved in social justice activism through mainstream and black press from 1949 to 2005. Results suggest that cultural identity and historical events were significant in dominant media frames; however, African American celebrities continued to face ideological undermining and reprimands as the result of their protests. While there are historical references of celebrity activism in the form of social justice statements, celebrities in recent years have used media channels to convey their ideology and opinions. In fact, social media has galvanized a new form of celebrity activism. Celebrities' images and persuasive rhetorical messages mobilize audiences and convince followers with no previous philanthropic activism to participate in their efforts (Bennett, 2014). Harlow and Benbrook (2017) further scholarship on race and social media in their analysis of hip-hop artists' social media contributions to the #BlackLivesMatter Movement and association of the social justice hashtag with black identity. The researchers examine opposing views, effects of celebrity support, and public perception. Their findings revealed that identification was essential in showing hip-hop artists' accord with the black community and faithful support of social justice issues through a call to action. Moreover, four themes emerged in their collective identity: speaking to whites, solidarity, black is beautiful, and equality.

METHODOLOGY

The method employed for this study is generative criticism which permits the construction of themes to characterize an artifact (Foss, 2009). First, I conducted a general web search of celebrity responses in support of or opposition to Kaepernick and Take-a-Knee incidences. Primary rhetorical artifacts included seventy-five celebrities' social media posts, pictures, and media statements. In the artifacts discovered, twenty-six celebrities conveyed opposition to Kaepernick and Take-a-Knee actions while forty-nine celebrities communicated support. After separating the findings into sets of opposition and support of the occurrence, I disaggregated the artifacts based upon celebrities' occupation and the communicative platform employed. Major features of each artifact were interpreted including accompanying images, date of the communicative statement, and applied social media hashtags or key expressions. These served as aspects of the terministic screens from Burke's theory of identification—the explanatory schema. Based upon Burke's (1966) supposition, terministic screens are a symbolic representation of objects that provide distinctions within celebrities' stances and "direct the attention" of the audience to their particular intent (p. 45). Thus, themes emerged that explicated their communicative approach in this controversy.

ANALYSIS

Celebrity Opposition to Colin Kaepernick and Take-a-Knee NFL Protests

Celebrities in opposition to Take-a-Knee protests viewed NFL stakeholders' actions as impudent demonstrations toward the representations of American symbols and a stratagem to create division within the country. American symbols—including the flag and national anthem—represented the sacrifice of military veterans, families, and police officers. Celebrity opponents collectively associated patriotic representations with freedom, pride, valor, and opportunity for Americans. Consequently, kneeling during the national anthem or perceived disrespect to the American flag indicated ingratitude and ignorance about these representations. Celebrity adversaries to the Take-a-Knee demonstrations generally suggested that their intention was to defend military service members and law enforcement officers. However, in several statements—even the explicit messages—celebrity adversaries were willing to acknowledge supporters' constitutional rights to protest and their right of free speech.

Celebrity Opposition Platforms and Timing of Statements

The analysis revealed several instances of an individual celebrity using multiple communication platforms to convey a singular position. Twitter was the primary medium employed to share statements opposing the protests. More than sixty percent of celebrities used the communicative mode which limited their sentiments to 140 characters per tweet. Media interviews or YouTube videos provided platforms for additional celebrity conveyances. Television, radio, and internet broadcasts allowed them to verbally state their views. Opponents used Facebook, the third employed platform, to share their views through lengthier discourse or editorials. One celebrity, Kate Upton—a model, used Instagram as a communicative medium to post an image of athletes kneeling at a September 11, 2016, NFL game. She accompanied the picture with commentary about their disregard for the freedoms and opportunities provided by American citizenship, as well as impudence toward military service members and veterans.

Nineteen celebrity opponents' statements in this analysis occurred after Kaepernick's initial kneeling demonstration and prior to President Donald Trump's comments about NFL stakeholders and the Take-a-Knee controversy. They also communicated frequently when other football players followed the 49ers quarterback's actions. The majority of celebrity critics maintained their views after Trump's 2017 comments and the NFL team demonstrations that resulted. Seven opponents made their initial public statements following this period; however, most of those in opposition initiated their commentary at the onset of the protest movement.

Opposition Theme 1: Compelling Images of Veterans and Family Stories

Famed personalities included compelling images or personal anecdotes in their statements against the Take-a-Knee protest. These distinctions were considered terministic screens in oppositional message statements. Some celebrities expressed personal discontent toward the protest due to their family members' service in the military and law enforcement. They included: Shaquille O'Neal, an NBA Hall-of-Famer; Curt Schilling, a former MLB pitcher; and Sage Steele, an ESPN anchor. Beyond conveying a general statement about the Take-a-Knee issue, personal experiences represented meaningful familial connections and displayed traditional American values that precipitated protest deviation.

The compilation of celebrities' social media images was meant to conjure empathy from audiences and underscore the basis of their patriotic beliefs. Their efforts displayed the poignant and courageous sacrifices of veterans as a response to NFL stakeholders' perceived reprehensible actions during the national anthem. In a Twitter post, Sage Steele included an image of a man kneeling beside a headstone at a veteran's cemetery. Scott Baio, an actor, posted a picture of a military amputee in salute to the flag while sustaining his body weight on a wheelchair. Baio also shared a picture of a veteran's widow mourning over his open casket as he lay in uniform. Kevin Sorbo, an actor, and Dean Cain—the actor who portrayed Superman on the television series *Lois & Clark: The New Adventures of Superman*—retweeted an image of Alejandro Villanueva, the Pittsburgh Steelers player and Army veteran who performed three tours in Afghanistan. Villanueva stood outside of the tunnel to salute the American flag during the national anthem while the remainder of his team remained in the locker room to refrain from taking sides during the height of the NFL protests. Cain captioned Villanueva's image with, "I'm a lesser Man of Steel #respect" (Cain, 2017).

Opposition Theme 2: Hashtags and Statements to Unify or Vilify

Celebrities included hashtags and Twitter handles for opposing protest views on Twitter and Instagram. These statements serve as an additional terministic screen to indicate unifying or divisive messages. Celebrities focused their hashtags on messages of collaboration and unity or insults toward Kaepernick and the Take-a-Knee movement. Celebrity protest adversaries shared unifying hashtags to encourage the public to collectively stand during the national anthem. The statements included: #unitedwestand, #buildabridge, #solution, #neverforget, #AllLivesMatter, #USA, and #GodBlessAmerica. Joy Villa, a singer and Fox News commentator, emphasized unity when she referenced the @NFL Twitter handle and said that the way to destroy America is from within and division is weakness (Villa, 2017a).

Political ideology and identification were apparent in at least two celebrities' tweets with unifying hashtags; correspondingly, posted a couple of days following the president's public comments regarding NFL stakeholders. Stacy Dash, an actress, included #MAGA, in her protest statement. Joy Villa—the singer and Fox News commentator—also inserted #MAGA in a retweeted picture of Thomas Davis, an NFL player with the Carolina Panthers, standing and praying during the national anthem. This hashtag represents Trump's campaign slogan—"Make America Great Again"—distinctly indicating these celebrities' support of him and alignment with his position on the issue. Villa also corroborates her personal identification with Christianity and evangelical beliefs in her stance on the protest with the image of the praying athlete. The supporting text in the tweet states that she is writing a song about unity and prayer because "divided we truly do fall" (Villa, 2017b).

Celebrity opponents included divisive hashtags to contradict supportive NFL stakeholders in the protest. They included #Boycott and #BoycottTheNFL. Beyond hashtags and handles, divisive messaging was evident after Trump's statements about the controversy. Neal McCoy, a country music singer, posted a video to Facebook with a debut of his original song called, "Take a Knee . . . My Ass." In a Twitter post, Nick Searcy, an actor, referred to kneeling NFL players as "classless asshats" (Bond, 2017). On Facebook, Kid Rock also said, "Fuck ANYONE who takes a knee or sits during our national anthem!" (Kid Rock, 2017). Celebrities' inclusion of pejorative terms toward NFL stakeholders in the controversy was consistent with Trump's reference to a protesting player as a "son of a bitch." Furthermore, the use of profanity was a method to intimidate and denigrate players through oppositional statements.

Opposition Theme 3: Kaepernick as Villain

Several celebrities directly addressed Kaepernick as the instigator of the actions they deemed unacceptable, primarily stated in the early stages of his protest. Multiple derogatory statements accompanied the hashtags #Kaepernick and #ColinKaepernick. Collectively, these terministic screens of name-calling as well as points emphasizing Kaepernick's inconsistency show communicative intent to implode and refute his credibility as the leader of the demonstrations. Tony Stewart, a famed NASCAR driver, and James Woods, an actor, applied Twitter hashtags to defame his character and actions including #idiot, #POS, and #dirtbag. Stacey Dash, the actress well-known from the movie *Clueless,* shared a Facebook post of an op-ed article by Sherriff David Clarke referencing Kaepernick as a "dumb jock," "elitist," "crybaby," and "misinformed" about civil rights and freedom (Clarke Jr., 2016; Dash, 2016). Kaepernick's quarterback performance and the timing of the Take-a-Knee protest was also criticized by celebrity opponents. Bill Maher—a comedian and television show host with millions of Twitter followers—referred to the quarterback as an "idiot" for his inconsistent season of interceptions and decision to kneel; Maher, however, admitted he supported the protest issues (Maher, 2016). In a *Fox and Friends* interview, Shaquille O'Neal—the NBA Hall-of-Famer—acknowledged injustices toward people of color yet questioned Kaepernick's activism prior to Take-a-Knee actions. O'Neal insinuated that the quarterback lacked the message consistency of previous athlete activists because he was not as vocal about social justice issues in the prime of his career.

Several celebrity opponents also referenced Kapernick's "error" of combining his professional football career with activism as well as subsequent repercussions. Jim Brown, the NFL Hall-of-Famer and activist, emphatically disagreed with the national anthem protest and explained the need for the quarterback to distinguish his career from activism. Brown also suggested that Kaepernick was not astute in his protest decisions. He said he would have solved the issues in an "intelligent manner" using donations and fame instead of violating the flag (The Postgame Staff, 2017). Britt McHenry, a former ESPN correspondent, criticized Kaepernick's receipt of the *Sports Illustrated* "Sportsperson of the Year" award and cited defaming occurrences associated with his proclaimed activism to deride the decision. She referenced socks he wore at the San Francisco 49ers' 2016 training camp depicting police officers as pigs and another instance when Kaepernick donned a shirt with Fidel Castro—a communist Cuban leader—in Miami, a city with a substantial Cuban immigrant population (McHenry, 2017). In another instance, Jay Mohr, an actor and podcast host, called the quarterback a "douchebag" and "disingenuous" in a 2016 tweet; however, nearly one year later, he tweeted that Kaepernick was "blackballed by NFL owners" and called the treatment "horrible" (Mohr, 2016; Mohr, 2017).

Opposition Theme 4: Racial Identification, Approach and Retraction

Although black and brown male celebrities were opponents to NFL national anthem protests, they were more willing to acknowledge the social justice issues of the protest than opponents of other ethnicities. In media interviews, Shaquille O'Neal referenced America's injustices and Jim Brown discussed the need to rectify systemic problems. Their criticism of Kaepernick involved his approach to raise awareness about the issues. Each celebrity male opponent of color who used social media to convey their Take-a-Knee views after the initial kneeling protest later removed their public posts. In September 2016, Latino American rapper Fat Joe tweeted that the national anthem protest was disrespectful to soldiers and said he disagreed; however, he later deleted his Twitter post. Jerry Rice, a legendary NFL wide-receiver and Hall-of-Famer, initially posted a Twitter message on August 30, 2016, that "All Lives Matter" and said while he respected the right to protest, Kaepernick should not "disrespect the flag" (Brinson, 2016). A few weeks later, Rice recanted his statement and replaced it with another tweet applauding Kaepernick's ability to raise "awareness to injustices" (Rice, 2016; Brinson, 2016).

This theme shows the significance of black and brown males' identification with the protest issues. While they were able to debate the Take-a-Knee approach, their audiences held them responsible for identifying with the protest issues of injustice and oppression toward minorities. Male celebrities of color who communicated their standpoints via media interviews were able to exhibit this awareness, develop their stances and comprehensively explain their oppositional justification. Cultural identification was not apparent in initial Twitter posts by male celebrity opponents of color. Consequently, their statements were recanted or restructured to include empathetic amendments due to public criticism. This finding emphasizes the cultural group's challenges to convey authentic contrasting views through social media in a polarizing climate involving race-related issues.

Celebrity Advocates of Colin Kaepernick and Take-a-Knee NFL Protests

Celebrities in support of Take-a-Knee protests viewed NFL stakeholders' actions as courageous demonstrations performed to stimulate critical social justice dialogue. Celebrity advocates reiterated protesters' First Amendment rights. Although kneeling actions occurred during the national anthem, supporters clarified the intent of the protests from contrasting anti-military and law enforcement condemnation standpoints. Their consciousness of protest issues regarding injustice against people of color, historical underpinnings of oppression, and systemic racism caused them to question adversaries' ideology. In a few cases, supporters emphasized opponents' conflicting views of Take-a-Knee protests compared to the apparent absence of debate regarding white nationalists' and Confederate monument rallies. This strategy implied critics' arguments were erroneous and connected to racist ideals.

Celebrity Advocate Platforms and Timing of Statements

Comparable to celebrity opponents, advocates used multiple communicative platforms exclusively and mutually to convey individual statements. Instagram and Twitter were the main channels employed to communicate supportive stances. Several celebrities posted personal messages and videos on Instagram to encourage NFL stakeholders, sympathetic Take-a-Knee protesters, and the public to participate in demonstrations. They also shared images of themselves with communicative expressions to convey support, as well as individual kneeling athletes and NFL teams with unified protest displays of kneeling or locking arms. Media interviews were also a platform for celebrities to expound upon supportive protest views and clarify their stance to audiences via journalists' questions. Celebrity supporters in this analysis did not use Facebook. However, advocates employed two distinct communicative platforms to convey their support of demonstrations—Kaepernick's San Francisco 49ers jersey and concerts or awards shows. These served as terministic screens of supporters.

While one half of the celebrities in this analysis advocated for Kaepernick following his initial protest stance during the national anthem, supportive expressions and rebuttals were slightly intensified after Trump's blunt rhetoric regarding athletes and NFL owners. Diversity of celebrity advocates was also more apparent—including ethnicity, gender, and representations—following his communicative statements. Prior to the president's comments, the majority of celebrity advocates were black or Hispanic males. The responses were also singular rather than group demonstrations. Following Trump's comments, white, black, and Hispanic female celebrities were more inclined to communicate their supportive stance regarding the protest. Additionally, images of casts or groups kneeling in support of the movement were apparent, which varied from the individual responses prior to the president's statements. These distinctions suggest that celebrities were offended by Trump's comments and perceived them as an insult toward kneeling stakeholders.

Advocate Theme 1: Hashtags and Statements to Unify or Vilify

Celebrities used hashtags and Twitter handles for supportive protest views on Twitter and Instagram. These statements serve as terministic screens to indicate unifying or divisive messages. To define support of the movement and exemplify a unified stance, celebrities frequently used variations of #takeaknee, as well as #weKNEEL, #kneelinonneedles, and #BendTheKnee. Additionally, celebrity advocates exemplified unity by posting images of group protest demonstrations. These images included pictures of NFL teams and owners kneeling or locking arms. Celebrity casts also imitated these unified representations. Images of kneeling cast and crew members from *Grey's Anatomy*, *The X-Files*, and *1984* on Broadway exhibited support for the Take-a-Knee cause, particularly after Trump's comments about NFL stakeholders.

Another celebrity expression supporting the protest was kneeling at concerts. This terministic screen indicated solidarity with Take-a-Knee movement stakeholders. In a video posted on Twitter, Pearl Jam vocalist and guitarist, Eddie Vedder, took a knee during a solo set at a concert. Stevie Wonder, a legendary R&B singer who is blind, received assistance from his son, Kwame, to kneel with both knees at the Global Citizen Festival in New York City. John Legend, an R&B crooner, also took a knee at a concert while singing with one fist in the air and wearing all black; thus, indicating racial identification with the issues. Grammy Award-winning singer and producer Pharrell Williams also took a knee while performing at the "Charlottesville Unity Concert." His actions were a response to white nationalists' protests the previous month in Charlottesville, Virginia, August 11–12, 2017, regarding the proposed removal of a Robert E. Lee statue. The protests led to one woman's death and multiple injuries.

Celebrity advocates' hashtags and statements also characterized Trump as a villain and bigot with xenophobic supporters. Their disapproval of his presidential election was also apparent in responses. Sophia Bush, an actress, referenced the president as "Donald Embarrassment-to-us-all Trump" and used the hashtag, #ImpeachOrange (Bush, 2017). Michael Moore—a stage and screen director—tweeted a picture of his Broadway show explaining that the audience was in "solidarity with the NFL players protesting Trump & owners" (Moore, 2017). Savion Wright, an alternative pop artist, called on black NFL players and the public to stand in "solidarity against racist Drump [sic]" (Wright, 2017). Correspondingly, Soledad O'Brien—a national news anchor—shared a video of the crowd's enthusiastic reaction to Trump's Take-a-Knee remarks and said the response resembled a Ku Klux Klan rally.

Advocate Theme 2: Kaepernick as Hero

Celebrity advocates aligned their statements with Kaepernick's stated intention for equality and justice for people of color. Consequently, they perceived the quarterback as a champion leading a commendable cause and NFL protest stakeholders as heroic warriors sacrificing their public platform for social change. Specific to this idea, celebrities included the following hashtags to display solidarity which also served as terministic screens: #ImwithKap, #KaepernickEffect, #VeteransforKaepernick. Additionally, celebrity advocates began to emulate the quarterback's identity—including visual and physical representations. John Leguizamo, an actor, encouraged "Latin stars and athletes" to "Be #Kaepernick" as he stressed their influence in the 2016 presidential election (Leguizamo, 2016). This statement references the quarterback's likeness and expression to initiate sociopolitical change. Kaepernick's San Francisco 49ers #7 jersey also represented a visual communicative symbol and terministic screen to demonstrate individual support of the quarterback and corroborate his cause. Eight male celebrities wore the jersey in social media pictures, at concerts, or on television appearances. The majority of advocates personifying this approach were hip-hop and R&B artists with socially-conscious, distinctive, or nonconformist personas—including rapper Jay-Z on a *Saturday Night Live* performance. However, NBA player Jabari Parker was one of the first celebrities to wear a #7 jersey after Kaepernick's initial stance. Michael Moore, a film and stage director, also expressed his support using this communicative approach during one of his Broadway shows.

Celebrity supporters' statements and actions also defended Kaepernick—their metaphorical hero—amidst the controversy, as well as encouraged racial equality discourse. "Charlamagne tha god," an author and host on *The Breakfast Club*—a popular radio show on urban networks, appeared on ESPN's *First Take* wearing a shirt displaying a kneeling Kaepernick silhouette—including his afro. When Stephen A. Smith—one of the *First Take* hosts—asked Charlamagne his views about the protest, social justice issues, and fact that Kaepernick did not vote in the last presidential election, he said that these actions do not discredit the quarterback as a leader and change agent.

The purpose of the protest personally resonated with several black celebrities, inciting their support of Kaepernick and NFL stakeholders' kneeling actions. Their communicative expressions showed a significant level of consciousness about the national anthem's history, as well as societal injustice toward people of color. In a series of tweets, Steve Harvey—a comedian and television host—explained that America is an inauthentic representation of freedom and opportunity. He stated, "'Land of the Free' aint [sic] true for all sadly" (Harvey, 2016). Erykah Badu—an R&B recording artist—shared a poem about impassiveness toward social justice issues in America. Tina Knowles-Lawson, R&B singers' Beyoncé and Solange's mother and former stylist, also mentioned indifference to injustice toward minorities, as well as her interpretation and defense of Kaepernick's stance. Yara Shahidi—a young actress—posted a poetic video reflection to Instagram about police brutality toward black males. Rapper T.I. shared a picture on Instagram of Francis Scott Key, composer of the national anthem, with a message that Key was a "white supremacist slaveowner" who described African Americans as a "distinct and inferior race" (T. I., 2016). John Legend paralleled Take-a-Knee issues to the civil rights movement and resembled Black Panther Party members during one of his concerts. As mentioned previously, Legend—wearing all black—knelt with his fist in the air symbolizing "Black Power." Meanwhile, the jumbotron displayed a black and white picture of a sign stating, "We March for Integrated Schools" (Legend, 2017).

Black celebrities were not the only Take-a-Knee advocates or ethnic group to display fervor for the issues. One-third of celebrity supporters were white. Megan Rapinoe, a professional women's soccer star, was one of the first celebrities to kneel following NFL players in 2016, conveying support toward Kaepernick's cause. Actress Susan Sarandon marched with more than one thousand protesters at a rally outside of the NFL headquarters in New York City after the quarterback remained unsigned by an NFL team in 2017. Joshua Malina, an actor, questioned Trump's support of First Amendment rights for white supremacists without the same compassion for black athletes. Meanwhile, Latino celebrities also conveyed support for the quarterback. Carlos Santana, a musician, commended Kaepernick for his bravery while actors John Leguizamo and Rosie Perez called attention to the issue among their fan bases. These instances, as well as others examined in this analysis, indicate that white celebrities and those of other ethnicities also showed passion and support for Take-a-Knee issues. A key distinction is that black celebrity advocates were more likely to point the issue to historical resistance periods for people of color and systemic injustice in America.

CONCLUSION

Celebrities shared critical and candid perspectives regarding Kaepernick and the Take-a-Knee controversy. They conveyed their own identification with or opposition to Kaepernick directly to audiences through discursive and non-discursive communicative platforms. Terministic screens of hashtags and rhetorical expressions indicated that celebrities communicated unified or divisive stances yet distinctly expressed their views using various demonstrations. Advocacy through clothing, kneeling at concerts, as well as awards show rhetoric exemplified their ability to support a divisive issue using complimentary representations of the change agent. These interpretations advance existing research on celebrity activism and communication approaches in public forums. The findings also suggest the beliefs, values, and behaviors that people may adopt during a social justice issue merely due to the processes of celebrity identification, parasocial interaction, worship, or transportation. Consequently, if more celebrities are willing to foster unity, civil understanding, and effective communication with opposing sides in divisive situations, their audiences may follow, potentially creating a favorable impact in society.

The researcher observed similarities between celebrity opponents and advocates examined in this analysis. Celebrity conveyances regarding this occurrence show a concern for humanity and loss of human life—whether fallen military soldiers, police officers, or persons of color. This finding suggests that celebrities use their influence to honor meaningful sacrifices, gain respect from public followers, and communicate their views to supporters and adversaries. Since celebrity posts supporting fallen soldiers preceded Trump's similar comments, perhaps Trump followed their lead.

The factor of race in this analysis also suggests the depth of identification with the issues emphasized in this situation, which is consistent with previous scholarship. Black celebrities, particularly males, on each side of the matter were more likely to identify with the principles of Kaepernick's stance regarding injustice and oppression toward people of color. Black celebrities were also more likely to convey support for him and the protests. Black opponents who did not support the demonstrations referenced Kaepernick's lack of patriotism, approach, and uncertainty about his genuine intentions; however, their preferred communicative vehicle and need to identify was critical for gaining audience approval. When they neglected these elements, statement retraction or removal resulted after public criticism. The implication shows the significance of communicative approach, empathy, and sociocultural awareness for male celebrities of color in contentious social justice matters. The finding is also a contribution to scholarship concerning cultural identification for black male celebrities, as well as practical application for publicists with prominent clients.

REFERENCES

Andrews, D.L., & Jackson, S.J. (2001). *Sport stars: The cultural politics of sporting celebrity* (1st ed.). London: Routledge Ltd. doi:10.4324/9780203463543

Basil, M.D., & Brown, W.J. (2004). Magic Johnson and Mark McGwire: The power of identification with sports celebrities. *Sports Marketing and the Psychology of Marketing Communication*, 159-171.

Bennett, L. (2014). 'If we stick together we can do anything': Lady Gaga fandom, philanthropy and activism through social media. *Celebrity studies*, 5(1-2), 138-152.

Bond, P. (2017, September 25). Hollywood conservatives ridicule NFL, back Trump. Retrieved from https://www.hollywoodreporter.com/news/hollywood-conservatives-ridicule-nfl-back-trump-1042834

Brinson, W. (2016, September 21). Jerry Rice changes his mind on Kaepernick kneeling during the anthem. Retrieved from https://www.cbssports.com/nfl/news/jerry-rice-changes-his-mind-on-colin-kaepernick-kneeling-during-the-anthem/

Brown, W.J. (2010). Steve Irwin's influence on wildlife conservation. *Journal of Communication*, 60(1), 73-93. doi:10.1111/j.1460-2466.2009.01458.x

Brown, W.J. (2015). Examining four processes of audience involvement with media personae: Transportation, parasocial interaction, identification, and worship. *Communication Theory*, 25(3), 259-283. doi:10.1111/comt.12053

Burke, K. (1966). *Language as symbolic action: Essays on life, literature, and method*. Berkeley: University of California Press.

Burke, K. (1969). *A rhetoric of motives*. Berkeley: University of California Press.

Bush, A.J., Martin, C.A., & Bush, V.D. (2004). Sports celebrity influence on the behavioral intentions of generation Y. *Journal of Advertising Research*, 44(1), 108-118. doi:10.1017/S0021849904040206

Bush, S. (2017, September 23). Sophia Bush Instagram Page. Retrieved from https://www.instagram.com/p/BZZr3r1DuXL/?utm_source=ig_embed

Cain, D. (2017, September 24). Dean Cain Twitter Page. Retrieved from https://twitter.com/RealDeanCain/status/912184094603190272

Campbell, C. (2012). The modern Western fashion pattern: Its functions and relationship to identity. *Identities through Fashion*. London: Berg.

Clarke Jr., D. (2016, September 9). Colin Kaepernick knows nothing about civil rights or freedom. Retrieved from http://www.patheos.com/blogs/davidclarke/2016/09/colin-kaepernick-knows-nothing-about-civil-rights-or-freedom/#X6iC5hCYLqX8Qlza.99

Dash, S. (2016, September 9). Stacey Dash Facebook profile. Retrieved from https://www.facebook.com/OfficiallyStaceyDash/posts/661994623977217

Diaz, D. (2016, September 2016). Obama defends Kaepernick's anthem protest. Retrieved from https://www.cnn.com/2016/09/28/politics/obama-colin-kaepernick-nfl-national-anthem-presidential-town-hall-cnn/index.html

Forbes Magazine. (2018). Beyoncé Knowles profile. *Forbes Magazine*. Retrieved from https://www.forbes.com/profile/beyonce-knowles/

Foss, S.K. (2009). *Rhetorical criticism: Exploration & practice* (4th ed.). Long Grove, IL: Waveland Press.

Fox News. (2017, December 6). Beyonce surprises Colin Kaepernick with SI's Muhammad Ali award. Retrieved from http://www.foxnews.com/entertainment/2017/12/06/beyonce-surprises-colin-kaepernick-with-sis-muhammad-ali-award.html

Fraser, B.P., & Brown, W.J. (2002). Media, celebrities, and social influence: Identification with Elvis Presley. *Mass Communication & Society*, 5(2), 183-206.

González, A.M., & Bovone, L. (2012). *Identities through fashion: A multidisciplinary approach* (1st ed.). London: Bloomsbury UK.

Gretzky, W. (2017, December 6). Colin Kaepernick accepts Sports Illustrated's Muhammad Ali Legacy Award. Retrieved from http://abcnews.go.com/Sports/colin-kaepernick-accepts-sports-illustrateds-muhammad-ali-legacy/story?id=51609957

Harlow, S., & Benbrook, A. (2017). How #Blacklivesmatter: exploring the role of hip-hop celebrities in constructing racial identity on Black Twitter. *Information, Communication & Society*. https://doi.org/10.1080/1369118X.2017.1386705

Harvey, S. (2016, September 14). Official Steve Harvey Twitter Account. Retrieved from https://twitter.com/IAmSteveHarvey/status/776038134350053376?ref_src=twsrc%5Etfw&ref_url=http%3A%2F%2Few.com%2Farticle%2F2016%2F09%2F14%2Fsteve-harvey-colin-kaepernick-anthem-protest%2F&tfw_site=ew

Jackson, S.J. (2010). *African American celebrity dissent and a tale of two public spheres: A critical and comparative analysis of the mainstream and black press, 1949–2005* (Order No. 3434270). Available from ProQuest Dissertations & Theses Global. (847026616). Retrieved from http://eres.regent.edu:2048/login?url=https://search-proquest-com.ezproxy.regent.edu/docview/847026616?accountid=13479

Kelman, H.C. (1961). Processes of opinion change. *The Public Opinion Quarterly*, 25(1), 57-78. doi:10.1086/266996

Kid Rock. (2017, September 11). Kid Rock Facebook page. Retrieved from https://www.facebook.com/kidrock/posts/10155502465850049

Kurtz, J. (2016, December 4). NFL great Brown on meeting Trump: 'He's got my admiration.' Retrieved from https://www.cnn.com/2016/12/13/politics/jim-brown-cnn-newsroom-black-community-brooke-baldwin-cnntv/index.html

Legend, J. (2017, September 24). John Legend Instagram Page. Retrieved fromhttps://www.instagram.com/p/BZcFXEWgnK5/?utm_source=ig_embed&utm_campaign=embed_profile_upsell_control

Leguizamo, J. (2016, September 3). John Leguizamo Twitter Page. Retrieved from https://twitter.com/JohnLeguizamo/status/772172282122960896?ref_src=twsrc%5Etfw

Lurie, A. (1981). *The Language of Clothes*. New York, NY: Random House.

Maher, B. (2016, September 27). Bill Maher twitter profile. Retrieved from https://twitter.com/billmaher/status/781020779534221312

McHenry, B. (2017, November 13). Britt McHenry twitter profile. Retrieved from https://twitter.com/BrittMcHenry/status/930090700498259971?ref_src=twsrc%5Etfw&ref_url=http%3A%2F%2Fwww.foxnews.com%2Fentertainment%2F2017%2F11%2F14%2Fbritt-mchenry-ex-espn-reporter-blasts-gq-for-naming-colin-kaepernick-citizen-year.html

Mohr, J. (2016, August 29). Jay Mohr twitter profile. Retrieved from https://twitter.com/jaymohr37/status/770358789279068160

Moore, M. (2017, September 24). Michael Moore Twitter Page. Retrieved from https://twitter.com/MMFlint/status/912068894004826113/photo/1?ref_src=twsrc%5Etfw&ref_url=https%3A%2F%2Fwww.globalcitizen.org%2Fen%2Fcontent%2Fcolin-kaepernick-takeaknee-celebrities-protest%2F

NBC News. (2017, December 6). Beyoncé surprises Colin Kaepernick to present SI Muhammad Ali Legacy Award. Retrieved from https://www.nbcnews.com/news/us-news/beyonc-surprises-colin-kaepernick-present-si-muhammad-ali-legacy-award-n826986

Nownes, A.J. (2012). An experimental investigation of the effects of celebrity support for political parties in the United States. *American Politics Research*, 40(3), 476-500. doi:10.1177/1532673X11429371

Nyren, E. (2017, December 5). Beyoncé presents Colin Kaepernick with SI Muhammad Ali legacy award. *Variety Magazine*. Retrieved from http://variety.com/2017/music/news/beyonce-colin-kaepernick-si-muhammad-ali-legacy-award-1202631812/

Polletta, F., & Jasper, J. M. (2001). Collective identity and social movements. *Annual Review of Sociology*, 27(1), 283-305. doi:10.1146/annurev.soc.27.1.283

Presnell, K. K. (2008). *Media, celebrities, and identification: An examination of fan relationships with dale earnhardt amid the culture of NASCAR* (Order No. 3321380). Available from Dissertations & Theses @ Regent University; ProQuest Central; ProQuest Dissertations & Theses Global. (304820291). Retrieved from http://eres.regent.edu:2048/login?url=https://search-proquest-com.ezproxy.regent.edu/docview/304820291?accountid=13479

Respers France, L. (2017, December 6). Beyoncé surprises Colin Kaepernick with award. CNN. Retrieved from https://www.cnn.com/2017/12/06/entertainment/beyonce-colin-kaepernick-award/index.html

Rice, J. (2016, September 20). Jerry Rice twitter profile. Retrieved from https://twitter.com/JerryRice/status/778301857529606144?ref_src=twsrc%5Etfw&ref_url=https%3A%2F%2Fwww.cbssports.com%2Fnfl%2Fnews%2Fjerry-rice-changes-his-mind-on-colin-kaepernick-kneeling-during-the-anthem%2F&tfw_creator=WillBrinson&tfw_site=cbssports

Rokeach, M. (1973). *The nature of human values*. New York: Free Press.

Skiver, K. (2017, December 6). Beyonce presents Colin Kaepernick with SI's Muhammad Ali Legacy Award. Retrieved from https://www.cbssports.com/nfl/news/beyonce-presents-colin-kaepernick-with-sis-muhammad-ali-legacy-award/

Sports Illustrated. (2018). Sports Illustrated Muhammad Ali legacy award. Retrieved from https://www.si.com/specials/muhammad-ali-sportsman-legacy-award/

T.I. (2016, August 28). Official Troubleman 31 Instagram account. Retrieved from https://www.instagram.com/p/BJqvDfdATrh/

The Postgame Staff. (2017, August 24). Jim Brown gives us the 'real deal' on Colin Kaepernick, flag, activism. Retrieved from http://www.thepostgame.com/jim-brown-colin-kaepernick-activist-flag-anthem

Time Magazine. (2017, September 2017). The difference between president Trump and president Obama's reactions to the nfl kneeling movement. Retrieved from http://time.com/4955050/trump-obama-nfl-nba-kaepernick-kneeling/

Villa, J. (2017a, September 24). Joy Villa Twitter Profile. Retrieved from https://twitter.com/Joy_Villa/status/912105531669495808?ref_src=twsrc%5Etfw&ref_url=https%3A%2F%2Fwww.lifezette.com%2Fpopzette%2Fcelebrities-speaking-out-against-national-anthem-protests%2F&tfw_creator=Lifezette&tfw_site=Lifezette

Villa, J. (2017b, September 26). Joy Villa Twitter Profile. Retrieved from https://twitter.com/Joy_Villa/status/912533677476909057?ref_src=twsrc%5Etfw&ref_url=https%3A%2F%2Fwww.lifezette.com%2Fpopzette%2Fcelebrities-speaking-out-against-national-anthem-protests%2F&tfw_creator=Lifezette&tfw_site=Lifezette

Winge, T.M. (2008). "Green is the new black": Celebrity chic and the "Green" commodity fetish. *Fashion Theory*, 12(4), 511-523. doi:10.2752/175174108X346968

Wright, S. (2017, September 24). Savion Wright Twitter Page. Retrieved from https://twitter.com/SavionWright/status/911958710146273280/photo/1?ref_src=twsrc%5Etfw&ref_url=http%3A%2F%2Fpeople.com%2Fcelebrity%2Fits-that-easy-celebrities-shoe-support-for-nfl-players-protesting-against-trump-with-takeaknee%2F

ELEVEN

The Role of Race in the Perceptions of and Response to the Protests

Nadine Barnett Cosby

Some scholars question the influence of race and culture in the way social movements are perceived and, specifically, the emotional effect experienced by the public. Palczewski (2011) argues that an accurate understanding of how social movements develop and proliferate requires that scholars extend their focus beyond how movements appeal to political leadership for legitimacy. The author highlights the need to foster an understanding of how "counterpublics develop oppositional communication practices" (p. 161), and states that ultimately, that relationship between a movement, its public and counterpublics "has as its precondition—and its directing force—the framework provided by the in-group discourse" (p. 161). Therefore, "attention to both state-focused political activism as well as culturally driven discursive politics is necessary" (p. 161).

Papacharissi (2014) discusses the likenesses and contrasts between three movements: the Arab Spring movement in Egypt, Occupy movements in Europe and the United States, and Indignados movements in Europe. The "absence of any explicit allegiance to existing political factions in Egypt, especially Muslim ones, comforted [a] Western public uneasy with the ramifications of the uprising" (p. 6) in the Arab Spring. Papacharissi argues that this also served to legitimize the Arab Spring movements by communicating to their publics their "unity and distance from partisan, and potentially corrupt, politics" (p. 6). By contrast, the Occupy movement in the United States and Europe, protesting global economic and social inequality, was swiftly criticized for its failure to express any specific agenda or leader. Meanwhile, the Indignados movements throughout Europe were similarly critiqued as devoid of any ideological consistency. The author contends, "All of these movements emerged out of different contexts but shared one thing in common: online and offline solidarity shaped around the public display of emotion" (p. 6). In these examples, the circumstances varied. However, the various participants of these counterpublics, despite their ideological differences, were united in their public display of affect and indignation for circumstances that had prevailed for too long. The "personal and affective expressions accumulated and dispersed virally through digitally enabled networks, discursively calling into being further publics of support" (p. 6).

Applying the theoretical framework of critical race theory, this study will use in-depth interviews and critical analysis of social media posts to examine how race and racial implications impact the experience of the individual participant, or the tone and tenor of conversations on social media.

THEORETICAL FRAMEWORK

Critical race theory, or CRT, is a theoretical framework that applies critical theory to the intersectionality of race, legal, and power structures. It provides a critical exploration of race and racism from a legal frame of reference. CRT assumes racism is a systemic social structure engrained in the fabric of American society. In other words, the individual racist need not exist to affirm that institutionalized racism is pervasive in the dominant culture. Critical race theory attempts to expose the assumptions held within predominant discourses and how these are represented in texts. This is the methodical lens through which CRT examines existing power structures. The central premise of critical race theory is that "racism is a normal and ordinary part of our society, not an aberration" (Wing, 2016, p. 48). The presupposition of a color-blind society and governing regulations and practices is not only false, but detrimental in its obtusity. The white over color hierarchy, and the power existing therein, is a critical aspect of how society develops and proliferates marginalization. It is also a pivotal factor in how some perceive digital texts and artifacts related to social movements. Critical race theory claims that in the United States, power structures are based on white privilege and white supremacy, which perpetuate and propagate the existence of a dominant group and marginalized groups. Specifically, critical race theory contends that, due to the racially divisive historical context of the United States, the marginalization of people of color is a systemic phenomenon within society even today. Legal discourse, which is one of several early contributing areas to critical race theory, posits that the law is neutral and color-blind.

CRT challenges this legal foundation by identifying constructs of liberalism and meritocracy as a vehicle for power, privilege, and self-interest. Despite its initial use in legal studies, critical race theory has been extended to areas such as women's studies (Wing, 1997) and sociology (Aguirre, 2000). For the purposes of this study, I introduce CRT to the discussion of the use of digital artifacts in online social justice discourse as it represents a paradigm shift in the existing discourse about race and social media. The following research question will be addressed.

RQ1: What is the Role of Race in the Perceptions of and Response to Protests?

Through examining this question, the researcher sought a greater understanding of attitudes toward racial relations in the United States. The function of successful social justice movements has historically relied upon collaboration and/or cooperation from various facets of society, regardless of the movement. In many cases, movements are judged by the people who participate in and/or are influenced by the causes or injustices in question. Race, whether consciously or subconsciously, is typically an inherent factor in how individuals view and make sense of their worlds. This study explored what relevance, if any, race has in the communication and perception of the Take-a-knee movement, as well as if and how race—of a movement's participants, supporters, detractors, or general audiences—or artifacts related to race, contribute to or detract from an individual's response to the social movement. In-depth interviews allow for a richer understanding of the level of racial consciousness that impacts the perception and reception of a movement.

METHODOLOGY

The primary methodology utilized for this study was in-depth interviews with participants who frequently posted unique commentary and artifacts on content related to the Take-a-Knee movement. This was done to provide further understanding of the relationship between social media artifacts of engagement, the influence of racial perceptions, and real-world participation. Using critical race theory to frame my analysis, I examine how our divergent positions within complex systems such as dominance and oppression, privileged and marginalized, affect how people perceive and interact with social movements via online and temporal spaces. Specifically, the researcher focused on the way in which activists and social media participants perceive or engage with racial content, as well as the responses they garner from the public when utilizing this type of engagement. Furthermore, a textual analysis of users' artifacts of engagement explore if and how race is incorporated into users' articulation of their viewpoints or perceptions of the message behind the movement.

RESULTS

As introduced in chapter seven, some social justice activists were selected to participate in in-depth interviews to provide their unique perspectives of the interplay of race and social media use in discussing social justice movements, and specifically, the Take-a-Knee movement. This section includes components gathered from discussions with Monte and Yvonne, a chaplain and filmmaker, as well as activists Quinton, former NFL player Larry, and sports radio announcer Mark. All names have been changed for anonymity.

Interviews

Monte, the thirty-four-year-old African-American male and associate chaplain, shared that he frequently includes racial language, content, or themes in his posts deliberately, often inspired by a desire to share his own personal experience or perspective with race in the United States. "I am a believer that Black people (people of African descent) have been marginalized wherever colonialism has been successful. So, I'll use language like that which I think is speaking to the race constructs . . . you have to engage in race constructs." The inclusion of racial content in his posts does, however, garner significantly different perceptions and responses. He shares that his racialized posts typically have a smaller numerical reach, as they are shared and/or retweeted less, but seem to attract way more bigotry and vitriol, or as Monte puts it, "trolls who are only there to incite anger and push their own ideology. . . . Rhetoric becomes a lot more tense and volatile when I post on race." Barring these responses, Monte is not deterred and will not change the frame of his conversation on social media simply because of the risk of disagreement or unpopularity. While Monte expresses an interest in his tweets being shared, he asserts that his main purpose and concern when authoring a post on social media is to incite dialog and possibly inform or educate. He states, "Yes, with my posts I am attempting to start dialog more so than just to speak my mind. I'm wanting the post to become a hub for conversation."

Yvonne, the 31-year-old biracial filmmaker, also includes racial rhetoric in her posts. She speaks in a very informed and unreserved manner, particularly on issues concerning race and gender, discrimination, and the Take-a-Knee movement. Her inherent interest in and concern for racial equity is evident in her propensity to focus on issues concerning the unique experiences of black Americans in her films and creative works, as well as in her activism. This may not necessarily have been as much a decision about race for Yvonne as it has been about humanity and advocacy. If we accept some of the basic perceptions of racial conventions, Yvonne straddles the proverbial fence with regard to race and representation. She could easily and seamlessly have made a choice to navigate the world as a white woman. This particular point will come up again and be further discussed much later in our interview. Nonetheless, these facts contribute to Yvonne having particularly unique and insightful perspectives on activism, race, and social media. When asked if she would categorize her social media engagement as the kind that frequently includes racial content, language, or themes, Yvonne laughs, and responds with an ease that is organic and built from a lifetime of tackling "the race question"—"Oh yeah, absolutely!" She then elaborates very seriously, "I also don't want to villainize whiteness, but I am very frank about what it means for people of color when they experience these things. I want to be very clear on that." In this moment it becomes clear to me, through her expression and inflection, that Yvonne's own personal and familial experiences have unequivocally made her an activist. She has traversed two existences, one in which she has an inherent familiarity with racial bias, marginalization, and injustice as a black woman in the United States, and the other as a part of a white Hungarian family that has always loved and supported her, and tried to protect her from those very experiences but were unmistakably clear about her being a black woman. For this reason, Yvonne presents as an important representation of the meaning behind the Take-a-Knee movement that often goes unseen in social media discussions. As she explains the dichotomy, "My correlation to Blackness is deeply rooted in some of my familial experiences growing up." She describes her early understanding of blackness being inextricably linked to a lot of complex and negative systems and, although realizing early on that she could live her life as a white woman should she so choose, her perspective and consciousness on race was always that she was a black woman. She says, "I don't look at Blackness in the abstract, I look at it from a solidarity perspective . . . it is important for me to identify that my politics are shared politics with a lot of other people of color." Referring back to the topic of misperceptions about a social movement and its participants, Yvonne states, "When I do engage in social media I am very consistent about my voice and what I want to talk about, so yes . . . race is always a lens that's very important to me when I think about things." She expresses a final, very pivotal thought on the topic of race, saying,

> I don't think my politics are race-based. If you look at the core of any of these issues . . . environmentalism, communities in North Carolina and Mississippi that live next to swamps, Flint and the water, etc., it's impossible not to talk about race, but race is not necessarily the only reason that those issues are important.

At twenty-five years old, Quinton has already positioned himself as an esteemed social justice activist. A native of Guyana, South America, Quinton works nationally in his role as a Social Change Strategist. In describing that self-appointed title, Quinton explains that he wears many hats in his justice work and tries to use a title that encompasses the diversity of his work. Quinton is clear on his purposeful and deliberate choice to explicitly reference various populations when he posts on social media. This includes the use of racial terms and gender-specific language. He observes that those posts may get even fewer likes, but notes that typically those who are engaging with racially specific posts are usually likewise interested in the work of social justice and understand the need for explicitness. He also expresses an understanding of the fear factor sometimes associated with racialized posts. For a multitude of reasons, people feel an inherent fear in posting using racialized content, as well as responding to posts that include racialized content. This also speaks to one of the drawbacks of the democratic nature of social media. Any original post or engagement with a post via commenting is a potential opening for an individual to be scrutinized or even ostracized by the public. Quinton notes that there have been times when he has posted racialized content on social media and people may not engage with it publicly on his post, but will privately message him to discuss the post. He describes this as a "fear of being called out, being wronged or being shamed" publicly. Quinton continues this thought, turning to the activist side of the same conversation, saying, "Any activist who is out there trying to make social change and is not willing to disrupt is just a fool out there trying to save the world . . . putting disruptive discourse through social media is productive to get conversations going." He explicates the point by sharing an interesting story related to the Take-a-Knee movement. Quinton discusses a situation that occurred when a former employer honored Colin Kaepernick with an award for his justice work. He notes how he personally feels that the award was well-deserved due to the courageous efforts of Kaepernick to take the stance that he has. He notes, however, that while employed by the same organization, he was told by a supervisor that "Amnesty is not a black power organization" in response to some of the initiatives he was driving. Recalling that incident, Quinton posted on social media his opinion about the irony that he saw in the organization publicly awarding Kaepernick after privately detaching itself from movements specifically geared toward black justice and equality. The post, at the very least, created a public dialog which the organization needed to have with some of its employees. Quinton emphasizes with this story,

> Change doesn't happen without discomfort . . . if there are problems in the world, we need to speak to those problems, put it on the table in its entirety, for us to start addressing it, and I think that's uncomfortable.

> Social media is also a think tank for [activists]. It's not always just about mobilizing or building.

He goes on to comment about the systemic racism in the professional football industry and the value of Take-a-Knee in the disruption of the blissful ignorance with which the fans and viewers, the majority of them white, generally view professional sports and black athletes, without ever having to think about the inequitable treatment of blacks who do not have the same privileges. He argues that NFL viewers may not necessarily see or believe the Black Lives Matter hashtag, or may be "a part of the huge vacuum of people in our country who say this doesn't affect me, I'm neither a black lives or blue lives or all lives supporter," and do not want to think about that when they enjoy the pastime of viewing NFL games. He stresses, "Kaepernick took the protest into people's daily lives." Quinton adds that Black Lives Matter created a conversation and challenge about acknowledging the treatment of Black people in America, and "Take-a-Knee took that challenge into American values."

Mark has had a long career—approximately twenty years—in sports broadcasting and has worked with many professional leagues and players. He is admittedly not an activist, and primarily uses social media to post information related to sports or the broadcasting industry. Having worked with athletes for his entire media career, he did have very strong feelings about the protests, as well as the impact they have had on professional football. Mark astutely began with his thoughts on protest in general, stating, "Freedom of speech is the greatest gift we have as Americans. . . . It's been almost 250 years since we fought for our independence from England for the right to speak, write, and worship in the manner and fashion we want as citizens of the United States." His next statement presents an interesting and unexpected dichotomy: "To honor our flag and the veterans, who have given so much, is the least we can do as a sign of respect for them." He goes on to share his views that people are not treated equally in this country, and that although that is one of the main tenets of the Constitution, it is disingenuous to suggest otherwise. Mark refers to Colin Kaepernick and the Take a Knee protests as a "slippery slope," and asserts that it would be naïve of anyone to think that police do not target young black males, and states, "I don't think the average person debates that." In that moment, I want to challenge him and ask him if he really believes his last statement. I want to show him the hundreds of social media posts procured in this study which suggest otherwise. But he continues his point and I choose not to interrupt him. "I think the issue is that athletes don't put their money where their mouth is. They flush money down the toilet on cars, jewelry, drugs, and the nightlife and it could be going towards something good in the community." From Mark's perspective, Colin Kaepernick and other athletes have a right to protest, and are highlighting a worthy cause in that there is a real issue with inequitable treatment of blacks by police. The disconnect for Mark lies in the hypocrisy, in his opinion, of them protesting during the games that provide their hefty salaries. It raises the question of how do we determine what protest should look like. Mark elaborates:

> Instead of taking a knee, wear an armband to signify your cause and start building community centers and hospitals in the inner city. Create labs with educational resources and have meals so impoverished kids can get off the street and have a place they feel safe. Bring in retired athletes as role models. Cease and desist the vulgarity of using the "N" word and truly understand its genesis.

After Mark has described his ideas regarding more effective efforts to address the issue at the nucleus of the Take a Knee movement, I ask him what aspect of the movement bothers him. He replies, "I agree with the message, just not the way it was delivered. Also, Americans need to address all the causes of this disease of racism, not just one."

Larry is a fifty-six-year-old retired African American NFL player. At the time of this research, Larry is primarily involved in his post-NFL business ventures, and specifically his work as a CBD advocate and product spokesman since being diagnosed in 2013 with Chronic Traumatic Encapholopathy (CTE), a degenerative brain disease commonly found in athletes, military veterans, and others with a history of repetitive trauma to the brain. In this work, he has come to utilize Facebook and Twitter quite significantly to market his platform, ideas, and products to a wider audience. He shares that Facebook and Twitter are great platforms to share information and to cultivate and grow an audience. Larry shares that he has had several conversations with both professionals working within and outside of the sports industry who wanted to know his stance on the issue of the anthem protests prior to engaging in business conversations about potential partnerships. At the mention of this, Larry is compelled to elucidate his thoughts on the issue. He shares that he used to have "mixed emotions" about the protests until he did "a deeper dive into the why and not the who" of the issue. He states that in doing his research he arrived at the opinion that "everyone has the right to free speech in this country and the right to protest in this country, and while you may not agree with it or like it, they have a right." Presenting a significantly different perspective on the issue, Larry goes on to articulate a business or professional aspect of the issue that has not been previously mentioned in this research, stating,

> You have a league that receives money on an annual basis from the armed forces, whether it be the Army, Navy, Marines, or Air Force, the National Football League receives compensation which forces them to honor and support the flag . . . honor and support everything that the armed forces represent.

That being said, Larry also states, "Those that own the toys control how and when the toys are played with."

As evidenced in our conversation, Larry is not averse to discussing contentious issues, nor is he apologetic for making his own personal choices. However, in scrutinizing his social media timelines, it became evident that Larry is less forthright with his postings related to the issue of protests. While he does post about topics of race, racial disparities, and social justice, all of these posts seem to serve the same purpose. In his social media discussions of these issues, Larry expresses disappointment or sadness at the current polarization in the race and social justice conversations in the country. However, he never directly references a particular side of the argument, nor does he mention any particular social justice movement or hashtag. Also conspicuous in my conversation with Larry is his unwillingness to condemn any player, regardless of whether he agrees or disagrees with the choices they might have made. As we discuss his social media postings, Larry again presents his unique perspectives on the issue, based on a few different variables. For one, he is wholeheartedly appreciative of the benefits he has experienced from playing professional football. His respect and appreciation of having had the opportunity to play professionally is consistently evident throughout the conversation. Secondly, he mentions a personal consideration that is not necessarily a common point of social justice discourse, but represents another underrepresented facet of society today on social media. Larry is in an interracial relationship with a white woman and has a biracial child, which forces him, in his own words, to see the race conversation from a different point of view. Lastly, he concedes to a concern about perceptions. He shares about his experiences trying to build and cultivate relationships for his current business ventures and in doing so, having to contend with people who assume to know his stance on the anthem protests, and other issues for that matter, simply based on the fact that he is a black male who used to play for the NFL. As Larry states it, "They figure we are all the same." As such, Larry relies more on opportunities to directly articulate his point of view, such as in individual interviews, as opposed to trying to articulate his nuanced points through a social media post or tweet.

SOCIAL MEDIA

In addition to the activist interviews, a textual and visual content analysis of Facebook and Twitter posts and comments, paying specific attention to the use of text, hashtags, and artifacts related to the Take-a-Knee movement as indicated with the hashtag #TakeAKnee were also reviewed for race themes. Race and/or racial rhetoric was often included in posts attempting to explain what the meaning was behind Take-a-Knee by specifically referencing its intent to highlight the inequitable treatment of blacks. In most cases, these posts showed a significant amount of redundancy in efforts to explain Colin Kaepernick's impetus for taking a knee, and what the symbolic stance meant and/or did not mean, as well as challenge readers to think of the hypocrisy of those that were upset by the act of kneeling. This is evident in a comment by a white, male Facebook user who responded to a post by CNN about the controversy. The official CNN Facebook page posted an article titled, *The #TakeAKnee protests have always been about race. Period.* The article received numerous comments on either side of the movement. However, this rhetorical stance was also used by those who disagreed with the movement and articulated in their posts the need for people of color to stop undermining what they deemed as standard rules of engagement in professional sports. In many instances, posts that included race or racial terminology were not only employed to discuss race, but they also discussed groups of people in a particularly biased way, commented on an entire race of people in a blatantly derogatory way, or used racial slurs or stereotypical comments or artifacts to express disdain for or disapproval of the movement at large. This was prominently the case in posts that attempted to attack or vilify black people and/or Colin Kaepernick for their outspokenness or stance on racial inequality, or a perceived disrespect of the flag or the anthem in taking that stance. President Donald Trump himself alluded to this notion in his own inflammatory tweets, stating, "If a player wants the privilege of making millions of dollars in the NFL, or other leagues, he or she should not be allowed to disrespect . . . our Great American Flag (or Country) and should stand for the National Anthem. If not, YOU'RE FIRED. Find something else to do!" These tweets reference the call for players to stand for the anthem as if it is an inherent part of their job description. Mark, while hesitant to express agreement with a president whom he voted for but now expresses disappointment and embarrassment by, adopted a similar sensibility regarding the anthem protests, stating, "To honor our flag and the veterans, who have given so much, is the least we can do as a sign of respect for them." This narrative of anti-patriotism has, for the most part, superseded much of the other discourse around the Take-a-Knee movement. It was developed as a counternarrative to the movement itself and has essentially forced people to choose a side based on their identification with any of the iconographic examples mentioned. At the same time, some supporters of the movement try to dispute this narrative by referencing a reverse dynamic, a disrespect by the country to black people, who also participate in many of these patriotic acts without being truly treated as equal citizens. Among users who associate the protests with antipatriotism, and specifically disrespect to the military, there seems to be a disconnect with the fact that there are black military or there are veterans who participate in the protests. A white female user on Facebook posted an article titled "Lynching in America: Targeting Black Veterans," and wrote:

> An important thing to remember in the debate over whether taking a knee dishonors veterans and the flag is the fact that black servicemen were murdered specifically for wearing their military uniforms after having fought for America. The lynching of black veterans is a historic American tradition as thousands of black veterans were assaulted, threatened, abused, or lynched following military service.

Variations of a similar or tangential sentiment were posted. Another Facebook user, a white female veteran wrote:

> This country is NOT offering liberty and justice for all as our pledge of allegiance states. . . . As a matter of fact—kneeling—especially as I recall in sports, was done when a teammate was down on the field. We serve this country to protect freedom. People of color serve too . . . and they do not enjoy the freedoms that white people do. If you ignore that, you're part of the issue #takeaknee.

DISCUSSION

The research question sought to examine how racial implications affect the nature of discourse in digital spaces. Specifically, the researcher sought to address the ways in which racial content impacts the way a movement is perceived, and/or the way the perception of race impacts the way others respond to a movement. During the content analysis and coding of posts, particular attention was paid to the ways in which race and racial terminology influenced and/or articulated users' perceptions of a social movement. The digital environment is as impactful and influential on behaviors as are real-world environmental concerns. Of the personal factors inherent in protest perceptions and behaviors, race was a critical biological factor. The identification of race as associated with a movement had a direct association with the way the movement itself was perceived, as well as users' attitudes toward the movement and its participants. For many users on either side of the movements, race was inextricably linked to the perceptions of each movement and the responses to each movement by the public. While this was particularly evident in social media movement discourse, the interview participants in this study also corroborate this notion. Admittedly, many activists intentionally include racial language and/or artifacts in their discourse in an effort to secure the relationship with race as the impetus for the movement.

While the more pervasive narrative around Take-a-Knee discourse has been patriotism, pride, and respect, there is also an intrinsic connection to race in the perception of this movement. This makes sense, as the very foundation and impetus behind the Take-a-Knee movement, as explained by Colin Kaepernick, was to bring awareness to the injustices and inequitable treatment of black people by law enforcement officers. Once again, this linking of the movement to a cause which specifically impacts or references a single racial demographic, is to some, reason enough to disregard or disagree with the movement without further exploration. In general, discourse in social media spaces mimics real-world behaviors in that to many, race is still a factor that is inextricably linked to perceptions and worldviews.

Race as a Floating Signifier on Social Media in Critical Race Theory

Taking what he calls a "discursive position" on race, Hall contends it is in "analyzing the metaphors, the antidotes, the stories, the jokes that are told by culture about what physical racial differences mean" (Jhally, 1997) that we see the historical meaning-making of things like race and skin color to classify and compartmentalize human beings by perceived difference. Hall goes on to explain why race is a floating signifier, referencing the different ways in which race is used to make meaning in different scenarios. Hall argues that race is never static or the same, and asserts that this foundational understanding is necessary in comprehending how racism works and how it can be combatted. Specifically, within discourse about blacks in the United States, Hall contends that black, in reference to race, is a "mark of difference" (Hall, 1997, p. 110). He argues that race has discursive qualities in that it assumes a different meaning based on how it is positioned within discourse or "organized within language, within discourse, within systems of meaning." This discursive engagement with race provides the framework for the manifestation of racist ideologies. This study adds to the scholarship of Hall and others in addressing the ways in which race is an inherent factor in the way we engage with the world, including the digital world of social media.

Of the various analyzed posts and tweets, some racial connotation or implication in reference to a conversation about the movement was quite common. For the vast majority of black social media users, the texts and artifacts related to black men and women being subject to unchecked abuses of power or uninhibited bigotry is unfortunately too familiar (Gay, 2015; Gay & Staff, 2015; Lundman & Kaufman, 2003; Morton, 2015; Mullainathan, 2015; Susman, 2015; Unnever, 2008; Wu, 2014), as are the counternarratives of such on social media. The understanding of these artifacts requires little cognitive effort to come to a clear understanding of the meaning and significance. In many cases, the familiarity of instances of injustice was admittedly based primarily on being privy to the numerous instances of unfair treatment that had been documented and shared via social media. However, a striking number of users also shared personal narratives indicating familiarity with situations of injustice due to similar encounters and/or their own firsthand experiences. Likewise, each interview subject perceived a bias based on behaviors that unjustly or disproportionately affected black people.

On the contrary, many white users communicated, through their rhetoric and artifacts, an inability to identify racial discrimination or bias as a real and systemic phenomenon in the current day and age. However, some of the same users that deny racial discrimination were able to easily attribute the committing of a crime to those who were victims of police abuse, or individuals having the police called on them. In one example, a user responded to an article posted about the police shooting of Philando Castile in Minnesota in July 2016. Castile was driving with his girlfriend and her four-year-old daughter when he was pulled over for a traffic stop. After the officer requested his identification, Castile informed the officer that he was carrying a concealed handgun which he did have a permit for. The officer told him not to reach for it and though Castile did not, he was subsequently shot seven times, two of those bullets fatally piercing his heart (Chan, 2016). In a response to the post, a user comments, "Flash [sic] car, low rider, big wheels, yeah—drug dealer. If he was driving a nice mid class car in nice condition, rolled down his window and said, 'Hello officer how are you today?' things would've gone much differently." Not only was Castile in his used white Oldsmobile when he was shot, but he was a cafeteria supervisor at a Minnesota magnet school and regarded as a role model among his colleagues and the students. The rhetoric of this user's post automatically ascribed a crime or criminal behavior to Castile. This phenomenon often occurred in responses to posts about black victims of police shootings, regardless of whether or not a crime had been committed. Another post referred to the March 2018 police shooting of Stephon Clark, a twenty-two-year-old black man who was shot eight times, most of the bullets hitting him in his back, while in his grandmother's backyard. When police responded to a report that someone was breaking car windows in the area, a user comments, "Wasn't he breaking into houses at the time?? That's 'thuggish' behavior. Didn't deserve to be shot but it is thuggish." In this case the user not only incorrectly ascribes a crime to the victim, but also attributes a crime that was not a part of the actual events. This often presented a disconnect that resulted in a conflict/confrontation/argument exchange via posts, narratives, and counternarratives.

The themes that emerged from narratives and counternarratives regarding instances of perceived systemic racism or injustice highlight an important implication of critical race theory in which reactions to perceived racist situations are uniquely surveyed and understood from the distinct perspective of the individual and his/her gaze. This echoes Anderson's (1996) conjunctive model of communication in which the individual is often the "site of the intersection of material, cultural, and social influences" (p. 86). In the realm of social media, this conceptualization of race as a floating signifier also includes digital artifacts of engagement, such as hashtags like #TakeAKnee.

REFERENCES

Aguirre, A. (2000). Academic storytelling: A critical race theory story of affirmative action. *Sociological Perspectives, 43*, 319-339.

Gay, R. (2015, October 31). Where are black children safe? *International New York Times*, p. 8.

Gay, R., & Staff. (2015, October 30). Where are black children safe? *The New York Times*, p. 27.

Hall, S. (1997). *Representation: Cultural representations and signifying practices* (Vol. 2). Thousand Oaks, CA: Sage.

Jhally, S. (Interviewer) & Hall, Stuart (Interviewee). (1997). *Race: the floating signifier* [Interview transcript]. Retrieved from Media Education Foundation Web site: http://www.mediaed.org/transcripts/Stuart-Hall-Race-the-Floating-Signifier-Transcript.pdf

Lundman, R. J., & Kaufman, R. L. (2003). Driving while black: Effects of race, ethnicity, and gender on citizen self-reports of traffic stops and police actions. *Criminology, 41*, 195.

Morton, R. (2015, December 6). Black men increasingly feel under siege in America. *Pittsburgh Post-Gazette*, p. D-2.

Mullainathan, S. (2015, October 18). Police killings of blacks: What the data says. *The New York Times*, p. 6.

Palczewski, C. H. (2011). Cyber-movements, new social movements, and counterpublics. (pp. 161-186). In R. Asen & D. Brouwer (Eds.), *Counterpublics and the State*. Albany, NY: SUNY Press.

Papacharissi, Z. (2014). *Affective publics: Sentiment, technology, and politics*. New York: Oxford University Press.

Susman, T. (2015, June 23). Black women also feel at risk; A new movement demands justice for the unarmed females who have been killed by police. *Los Angeles Times*, p. A6.

Unnever, J. D. (2008). Two worlds far apart: Black-white differences in beliefs about why African-American men are disproportionately imprisoned. *Criminology, 46*(2), 511-538.

Wing, A. (Ed.). (1997). *Critical race feminism: A reader*. New York: New York University Press.

Wing, A. K. (2016). Is there a future for critical race theory? *Journal of Legal Education, 1*, 44-54.

Wu, Y. (2014). Race/ethnicity and perceptions of the police: A comparison of white, black, Asian and Hispanic Americans. *Policing and Society, 24*(2), 135-157.

TWELVE
Rights and Respect

How Politicians and Their Followers View Anthem Protests

Michael Rhett and Joshua Weiss

While many people may run from confrontation and controversy, politicians sprint toward it like lions chasing down an antelope, devouring every last piece of flesh. They conspire to create and control the narrative hoping it will "chain out" to the public (West & Carey, 2006, p. 388). The Take-a-Knee protest, for example, was heavily publicized as being motivated due to police brutality toward young African-American men, though others saw it as disrespectful to the military. So, since party identification and political ideology is linked (Levitin & Miller, 1979; Norpoth & Lodge, 1985), and political party identification and political ideology are both informed in part by racial psychological attachments (Mangum, 2013), an investigation into the political responses and communication elements among politicians and the grass roots of their respective parties is warranted.

Fantasy theme analysis, which "is the shared fantasies of a group of people" that seeks to determine a group's "shared consciousness," can be used to extrapolate the themes these narratives create (Bormann, n.d., para. 1). The current research seeks to not only identify the themes Republican and Democrat Congresspersons conveyed regarding "Take-a-Knee," but also the effect those communication efforts had among the political bases. A fantasy theme theoretical framework was utilized in the evaluation of the political leaders while social identity theory influenced the grassroots element of this study. Social identity theory (see also Bullock, 2019, ch. 14 of this book) postulates that individuals categorize themselves and everyone else automatically (Transue, 2007).

LITERATURE REVIEW

Preeminent African American support of the Republican and Democratic Parties has changed throughout American history. Black voters were aligned with Republicans following the Emancipation Proclamation by Abraham Lincoln. They switched to Democrats when Republican president Theodore Roosevelt, in the early 1900s, claimed 350 blacks were lynched as the result of sexual assaults of white women (Wickham, n.d.). Others attribute the Republican to Democratic Party shift of black voters to the mid-1960s when the civil rights movement supported Democratic presidential candidate John F. Kennedy. This support carried over to Democrat Lyndon B. Johnson following the coded racial appeals by the Republican presidential candidate Barry Goldwater (Carmines & Stimson, 1989; Hughey, 2014; Mangum, 2013) and the passing of the Civil Rights Act of 1964. Strom Thurmond, a notorious civil rights opponent, shifted parties to join the Republican Party in 1964, yet another event credited with black voters changing parties (Rosino & Hughey, 2016).

The overwhelming support of the Democratic Party by the African American population continues in the twenty-first century with recent evidences exhibited toward the treatment of Republican president George W. Bush by the civil rights movement, the support of the first black president, Democrat Barack Obama, and vitriol toward Republican president Donald Trump, often called a "racist" by news organizations like CNN (Schmidt, 2018). Republican congressman Sean Duffy articulately points out that, "There's a viewpoint that says, 'I can fight for minorities, and I can fight for women,' and if you get that, you make up a vast majority of the voting block and you win. And white males have been left aside a little bit in the politics of who speaks to them" (Craig & Richeson, 2017, p. 1). Essentially, Congressman Duffy suggests that the current Republican Party is speaking on behalf of white males. Additionally, Black Lives Matter as an influencer of "Take-a-Knee" helped some draw the conclusion that supporters of the protest would be Democrat while detractors would be Republican. "Whites perceive Black complaints about police mistreatment as exaggerations, [while] many African Americans see police misconduct as real examples of the cost of being Black in America" (Dixon et al., 2008, p. 531; See also Bergesen & Herman, 1998; Cochran, 2001; Kinnon, 1999; Olzak et al., 1996).

Social identity theory denotes "People use these social comparisons to create in-groups (people who are similar) and out-groups (people who are dissimilar), which results in an accentuation of sameness among those in the in-groups, and differences between those in the out-groups and also indicates that people categorize themselves and others based on a shared social identity; they learn from popular conceptions of the group, and then adopt those conceptions and internalize them (Hogg, Terry, & White, 1995; Mangum, 2013; Stets & Burke, 2000; Tajfel, 1978; Turner, 1985). Racially speaking, social identity theory explains the historical alignment of African Americans' political affiliations. Compound this with the theory of issue ownership which contends a relationship exists between the position taken by political parties on specific issues, and the social groups that make up those parties (Petrocik, 1996). For "Take-a-Knee," if the group consciousness believes there is social injustice to young black men, social identity theory posits those who agree gravitate to the party that supports this belief while dismissing those who disagree. "Racial minorities are most likely to sense that their group has been treated unfairly by society and to experience race discrimination" (Mangum 2013, p. 1228).

Scholarship on fantasy theme analysis and political rhetoric seems limited. The 1972 Presidential race between Republican Richard Nixon and Democrat George McGovern saw Thomas Eagleton, McGovern's running mate, drop out eighteen days after being selected, due to health reasons. Bormann (1973) analyzed the entire Eagleton affair for fantasy themes; these included Eagleton's health, campaign finances, the themes surrounding McGovern and Nixon before and during the affair, and the role mass media played (see also Phillips & Higgs, 2019, ch. 3 of this book) in creating a fantasy that would chain out to the public and get them to think, and then act, in a certain way. Bormann explains, "When a fantasy begins to catch on with a large group of people the evidence of public interest tends to draw outsiders into the social reality for self-serving reasons (1973, p. 153).

West and Carey (2006) describe President George W. Bush and Vice President Dick Cheney as having created a Wild West mythos to surround post-9/11 American foreign policy. They advance that in the context of political communication and the presidency, fantasy theme analysis can be "a tool for evaluating a rhetorical discourse, which focuses on the message" (Bormann, as cited in West & Carey, 2006, p. 404).

Vultee extrapolated themes he claims Fox News created for President Obama that "chained out" to online forum participants. Obama was "the first president to be a Nazi and a Communist at the same time, at once an idiot and an effete Harvard professor, an empty-suited puppet and a master conspirator, a street thug and a pantywaist" (2012, p. 54).

METHODOLOGY

To decipher the fantasy themes of the Take-a-Knee protest among Democratic and Republican politicians, speeches, interviews, or letters were coded from transcripts of recordings and printed documents. Article quotes were not used as these could be taken out of context. Republicans included House Speaker Paul Ryan, Senator Ted Cruz, who ran in the 2016 Presidential primary, Libertarian-leaning Senator Rand Paul, Senator John Cornyn, Senator Cory Gardner, and Senator Tim Scott, the only black Republican senator. Democrats included House Minority Leader Nancy Pelosi, Senators Cory Booker and Kamala Harris, both probable Democratic presidential candidates in 2020, 2016 presidential candidate, Senator Bernie Sanders, and Congressman Cedric Richmond, chair of the Congressional Black Caucus.

After coding these politicians' responses to the protest, independent focus groups, and one-on-one interviews were conducted among fifteen Democratic and Republican grassroots respondents, respectively, to see if there was correlation between messaging disseminated from the two primary political parties and their respective bases. The qualitative research spanned men and women evenly, with respondents ranging from twenty-seven to seventy-one years of age. The question, "Was the Take-a-Knee protest a political issue?" underscored the shallow surface of this grassroots research. If party identification and political ideology are a function of racial psychological attachment (Mangum, 2013), then assumptions could be made that this protest would find polarizing responses from each of the primary political parties since Democratic and Republican are arguably racial labels as well as political labels (Mangum, 2013). Focus groups and one-on-one interviews were then transcribed and coded to compare to politician responses in light of social identity theory.

THE THEMES FOR "TAKE-A-KNEE" AMONG POLITICIAN RESPONSES

Two major themes arose: rights and values, and progress, or the lack thereof.

Rights & Values

Democrats

Free speech and expression is intrinsically American. Democrats therefore create the narrative that NFL players are acting out American values, doing nothing wrong, because it is their *right* to protest. Pelosi notes, "Our Constitution guarantees people the right to express themselves freely" (Pelosi, 2017b). Harris goes even further:

> One of the beautiful things about our country is that we were founded on certain principles that were articulated in 1776 . . . in our constitu-

tion . . . part of what we decide, what makes a fair and just and noble society (pause) and a democracy, a true democracy is freedom of religion, freedom of association, the First Amendment. That is part of who we are as a country, and I will defend it to the core (Harris, 2017).

Mentioning freedom of association refers to the landmark 1958 Supreme Court case, *NAACP vs. Alabama*, which stated the NAACP did not have to reveal their members' names, mostly African American, nor addresses.

In describing "basic rights of citizenship," Booker (2017) also references the many African Americans, and women too, who fought for rights still denied them. Several black and white photos of civil rights leaders loom behind him, a historical reminder manifested in Booker's rhetoric of people who protested nonviolently, which is a "noble tradition" (Booker, 2017).

In a letter to NFL commissioner Roger Goodell and other National Football League (NFL) leaders, Richmond lauds Colin Kaepernick, and other kneelers, as patriots, asserting "Peacefully protesting is one of the most American things any citizen can do . . . African Americans are just as patriotic as any other Americans," and still don't have the same rights the First Amendment guarantees (Tynes, 2017, para. 12, 26). He boldly bands together "Take-a-Knee" to the Boston Tea Partiers, abolitionists, suffragettes, the Little Rock Nine, and Freedom Riders (Tynes, 2017, para. 31).

Republicans

Republicans also acknowledge the right to protest. However, they maintain that kneeling for the anthem is wrong and misguided. Moreover, Republicans, and thus other Americans, have the *right* to disagree with kneeling.

Though Paul Ryan initially agrees with his Democratic counterpart Pelosi in the House of Representatives, he sees kneeling as inappropriate in the context of the anthem. "Clearly people have a right to express themselves as they want to, that's the First Amendment, but what I don't think people seem to get is when you do it on the flag and the anthem, it looks like you're against the ideals of America, the patriotism, the military" (Ryan, 2017).

"I believe in free speech," Cruz says (2017), and because of that right, Cruz has the right to disagree with Kaepernick's "right to disrespect the flag," "we have every bit of right to say, 'I disagree with your speech.' That's how free speech works." Cornyn also believes people can express themselves but should stand for the anthem; both he and Cruz reaffirm freedom of expression in that people may choose not to patronize the NFL (Cornyn, 2017 & Cruz, 2017).

Rand Paul acknowledges there is racial injustice, something most Republicans won't necessarily admit. "I don't hesitate to criticize policy when I think it needs it, but I stand and say the Pledge and I think people should . . . still complain. . . . We need to be proud of our country and at the same time try to make it a better place" (Paul, 2017).

Senator Tim Scott is both black and Republican. He has been called, by other blacks, a "House Negro" and "Nigger" among other slanders, for certain Republican stances (Jashinsky, 2017). However, he entreated President Donald Trump to consider America's racial challenges (Alcindor & Thrush, 2017). "Every man, woman, child in this country should stand for the national anthem. That should go without question. We should also ask ourselves the questions, 'Why are they kneeling?' If we were able to A. reinforce the fact that we all should stand, and B. delve into the challenges that have some players kneeling, we'll be in a better place as a country" (Scott, 2017).

In summary, patriotism, peaceful and nonviolent protests, the First Amendment, and the right to disagree encompass the rights and values politicians believe Americans hold dear.

Progress (or Lack Thereof)

Unity & Division

The second theme of progress is also integral to the American ethos, and the battle for progress is never ending. It could be argued other nations seek progress too, but since "the United States represents approximately 5% of the world's population but has created more new wealth than the rest of the world combined (that is wealth for the entire world, Skousen, 2009, p. xvii), it could then be argued America equals progress. What is more, Americans never stop fighting. The American Civil War was fought over progress. Civil rights leaders, such as those behind Senator Booker, marched, were attacked by dogs, sprayed with fire hoses, and even lynched for the progress promised by America's Declaration of Independence and Constitution.

Progress is often slow, and it is hindered through lack of empathy and understanding. While Republicans do not directly address Trump's comments, Democrats attack his divisiveness saying things like, "I'd like him to do what he said he would do when he ran . . . to bring people together" (Pelosi, 2017a). "This is a time when we should have leaders trying to pull our country together. . . . A real patriot find(s) ways to advance our country and unite this nation to greater understanding and a more courageous empathy" (Booker, 2017), and "I think he knows exactly who he's pitting against each other" (Richmond, 2017). However, according to Richmond, many of these people are of "good will" just as the clergy were to whom Dr. King wrote (Richmond, 2017). Harris sees good will also saying, "The vast majority of us have so much more in common than what separates us" (Harris & Key, 2017).

Ignorance

Progress is also impeded by ignorance, willful or otherwise, the failure to focus on important issues, the challenge to create reform, change, and greater equality and fairness, and an understanding of history.

"He is the deflector in chief," declares Pelosi (2017b). He is deflecting from America's true priorities, which in the fall of 2017 were the ravages of hurricanes that affected Florida, Houston, and Puerto Rico, health care reform, and the protest's true purpose, at least according to the Democrats, of bringing awareness to racial injustice, police brutality, and the police system, which both Booker and Sanders note at the beginning of their interviews.

Booker and Sanders immediately seek to control the interview, the narrative, with their calls for criminal justice and police department reform. "We have a real crisis in criminal justice [that] I think what the players are talking about is the need for criminal justice reform, the need for police department reform" (Sanders, 2017). Richmond believes players are kneeling "to protest police officers who kill unarmed African Americans—men and women, adults and children, parents and grandparents—with impunity. They are taking a knee to protest a justice system that says that being black is enough reason for a police officer to fear for his or her life" (Richmond, 2017). Republicans only see the flag and military being disrespected, something Richmond addresses.

Richmond underisively calls Trump a "smart man" who, aware of the divisiveness among "people of good will who believe in equality and justice and peace," are "get[ting] sidetracked on whether you're standing or kneeling at the flag"; the real question, he continued, is why are there black men and women lying in caskets? (Richmond, 2017). Using history as a reminder, Richmond seeks to resolve what he sees as a misunderstanding by reaching out to "the good guys on the wrong side" (Tynes 2017, para. 9), those who disagree with the protesters' tactics, as did many whites in King's day, but who believe in equality. Richmond conveys, "I understand your discomfort with kneeling during the national anthem, but please understand our pain" (Tynes, 2017, para. 10). Richmond demonstrates unity, not only in his attempt to reconcile the two sides but also because the CBC website, on which the press release was written, features a photo of all 37 members of the CBC, both Republican and Democratic (Congressional Black Caucus, 2017).

Focus & Priorities

One Republican, Senator Gardner of Colorado, though not mentioning Trump by name, stated "There are far more things that we ought to be focusing on: North Korea, Iran . . . healthcare bill. That's what I'm going to continue to focus on" (Gardner, 2017).

Trump was elected "to be the leader" (2017), Booker asserts, "of the United States of America, all of us" (2017). He should be "call(ing) us to come together despite differences to answer the call of country right now which should be focusing on places like Puerto Rico (or) talking about something that's affecting every American (healthcare). . . . To focus just on the protest and miss entirely the purpose of the protest, you have to understand these folks are not just taking a knee because they want to disrespect the flag, they're doing this because of real issues in this country" (Booker, 2017).

(Dis)respect

By disrespecting someone, even if the disrespect is misperceived, there cannot be unity and thus there cannot be progress.

Cornyn says, "I think it is profoundly ungrateful given the sacrifice that our military personnel have made and their families, and some of whom have made the ultimate sacrifice, not to demonstrate respect for the flag" (Cornyn, 2017). Though Democrats insist disrespecting the flag or military is not the intent, Cornyn maintains, "I think they need to reassess what the message is because that's the message many receive is one of profound ungratefulness and disrespect" (Cornyn, 2017). Booker (2017) posits that when Trump "has harsher words" for patriotic protesters than white supremacists in Charlottesville, VA, there is disrespect.

The Grassroots

Those close to whites attach themselves to the Republican Party, and against the Democratic Party, while those close to blacks do the opposite (Mangum, 2013). Philpot (2004) goes so far as to suggest that "Citizens support political parties in large part (although not necessarily exclusively) based on their perception of a party's racial symbolism or the party's reputation with respect to race" (p. 255). "Take-a-Knee" was heavily rooted in racial and social justice issues, particularly of young black men experiencing police brutality. As identified in the analysis, Democratic Party voices were supportive of the protest concerning black plight, while the Republican Party found it disrespectful.

Influenced by Politicians

For the grass roots research, no respondent exhibited signs that his or her position on the topic was fed from a political leader, except Trump. This could be because "The proportion of Americans who trust their leaders has fallen from 70% in the 1960s to around 20% at the end of the century" (Newman, 1999. p. 32).

Many respondents to this research got their information on the protests from sports talk shows, social media platforms, and news outlets such as CNN, the *New York Times*, and the *Washington Post*. When asked what specific messages were communicated by leaders of the two primary political parties, the fantasy themes previously mentioned did arise. However, it seems the perspectives on both sides of the aisle were close to one another even though the perception was that the issue was polarizing.

Members from both parties agreed that the motivation of the protest spawned from one of two reasons, Kaepernick's career was floundering and "he needed attention," or "He was trying to bring attention to perceived police brutality and the government discrimination against minorities." Several participants in both party groups agreed that police brutality was a real issue, but that it was a result of "a few bad apples" rather than all police.

Anti-Military and Anti-American

Another consistency among every interview and focus group was that everyone recognized the protest was not against the military, but the situation was made to be about the military. One Democrat felt this was a "propaganda" ploy that came "from the other side" and was a "PR line that it is anti-military and that it's not patriotic because of the flag." Another Democrat heard often that the protest was "anti-American" which she found ironic. A different Democrat voiced her solid support for somebody utilizing freedom of speech and expression for a cause he believed in; however, she followed that up by saying, "I just can't understand how they could disrespect our military and those families and individuals who sacrificed so much for this country with the ultimate sacrifice." She emotionally mustered up the strength after long pauses to share her personal story of losing her father in military combat. For her, "The flag and the national anthem is a time that honors him and his sacrifice." Even though the Take-a-Knee protest was not directed at the military, for her, kneeling during the national anthem was disrespectful.

Republican participants also agreed the protest was not about the military, but disrespectful toward the military nonetheless. The oldest participant at seventy-one had even protested against Vietnam by not standing for the flag. Yet, she felt Kaepernick kneeling was a "blatant disrespect [of] the flag." Her justification was he used a large platform while hers was done quietly. But other Republican respondents called out her double standard. One person reprimanded Republicans in general saying, "It's not like they are ripping the flag in half or tearing it down off the pole." For her, kneeling was just a passive aggressive protest. She elaborated, "If you are offended by a guy who takes a knee, but you aren't offended by these guys who beat women and take drugs. . . . Let's not pretend like all these other guys who are standing up for [the flag] are like good Americans because they stood."

President Trump

In total, very few participants articulated any actual response from any politician, except Trump, and both sides were unhappy with his involvement. The Republicans, on multiple occasions, indicated that the whole protest was more of a "we hate Trump" reaction than a racial one. Both sides felt other players knelt in unity because of Trump's "SOB" comments. Several Republicans asserted that the motivation to kneel was a response to being told not to. It became "about my freedom of speech, and you can't tell me I can't do this." Another said that he "was bothered by the president's response. I feel like he overreacted and inflamed the situation."

Democrats said that even though the comments came from a Republican president, they still didn't seem to feel it was a red or blue issue. It was a personal vendetta that the president had toward the NFL. "Trump wanted to make the statements a long time ago, it was on his list of grievances" and "Donald Trump was saying stuff he wanted to say 20 years ago when he was kicked out of the NFL." It was personal, not political. But then later in the interviews, Democratic participants indicated Republicans were blowing up the issue to divide people and get people upset because of an upcoming election. Another Democrat thought that "things are being publicized by the political leaders on the right so that they can shift public focus onto the NFL issue rather than the other areas that Trump was crooked."

Other Politicians and the Partisan Divide

Only one Republican member could recall a single politician, other than Trump, speaking up: Claire McCaskill. Likewise, one Democrat was able to recall a response by Maxine Waters while another painted Republican politician responses with a broad brush. She said, "I do know that Paul Ryan came to say that he agreed with the president. One more in the long list of, 'I agree with what he is saying. I've got my fingers crossed behind my back so nobody calls me on it later.' . . . Mitch McConnell was very vocal about it on the Republican side." However, Ryan never addressed Trump's comments directly and Mitch McConnell was silent on the topic. When Paul Ryan's name was mentioned, others in the group would scoff and roll their eyes while the participant spoke derogatorily. The word "propaganda" was used on multiple occasions to describe the Republican narrative.

It seems that participants in both groups felt that the topic was partisan in that the opposing side disagreed completely. Democratic responses included:

> I think there was a very definite partisan line on it. . . . You had your conservative Republicans who were, "Well the president is right, you

know, he needs to handle this and you know, if they won't handle it, we'll handle it . . ." while Democrats would think Kaepernick "has the right of freedom of speech, has the right of freedom of expression and these are things, these are injustices that somebody needs to speak out against."

The Republican members also felt it was a very polarizing political issue. "Once you get such a polarizing issue and something like that, you're going, eventually, I believe you're gonna get to straight up down the line red and blue." Another pointed out, "It's obvious that it's polarizing, but we don't know how much is along party lines." The most passionate of the Republican group, who also referenced political responses with a broad brush much like the Democratic respondent, made the statement, "I think you got into party lines at that point. I think Democrats went into freedom of speech, um, minority support, and then the Republicans went into pro-military, patriotism, all that kind of stuff. I think your camps divided pretty quickly into their normal encampments." She pointed out that it was such a major topic that "every senator and everyone is asked about it." The Democrats were in support of everything. "Then we'd have Cruz and different people who tend to be the loud voices of patriotism and, um, pro-military. They all had something to say supporting standing and they should be standing and all this kind of stuff. . . . This is down the aisle stuff."

CONCLUSION

The "Take-a-Knee" controversy saw Republicans create a narrative that acknowledges freedom of expression, as evidenced in America's founding, and that such freedom allows for disagreement, in this case, of kneeling even when it is disrespectful. Democrats also acknowledge the same freedom, referencing the founding as well; however, they add that Trump's divisiveness is preventing progress on equality and justice. Each side believes the other is ignorant of the message being sent, Republicans saying Democrats are disrespecting the flag and the military, with the Democrats insinuating disrespect toward the protesters. The reality, according to the grass roots people, is a need for greater racial equality even though America has made progress. Nevertheless, there is still work to be done:

> This is the country where it is now un-American to be racist even if some leaders such as the President have been accused of racism. That is a form of progress and a picture of evolution that has occurred . . . many people are standing up and saying let's figure this out together. Let's always, always support the American flag and the American people and challenge those within our country who seem to have some prejudice towards some of the folks who are Americans. That is an

equilibrium that needs to be emphasized, and frankly the history of this country says it's been black folks and white folks working together to solve some of these issues. We can do that again (Scott, 2017).

LIMITATIONS AND FURTHER RESEARCH

The qualitative portions of this research were done in and around the Dallas-Fort Worth metroplex and consisted of people who regularly attend evangelical denominational churches. Although they were all either firm Democratic or Republican respondents, it is reasonable to assume that those outside a major metropolitan area may feel and respond differently. Likewise, although "the South is increasingly like the rest of the United States in terms of racial attitudes" (Tuch & Hughes, 1996, p. 782), Texas is solidly Republican, though Dallas-Fort Worth is solidly Democratic as evidenced by Hillary Clinton's victory margin over Trump in the 2016 election (Ramsey, 2016, para. 3, 5), and would likely draw a different intensity of responses from participants than perhaps those in solid Democrat states, or at least cities. Additional qualitative research would benefit from a larger number of respondents, including a mixture of people from various geographic areas and of different socioeconomic backgrounds.

While it appears the given fantasy themes have reached saturation, it would be interesting, for example, to see if more Republicans indirectly criticized Trump as did Gardner, or even directly criticized him. Additionally, given that much of the information that influenced the respondents came from sports talk personalities and news outlets, it would be beneficial to identify what level of influence politicians had on those platforms (see King & Frederick, 2019, chapter 5 in this book). Perhaps agenda setting theory would be able to make stronger connections between politicians' rhetoric and grass roots respondents.

REFERENCES

Alcindor, Y., & Thrush, G. (2017). After Charlottesville, black Republican gives Trump a history lesson on racism. [video recording]. *Nytimes.com*. Retrieved from https://www.nytimes.com/2017/09/13/us/politics/trump-tim-scott-charlottesville-race.html

Bergesen, A., & Herman, M. (1998). Immigration, race, and riot: The 1992 Los Angeles uprising. *American Sociological Review, 63*(1), 39-54.

Booker, C. (24 Sept. 2017). Interview with Chris Hayes. [video recording]. *All In*. MSNBC. YouTube. Retrieved from https://www.youtube.com/watch?time_continue=1&v=yPlvH4NhEC0

Bormann, E. (n.d.) Fantasy theme analysis. Vayne.com. Retrieved from http://www.vayne.com/fantasy_theme_analysis.htm

Bormann, E. (1973). The Eagleton affair: A fantasy theme analysis. *Quarterly Journal of Speech, 59*(2), 143-159. http://dx.doi.org/10.1080/00335637309383163

Bullock, C. (2019). A great American race: Visual rhetoric in NASCAR's national anthem ceremonies. In S.D. Perry (Ed.), *Pro football and the proliferation of protest: Anthem posture in a divided America*. Lanham, MD: Lexington.

Carmines, E., and J. Stimson (1989). *Issue evolution: Race and the transformation of American politics*. Princeton, NJ: Princeton University Press.

Cochran, J. (2001). Controlling our destinies. In T. Smiley (Ed.), *How to make Black America better: Leading African Americans speak out* (p. 71). New York: Anchor Books.

Congressional Black Caucus. (2017). Statement from CBC chairman on Trump, Kaepernick and the NFL. Retrieved from https://cbc.house.gov/news/documentsingle.aspx?DocumentID=732

Cornyn, J. (25 Sept. 2017). @TexasTribune. ".@johncornyn and @tedcruz on #TakeAKnee." [video recording]. [Tweet]. 10:17am. Retrieved from https://twitter.com/TexasTribune/status/912365401819901952

Craig, M. A., & Richeson, J. A. (2017). Information about the US racial demographic shift triggers concerns about anti-White discrimination among the prospective White "minority." *PLoS ONE, 12*(9), 1–21.

Cruz, T. (25 Sept. 2017). @TexasTribune. ".@johncornyn and @tedcruz on #TakeAKnee." [video recording]. [Tweet]. 10:17am. Retrieved from https://twitter.com/TexasTribune/status/912365401819901952

Dixon, T. L., Schell, T. L., Giles, H., & Drogos, K. L. (2008). The influence of race in police-civilian interactions: A content analysis of videotaped interactions taken during Cincinnati police traffic stops. *Journal of Communication, 58*(3), 530–549. https://doi.org/10.1111/j.1460-2466.2008.00398.x

Gardner, C. (24 Sept. 2017). Transcript: Sen. Cory Gardner on "Face the Nation." [video recording]. Interview with John Dickerson. *Face the Nation*. Cbsnews.com. Retrieved from https://www.cbsnews.com/news/transcript-sen-cory-gardner-on-face-the-nation-sept-24-2017/

Harris, K., & Key, P. (1 Oct. 2017)."Kamala Harris: NFL Players 'should not be threatened or bullied' for protests by Trump." [video recording]. Atlanta's First Congregational Church. Breitbart. Retrieved from http://www.breitbart.com/video/2017/10/01/kamala-harris-nfl-players-not-threatened-bullied-protests-trump/

Harris, K. (5 Oct. 2017). "Kamala Harris: My opinion of NFL national anthem protests." David Nazar News. [video recording]. YouTube. Retrieved from https://www.youtube.com/watch?v=MvOckEkwfaY

Hogg, M.A., D.J. Terry, & K.M. White (1995). A tale of two theories: A critical comparison of identity theory with social identity theory. *Social Psychology Quarterly, 58*(4): 255-269.

Hughey, M.W. (2014). White backlash in the 'post-racial' United States. *Ethnic and Racial Studies Review, 37*(5), 721-730.

Jashinsky, E. (2017). Tim Scott #Persisted. *Washington Examiner*. Retrieved from http://www.washingtonexaminer.com/tim-scott-persisted/article/2614370

King, K. & Frederick, E. (2019). Influencing America: Conservative and sports talk radio. In S. D. Perry (Ed.), *Pro football and the proliferation of protest: Anthem posture in a divided America*, Lanham, MD. Lexington.

Kinnon, J. B. (1999). DWB Driving while Black: What's behind the wave of attacks on Black motorists. *Ebony*, 54, 62-64, 66.

Lang, H. (28 Sept. 2017). Congressional Black Caucus chair slams Trump's response to NFL protests. [video recording]. Interview with Don Lemon. CNN. Retrieved from https://www.cnn.com/2017/09/28/politics/congressional-black-caucus-trump-letter/index.html

Levitin, T.E., and Miller, W. (1979). Ideological interpretations of presidential elections. *American Political Science Review, 73*(3): 751-771.

Mangum, M. (2013). The racial underpinnings of party identification and political ideology. *Social Science Quarterly, 94*(5): 1222–1244.

Newman, B. (1999). *The mass marketing of politics: Democracy in an age of manufactured images*. Thousand Oaks, CA: Sage.

Norpoth, H., & Lodge, M. (1985). The difference between attitudes and nonattitudes in the mass public: Just measurements. *American Journal of Political Science, 29*(2): 291-307.

Olzak, S., Shanahan, S., & McEneaney, E. H. (1996). Poverty, segregation, and race riots: 1960 to 1993. *American Sociological Review, 61*(4): 590-613.

Paul, R. (2017). "Rand Paul on the NFL Protests | Kneeling National Anthem." [video recording]. Interview with Chuck Todd. *Meet the Press*. YouTube. Rand Paul. Retrieved from https://www.youtube.com/watch?v=lEN_HK5eM9I

Pelosi, N. (24 Sept. 2017a). "Leader Pelosi on Meet the Press." [video recording]. Interview with Chuck Todd. *Meet the Press*. Nancy Pelosi. YouTube. Retrieved from https://www.youtube.com/watch?v=E-IDVcGftX8

Pelosi, N. (28 Sept. 2017b). Nancy Pelosi Reacts to Trump's NFL players comments & Tom Price private jet flights conference. [video recording]. YouTube. CasonVids. Retrieved from https://www.youtube.com/watch?v=0sGCXVrlV_8

Petrocik, J. (1996). Issue ownership in presidential elections, with a 1980 case study. *American Journal of Political Science, 40*(3): 825-850.

Phillips, D. & Higgs, H. (2019). Government v. protesters: A historical look at how the media chooses a winner. In S.D. Perry (Ed.), *Pro football and the proliferation of protest: Anthem posture in a divided America*. Lanham, MD: Lexington.

Philpot, T. S. (2004). A party of a different color? Race, campaign communication, and party politics. *Political Behavior, 26*(3), 249–271.

Ramsey, R. (2016). Analysis: The blue dots in Texas' red political sea. Retrieved from https://www.texastribune.org/2016/11/11/analysis-blue-dots-texas-red-political-sea/

Rosino, M. L., & Hughey, M. W. (2016). Who's invited to the (political) party: Race and party politics in the USA. *Ethnic and Racial Studies, 39*(3): 325–332.

Ryan, P. (28 Sept. 2017). Paul Ryan weighs in on NFL protests. [video recording]. *The Washington Post*. Retrieved from https://www.washingtonpost.com/video/politics/paul-ryan-weighs-in-on-nfl-protests/2017/09/28/09f65eb8-a46a-11e7-b573-8ec86cdfe1ed_video.html?utm_term=.4d48c3cb4152

Sanders, B. (1 Oct. 2017). Sanders: NFL protest about police, not politics. [video recording]. Interview with Jake Tapper. CNN. Retrieved from https://www.cnn.com/videos/politics/2017/10/01/sotu-sanders-nfl.cnn

Schmidt, S. (2018). 'This is CNN Tonight. I'm Don Lemon. The president of the United States is racist.' [video recording]. Retrieved from https://www.washingtonpost.com/news/morning-mix/wp/2018/01/12/this-is-cnn-tonight-im-don-lemon-the-president-of-the-united-states-is-racist/?utm_term=.b5f4e364dc14

Scott, T. (27 Sept. 2017). Sen. Tim Scott: 'Every man, woman, child' should stand for the national anthem. [video recording]. Interview with Joe Kernen. *Squawk Box*. CNBC. Retrieved 19 April 2018, from https://www.cnbc.com/2017/09/27/sen-tim-scott-on-nfl-everyone-should-stand-for-the-national-anthem.html

Skousen, W. (2009). *The 5,000 year leap* (p. xvii). Franklin, TN: American Documents Publishing, L.L.C.

Stets, J.E., & Burke, P.J. (2000). Identity theory and social identity theory. *Social Psychology Quarterly, 63*(3): 224-237.

Tajfel, H. (1978). Social categorization, social identity, and social comparison. In H. Tajfel, ed., *Differentiation Between Social Groups, Studies in the Social Psychology of Intergroup Relations*. New York: Academic Press.

Transue, J. (2007). Identity salience, identity acceptance, and racial policy attitudes: American national identity as a uniting force. *American Journal of Political Science, 51*(1):78-91.

Tuch, S. A., & Hughes, M. (1996). Whites' opposition to race-targeted policies: One cause or many? *Social Science Quarterly, 77*(4): 778–788.

Turner, J. (1985). Social categorization and the self-concept: A social-cognitive theory of group behavior. In E. Lawler, (Ed.), *Advances in group processes: Theory and research* (Vol. 2). Greenwich, CT: JAI Press.

Tynes, T. (2017). "Read the Congressional Black Caucus' letter to the NFL about police brutality." *SBNation.com*. Retrieved from https://www.sbnation.com/2017/10/16/16482694/congressional-black-caucus-letter-nfl-police-brutality

Vultee, F. (2012). Man-child in the White House. *Journalism Studies, 13*(1): 54-70. doi 10.1080/1461670x.2011.580946

West, M., & Carey, C. (2006). (Re)Enacting frontier justice: The Bush administration's tactical narration of the Old West fantasy after September 11. *Quarterly Journal of Speech, 92*(4), 379-412. doi 10.1080/00335630601076326

Wickham, D. (n.d.). Remembering Roosevelt: Reflections on race and the Republican Party. *Harvard Journal of African American Public Policy*, 27–32.

THIRTEEN

Together We Tweet

A Cloud Protest Exploratory Study Examining the Evolution of #TakeAKnee

Jana Duckett and Deborah Sacra

Before the advent of digital communication, social movement scholars were challenged by the descriptive nature and elite bias of their research, largely due to the limitations of their sources: official documents produced primarily by the leaders of social movements and mainstream media (Benford, 1997; Downing, 2008). Social media has revolutionized this research field, as platforms like Twitter make visible the processes of identity and meaning construction in collective action (Milan, 2015b; Rogers, 2013). At the same time, new technology has shaped these negotiations through its algorithms and affordances (Langlois, 2011; Milan, 2015).

Milan (2015a) proposes the notion of *cloud protesting* to bracket the intersection of social movement studies (SMS) and science technology studies (STS), to consider how "the specific materiality of social media" remakes the dynamics of collective action (p. 893). The cloud is an imagined, symbolic place that provides virtual infrastructure for networking, communication, and storage of the cultural and symbolic resources needed to create social movements. Applying the theoretical framework of cloud protest, this study will use network analysis tools to discover how symbolic resources, embodied in frequently-used hashtags, were adopted and manipulated by Twitter users to negotiate narratives of meaning, or frames, around the National Football League (NFL) national anthem protest.

LITERATURE REVIEW

In the context of social movements, frames are semantic structures that define social experience in relation to the imperative for change, through the identification of a problem and its cause, prescription of a solution, and motivation for individual action (Benford & Snow, 2000). The development of collective action frames (CAFs) is a discursive and contested process, evidenced by frame disputes within the movement, counter-framing by opponents, bystanders, and media, and by adjustments made in response to real-world events (Benford & Snow, 2000).

On the microblogging platform Twitter, hashtags are an addressivity function used to locate the narratives surrounding a certain topic (Guo & Saxton, 2014; Messina, 2007). Certain hashtags have become memes that represent social movements, both online and off, such as #MAGA (make America great again), #Occupy and #BlackLivesMatter. In the case of the NFL national anthem protests, #TakeAKnee is the meme around which the framing of the social movement has been contested by adherents, bystanders, and antagonists.

Because hashtags on Twitter are public from their inception, their meaning is publicly negotiated, as in the case of the challenge to #BlackLivesMatter by #AllLivesMatter in its early stages of use (Carney, 2016). The dispute over the #BlackLivesMatter sign overshadowed discussion of the racial injustice narrative until strategic engagement by its users clarified and strengthened it in response to the #AllLivesMatter counter-narrative. Quantitative data from a similar time period shows that the most active participants in the Twitter discourse for #BlackLivesMatter were non-journalists and online journalists (Groshek & Tandoc, 2016), indicating that the negotiation was a grassroots phenomenon.

One strategy conversants use to build and dispute frames is combining different hashtags, which may represent resonant, antagonistic, or even peripheral narratives (Yang, 2016). Therefore, semantic communities in a network analysis of a Twitter hashtag co-occurrence network can reveal the narratives of social groups in cloud protesting (Bennett, 2012; Bruns & Burgess, 2015; Groshek & Tandoc, 2016; Tremayne, 2014; Wang, Jin, Cao, Yang, & Zhang, 2016). Hashtag co-occurrence networks are multi-purpose, allowing Twitter users to connect two or more movement messages and influence public opinion by increasing virality (Gleason, 2013; Milan, 2015a). Degree centrality positively correlates with hashtag frequency usage in combination with other hashtags (Wang et al., 2016) to create "higher symbolic salience" creating a dimension of "structural virality" that drives increased visibility of the movement (Wang et al., 2016, p. 854).

The modularity of hashtag co-occurrence networks corresponds closely to the social network structure on Twitter. Network visualization of influencers among 2500 Twitter users revealed that linguistic groups correspond to network clusters in social media movements (Grandjean, 2016). Political sub-groups were distinguished by examining hashtag co-occurrence in nine million tweets posted during the 2010 United States midterm elections (Bode, Hanna, Yang, & Shah, 2015). Romero, Tan, and Ugander (2013) found significant correlation between hashtag clusters and "the topology of the connections among users" (p. 524) on Twitter, implying that hashtag networks can predict social networks. Based on these studies, the #TakeAKnee hashtag co-occurrence network should reveal frames of meaning of Twitter users who participated in the cloud protest.

THEORETICAL PERSPECTIVE

Cloud protesting is attentive to the ways in which "communication logic has the power to drive social action" (Milan, 2015a, p. 888) through its affordances and algorithms. The asynchronicity, visibility, mobility, virtual copresence, and platform software of social media create a *politics of visibility*, a constant negotiation and invigoration of meanings, which underlies and shapes the way individuals engage in cloud protesting (Milan, 2015b).

In a similar vein, Meraz and Papacharissi (2013) proposed the term *networked framing* for the negotiation of collective action frames on social media. However, while they note that socio-technical architectures "amalgamate collective intelligence in an effortless aggregation" (p. 160), cloud protesting suggests a new dynamic exists in social media-based social movements, in which meanings and identities do not converge into collective ideologies, but remain individualized. This failure to form a collective narrative impacts the life cycle and sustainability of social action (Milan, 2015a; 2015b).

The explosiveness, limited time frame, and conflicting narratives of the NFL player national anthem protests in 2017–2018 provide a scenario in which the assertions of cloud protest can be examined in the evolution of collective action frames constructed around #TakeAKnee as it transpired on Twitter. The graphs and statistics of social network analysis will provide supporting evidence for Milan's predictions for social movement dynamics.

Three research questions will be addressed:

RQ1: What are the dominant semantic communities that cluster in connection with the hashtag #TakeAKnee?

RQ2: How do the semantic communities change in response to social media-amplified events?

RQ3: How does network analysis of hashtag co-occurrence reveal the processes of collective action frame negotiation in the context of cloud protesting?

METHODS

Data collection and analysis for this study consisted of administering the following procedures. The initial step involved collecting 539,978 tweets from 287,690 users from the #TakeAKnee data set using the Boston University Twitter Content and Analysis Toolkit (BU-TCAT). This tool curates Twitter content using the public streaming Twitter application programming interface (API). Initially developed as part of the Digital Methods Initiative (Borra & Reider, 2014) the system provides customized sampling of public Twitter data using a system that "has been shown to produce generalizable samples of Twitter content" (Groshek & Tandoc, 2016, p. 4).

For the examination of this study's research questions, network data files of the top 50 co-occurring hashtags within the #TakeAKnee data set were downloaded from TCAT. For the purpose of this study, hashtag "co-occurrence" is defined as hashtags grouped together or appearing within the same tweet. Hashtags are represented as vertices, or nodes, in the network data, and co-occurrence is represented by undirected edges, or links, between nodes. The network files were then imported into Gephi, an open-source program developed for network analysis that allows users to sort and visualize large data sets.

Metrics were calculated for modularity, degree centrality, and graph density. Modularity is a statistic ranging from −1.0 to +1.0 that represents the strength of the clustering in the network. A higher modularity score indicates denser clusters that are more dispersed from others. Degree centrality designates the number of edges connected to a node, demonstrating the most popular or influential hashtags. Average degree centrality is the average number of edges connecting nodes throughout the system. Graph density is a calculation of the actual number of edges divided by the total possible edges if all nodes were connected to each other. Higher graph density indicates a more interconnected network.

Applying the Yifan Hu visualization dispersed nodes gravitationally to identify more densely connected semantic communities. Nodes were given a size proportional to their degree centrality. The larger the node, the more connected it is within the network. Thus, #TakeAKnee is the most symbolically salient node within each graph, which are available for online viewing through listed links. In addition, to distinguish semantic communities, nodes were grouped according to their modularity class. The prevent overlap setting was applied to untangle the network and create more comprehensible visualization.

The data in the sample included the top fifty co-occurring hashtags within tweets that mentioned the tag #TakeAKnee from October 6, 2017, through January 31, 2018. The beginning date marks when TCAT began collecting the Twitter data. Although it comes a few weeks into the 2017–2018 NFL season, we do not see it detracting from the results due to the longitudinal and evolutionary nature of our study.

RESULTS

In order to model both semantic communities and how the hashtag narrative shifted based on social media-amplified events, this study separated the co-occurring hashtag data into monthly periods: October 6 to 31, 2017; November 1 to 30, 2017; December 1 to 31, 2017; and January 1 to 31, 2018.

October 2017

The October 2017 network consists of 50 nodes with 749 edges with a density of 0.611 and an average degree centralization score of 29.96. The modularity score was 0.177 with a resolution of 0.5. Six semantic communities were identified. The top ten nodes with the highest degree centrality scores following #TakeAKnee for the month of October were: #Maga (47 connections), #NFL (47 connections), #BlackLivesMatter (46 connections), #TakeTheKnee (45 connections), #BLM (44 connections), #TakeAKneeNFL (43 connections), #Trump (43 connections), #ColinKaepernick (42 connections), #NFLBoycott (41 connections), #Resist (41 connections), #BoycottNFL and #Kapernick [sic] (39 connections), and #ImpeachTrump (38 connections).

Semantic Communities

In October, the hashtag network, viewable in Gephi at https://goo.gl/yzfG3D, or by using the QR code for October in Figure 13.1, was not well-defined, verified by a modularity score of 0.177. Most hashtags fell into a single community around the central node (#TakeAKnee) and graphically did not have a distinct narrative or perspective. In addition to the #TakeAKnee node, the community included 7 of the 10 nodes having the highest degree centrality (#NFL, #BlackLivesMatter, #BLM, #Resist, #ColinKaepernick, and #NFLBoycott). It also included anti-sentiment hashtags that directly related to the national anthem conflict: #TakeAStand, #NationalAnthem, #StandForTheFlag, #StandForAnthem. Another community grouped around politically conservative hashtags such as #MAGA (make America great again), #TCOT (Top Conservatives on Twitter), and #PJNet (Patriot Journalist Network). The smallest, peripheral community embodied an anti-Trump narrative, including #ImpeachTrump from the top 10 hashtags, and the #Resistance and #Boycott related communities showed the initial formation of the boycott narrative.

Response to events

October was the most active month for the #TakeAKnee hashtag, with 361,171 tweets from October 6 to 31. In October, the peak of Twitter activity in relation to #TakeAKnee was seen on the 9th, the day after Vice President Mike Pence walked out of an Indianapolis Colts–Green Bay Packers game because players knelt during the national anthem. Also in the same time frame, rapper Eminem released a video, shown at the BET Hip Hop Awards, that criticized President Donald Trump, racism, and insufficient U.S. support of Puerto Rico's recovery from Hurricane Maria, while supporting the principles of the kneeling protest. Both events appeared in co-occurring hashtags that include #MikePence, #Pence, #Eminem, and #PuertoRicoRelief. These hashtags did not reappear in later months.

A second peak in #TakeAKnee activity occurred during the second weekend of the month, after Colin Kaepernick filed a formal grievance against the NFL. From October 18 to 28, the hashtag declined to less than 6,000 tweets a day, a large drop from over 18,000 the first weekend of the month. Then, the last weekend of the month shows one last peak (to over 12,500 tweets), after news broke that the Houston Texans owner referred to NFL players as "inmates running the prison" (Chiquillo, 2017). Interestingly, this event is not marked by new hashtags, but perhaps served to reinforce the existing protest narrative, and add to the boycott communities who may have had a desire to penalize the team owners.

November 2017

The November 2017 network consisted of 51 nodes with 464 edges, with a density of 0.364 and an average degree centralization score of 18.196. The modularity score was 0.236 with a resolution of 0.5. Eight semantic communities were identified. The top ten nodes with the highest degree centrality scores following #TakeAKnee for the month of November were: #NFL (43 connections), #BoycottNFL (36 connections), #Maga (36 connections), #NFLboycott (34 connections), #BlackLivesMatter (32 connections), #Kaepernick (29 connections), #ColinKaepernick (28 connections), #TakeTheKnee (28 connections), #Trump (28 connections), #BLM (26 connections), #BoycottNFLSponsors and #TheResistance and #TakeTheKneeNFL (26 connections).

Figure 13.1. QR codes to full color diagrams of co-occurring hashtags

Semantic communities

In November, the increased modularity score (0.236) corresponds to more dispersion of the top hashtags among different semantic communities [View at https://goo.gl/k16CKBor through the November QR Code in Figure 13.1]. The community with the most nodes included only 3 of the top 10 (#NFL, #MAGA, and #TheResistance) and the rest of its hashtags, all considerably less cited, were characterized by an anti-Trump perspective. The community encompassing Kaepernick and Black Lives Matter tags contained 5 of the top 10 hashtags, reflecting a resurgence of

Kaepernick's stated reason for the kneeling protest: To highlight racial bias. Two of the remaining top 10 hashtags fell into a community promoting the NFL boycott in connection with the #StandForTheFlag/Anthem hashtags. A conservative, pro-Trump community was formed that included a Veterans' Day tag, and was in close proximity to the various boycott nodes. Interestingly, it did not include #MAGA, which was a top 10 hashtag in the largest community. Finally, an additional isolated strongly liberal community was also seen clustered around #Resist.

Response to events

The overall scale of #TakeAKnee activity was greatly reduced in November, as the total number of tweets (80,070) dropped to less than 20 percent of the previous month (though the month of October included four fewer days of tweets that were captured). However, activity remained volatile. The highest daily activity was seen in the first days of November (around 4000 tweets), after the Houston Texans players' protest. Other peaks in #TakeAKnee activity continued during the weekends and Mondays in November. On November 12, Veterans' Day Sunday, the NFL made a special effort to honor veterans, restraining all but three players from kneeling in an attempt to show the protest was not meant to dishonor the military. While the #VeteransDay hashtag is not in the same community, it is seen to be closely connected to the stand for the anthem/flag and boycott hashtags. The financial impact of the boycott was a focus in the mainstream media (McCarthy, 2017).

The primary outside story that emerged in connection to #TakeAKnee was #MeToo, a sign women began to use in mid-October to demonstrate the prevalence of sexual harassment in American society, after Hollywood producer Harvey Weinstein was accused by multiple women. Perhaps some felt their experience was connected to racial discrimination, so they cited #TakeAKnee as well. Also, it is noted that during the election week, #TakeAKnee activity dropped.

December 2017

The December 2017 network consisted of 50 nodes with 348 edges with a density of 0.284 and an average degree centralization score of 13.92. The modularity score was 0.329 with a resolution of 0.5. Six semantic communities were identified. The top ten nodes with the highest degree centrality scores following #TakeAKnee for the month of December were: #Resist (30 connections), #MAGA (28 connections), #BlackLivesMatter (27 connections), #NFL (26 connections), #TheResistance (25 connections), #BLM (25 connections), #BoycottNFL (23 connections), #ImpeachTrump (23 connections), #NFLBoycott (20 connections), #Boycott-

TheNFL (19 connections), #BoycottNFLSponsors, #ImWithKap, and #TakeTheKnee (18 connections).

Semantic Communities

In December, the number of tweets (28,300) decreased by more than 50 percent from November. The modularity score increased to 0.284 as communities become more defined [View at https://goo.gl/fNsM63]. The semantic community that dominated the narrative included high centrality nodes #ImpeachTrump, #Resist, and #BlackLivesMatter, plus 3 of the boycott hashtags clustering together. Thematically, it is comprised primarily of anti-Trump and pro-kneeling sentiment. The semantic community anchored by high centrality tag #NFL connects with more anti-protest language such as #StandForTheFlag and #TakeAStand. A smaller community is political, with tags containing both pro-Trump and anti-Trump sentiment with high centrality nodes #MAGA and #TheResistance. Unlike the previous month, the #MAGA node is no longer in the same semantic community as #TakeAKnee. Two smaller communities are less related to the central node, which include: #ImStillWithHer, #LGBTQ, #VoteVets, #WeRise, #Indivisible, and #RussiaGate. These may represent separate causes attempting to enter or spin off the #TakeAKnee conversation.

Response to events

In December, the boycott narrative sees a significant increase in usage compared to previous months. Four different boycott hashtags enter the top ten, illustrating sharp polarization among the dominant semantic communities with one boycott-related tag connected to #StandForTheFlag and #NFL in the pro-sentiment community and others connected to #Resist and #ColinKaepernick in the larger anti-sentiment community. Additionally, the most centralized nodes in the data, #MAGA and #Resist, were connected with the #MeToo tag.

January 2018

The January 2018 network consisted of 50 nodes with 330 edges, with a density of 0.269 and an average degree centralization score of 13.200. The modularity score was 0.404 with a resolution of 0.5. Six semantic communities were identified. The top ten nodes with the highest degree centrality scores following #TakeAKnee for the month of January were: #Maga (30 connections), #TheResistance (26 connections), #BLM (25 connections), #Resist (25 connections), #Trump (24 connections), #BlackLivesMatter (23 connections), #NFL (23 connections), #ImpeachTrump (22 connections), #TrumpShutdown (20 connections), #BoycottNFL (19 connections), #Indivisible, #LGBTQ, #MeToo, and #MLKDay (16 connections).

Semantic Communities

In January, modularity scores increased from the previous month (0.404), as well as the number of tweets (36.086). Surprisingly, the hashtags with the highest degree centrality, #MAGA and #TheResistance, were outside the largest community [as shown at https://goo.gl/Ktbw7E]. Similar to October, the largest semantic community is comprised of multiple narratives. High centrality nodes in this community, such as #NFL, #Resist, #BLM, and #BlackLivesMatter, are connected with diverse stances represented by #Republican, four different pro-standing hashtags, and #NFLBoycott, which was located in the counternarrative in December. Peripheral nodes from December, such as #LBGTQ, #Democrat, and #Republican, increase in degree centrality and are absorbed into the dominant semantic community. The second largest semantic community is distant from the #TakeAKnee node, clustered densely around #TrumpShutdown, and connected to political conspiracy language such as #ReleaseTheMemo, #TrumpDossier, and #FusionGPA. Another top ten hashtag, #Trump, serves as a central node for a community clustering hashtags related to protests in Iran early in January. This was the first month #Trump was separated from the primary semantic community throughout the season. Another secondary semantic community shows a polarized political narrative containing both pro- and anti-Trump sentiment with both #MAGA and #ImpeachTrump nodes, both of which were in the top ten. The #MeToo node increased in degree centrality and became a semantic community with #TheResistance.

Response to Events

January co-occurrences were amplified by two spikes: Trump's appearance at the NCAA college football national championship game between the Alabama Crimson Tide and the Georgia Bulldogs in Atlanta, and the State of the Union address. The #Trump and #NationalAnthem nodal connection supports the January 9 spike when a flood of social media Twitter commentary suggested Trump was stumbling over the words to the national anthem on the ABC live broadcast. Also, the #MAGA tag was connected to the #SOTU (State of the Union) in connection with his address on January 30. Perhaps an indication of the waning of the social movement, only a slight surge for #TakeAKnee overall and the co-occurrence of #MLKDay and #MartinLutherKing was seen during marches for Martin Luther King Day weekend. Another semantic cluster revealed the government shutdown and incidents related to the investigation into Russian interference in the 2016 Presidential election.

DISCUSSION

In this discussion we will summarize the evolution of the semantic communities from October 2017 through January 2018. From these observations, we will answer the third research question, explaining how the analysis of the hashtag co-occurrence network reveals frame negotiation in the context of cloud protesting.

Network Analysis Statistics

As mentioned earlier, modularity is a statistic ranging from −1.0 to +1.0 that represents the strength of clustering within a network. A higher modularity score indicates denser clusters that are more dispersed from others. The modularity algorithm showed with each month the scores increased, getting closer to 1.0. This implies the nodal structures of semantic communities became more connected over the course of the four months observed. This "homophily effect" reflects what previous studies have found. That is, in the initial stages, social media movements experience high participation and momentum around multiple narratives, but they are sustained by the organizational strength of shared ideology, a dynamic seen in the network when nodes shift to align more closely with hashtags and narratives similar to their core belief systems (Bennett, 2012; Carter, 2013; Tremayne, 2014; Wang, Liu, & Gao, 2015). For example, October indicates an average centrality score of 29.96; however, in January this statistic drops by more than 50 percent as symbolic meaning and significance of the most influential hashtags is negotiated during the movement (Milan, 2015).

Likewise, the downward trend in the density statistic indicates that as the protest went on, the participants were less interconnected overall. The statistic shows the degree to which communities form and strengthen as nodes become more compactly connected around hashtag narra-

Table 13.1. Network Analysis Statistics

Statistic	Oct 2017	Nov 2017	Dec 2017	Jan 2018
Number of Communities	6	8	6	6
Modularity (resolution = 0.5)	0.177	0.236	0.284	0.404
Average Centrality	29.96	18.20	13.92	13.20
Graph Density	0.611	0.364	0.329	0.259

tives, as individuals broker meaning by selecting and appropriating "the elements that best match their identity, history, and feelings" (Milan, 2015b, p. 8). Through this selection process, participating individuals determine which hashtags are the most meaningful embodiment of the collective action frames as "the cloud collectively 'votes' by selecting, emphasizing, and sharing content" (Milan, 2015b, pp. 6-7), and are less likely to interact with other narratives.

Thus, co-occurring hashtag usage with #TakeAKnee became about individuals not only engaging the universal conversation, but also segmenting the narrative into divergent collective ideologies, thereby forming the semantic communities around #TakeAKnee. Through the customization of protest narratives in this way, the cloud creates an environment of high symbolic salience, in which social movement activism is shaped by the affordances and algorithms of the platforms (Milan, 2015b). Milan calls this influence on the social movement narrative the politics of visibility, indicating that the platforms themselves become political actors. Milan asserts the politics of visibility replaces the politics of identity creating, "individuals-in-the-group, whereby the 'collective' is experienced through the 'individual' and the group is the means of collective action, rather than its end" (Milan, 2015a, p. 1).

Narrative Evolution and Maintaining Visibility

This section will explore the study's research questions addressing collective action frames, the emergence of dominant semantic communities, and the use of social media events to amplify hashtag visibility using Milan's four mechanisms shaping the politics of visibility: *centrality of performance, interpellation to fellows and opponents, expansion of the temporality of the protest, and reproducibility of social action* (Milan, 2015b).

The social network data over the course of four months illustrated widely dispersed action in the beginning that eventually became narrow and compacted by the final month. Initial data revealed dispersed network structure where communities were sparsely clustered around the central node, #TakeAKnee. In October multiple hashtag narratives connected with the central node #TakeAKnee as groups vied for visibility. *Centrality of performance* is evident as many of the nodes appeared similar in size to the central node, suggesting it was early in the meaning-negotiation phase. Actors were learning which hashtags to identify with and selecting tags that contributed to the "collective representation" of "we" (Milan, 2015b, p. 5). This is primarily observed as multiple variations of #TakeAKnee appeared highly centralized early in the conversation but eventually lost influence. Segmentation of dominant narratives around #TakeAKnee began to form in November, "making protest visible" (Milan, 2015b, p. 7). In addressing the first research question, social actors consistently enacted dominant semantic community storylines around political conservatism or pro-Trump semantic units such as #MAGA, #TCOT, and #Trump, followed by pro-Kaepernick social justice semantic units such as #BlackLivesMatter, #Resist, #PoliceBrutality, and #TakeTheKnee. Secondary narratives included #NFL, #NFLBoycott, #NationalAnthem, #TakeAStand, and #BoycottNFLProtest co-occurences.

In October, Vice President Pence appeared among the #TakeAKnee conversation in Twitter, seemingly aligning the conversation with pro-anthem tags such as #StandForTheAnthem and #Respect. This illustrates the mechanism of *interpellation,* as Twitter enables "users to call other people into action" through "the use of hashtags . . . which spur conversations and content exchange" (Milan, 2015b, p. 7). Initial social network data in October and November indicated conversations around Kaepernick and Trump were more centralized; however, narratives emerged around political conservatism, police brutality, social justice, and patriotism toward the national anthem. November specifically showed stronger grouping of semantic communities and a consolidation of hashtags as the mechanism of visibility politics continued. The increase of semantic communities in the top fifty was in part a result of hashtag narratives surrounding the boycotts. This was another instance of interpellation as new call-to-action messages engaged social actors, leading to the emergence of a new semantic community. Kaepernick and Trump hashtags became less centralized, while the ideas they represented became more central. Signs of symbolic negotiation and refinement remained evident, as several opposing sentiment hashtags appeared in the same community, with #ImWithKap, #Trump, #BlackLivesMatter, and #NationalAnthem grouped together, implying social actors from multiple sides could have used anti-sentiment hashtags as a tactic to break down and reshape the conversation.

In December, we finally began to see the pro- and anti-kneeling communities characterized by defined clusters. Anti-Trump or political liberalism narratives dominated the network with #Resist, #BlackLivesMatter, and #ImpeachTrump tags in direct community with #TakeAKnee. This segmentation illustrates the third mechanism of *expansion* whereby protest actions are reproduced, in this case through co-occurring hashtags, and the life cycle of the protest extended beyond the initial occurrence. #MAGA continued to be highly centralized but was unable to maintain semantic cohesion as opposing sentiment tags also attached to the node, destabilizing and disrupting the political conservatism narrative. Finally, the #NFL tag was highly centralized and clustered around pro-anthem language including: #StandForTheFlag and #TakeAStand. Thus, pro- and anti-sentiment dominant semantic communities emerged around three key segments of the #TakeAKnee conversation: national anthem and the NFL, Trump and political conservatism, and racial justice and political liberalism. This supports what Tremayne's (2014) hashtag co-occurrence study observed in social movements—they grow and evolve as individuals "cluster around shared interest in an idea" (p. 113).

January social network data showed hashtag co-occurrences advancing the social justice and political liberalism narrative were stabilized in the process of meaning negotiation, collectively contributing to the "who we are" factor, encouraging joint action among social actors (Milan, 2015, p. 7). As it relates to the third research question, we observed that as collective frames were co-created by individuals through hashtag combinations they were selecting and *reproducing social action*, which eventually created rituals. The most evident frame negotiation ritual seen in the hashtag network was the "choice" of a central hashtag for the movement. In October and November, there were multiple versions of the hashtag: #TakeAKnee, #TakeTheKnee, #TakeAKneeNFL. Numerous variations were seen in the data that did not make it into the top fifty hashtags, many of which mocked #TakeAKnee. However, by December and January #TakeAKnee dominated.

Over the course of four months, we explored how digitally-mediated protests clustered around collective action frames in order to create group solidarity through social networks, in this case Twitter. Using the lens of cloud protesting, we examined what Milan (2015a) referred to as the "symbolic place between technology devices and platforms" or the imaginary space where cultural and symbolic production takes place using the Twitter platform. Hashtag co-occurrences in the cloud provide affordances where both individual and universal narratives work together to accomplish "the politics of visibility" (p. 11) through continued reactivation. By combining hashtags, protest movements are able to expand reach in the Twittersphere and align groups around collective action frames, symbolically represented by nodes with high centrality. In comparing the monthly findings from October through January, the results revealed the process of developing consistent patterns of hashtag co-occurrences, anchored around ideological beliefs, namely pro- and anti-sentiment related to the national anthem and the NFL, Trump and political conservatism, and racial justice and political liberalism.

A final observation speaks to the deterioration of the movement over time. In just a few months, the data showed the number of Twitter users in the available sample diminished from over 174,000 in October to close to 24,000 in January, highlighting one of the major challenges with cloud protest movements. In the end, while the cloud proves to be an exceptional organizing space for surface idea exchange and "short-lived loyalties" of collective action, it becomes "fragile" in terms of the long-term sustainability of the overall movement as it lacks the ability to incite accountability toward offline, action-oriented social responsibility (Bennet, 2012; Milan, 2015b, p. 7; Spiro & Monroy-Hernandez, 2016).

CONCLUSION

This study provides quantitative evidence for the predictions of Milan's theory of cloud protesting, which contends that the algorithms and affordances of socio-technologies have changed social movement dynamics. While social media has made visible the processes of frame definition and negotiation, it cannot be assumed that narratives of meaning are truly collective. The social network analysis represents the aggregation, rather than the convergence, of the meanings of participants in the negotiation. These meanings may be discursively impacted by social media interactions via the politics of visibility, but in the end, each user maintains a personal frame of meaning.

The #TakeAKnee hashtag co-occurrence network provided a robust data set for this examination due to the variety of frames with which users perceived the NFL players national anthem protests. As Milan predicted, the online social movement waned when ongoing events failed to revitalize the narratives. This phenomenon has some correspondence to the results of Nowak, Szamrej, and Latané's (1990) computer simulation of social impact theory, in which a theoretical social group achieved a condition of "partial polarization": after a period of dispersion, the social network settled into a sort of consensus, with subgroups on the fringes that did not disturb the stability of the center.

Although the social movement breaks down online, it does not necessarily have to end. Those who have engaged with the narrative must decide how it will impact their offline identity and actions. Kaepernick himself took "real life" action long before the 2017 NFL season. In October 2016 he held his first "I Know My Rights" camp to educate young people of color about their rights and staying safe in their interactions with police (King, 2016). Also, he gave away one million dollars to community organizations working with oppressed social groups ("Million Dollar Pledge," 2018). Neither of these activities appeared in the #TakeAKnee narrative. The results of this study, and Kaepernick's example, suggest that the "social movement" in the cloud can only be a starting point for conversation, a place where all the perspectives are "visible" for consideration and discussion, but not a place where productive social change can take place.

This study was limited in its ability to represent the full scope of the Twitter narrative around #TakeAKnee. We restricted our data set to the hashtag co-occurrence network, but not all participants use the addressivity convention (Hwang, 2009). Furthermore, we made inferences about the meaning of the hashtags, without examining the tweets qualitatively to determine whether individual users meant to use the language sincerely or ironically. In addition, standards and methods for "cleaning" Twitter data to eliminate the work of automated posting "bots" are still in development, and we did not attempt to detect illegitimate Tweets. However, the quantity of the data—over 500,000 tweets—gives substance to our claims that it represents the narrative accurately.

Finally, a weakness of this study is the possibility that the social movement narrative waned simply because the NFL season ended. Additional studies should investigate movements that do not have a natural timeline constraining the evolution of the narrative.

REFERENCES

Benford, R.D. (1997). An insider's critique of the social movement framing perspective. *Sociological Inquiry*, 67(4), 409–430. doi:10.1111/j.1475-682X.1997.tb00445.x

Benford, R.D., & Snow, D.A. (2000). Framing processes and social movements: An overview and assessment. *Annual Review of Sociology*, 26(1), 611–639. doi:10.1146/annurev.soc.26.1.611

Bennett, W.L. (2012). The personalization of politics: Political identity, social media, and changing patterns of participation. *The Annals of the American Academy of Political and Social Science*, 644(1), 20-39. doi:10.1177/0002716212451428

Bode, L., Hanna, A., Yang, J., & Shah, D.V. (2015). Candidate networks, citizen clusters, and political expression: Strategic hashtag use in the 2010 midterms. *The Annals of the American Academy of Political and Social Science*, 659(1), 149–165. doi:10.1177/0002716214563923

Bruns, A., & Burgess, J. (2015). Twitter hashtags from ad hoc to calculated publics. In N. Rambukkana (Ed.), *Hashtag Publics: The Power and Politics of Discursive Networks* (pp. 13–28). New York: Peter Lang.

Carney, N. (2016). All lives matter, but so does race: Black Lives Matter and the evolving role of social media. *Humanity & Society*, 40(2), 180–199. doi:2048/10.1177/0160597616643868

Carter, M.J. (2013). Advancing identity theory: Examining the relationship between activated identities and behavior in different social contexts. *Social Psychology Quarterly*, 76(3), 203-223. doi:10.1177/0190272513493095

Chiquillo, J. (2017, October 28). Most Houston Texans kneel during anthem after owner's comment about "inmates running the prison." Retrieved April 20, 2018, from https://www.dallasnews.com/news/texas/2017/10/28/inmates-running-prison-texans-owner-apologizes-twice-remark-nfl-protests

DiGrazia, J., McKelvey, K., Bollen, J., & Rojas, F. (2013). More tweets, more votes: Social media as a quantitative indicator of political behavior. *PLoS One*, 8(11). doi:10.1371/journal.pone.0079449

Downing, J. (2008). Social movement theories and alternative media: An evaluation and critique. *Communication, Culture and Critique*, 1(1), 40–50. doi:10.1111/j.1753-9137.2007.00005.x

Evans, J.H. (1997). Multi-organizational fields and social movement organization frame content: The religious pro-choice movement. *Sociological Inquiry*, 67(4), 451–469.

Grandjean, M. (2016). A social network analysis of twitter: Mapping the digital humanities community. *Cogent Arts & Humanities*, 3(1). doi: 10.1080/23311983.2016.1171458

Groshek, J., & Tandoc, E. (2016). The affordance effect: Gatekeeping and (non)reciprocal journalism on twitter. Paper presented at the 7th International Conference on Social Media & Society. doi: 10.1145/2930971.2930993

Guo, C., & Saxton, G.D. (2014). Tweeting social change: How social media are changing nonprofit advocacy. *Nonprofit and Voluntary Sector Quarterly*, 43(1), 57–79. doi:10.1177/0899764012471585

Himelboim, I., McCreery, S., & Smith, M. (2013). Birds of a feather tweet together: Integrating network and content analyses to examine cross-ideology exposure on Twitter. *Journal of Computer-Mediated Communication, 18*(2), 40–60. doi:10.1111/jcc4.12001

Hwang, T. (2009). The Iran election on Twitter: The first eighteen days. Retrieved from http://www.webecologyproject.org/wp-content/uploads/2009/08/WEPtwitterFINAL.pdf

King, S. (2016, October 29). Kaepernick's camp cements his status in the black community. Retrieved April 20, 2018, from http://www.nydailynews.com/news/national/king-kaepernick-camp-cements-status-black-community-article-1.2850326

Langlois, G. (2011). Meaning, semiotechnologies and participatory media. *Culture Machine, 12*. Retrieved from http://culturemachine.net/wp-content/uploads/2019/01/7-Meaning-437-890-1-PB.pdf.

Leopold, J & Bell, M.P. (2017). News media and the racialization of protest: an analysis of Black Lives Matter articles. *Equality, Diversity and Inclusion: An International Journal, 36*(8). 720-735, doi:10.1108/EDI-01-2017-0010

McCarthy, M. (2017, November 5). NFL TV numbers' plunge deepens; one major sponsor points finger at Goodell. Retrieved April 20, 2018, from http://www.sportingnews.com/nfl/news/nfl-tv-ratings-cbs-nbc-fox-espn-sponsors-anthem-protests-kaepernick-goodell-papa-johns-schnatter-mnf-tnf-snf/1ev0o829z5cen1qna0rgai7fuw

Meraz, S., & Papacharissi, Z. (2013). Networked gatekeeping and networked framing on #Egypt. *The International Journal of Press/Politics, 18*(2), 138–166. doi:10.1177/1940161212474472

Messina, A.C. (2007, August 26). Groups for Twitter; Or a proposal for Twitter tag channels. Retrieved March 7, 2018, from https://factoryjoe.com/2007/08/25/groups-for-twitter-or-a-proposal-for-twitter-tag-channels/

Milan, S. (2015a). From social movements to cloud protesting: The evolution of collective identity. *Information, Communication & Society, 18*(8), 887-900. Available at SSRN: https://ssrn.com/abstract=2882067

Milan, S. (2015b). When algorithms shape collective action: Social media and the dynamics of cloud protesting. *Social Media & Society, 1*(2). doi: 10.1177/2056305115622481

Million Dollar Pledge. (2018). Retrieved April 20, 2018, from http://kaepernick7.com/million-dollar-pledge/

Nowak, A., Szamrej, J., & Latané, B. (1990). From private attitude to public opinion: A dynamic theory of social impact. *Psychological Review, 97*(3), 362–376. doi:10.1037/0033-295X.97.3.362

Romero, D.M., Tan, C., & Ugander, J. (2013). On the interplay between social and topical structure. In *Proceedings of AAAI International Conference on Weblogs and Social Media*.

Spiro, E.S., & Monroy-Hernández, A. (2016). Shifting stakes: Understanding the dynamic roles of individuals and organizations in social media protests. *PLoS One, 11* (10) doi 10.1371/journal.pone.0165387

Tremayne, M. (2014). Anatomy of a protest in the digital era: A network analysis of twitter and Occupy Wall Street. *Social Movement Studies, 13*, 110-126. doi: 10.1080/14742837.2013.830969.

Wang, R., Liu, W., & Gao, S. (2016) Hashtags and information virality in networked social movement: Examining hashtag co-occurrence patterns. *Online Information Review, 40* (7), 850-866. doi:10.1108/OIR-12-2015-0378

Yang, G. (2016). Narrative agency in hashtag activism: The case of #BlackLivesMatter. *Media and Communication, 4*(4). doi: 10.17645/mac.v4i4.692

FOURTEEN

A Great American Race

Visual Rhetoric in NASCAR's National Anthem Ceremonies

Christina Bullock

INTRODUCTION

Colin Kaepernick's choice to kneel during the national anthem ignited debates beyond the nature of his cause. Publics questioned whether the timing and *location* of his protest were appropriate for a sporting event. The site of the protests—during the playing of the United States National Anthem—was especially unsettling for some, while others were inspired to echo the protests in various settings across the country (Gregory, 2016). Scholars have considered the power of *place* in political protests. Endres and Senda-Cook (2011) assert that location is used as a "rhetorical force" to help demonstrators achieve the goals of social movements (p. 257). This was especially true of the Take-a-Knee movement, where some of America's favorite athletes disrupted a once-unifying time of collective patriotism (Dunst, 2018). Anti-National Football League (NFL) anthem protest campaigns like #StandfortheAnthem on social media ensued, where "protesting athletes decreased viewership and attendance and tarnished [NFL's] multibillion-dollar brand" (Hanson, 2017, para. 4). And, public figures like long-time Pittsburg Steelers fan and politically-conservative radio host Rush Limbaugh refused to attend an NFL game "for the first time in over four decades" (Ernst, 2017, para. 5).

With Kaepernick positioned as the most polarizing figure in the NFL community (Haugh, 2016), audiences naturally turned their attention to media reactions from civic leaders and other large, American athletic leagues. Along with President Donald Trump, one of the most outspoken rebukes of Kaepernick (and other protesting NFL players) came from the legendary NASCAR champion Richard Petty, "Anybody that don't stand up for the anthem ought to be out of the country. Period. What got 'em where they're at? The United States." Petty also confirmed that he would fire any Richard Petty Motorsports team member who protested the anthem (Bieler & Hamilton, 2017).

Petty's decree paid homage to the anthem as a symbol of American identity and heritage—a concept effervescent in NASCAR's history. Since its 1947 inception, the National Association for Stock Car Auto Racing (NASCAR) has risen to become arguably the most popular sport in the United States. With over one thousand races and circuits throughout the world, NASCAR holds roots in the American southern states with headquarters in Daytona Beach, Florida. The sport also boasts humble, family-owned beginnings. This "self-made" story of a single founder with a fierce vision (Bill France, Sr.), passing on a legacy to his sons, turned multimillion dollar industry, is an exemplum of the American dream (Alderink, 2011). In September 2017, media reports covered the numerous NFL-anthem kneeling protests that included individual players and even entire teams that boycotted the field. Bieler and Hamilton (2017) reported that "the scene was much different" at NASCAR races where, "No drivers or other team members were seen demonstrating in any way" (para. 1).

While some have attributed NASCAR's lack of protests to the organization's politically conservative ties (Gibbs, 2016), little academic scholarship exists to address the rhetorical nature of NASCAR's national anthem through symbols of American heritage. The purpose of this study is to examine symbols of nationhood presented in the 2016–2018 national anthem ceremonies of the Daytona 500, also known as the "Great American Race." The chapter is structured as follows: First, it will review literature related to NASCAR's deep-rooted sociocultural and organizational identity in the United States. Next, it will employ a visual rhetorical analysis of televised images of the 2016–2018 Daytona 500 national anthem ceremonies. The last section of the chapter will follow with a discussion of how NASCAR national anthem symbols resonate and reflect the community. Finally, the chapter will follow with a conclusion to discuss implications and opportunities for future research.

NASCAR, SOUTHERN AMERICAN CULTURE AND NATIONAL CITIZENSHIP

Scholars have asserted that NASCAR represents a specific community of "white American cultural citizenship" (Scott, 2013, p.15). This citizenship is rooted in the idea that automobiles are a quintessential facet of American life. "Cars embody, express and enable all the great American values: freedom, mobility, independence, self-sufficiency, status, leisure, control, speed, mastery, sensuality, affluence, power" (Wright, 2002, p. 33). Cars also represent the "quaintly traditional" aspects of American life, which typically portray males as the dominant gender in the American household. Scholars have also explored how auto-mobility literally transports and divides people from place to place, and has established and reaffirmed gendered perceptions of geographical locations like work and home (Scott, 2013, p. 19).

From a historical perspective, researchers assert that the NASCAR community holds several stereotypes based on stock car racing practices in the South and the organization's large following of white male audiences (Hurt, 2005). During 1940s prohibition, alcohol traders would enhance their vehicles to reach high speeds to avoid arrest by authorities (Hagstrom, 2001). This history developed over the years to create an image of the NASCAR community as one that attracts "rednecks," rebels, and the "good ol' boys" (Amato et al., 2005; Johnson, 2001; Lapio & Speter, 2000).

NASCAR Fandom Studies

Scholars have written on the significance of NASCAR to the American sports landscape in comparison to other sports in the United States. Through collective identification and motivation approaches to understanding sports attachment, researchers studied which factors drive fans' identification with NASCAR. Key factors included strong dependencies on national media due to the inability to follow hometown coverage of drivers. This distinguished NASCAR from other sports like professional football that hold "homefield" advantage for teams (Keaton et al., 2015 p. 46). Studies have also found that fans create imagined camaraderie with individual NASCAR athletes based on perceived, shared characteristics such as patriotism (Hugenberg & Hugenberg, 2008). In a survey of nearly one thousand sports fans, results found that NASCAR followers were more likely to have the time and financial resources to attend and travel to nationwide events than in other sports. Fans also reported being motivated to watch races due to the thrill and risk associated with expert skills of individual drivers to reach speeds of nearly 200 mph (p. 47). Little research has been done to study the intersections of the NASCAR community's collective identity perceptions and relevant social and political events. Thus, an analysis of NASCAR's performed symbols of nationhood during the same time frame as the Take-a-Knee anthem protests could help fill gaps in literature related to relevant sport-fan interests and political communication.

NASCAR Symbolism and Organizational Brand

Symbolism within NASCAR plays an integral role in the communication of its southern American identity. Gibbs (2017) writes,

> As sophisticated as NASCAR technology may be these days, it's still very much a sport controlled by flags. The green flag starts the race, the checkered flag ends it. The yellow flag signals caution, the red flag signals a stoppage, and the white flag indicates there's only one lap remaining. Flags are a key component of the fan experience as well. Driving south to the Richmond International Raceway, driver flags line the route — appearing on car windows and mailboxes, outside makeshift roadside RV campgrounds and on the pop-up tents selling unofficial NASCAR merchandise (para.1).

Scholars assert that symbols in sport create a sense of common identity that can be both positive and detrimentally divisive (Eitzen, 2006). Strategic communication researchers have examined the symbols associated with NASCAR, their impact on audiences, and the subsequent benefit for its Fortune 500 sponsors and marketing agencies. Lee et al. (2010) noted that the Confederate flag is a common and significant symbol within the NASCAR brand. The prominence of the flag and its variations at races has caused difficulties for marketing the organization to diverse populations. For many groups, the Confederate flag is a symbol of "hatred, intolerance and racial oppression" (p. 174).

In recent years, response to criticism from NASCAR has been multifaceted diversity campaigns, including programs to increase underrepresented racial groups in the motorsports industry on an international level (p. 175). In February 2018, Darrell "Bubba" Wallace was featured in the media as the first African American to race in the Daytona 500 in nearly fifty years (Mayer, 2018). Research shows that the organization has seen significant growth in participation in NASCAR events from minorities and women (Amato et al., 2005). However, the organization has not made aggressive efforts to ban the Confederate flag at its races or affiliate events, which continues to curtail the organization from rebranding itself as one that is inclusive to all demographics (pp. 175-176).

A small number of communication studies have focused on reputation management efforts of the NASCAR organization and its athletes. Jerome (2008) studied image repair efforts and rhetoric of atonement used by well-known NASCAR athlete Tony Stewart after he physically assaulted a photographer following the 2002 Brickyard 400 race. Bodkin et al. (2009) examined how conflict might act as a catalyst for fans attitudinal commitments to sponsors based on their favored-athlete's endorsements. Research points to the overall NASCAR brand as one with a reputation that "has many favorable image associations (e.g., speed, excitement, success) with which prominent companies . . . desire to connect in order to shape and strengthen their own brand image" (Lee et al., 2010, p. 173).

Rhetorics of Nationhood

This study explores visual rhetoric and symbols of nationhood in the Daytona 500 national anthem ceremonies. Reicher and Hopkins (2001) define nationhood as a socially constructed phenomenon by which individuals gain knowledge through activities and social identity processes. Lauenstein (2013) studied how the metaphor of family (through ideas of fatherland and belonging) is used as a rhetorical device in public mobilization content to include political debates and national anthems (p.1). Scholars have also surveyed the history of rhetorics of nationhood in American advertising from the 1920s, and found that the imagery of commemoration and remembrance is effective in achieving experiences and ideals of a national and ethnic past for audiences (Mayer, 1998).

Rhetorics of nationhood can be found in the communication of some of America's most celebrated political figures. Browne (2002) analyzed rhetoric of nationhood in Thomas Jefferson's first inaugural address which included descriptive language that portrayed the drama of America's nationhood (a victorious revolution). Jefferson also spoke on the experience of citizenship and celebration of freedom, while referencing American traditions and rituals to include sermons, memorials, and debates (pp. 432-436). Building on previous research that echoes the deep heritage and rhetoric of nationhood in America, this study may contribute to knowledge of how present-day NASCAR's visual rhetoric connects with American history.

RHETORICAL ARTIFACTS

The Daytona 500, affectionately known as the "Great American Race" is the most important in the NASCAR Cup Series of motor races. Since its first run in 1959, the event has a legacy of "sizzling non-stop stock car action" (Daytona International, 2008). The Daytona 500 also symbolizes the quintessential American dream. In 2018, the Daytona 500 celebrated its 60th anniversary and *USA Today* honored this achievement through a special, digital publication devoted to NASCAR's track marks in American history. An image of Miss USA Diana Batts is featured kissing Mario Andretti after he won the 1967 Dayton 500 (image 9). Petty, seven-time Daytona 500 champion, is captured with his family, racers are shown wearing paraphernalia from some of America's favorite brands including Budweiser, Tide, and Goodyear. Images of the American flag serve as backdrops to racers in revel of their Great American victories. With over 100,000 fans in attendance each year, the strong modern-day following and historical reputation of the Daytona 500 make the event an ideal source for analyzing the visual rhetoric of NASCAR's national anthem ceremonies.

THEORETICAL FRAMEWORK

Social Identity Theory and Nationhood

This study uses social identity theory (SIT) to inform knowledge about the behaviors and practices of the NASCAR community during its most-coveted sports event of the year. Tajfel and Turner (1979) define groups as collective, with shared social categories, emotional participation, and commonalities of membership (p. 15). Scholars note that "social categorizations are conceived as cognitive tools that segment, classify and order the social environment, and thus enable the individual to undertake many forms of social action." Individuals who hold membership in groups also seek high self-esteem through forming positive ideals of themselves compared to others (p. 16). More specifically, self-categorization asserts that people view themselves as representations of the common values of their larger group memberships (Figueiredo et al., 2014). There are emotional attachments associated with group identity which also includes a sense of group pride (Zuo, 2000).

Scholars have found that one of the strongest forms of social identity is national identification (Huddy & Khatib, 2007; Schatz et al., 1999). Studies across a number of fields have explored how group identities and patriotism intersect. For example, Yang et al. (2014) studied the intersections of national identity and conflict, and found that historical representations of the Japanese influenced China's empathy toward Japan in the aftermath of the 2011 Japanese earthquake (pp. 187-188). Bulmer (2011) examined how groups hold a sense of national pride and identity through interactions with their favored product brand messages. Critical approaches of national identity have explored overt, "uncritical patriotism" where individuals experience positive emotions toward their respective nations despite negative facts, where it's "my country—right or wrong" (Sahar, 2008; Schatz et al., 1999). Researchers have also pointed to the influential power of sports to bring together the overlapping experiences of social identity and nationhood. Sports are enjoyed by people from a diversity of backgrounds and can be utilized to share specific beliefs and perspectives with their audiences (Giulianotti, 1996). To this end, this study seeks to examine the intersections of the NASCAR sports' symbols and definitions of a collective, national identity.

METHODOLOGY

A visual rhetorical approach was utilized to examine televised images from NASCAR's Daytona 500 national anthem ceremonies. Scholars have employed visual rhetorical analysis to better understand how images transmit meanings and influence the perceptions of audiences (Foss, 1994; Foss, 2005). The rhetorical approach to studying images has extended to knowledge of public phenomena such as memorials (Foss, 1986), advertising (Kaplan, 1990), movies and editorial photography (Vinson, 2012). Foss (1994) asserts that rhetorical judgments of images must be based on the function of the images to determine what is communicated to collective audiences (pp. 215-216). There are three components to analyzing images from a rhetorical perspective to include: (a) identification of the function(s) communicated by the image, (b) assessment of how well the function(s) is communicated and the support available for that function, and (c) critique of the legitimacy of the function of the images (pp. 217-218). The research questions were as follows:

RQ1: What are the primary images presented during the televised, 2016–2018 Daytona 500 national anthem ceremonies?

RQ2: How do televised images of the 2016–2018 Daytona 500 national anthem ceremonies function to communicate symbols of nationhood?

Primary data for analysis were three recordings of the Daytona 500 national anthem ceremonies found on Youtube.com, originally televised on FOX Sports channel. To closely align the data with the years of the ongoing NFL national anthem protests, the researcher selected to examine the Daytona 500 national anthem ceremonies from the February 21, 2016, February 26, 2017, and February 18, 2018, events. It is important to note that the 2016 Daytona 500 took place before Kaepernick's protests. The 2017 race was after the protests, but preceded Trump's and Petty's public criticism of the protests. The 2018 Daytona 500 was held at the height of the national anthem protests. To analyze the data, images were carefully reviewed in each frame of the ceremonies and coded based on the images' function pertinent to the research questions (using the approach to codable data as outlined by Foss & Waters, 2007). Afterward, the coded images were categorized, and evaluated based on whether the images accomplished their function within the larger context of the national anthem ceremonies.

IMAGES IN THE 2016–2018 DAYTONA 500 NATIONAL ANTHEM CEREMONIES

The first research question sought to identify the primary images used within the 2016-2018 Daytona 500 national anthem ceremonies. This section will identify the imagery presented, the characteristics and features of the televised images.

The United States Armed Forces

Images and representations of the United States (U.S.) Armed Forces appeared throughout the national anthem ceremonies first in the form of men and women in military uniform. In the 2016 Daytona 500, the United States color guard leads the ceremony and nineteen service men and women from the 82nd Airborne Division of Fort Bragg stand in full, matching uniforms to sing the national anthem (:03). A line of men wearing white uniforms (recognizably Navy service uniforms) are shown standing at attention with their arms raised in salute to the United States flag (:03).

Similar images are displayed in the 2017 Daytona 500, where the color guard is pictured holding flags, sabres, and rifles behind Jordin Sparks (multiplatinum American recording artist) who sang her rendition of the national anthem (:07). Along with the U.S. color guard, the sixteen members of the U.S. Navy Band Southeast stood at attention to play the national anthem at the 2018 Daytona 500 (:39, 1:27). Pictured high in the blue sky after the 2016-2018 Daytona 500 national anthem ceremonies were the U.S. Air Force Thunderbirds performing aerobatic formations over the Daytona International Speedway (2016, 1:06; 2017, 1:31; 2018, 2:24, 2:41). Other representations of the armed forces included race spectators with their arms raised, saluting during the anthem (2016, :26), and a woman holding a child with a military camouflage hat in her right hand pressed against her chest, near her heart (2018, 1.53).

The United States Flag

Each national anthem ceremony depicted the American flag waving in the wind with a blue sky, trees, and the sun in the background (2016, :15, :53; 2017, :36, 1:13; 2018, :09). The American flag is also pictured waving in the distance behind the 82nd Airborne Division of Fort Bragg (2016, :03), while Jordin Sparks sings the anthem (2017, :07) and as the U.S. Navy Band Southeast plays the anthem (2018, 1:27). The color guards prominently hold the U.S. flag during the 2017 and 2018 events for the duration of the anthem (2016, 2017, :07; 2018, :39). It is important to note that for the 2018 event, the American flag was shown at half-staff (:09).

Families

Images of families are frequent throughout the anthem ceremonies. For example, all the events featured images of male drivers in their respective athletic uniforms, standing next to their race cars very close to women (dressed in formal wear) while holding children (2016, :04, :12, :20, :39, :43, :56, 1:02, 1:17; 2017, :23, 1:19, 1:27; 2018, 1:38, 1:53, 2:27, 2:52, 2:54). These images were interpreted as marriage relationships. The 2018 event showed several depictions of public displays of affection between drivers and their families. After the anthem, a driver kisses a woman (assumed to be his wife as a ring is shown on her left ring finger) and an infant child, and another driver in uniform kisses a young child (presumed to be his daughter) before walking to his race car after the anthem (2:52, 2:54). A similar interaction is depicted in the 2016 Daytona 500, when a driver, holding a child, gets a young girl's attention to view the Thunderbirds, and another driver kisses what appears to be his family at the end of the anthem (2016, 1:02, 1:17).

Reverence

Images of people performing gestures of reverence and allegiance are shown throughout the 2016–2018 Daytona 500 national anthem ceremonies. The first image of NASCAR drivers during the anthem segment is of a driver and what appears to be his family with their hands over their hearts (2016, :04). In the 2017 event, a driver holds his hand over his heart as a child, who appears to be his son, sits on his father's shoulders (1:27). Fans are captured removing their hats and placing them over their hearts before the anthem begins at the 2018 run (:39). Other images of reverence include the salute, which is a gesture made by Navy servicemen (2016, :03), fans in the stands (2016, :26) and viewed as the director of the U.S. Navy Band turns, faces the direction of the camera, and salutes as the Thunderbirds fly over the Daytona International Speedway (2018, 2:52). The beginning of the 2018 national anthem ceremony featured a special invocation and prayer in which drivers and fans are seen with bowed heads and closed eyes (:54, 1:13), but they did not kneel.

SYMBOLS OF NATIONHOOD

The second research question sought to explore how the televised national anthem images worked in concert with one another to create visual symbols of nationhood in the larger context. This section will explore the strength and legitimacy of the imagery (outlined by Foss, 1994) to better understand how the function of the images accomplished this purpose.

United States Armed Forces: Protecting NASCAR Nation's Families

Images of the U.S. Armed Forces contributed to an overall visual rhetoric of nationhood through symbols of military protection. In the 2016 run, the nineteen service men and women of the 82nd Airborne Division stand with an American flag waving in the background. The lofty, mounted signage reading "Daytona International Speedway" serves as a backdrop in full view for the audience (:03). This imagery created a strong association between the U.S. military and the NASCAR brand. The anticipated Daytona 500 Air Force Thunderbird flyover after the anthem was impeccably staged with the vocalized lyrics, "Oh say does that star-spangled banner yet wave. O'er the land of the free, and the home of the brave?" (2017, 1:54). These images follow with drivers and their families smiling and embracing (2016, 1:02, 1:17; 2018, 2:52, 2.54). The Thunderbird "fighter jets" literally soar above the event and cover the people. (2016, 1:06; 2017,1:31; 2018; 2:24, 2:41) This image functions as a symbol of the U.S. military as a shield and defense of freedom for the NASCAR nation.

As discussed in the first section of the results, many images of drivers and their families were captured during the national anthem ceremonies. Perhaps one of the most compelling images creates a message of rich filial ties between the armed forces, drivers' families, and the sport itself. In the 2016 ceremony, Marines stand in a single-file line with their arms raised saluting the flag. At the end of the line is a driver, with his hand over his heart, standing next to his race car, wife, and three young children (:08). The camera shifts from images of stately Naval officers, to the playful innocence of children and the flash of a yellow, powerful race car. The image of the Naval officers in formation leading down to the drivers' family, functions to position the U.S. military as a line of defense and protection for the NASCAR family and athlete.

The United States Flag: Strength and Memorial

The American flag was used throughout the national anthem ceremonies to function as a symbol of strength and commemoration. This is evidenced in the prominence of the American flag in the 2017 ceremony when Jordin Sparks sings, "Whose broad stripes and bright stars through the perilous fight" and "The rockets' red glare, the bombs bursting in air, gave proof through the night that our flag was still there" (2017, :36, 1:12). The waving flag (positioned with background imagery of a blue sky and green land) is elevated as a reminder of the nation's resilient history. Images of the flag were particularly effective in the 2018 ceremony, where a special prayer and invocation were given to remember the young students and faculty who tragically lost their lives in a high school shooting on February 14, 2018, in Parkland, Florida. A flag waves at half-staff in their memories, and the announcer solemnly declares, "Every victim will always be remembered as individuals, and as part of our American family. We think of them and their families today" (.09).

Reverence: Unifying Pride in a Nation

Images and representations of reverence during the national anthem ceremonies function to create symbols of unified pride in a nation. People of all ages are shown reverencing the country. For example, a multitude of NASCAR fans are seen in the audience with their hands and hats placed over their hearts looking toward the American flag (2016, :30). In the 2017 ceremony, drivers and their families stand with their hands over their hearts as Sparks sings, "What so proudly we hailed at the twilight's last gleaming" (:29). A female driver is shown with an elderly man and woman looking toward the flag with their hands over their hearts (2016, 1:04). Multiple individuals were visually identifiable as people of color within the national anthem images to include the vocalist Jordin Sparks and military officers in the 82nd Airborne Division of Fort Bragg and Navy Band Southeast. A driver and his father stand with their hands over their hearts immediately after the American flag is seen waving while Sparks sings, "Gave proof through the night, that our flag was still there" (2017, 1:19). Images of people from a diversity of backgrounds create a sense of pride and unifying representations of respect and reverence for the nation.

DISCUSSION

This study contributes to knowledge in the field about the NASCAR community and its identity-related experiences of national citizenship. Echoing the work of Wright (2002), the research sheds light on the importance of the automobile to NASCAR culture and American life. This is achieved through visual-rhetorical images of race cars parked alongside U.S. military service people, NASCAR drivers, and their families. While research on NASCAR's cultural stereotypes of "rednecks" and "good ol' boys" (Amato et al., 2005; Johnson, 2001; Lapio & Speter, 2000) has presented the many negative, social-identity categorizations of the sport and its fans, the Daytona 500 national anthem ceremonies reveal a communal system of meaning driven by the NASCAR community's deep-connection to its American heritage.

Images of nationhood are performed in the Daytona 500 national anthem ceremonies through imagery representations of collective identity and pride. Despite the growing popularity of the Take-a-Knee protests between 2016 and 2018, the study shows that NASCAR's visual rhetorics of patriotism and nationhood remained steadfast. The findings confirm the value of analyzing sports events to gain insights into a community's social identity practices and experiences. While the vast majority of televised images of people could be visually identified as white males, the camera focused on a female driver at all the ceremonies. The presence of a woman-vocalist of color and military officers of color in the 2017 and 2018 runs, along with images of people of all ages seem to confirm Amato et al.'s (2005) position that the NASCAR organization has turned its attention to issues of diversity. Through activities such as bowing one's head in prayer, placing a hand over the heart, and saluting, common behaviors create representations of a unified nationhood that seem to visually transcend differences.

There was a strong presence of children and families throughout the national anthem imagery. This finding extends knowledge of how the NASCAR community tradition asserts nationhood through what Lauenstein (2013) references as "fatherland" and "belonging" in a group's social-identity processes. The American flag is prominently featured during a prayer to commemorate the tragic loss of innocent children in a school shooting—an image of remembrance and respect for a nation's past. These findings suggest an emotional attachment to representations of country, and seem to add arguable legitimacy to the opposition to any notion of protest or disrespect during NASCAR's sacred time of memorial.

CONCLUSION

With heavy media coverage of several NFL athletes' Take-a-Knee protests during the national anthem at competitive events, this study was inspired to gain insights into the visual rhetoric of national anthem ceremonies of another popular American sport—NASCAR. Many of the televised images presented in NASCAR's 2016–2018 Daytona 500 national anthem ceremonies functioned to communicate symbols of nationhood. Depictions of the United States Armed Forces created images of protection and defense of a nation, and more specifically, the NASCAR family. Images of the American flag breathed strength of country, memorialized the past, and commemorated victims of tragedy.

A tremendous respect for the national anthem itself is visually performed by NASCAR community members during the Daytona 500 anthem ceremonies. Images from the ceremonies also reflect the core thrusts of the #StandfortheAnthem movement, where ideals of a unified nation were elevated through devotion to honoring the flag and military. Reverent rituals portrayed through gestures of prayer, salute, and respect, bonded the NASCAR community to a collective identity of patriotic pride in the nation. This chapter contributes rhetorical knowledge to the study of the NASCAR community through the political lens of the national anthem and has implications for visual, political, and sports communication scholars.

A plethora of factors contribute to a community's identity beyond images and practices in public ceremonies. While NASCAR's Daytona 500 anthem ceremonies serve as significant and relevant events for data analysis, future studies might consider a wider data set to include national anthem ceremonies at other NASCAR Cup Series events. Future scholarship might also perform a visual rhetorical comparative analysis of ceremonies from a variety of American and international sports events and industries. This study reviewed only the FOX televised images of the Daytona 500 national anthems, but was limited in its perspective based on the channel that aired the event. As 2018 marks the sixtieth anniversary of the running of the Great American Race (and seventieth anniversary of the larger organization), more studies should consider the communicative aspects of NASCAR's social, cultural, and technological achievements.

REFERENCES

2016 Daytona 500 National Anthem. (2016, February 21). Retrieved from https://www.youtube.com/watch?v=eVvKQ26Ogs8

2017 Daytona 500 National Anthem. (2017, February 26). Retrieved from https://www.youtube.com/watch?v=3cfsc2oUYpU

2018 Daytona 500 National Anthem. (2018, February 18). Retrieved from https://www.youtube.com/watch?v=B6sWF9YJmf8

Alderink, Kiley. (2011). All About NASCAR. Retrieved from http://www.shavemagazine.com/cars/090601.

Amato, C. H., Peters, C. L. O., & Shao, A.T . (2005). An exploratory investigation into NASCAR fan culture. *Sport Marketing Quarterly, 14*, 71-83.

Bieler, D., & Hamilton, T. (2017, September 25). Richard Petty, other NASCAR owners decry protests, but Dale Earnhardt Jr. offers support. *The Washington Post.*

Bodkin, C. D., Amato, C., & Peters, C. (2009). The role of conflict, culture, and myth in creating attitudinal commitment. *Journal of Business Research, 62*(10), 1013-1019. doi:10.1016/j.jbusres.2008.05.005

Browne, S. H. (2002). "The circle of our felicities": Thomas Jefferson's first inaugural address and the rhetoric of nationhood. *Rhetoric & Public Affairs, 5*(3), 409-438. doi:10.1353/rap.2002.0050

Bulmer, S. (2011). How do Brands Affect National Identity? (Doctoral dissertation, The University of Auckland. 1-361.

Daytona International Speedway. (2008). Retrieved from http://www.daytonainternationalspeedway.com/images/DIS_DUSA%20SALES%20KIT%2008.pdf

Dunst, C. (2018, January 10). Colin Kaepernick makes us uncomfortable because he disrupts an American fantasy. *International Business Times.* Retrieved from http://www.ibtimes.com/colin-kaepernick-makes-us-uncomfortable-because-he-disrupts-american-fantasy-2639782

Endres, D., & Senda-Cook, S. (2011). Location matters: The rhetoric of place in protest. *Quarterly Journal of Speech, 97*(3), 257-282. doi:10.1080/00335630.2011.585167

Eitzen, D. S. (2006). *Fair and foul: Beyond the myths and paradoxes of sport* (3rd ed.). Lanham, MD: Rowman & Littlefield Publishing Group.

Ernst, D. (25 September 17). Limbaugh mocks NFL national anthem protests: "There's no way Donald Trump loses this." *The Washington Times*. Retrieved from https://www.washingtontimes.com/news/2017/sep/25/rush-limbaugh-mocks-nfl-national-anthem-protests-t/

Figueiredo, A., Valentim, J., & Doosje, B. (2014). *Theories on intergroup relations and emotions: A theoretical overview*. Coimbra: Imprensa da Universidade de Coimbra. http://dx.doi.org/10.14195/1647-8606_57 -2_3

Foss, S., and Waters, W. (2007). *Destination dissertation: a travelers guide to a done dissertation*. Lanham, MD: Rowman and Littlefield Publishers.

Foss, S.K. (1986). Ambiguity as persuasion: The Vietnam Veterans Memorial. *Communication Quarterly, 34*, 326-340.

Foss, S. K. (1994). A rhetorical schema for the evaluation of visual imagery. *Communication Studies, 45*(3-4), 213-224. doi:10.1080/10510979409368425

Foss, S. K. (2005). Theory of Visual Rhetoric. In *Handbook of Visual Communication: Theory, Methods, and Media*, K. Smith, S. Moriarty, G. Barbatsis, & K. (Eds.). New York: Routledge.

Frentz, T.S., & Rushing, J.H. (1993). Integrating ideology and archetype in rhetorical criticism, part II: A case study of *Jaws*. *Quarterly Journal of Speech, 79*, 61-81.

Gibbs, L. (2016, November 3). NASCAR's quest to separate the heritage from the hate. *Think Progress*. Retrieved from https://thinkprogress.org/nascars-quest-to-separate-the-heritage-from-the-hate-59c96fa0b266/

Gibbs, L. (2017, November 17). NASCAR provides the ultimate proof that the NFL's rating decline isn't because of politics. *ThinkProgress*. Retrieved from https://thinkprogress.org/nascar-provides-the-ultimate-proof-that-the-nfls-rating-decline-isnt-because-of-politics-8825ba535701/

Giulianotti, R. (1996). Back to the future: An ethnography of Ireland's football fans at the 1994 World Cup finals in the USA. *International Review for the Sociology of Sport, 31*(3), 323-344.

Golenbock, P. (1993). *American zoom: Stock car racing from the dirt tracks to Daytona*. New York: Macmillan.

Gregory, S. (2016, September 22). All Across the Country, Athletes Are Fueling a Debate about How America Defines Patriotism. *TIME*. Retrieved from http://time.com/4504023/athletes-america-patriotism/

Hagstrom, R. G. (2001). *The NASCAR way: The business that drives the sport*. New York: John Wiley & Sons, Inc.

Hanson, V. (2017, October 17). Status Quo Blues. *National Review*. Retrieved from https://www.nationalreview.com/2017/10/status-quo-mainstream-institutions-are-failing-public-turns-away/

Haugh, D. (2016, December 2). Colin Kaepernick a compelling figure, no matter where you stand on his message. *Chicago Tribune*. Retrieved from http://www.chicagotribune.com/sports/columnists/ct-colin-kaepernick-anthem-protest-haugh-spt-1204-20161203-column.html

History of the Daytona 500 (2018). Retrieved from https://www.usatoday.com/picture-gallery/sports/nascar/2013/02/14/history-of-the-daytona-500/1913949/

Huddy, L., & Khatib, N. (2007). American patriotism, national identity, and political involvement. *American Journal of Political Science, 51*(1), 63–77. doi:10.1111/j.1540-5907.2007.00237.x

Hugenberg, L. W., & Hugenberg, B. S. (2008). If it ain't rubbin', it ain't racin': NASCAR, American values, and fandom. *The Journal of Popular Culture, 41*(4), 635-657. 10.1111/j.1540-5931.2008.00540.x.

Hurt, D. A. (2005). Dialed in? Geographic expansion and regional identity in NASCAR's Nextel Cup Series. *Southeastern Geographer, 45*, 120-137.

Jerome, A. M. (2008). Toward prescription: Testing the rhetoric of atonement's applicability in the athletic arena. *Public Relations Review, 34*(2), 124-134. doi:10.1016/j.pubrev.2008.03.007

Johnson, K. (2001). Forget football. *American Demographics, 23,* 34-37. Retrieved from http://adage.com/article/american-demographics/forget-football/42224. August 8, 2015.

Kaplan, S.J. (1990). Visual metaphors in the representation of communication technology. *Critical Studies in Mass Communication, 7,* 37-47.

Keaton, S. A., Watanabe, N. M., & Gearhart, C. C. (2015). A comparison of college football and NASCAR consumer profiles: Identity formation and spectatorship motivation. *Sport Marketing Quarterly, 24*(1), 43, 55

Lapio, Jr., R., & Speter, K. M. (2000). NASCAR: A lesson in integrated and relationship marketing. *Sport Marketing Quarterly, 9,* 85-95.

Lauenstein, O. (2013). *From family metaphor to national attachment? a social identity approach towards framing nationhood* (Master's thesis, Saint Andrews University). St. Andrews Research Repository. doi:http://hdl.handle.net/10023/3627

Lee, J. W., Bernthal, M. J., Whisenant, W. A., & Mullane, S. (2010). NASCAR: Checkered flags are not all that are being waved. *Sport Marketing Quarterly, 19*(3), 170.

Levin, A. M., Beasley, F., & Gamble, T. (2004). Brand loyalty of NASCAR fans towards sponsors: The impact of fan identification. *International Journal of Sports Marketing & Sponsorship, 6*(1), 11-21.

Mayer, M. (2018, February 18). 'Bubba' Wallace to be first African-American driver at Daytona 500 in nearly 50 years. *CBS Sports.* Retrieved from https://www.cbssports.com/general/news/bubba-wallace-to-be-first-african-american-driver-at-daytona-500-in-nearly-50-years/

Mayer, R. (1998). 'Taste it!' American advertising, ethnicity, and the rhetoric of nationhood in the 1920s. *Amerikastudien/American Studies, 43*(1), 131.

Pierce, D. S., & Jackson, H. H. (2012). NASCAR vs. football: Which sport is more important to the South? *Southern Cultures, 18*(4), 26-42. doi:10.1353/scu.2012.0034

Reicher, S., & Hopkins. (2001). *Self and nation: Categorisation, contestation and mobilization.* London: Sage.

Sahar, G. (2008). Patriotism, attributions for the 9/11 attacks, and support for war: Then and now. *Basic and Applied Social Psychology, 30*(3), 189–197. doi:10.1080/01973530802374956

Schatz, R. T., Staub, E., & Lavine, H. (1999). On the varieties of national attachment: Blind versus constructive patriotism. *Political Psychology, 20*(1), 151–174. doi:10.1111/0162-895X.00140

Scott, R. R. (2013). Environmental affects: NASCAR, place and white American cultural citizenship. *Social Identities, 19*(1), 13-31. 10.1080/13504630.2012.753342.

Tajfel, H. & J. C. Turner (1979), "An Integrative Theory of Intergroup Conflict," in *The Social Psychology of Intergroup Relations,* W. G. Austin & S. Worchel, (Eds.). Monterey, CA: Brooks/Cole, pp. 33-47.

Turner, J. C., M. A. Hogg, P. J. Oakes, S. D. Reicher, & M. S. Wetherell (1987). *Rediscovering the Social Group: A Self-Categorization Theory.* Cambridge, MA: Blackwell.

Vinson, J. (2012). Covering national concerns about teenage pregnancy: A visual rhetorical analysis of images of pregnant and mothering women. *Feminist Formations, 24*(2), 140-162. doi:10.1353/ff.2012.0017

Wright, J. (2002). *Fixin' to git: One fan's love affair with NASCAR's Winston Cup.* Durham, NC: Duke University Press.

Zuo, Bin (2000), "On the Children's Acquisition of a National Identity." *Educational Research and Experiment, 2,* 33-37.

FIFTEEN

Articulating Christianity and Patriotism

Identifying a Hermeneutical Impasse through Emerging Meanings

Brian Mattson and Andrew Phillips

What does Christianity have to do with patriotism? Those who claim Christianity make up a large portion of the American populace and have participated in important ways throughout the history of the United States. In fact, the United States has come to be known as a "Christian nation." Because Christians have had a bold impact upon American society, it is important to understand how Christians in America have understood the national anthem protest. The Colin Kaepernick national anthem protest originally attempted to draw attention to apparent social injustices in American society. According to historic Christianity, justice and mercy have always served as outward signs of one's commitment to the Christian faith. However, the anthem protest sparked an apparent seismic shift in Christian practice toward calling attention to patriotism rather than religious ideals. In this chapter, the researchers explore how various secular and religious outlets frame Christianity within the national anthem protest debate. The study draws upon articulation theory and content/frame analysis to discover how Christianity and patriotism are linked in news outlets. Four primary articulations employed by Christians—ceremonial, moral obligation, American sacramentalism, and activist ideology—are analyzed. These four articulations point to a deeper hermeneutical problem that seeks to explain the meaning of a nation as an entity or as individuals. In response to the hermeneutical impasse present among Christians concerning the Take-a-Knee protests, this chapter will present a return to neighborliness and Christian anarchy as viable options to move forward.

CHRISTIANITY AND PATRIOTISM

Scholars have demonstrated interest in the link between religion and patriotism. Bellah (1967) and Marvin (2002) identify this link as national civil religion. In this view, the nation serves as a transcendent "god" and the constitution, flag, and national anthem all serve as symbols of the national god (Perry & Kang, 2012; Hariman & Lucaites, 2002). These symbols, as well as the nation's military are often presented in what Burke (1984) called tragic framing. Butterworth (2013) illustrated how tragic framing applied to sports media coverage of Tim Tebow, a Christian. The media often spoke of Tebow in tragic frames, or absolutes, which pointed to hero language. He was often referred to as "*the* miracle" or "*the* one." In the same way, national civic religion, or patriotism, will refer to the nation's symbols as "*the* flag," "*the* anthem," or "*the* military." Forst (2017) and Hafen (2009) concluded that this kind of framing is an act of "hegemonic civility" (Forst, p. 4). According to Hafen (2009), this hegemonic civility begins in the elementary school as an attempt to indoctrinate its citizens into the national civil religion.

During 1980-2000, a study showed Christians displayed minimal patriotism (Kerr, 2003), but in a post-9/11 America a rhetorical shift from a "rhetoric of freedom" to a "rhetoric of patriotism" emerged (Hafen, 2009, p. 62). According to Hafen, the rhetoric of patriotism is often laced with racism and xenophobia: "When patriotic/nationalisic fervor is aroused, the question of citizenry arises, which is less a legal issue than a question of who shares a shared or dominant sense of national identity" (p. 64). In other words, the national narrative provides a sense of identity to the masses and problems arise when there is a challenge to the national narrative of civil religion.

Contrary to the civil religion perspective, Ellul (2011) coined the idea of "Christian anarchy" as a way to think about the relationship between the Christian and the government. He challenged Christians to assess to whom their true allegiance and respect is given: to God or to government. Ellul suggested that the way Christians can break through the hegemonic grip of government is through the recovery of neighborliness. Neighborliness creates an environment where people can connect with each other despite governmental powers (Ellul, 1989). This aligns with one of the central tenets of Christianity, which urges Christians to "love your neighbor as yourself" (Matthew 22:34-40).

Articulation Theory

While articulation theory has its origins in sociology, communication scholars have found it useful because it assigns meaning to elements of communication. Articulation theory contends that a term, phrase, or other element of communication derives its meaning from the context instead of the thing itself. DeLuca applies articulation theory to discourse, stating that discursive elements do not discover meaning in a discourse but instead create shared meaning (1999). There are structural constraints that form boundaries for articulation theory, however, so that the assigning of meaning is not completely subjective (Curtin, 2016).

Articulation theory has been used to examine media response to major decisions. Whether it is the media response to a government decision (Kumar, 2014), or an examination of political activism (Bishop, 2015), it is a useful grid for understanding varying perspectives. While he does not specifically cite articulation theory, Anderson highlights different interpretations of key phrases in the Black Lives Matter movement, describing them as "hermeneutical impasses" (2017).

Articulation theory has been useful in examining the contrasting ideological perspectives on previous communication events. The theory of articulation both shows how "ideological elements come, under certain conditions, to cohere together within a discourse, and . . . how they do or do not become articulated, at specific conjectures, to certain political subjects (Hall, 1986, p. 53).

Hanczor explored the role of articulation theory in controversy analysis, specifically examining the responses to graphic content in the television series *NYPD Blue*, which debuted in 1993 (1997). Here, he also identified a confluence of religion and politics, noting the way conservative policians and religious leaders both conceptualized elements of the show as a challenge to morality. As a result, the perception grew that the ideological forces of political conservatives and Christians had always been linked on this issue.

Does articulation theory, when applied to Christian responses to the Take-a-Knee movement, show a confluence of Christian faith and patriotism, in a way similar to Hanczor's discovery? Christian responses will be examined to discover what articulations are used. A communicator, in this case a Christian, makes conscious or unconscious decisions about which articulations, or frames, to select (Sitten, 2011). Frames can exert a great deal of power, and when a frame is used often enough, it can influence other communicators to use it in an effort to avoid misunderstanding (Kerr & Moy, 2002).

The unique contribution this research will make is the examination of the linkage between "Christianity" and "patriotism." DeLuca (1999) suggested that "though elements preexist articulation as floating signifiers, the act of linking in a particular discourse modifies their character such that they can be spoken of anew" (p. 335). In other words, the link between "Christianity" and "patriotism" allows the two terms to become conjoined and formulate a new meaning. Through the examination of Christians in media frames, this research sets out to explain the new meanings that are produced by conjoining "Christianity" and "patriotism."

RESEARCH METHOD

Through Lexis-Nexis searches and simple Google searches, the researchers set out to discover the ways that Christians articulated Christianity and patriotism in the media in relation to the National Football League (NFL) anthem kneeling controversy.

Parameters

The study was limited to television, print, internet news, and blogs with the following parameters for consideration:

1. Any article or news segment that was printed, posted, or broadcast through television, print, internet news, and blog mediums.
2. Any reprinted article was rejected, only the original article was accepted and evaluated.
3. The person interviewed or who posted identified and represented the Christian (Mainline Protestant, Evangelical, or Roman Catholic) community. In the case of blogs, there was a clear connection between the author and Christianity (e.g., a church blog with the pastor as the blog author).

The researchers excluded Mormon commentators from the research due to theological differences that were deemed significant enough to potentially muddle interpretation of the findings.

Coding Definitions and Rules

Unit of Measurement

The unit of measurement consisted of the response of a Christian interviewee within a given article or broadcast. The interviewee claimed to be a Christian or identified as one who works in a Christian vocation (i.e., pastor, priest). In order to be evaluated, the statements for the Christian personality had to be a direct quote for both the print or broadcast segment, or an entry on a blog written by the Christian personality. Each Christian personality in an article/segment who was quoted was assigned their own separate coding sheet in order to analyze the articulations they present. The research will also analyze the following: type of news organization, articulations, interviewee position, and Christianity type.

Types of News Organization

This chapter employs three categories to determine the type of news organization providing the Christian interview: Left-leaning (liberal), Right-leaning (conservative), and Christian. In order to determine the political leanings of the news organization, the researcher consulted www.mediabiasfactcheck.com, a comprehensive website that identifies such leanings.

Articulations

This chapter is interested in the new meaning that emerges when Christians frame the terms "Christianity" and "patriotism" together. Bellah (1967) explored what he called "American civil religion" and how it was presented in light of presidential speeches. His research yielded three helpful frames: ceremonial, moral obligation, and American sacramentalism. He determined these frames through the evaluation of the juxtaposition of the term "God" with citizenship. In addition to Bellah's frames, this research will employ the frames of "activist ideology" and "other" as it seeks to understand the emerging articulation of Christianity and patriotism. These frames reflect the emerging meaning in the articulation of Christianity and patriotism.

Ceremonial

Articles that link Christianity and patriotism directly to the ceremonial aspects of public life. The ceremonial aspects of public life include standing for the national anthem, pledging allegiance to the flag, taking of public oaths. In other words, the person being interviewed emphasizes the ceremonial significance of Christianity and patriotism. Direct mention of respect for the flag, anthem, or military would indicate this category.

Moral Obligation

Bellah suggested that this category be used when speakers refer to one's duty to carry out God's plan or obedience to the State (p. 44). For instance, this may show up when a Christian emphasizes that Christians display their commitment to God by supporting or obeying the State. Advocates of this perspective often cite Paul's description of human authority being established by God in Romans 13. If God established national authority, then disrespect of that authority is disrespect of God.

American Sacramentalism

A sacramental frame emphasizes someone's death in order to provide freedoms for another person. It emphasizes honor to those who have died, "the war dead," in service to their country. Perhaps, it appears in terms of "oughtness" (Bellah, 1967, pp. 48-49). The juxtaposition of Christianity and patriotism becomes then an expression of honor or remembrance of sacrifice made by others.

Activist Ideology

A final frame that this chapter will identify is what we are calling "activist ideology." It suggests that a person is most Christian and most patriotic when citizens are looking out for the rights of others. The interviewee expressed a desire to right perceived injustices.

Articulations that do not align with the categories identified above will be labelled "other." If there are numerous categories labelled "other" the researchers will investigate further in order to discover new, emerging categories.

In the event that an interviewee or author refers to more than one expression of Christianity and patriotism, then the coder will count the number of expressions to which the interviewee refers. These will be counted as separate frames within the article/segment. Coders will determine primary and secondary frames by notating the number of sentences dedicated to a particular articulation. Primary frames will have the most sentences with secondary frames having fewer sentences.

Types of Christian Representation

This chapter is not only interested in how Christians articulate a new meaning of Christianity when combined with patriotism but also in how various expressions of Christianity articulate the meaning of Christianity and patriotism. The evaluation will not only evaluate the position the interviewee holds but also the kind of Christianity the individual represents. In the United States there are three primary representations of Christianity: Evangelical, Mainline Protestant, and Roman Catholic. Other groups exist, but these three represent the majority of Christian expressions in the United States. There are two ways to determine to which group an interviewee belongs: (1) identification in the article/segment; or (2) an internet search about the interviewee.

Mainline Protestantism

Bradshaw (2014) explained that Mainline Protestantism is represented by the following groups: United Methodist Churches, Evangelical Lutheran Churches, Presbyterian Churches of America, Episcopal

Churches, American Baptist Churches, United Church of Christ, and Christian Churches (Disciples of Christ). These types of Christian organizations tend to emphasize social activism and social issues regardless of congregational ethnicity. Politically, they tend toward left-leaning and Democratic policies.

Evangelical

According to the National Association of Evangelicals (NAE), Evangelical denominations tend to emphasize and adhere to four core philosophies (2018). The first core philosophy teaches the importance of conversionism. In this sense, Evangelicals believe that lives need to be changed through the proclamation of the Gospel in order for real societal change to take place. This leads into the second core philosophy which is called "Gospel activism" which often is expressed through missionary efforts by adherents. The third emphasis in Evangelicalism is a strong stance on "Biblicism." For Evangelicals, the Bible stands as the ultimate authority not only in the church but also in a Christian's life. Finally, Evangelicals emphasize the sacrifice of Jesus as the means for the redemption of humanity. Politically, Evangelicals tend toward conservative and Republican ideals. Typically, denominations that do not belong to the Mainline Protestants are lumped into the Evangelical category. However, Southern Baptist Churches, non-denominational churches, and many Christian Reformed Churches would be considered among the largest adherents to Evangelicalism. Smaller denominations such as those with Charismatic and Pentecostal leanings would also be considered Evangelical.

Roman Catholicism

With over 1 billion adherents worldwide, Catholics within the United States represent a major voice in the American religious landscape.

In the case where multiple Christians appear in an interview, such as a panel discussion, each interviewee or panel member would count as a separate unit of measure within the article/segment.

Intercoder Reliability

The researchers conducted a test to determine intercoder reliability. Fifteen articles were chosen at random and two researchers, both doctoral students, explored the articulations in the articles. The researchers reached high reliability (Krippendorf *Alpha* = .85) on assigning articles to the same subject frame.

FINDINGS

Through Lexis-Nexis searches and simple Google searches, 130 Christian representatives were identified in various articles, transcripts, and blog posts. The following search terms were used in various combinations in Lexis-Nexis searches, including a few names of well-known ministers: "pastor," "take a knee," "Evangelical," "patriotism," "Kaepernick," "Christianity," "respect," "flag," "NFL," "controversy," "interview," "anthem," "Pat Robertson," "Robert Jeffress," and "T.D. Jakes." To discover blog posts from various churches, the terms "Kaepernick," "NFL," "kneeling," and "national anthem" were used in conjunction with the names of various churches, such as "Catholic," "Presbyterian," "Methodist," "Episcopal," "Baptist," "Church of Christ," and "Christian church." All articles or blogs that fit the parameters from any of these searches were included in the data to be analyzed.

Christian Articulations

The researchers found 130 artifacts which consisted of 28.5 percent ceremonial, 6.9 percent moral obligation, 10.8 percent American sacramentalism, 44.6 percent activist ideology, and 9.2 percent other. Ceremonial articulations often included Christians reminding others of the meaning of the flag or urging the audience to respect the troops by standing. One NFL player, Cyrus Kouandjio, exhibited the ceremonial articulation when he said, " I'm a Christian, and I feel like the forefathers of this country built it around spiritual values—Christian values like freedom, liberty, and the pursuit of happiness, and I'm just glad to be part of it. . . . I can't kneel during the anthem. I don't blame Colin Kaepernick for doing what he did. But for me, I have too much respect for a flag and anthem that represent freedom and liberty" (Breitbart Sports, 2016).

Robert Jeffress, an Evangelical pastor, offered another articulation of the ceremonial perspective in comments on a broadcast of *Fox and Friends* (Chiquillo, 2017). While appealing specifically to Christian NFL players, he mentioned Matthew 22:21, "Render to Caesar the things that are Caesar's' and to God the things that are God's." In order to explain what belongs to God, he combined that passage with a principle in 1 Timothy 2:2, where Christians are called to pray for all those in authority. Jeffress stated, "We owe the government not just our taxes, but owe them our respect and our prayers, and I think that needs to be kept in mind in all of this discussion."

Only 6.9 percent of the primary articulations could be classified as moral obligation. References to moral obligation typically referred to the government as established by God, with the implication that one's disrespect of a governmental symbol, such as the flag, was equivalent to disrespect of God. Mel Brindley, a Baptist preacher, provided a prime example of this approach in a blog post he wrote in response to Kaepernick's protest: "We must understand that government has a two-fold responsibility—Godward and manward. The Bible teaches that God frowns on civil disobedience and is always on the side of constituted authority. Human government derives its authority from God" (Brindley, 2017). Those who articulated the moral obligation perspective also used the term "respect," and it is often connected to respect for God's authority. Pat Robertson, Evangelical preacher and television personality, put it this way during a broadcast of the 700 Club:

> There is disrespect now for our national anthem, disrespect for our veterans, disrespect for the institutions of our government, disrespect for the court system. All the way up and down the line, disrespect. . . . Until there is biblical authority, there has to be some controlling authority in our society, and there is none, and when there is no vision of God . . . the people run amok. (Robertson, 2017)

American Sacramentalism also found a voice in the writings of some Christians, amounting to 10.8 percent of the primary articulations. These references often compared the sacrifices of soldiers and their families with the perks of being an American football player. Jeff Cavins, known for being an evangelist and Biblical scholar, posted a picture on his Facebook account of a veteran with an amputated leg, along with a caption which read: "What taking a knee for your country actually looks like." George Culley, in a letter to the editor in the *Chicago Tribune*, linked the anthem to honoring the sacrifice of others and acknowledging God's power: "When I stand to [sic] the national anthem, I am proud to be an American . . . born in the land of the free and home of the brave! To remember the price the American soldiers gave their lives for freedom isn't free without a sacrifice. . . . Being Christian American citizens is the greatest blessing and being born in the United States of America is a blessing from the God of Israel and Jesus the Savior!" (Culley, 2017).

The activist ideology articulation was found more than any other group, in 44.6 percent of the artifacts. Many Christian activists applauded Kaepernick's actions, and some even planned special Sunday worship services where members would wear Kaepernick jerseys in solidarity. Those who espoused an activist ideology professed concern for individuals but it was in the narrative of faith and systemic injustices such as racism. In addition, those who use this articulation often draw comparisons between Jesus's relationship to Roman rule and Americans' relationship to the government. Natalie Finstead, an author and staff member of the Leadership Development Initiative (an Episcopal organization), explained that the Pharisees' allegiance to Roman authorities allowed them to maintain a place of cultural power in Rome. She saw this cooperation fully manifested in Jesus's crucifixion and attention to those who were marginalized by the establishment—those who were weary and burdened such as the poor, persecuted, or captive—challenging the authorities. This way of being was passed onto the early Church that understood it was to be part of the world without conforming to its oppressive ways (Finstead, 2016).

Statistical Results

According to the parameters set by the researchers in the method section, articulations from 130 different pastors, organization representatives, politicians, and athletes with a wide range of Christian backgrounds: Mainline Protestant, Evangelical, and Catholic were analyzed. These Christian personalities with diverse Christian backgrounds spoke through a number of differing mediums: print, television, internet news, and blogs.

An ANOVA test revealed a significant difference between the type of medium (independent, categorical variable) and the number of articulations (dependent, continuous variable, $F(3, 126) = 2.8$, $p < .05$). According to a Bonferroni follow-up test there were no statistical differences between the number of articulations found on blogs or internet news. However, a statistical difference ($p < .05$) was discovered between the number of articulations found on television and print media. Format seems to be the most reasonable explanation for this phenomenon. Print media articulations are limited by space and word count. The majority of television articulations occurred during news-talk formats such as *Hannity* on Fox News. These news-talk formats often featured a panel discussion which allowed for a greater diversity of viewpoints. According to the data, there was no significant difference between the kind of medium and the kind of articulation. In other words, medium, whether left-leaning, right-leaning, or Christian, does not predict how Christians will articulate their position on Christianity and patriotism.

The research primarily focused on primary articulations because there were insufficient secondary and tertiary articulations to demonstrate significance of any kind. A Chi-Square Analysis demonstrated a slight relationship between background and primary type of articulation. The results were $\chi^2(8) = 20.81$, $p < .05$ with a moderate effect size (Cramer's V = .278). Because of this, some follow-up Chi-Square tests were done to isolate where the relationships occurred. For instance, both Mainline Protestants and Evangelicals articulated an American Sacramental position. Of the two groups, Evangelicals were more likely to articulate a Sacramental position than Mainline Protestants: $\chi^2(2) = 6.783$, $p < .05$. Chi-Square also showed that an Activist Ideology is mostly to be articulated by either Mainline Protestants or Evangelicals $\chi^2(2) = 9.223$, $p < .01$. No instances of an activist ideology were found among Roman Catholic personalities.

Within Evangelicalism, however, the data suggests a non-significant relationship between Evangelicalism and type of articulation ($p > .05$). In other words, based on this data set, one cannot fully predict how an Evangelical will articulate the juxtaposition between Christianity and patriotism. This came as a surprise to the researchers because of the working hypothesis that Evangelicals are more likely to use a ceremonial articulation but that is simply not the case. A significant relationship exists, however, between Evangelicalism and the American Sacramentalism articulation, $\chi^2(1) = 6.635$, $p < .01$. In other words, if an American Sacramentalism view is articulated, then it most likely came from an Evangelical.

A surprising phenomenon appeared in the data in the relationship between the pre- and post-Trump intervention. The moral obligation articulation did not appear until after President Trump intervened. A total of nine cases displayed the moral obligation articulation. These were articulated by those with a Mainline Protestant, Evangelical, and Catholic background. As a result, there was no significant relationship between moral obligation and type of background. While this is a small number (7 percent) out of the numerous responses, it is reasonable to hypothesize a connection to Trump's comments about respect for our country and an increased emphasis from Christians on respecting God by respecting our government. This may be one tangible way that Trump's comments seem to have influenced the larger discussion. Another tangible way that Trump's comments may have impacted the discussion is by the number of before and after articulations. The number of Christian responses discovered through the parameters of this study nearly tripled. There were thirty pre-Trump articulations, while after Trump intervened there were one hundred.

In the research, twelve cases did not fit the articulation categories outlined in the method for research. As such, they were labelled "other." Upon further investigation, in nine of the cases the Christian personality presented his or her discussion of the protest, Christianity, and patriotism in terms of what Jacques Ellul called "Christian anarchy." These articulations often suggested that Christians should recognize—and avoid—the inherent religious symbols and gestures (i.e., hand over heart, pledging allegiance, standing, etc.) often associated with patriotism. A common theme among these Christian anarchists suggested that Christians should avoid participating in patriotic gestures because of their connection to civil religion, which is an affront to allegiance to Jesus Christ.

Morgan Guyton, a Methodist pastor, provided an example of a Christian anarchy articulation. First, he pointed out that much of the New Testament was written during a period of time where Christians were forced to recognize the power of the Roman government and their inherent forms of nationalistic worship. Second, he set out to expose what he called "nationalistic idolatry" that has emerged among Christians in the Take-a-Knee protests. He claimed "the national anthem is being used as a pious hymn that turns the spectacle of male gladiators beating each other up into a legitimate religious ceremony. The early fathers of the Christian church would have zero ambivalence about our duties as Christians to declare Jesus as Lord in the face of obvious idolatry" (Guyton 2017, para. 17).

Another example of a Christian anarchy articulation came from Andrew Hudgins, a program director for ncchurches.org. In light of the protests, he encouraged Christians "to raise questions about our relationship to the government and where our allegiances lie" (Hudgins, 2017).

DISCUSSION

This analysis demonstrates that American Christians are divided concerning the way that Christianity and patriotism relate to each other. The researchers expected stronger relationships between the background and articulation type. However, such relationships were not predictable. The results did show, however, that Christians have a deep interest and concern for what happens in the United States. The Take-a-Knee protests have prompted Christians to scuffle over the meaning of Christianity and patriotism in all sorts of public forums. The protests have exposed wide-ranging responses in the attempt to understand the relationship between Christian individuals and the government in which they reside. For instance, these Christians debate the meaning of Romans 13 where the Apostle Paul explained that God has given the State the power of the sword. Elsewhere in scripture, the writers call Christians to pray for their national leaders, to pay taxes, and to lead quiet lives. Varying interpretations of these passages only complicate matters in regard to Christianity and patriotism.

The Christianity and patriotism debate over the Take-a-Knee protests has exposed differences within the Christian community. For example, the articulations explored in this chapter demonstrate concern about the United States either as an entity or as individuals who make up subcultures. Those who articulated Christianity and patriotism in ceremonial and moral obligation terms often demonstrated their concern about the United States as an entity. On the other hand, those who employed American sacramental and activist ideology terms tended to focus more upon the individuals that make up the United States. The American sacramental view demonstrated concern for members of the military while the activist ideologues displayed concern for members of particular subcultures. The Christian Take-a-Knee debate, then, has exposed the ignorance or, at least, the confusion over the meaning of a nation. Is a nation an entity or is it the individuals that make up the entity? Again, the hermeneutical impasse is on full display. How can the Christian community go beyond the hermeneutical impasse exposed by the Take-a-Knee protests?

This chapter presents two viable options for the Christian community: Christian anarchy and neighborliness.

Christian Anarchy

Among the case studies where the "other" category was assigned, an interesting articulation emerged that was not found among Bellah's categories. This emerging articulation suggested that Christians ought not to be connected with any national symbolic gestures or any type of nationalism. This seems closely related to what Jacques Ellul called "Christian Anarchy." The term "anarchy" does not refer to the chaotic and violent resistance movements found throughout history. Rather, the term "anarchy," for Ellul, comes from the Greek terms *"an"* and *"arche"* which can simply be translated "No head." In other words a practice of Christian anarchy suggests that Christians ought not to be bound by national allegiance for Christians belong to the kingdom of God. According to Ellul, the only things the Christian ought to give the government are prayer for the leaders and taxes (Ellul, 2011). Smith (2009) suggested that nations exceed their God-given boundaries when they ask people for their allegiance. He claimed that the language of allegiance is borrowed from religious ritual language (p. 111). In other words, if a Christian comes to understand national allegiance is a form of worship then they may understand that patriotism is a form of idolatry.

While this seems like a harsh solution for a number of Christians, it does create unique opportunities for Christians to adopt the kind of language that goes beyond rational sterility and emotional subjectivism. It can put the Christian in the middle between two polarizing interpretations of defending the symbols of the nation and defending the rights of individuals. From the middle, then, Christians may be able to help both sides in finding common ground and paving a way through this impasse.

Neighborliness

Each of the case studies provided a Christian response to the national anthem protest. In doing so, these cases exposed how Christians articulate the relationship between Christianity and patriotism. However, these articulations did not provide tangible solutions to the divisive issue sparked by the protests. Across the differing Christian articulations, the Christian idea of "loving neighbor" was surprisingly absent. The social activist theme came close to what is meant by neighborliness but social activism addresses a concern for systemic issues such as racism. Neighborliness seeks to emphasize individual responsibility and calls individuals to meaningfully connect with other individuals. Unfortunately, none of the Christians in the cases that were found discussed one of the central tenets of Christianity "to love your neighbor as yourself" (Matthew 22:34-

40). Again, Ellul (1989) helpfully suggested that there are systemic forces working behind the scenes, not just civil debates that force people to become estranged from one another. Certainly, the national anthem protests have exposed and caused deep divisions in America concerning the meaning of being an American, and in the case of the protests, what it means to be a Christian in America.

Unfortunately, various mediums have presented the divisive issue in small segments or sound bites. These short speech-acts displayed across the mediums do not allow for a fully developed conversation concerning the protests. The same could be said of social media platforms where intensely complicated matters are discussed in terse form. Ellul would say that sound bites are a result of culture's desire for efficiency. In Ellul's schema, the craving for efficiency has divided people. The sound bite fetish, while attractive to audiences, actually serves to divide them (Rinke, 2016). It seems then that one of the ways to get past the hermeneutical impasse created by the protests would be to reject the efficiency of sound bite communication. Ellul suggested that the way to break the spell of efficiency is for people to be neighborly to one another again, "it is the duty of every Christian to become neighbor to someone" (Ellul, 1989, p. 104). Communicatively, to be a neighbor means, "to discover a new language, a language which helps men to understand one another, in spite of publicity, a language which permits men to abandon their despairing solitude, and avoids both rational sterility and subjective emotionalism" (Ellul, 1989, p. 105). This means that Christians, in particular, ought to seek out common ground on this divisive issue instead of following the polarizing public narrative on the issue. This perspective remains closely related to what is called "invitational rhetoric" as discussed by Connelly and Clarke in chapter 19 of this volume.

CONCLUSION

This chapter explored the emerging meanings from the articulation of Christianity and patriotism. The research affirmed Bellah's articulations of ceremonial language, moral obligation, and sacramental definitions of Christianity and patriotism. In addition, the category of activist ideology emerged as a viable option for the articulation of Christianity and patriotism. These articulations stem from Christians with various backgrounds and they show up in unpredictable ways. These articulations exposed a deeper rift on the meaning of a nation. For many, a nation exists either as an entity or as a community of individuals. Depending on the articulation, Christians will either demonstrate more concern for the nation and its national symbols or for individuals impacted by sources of social power.

In order to move beyond the hermeneutical impasse exposed by the Take-a-Knee protests, the Christian individual should consider the validity of Ellul's call to neighborliness. The call toward neighborliness will require resolve to be open to the other. The power of neighborliness rests in the fact that it happens on an individual-to-individual basis and not on governmental programs or solutions. In fact, Ellul stated that the government cannot fix anything for it is beyond the power of the government to do so (Ellul, 2004, p. 18). Individuals acting as neighbors toward others can create bridges over the hermeneutical impasse exposed by the Take-a-Knee protest.

REFERENCES

Anderson, L. (2017). Hermeneutical impasses. *Philosophical Topics, 45*(2), 1-19.
Bellah, R. (1967). Civil religion in America. *Daedalus, 96* (Winter), 1-21.
Bishop, E. (2015). Articulation theory in activist literacy research. *Theory in Action 8*(3): 65-78.
Bradshaw, W. (2014). *Mainline Churches.* Huffingtonpost.com. Retrieved from www.huffingtonpost.com/William-b-bradshaw/mainline-churches. Accessed 22 February 2018.
Breitbart Sports. (2016, November 18). 'I can't kneel during the anthem,' Bills lineman says upon becoming citizen. Retrieved from http://www.breitbart.com/sports/2016/11/18/bills-lineman-becomes-citizen-cant-kneel-anthem.
Brindley, M. (2017, September 29). I will stand. Retrieved from https://www.chestertownbaptistchurch.org/single-post/2017/09/29/I-Will-Stand.
Burke, K. (1984). *Attitudes toward history.* Berkeley: University of California Press.
Butterworth, M. L. (2013). The passion of the Tebow: Sports media and heroic language in the tragic frame. *Critical Studies in Media Communication, 30*(1), 17-33.
Chiquillo, J. (2017, September 25). Dallas pastor Robert Jeffress says kneeling NFL players would be shot in the head in North Korea. Retrieved from https://www.dallasnews.com/life/faith/2017/09/25/dallas-pastor-robert-jeffress-says-kneeling-nfl-players-thank-god-shot-head.
Culley, G. (2017, October 13). Letter to the editor: Standing for the anthem is a blessing from God. *Chicago Daily Herald: Du Quoin Evening Call Edition,* p. 12.
Curtin, P. (2016). Exploring articulation in internal activism and public relations theory: A case study. *Journal of Public Relations Research, 28*(1), 19-34.
DeLuca, K. (1999). Articulation theory: a discursive grounding for rhetorical practice. *Philosophy and Rhetoric 32*(4), 334-348.
Ellul, J. (1989). *The presence of the kingdom* (2nd ed.). (O. Wyon, Trans.) Colorado Springs, CO: Helmers & Howard.
Ellul, J. (2004). *Perspectives on our age: Jacques Ellul speaks on his life and eork* (Revised ed.). (W. H. Vanderburg, Ed.) Toronto: House of Anansi Press.
Ellul, J. (2011). *Anarchy and Christianity.* (G. Bromily, Ed.) Eugene, OR: Wipf & Stock.
Finstead, N. (2016, November 14). Colin Kaepernick—take us to church. Retrieved from http://www.leadership-development-initiative.org/blog/2016/9/14/colin-kaepernick-take-us-to-church-september-reflections-from-ldi.
Forst, M. L. (2017). Kneeling but still singing: Threshold identity, disidentification, and invitation in U.S. American national anthem protest. *Kaleidoscope: A Graduate Journal of Qualitative Communication Research, 16*(2), 1-33.
Guyton, M. (2017, September 23). When it became my duty not to stand for the national anthem. Retrieved February 2018, from Mercy not Sacrifice: http://

www.patheos.com/blogs/mercynotsacrifice/2017/09/23/became-duty-not-stand-national-anthem.

Hafen, S. (2009). Patriots in the classroom: Performing positionalities post 9/11. *Communication and Critical Studies, 6*(1), 61-83.

Hall S. (1986). On postmodernism and articulation: An interview with Stuart Hall. *Journal of Communication Inquiry, 10*(2) 45-60.

Hanczor, R. (1997). Articulation theory and public controversy: Taking sides over *NYPD Blue. Critical Studies in Mass Communication, 14*(1), 1-30.

Hariman, R. & Lucaites, J. (2002). Performing civic identity: The iconic photograph of the flag raising on Iwo Jima. *Quarterly Journal of Speech, 88*(4), 363-392.

Hudgins, A. (2017, September 29). Time to take a knee. Retrieved from https://www.ncchurches.org/2017/09/time-take-knee.

Kerr, P. A. (2003). The framing of fundamentalist Christians: Network television news, 1980-2000. *Journal of Media and Religion, 2*(4), 203-235.

Kerr, P. & Moy, P. (2002). Newspaper coverage of fundamentalist Christians, 1980-2000. *Journal and Mass Communication Quarterly 79*(1), 54-72.

Kumar, S. (2014). Articulation as a site of discursive struggle: Globalization and nationalism in an India media debate. *Journal of Communication Inquiry, 38*(2), 113-130.

Maadi, R. (2017, November 18). Christian players frustrated by protest criticism. Associated Press.

Marvin, C. (2002). Scapegoating and deterrence: Criminal justice rituals in American civil religion. In Hoover, S. and Clark, L. *Practicing religion in the age of the media: explorations in media, religion, and culture,* (203-218). New York: Columbia University Press.

National Association of Evangelicals. *What is an Evangelical?* www.nae.net/what-is-an-evangelical/. Accessed 22 February 2018.

Perry, K. E., & Kang, H. (2012). When symbols clash: Legitimacy, legality and the 2010 Winter Olympics. *Mass Communication and Society, 15,* 578-597.

Rinke, E. M. (2016). The impact of sound-bite journalism on public argument. *Journal of Communication, 66,* 625-645.

Robertson, P. (2017, October 2). *700 Club* [Television broadcast]. Virginia Beach, VA: CBN.

Sitten, R. Framing Christianity: A frame analysis of fundamentalist Christianity from 2000-2009. (Doctoral dissertation, University of South Florida, 2011). Proquest, No. 1497455.

Smith, J. K. (2009). *Desiring the kingdom: worship, worldview, and cultural formation.* Grand Rapids: Baker.

SIXTEEN

Pigskins and Protests

An Examination of the NFL Boycotts in Response to the Take-a-Knee Movement

Megan Westhoff and Jennifer Saint Louis

Professional athletes' decision to kneel for the national anthem has inspired heated debate about injustice, patriotism, and free speech in the United States (see chapter 1 for details on the kneeling debate). As boycott calls against the National Football League (NFL) began to surface (Bieler, 2017; Blake, 2017; Mediaite, 2017; Talking Points Memo, 2016; Ripple, 2017), talk has turned to action as individuals are heeding those calls. What makes these boycotts particularly interesting is that individuals are boycotting for different reasons in response to the Take-a-Knee protests. While some individuals are boycotting in opposition to the players kneeling, others are boycotting to support the players' protests, and in many cases, in direct opposition to the treatment of Colin Kaepernick. It is our intent to contribute a theoretical communication perspective to the existing consumer marketing research literature on boycott behavior, while at the same time contributing to understanding the division in America exemplified through the anthem controversy. The purpose of this study is to explore the factors that significantly contribute to NFL boycotting behaviors from both sides of the Take-a-Knee controversy.

LITERATURE REVIEW

Political Consumerism, Boycotts, and Buycotts

Consumers are vocal in their support of or opposition to products, companies, and organizations. Known as political consumerism, this behavior is defined as a form of "lifestyle politics" that enables individuals to address personal and political problems related to quality of life concerns outside the realm of electoral politics (Copeland, 2014, p. 174). Further, political consumerism refers to the decision to deliberately support or avoid specific products, companies, and organizations for political, ethical, or environmental reasons (Copeland, 2014; Stolle et al., 2005). Two distinct modes of political consumerism are boycotts and buycotts. Boycotting is conflict and punishment oriented, while buycotting is cooperative and reward oriented (Copeland, 2014, p. 173; Friedman, 1999; Neilson, 2010, p. 214). Boycotting, or anti-consumption, is a form of symbolic self-expression in which the avoidance of consuming controversial goods or services prevents individuals from associating their identity and self-concept to the undesired perceptions or effects of that good or service. Conversely, buycotting, or selective consumption, are attempts to support entities because individuals are closely connected to desirable perceptions or effects. Individuals choose to boycott or buycott and both are viewed as collective acts and prosocial behavior (John & Klein, 2003; Klein et al., 2004).

Extant literature offers insights into the demographic characteristics of individuals who are likely to boycott or buycott. Research is inconsistent regarding sex and boycotting. One study suggests that sex does not influence the likelihood to boycott (Neilson, 2010), while another suggests that women are more likely to boycott than men (Klein et al., 2004). Furthermore, two other studies found that women are less likely to boycott than men (Gardberg & Newburry, 2009; Sherkat & Blocker, 1994).

With respect to age and boycotting, Copeland (2014) posits that there are no statistically significant effects for age. As far as the influence between race and boycotting, blacks have been responsible for more boycotts than all other minority groups combined (Friedman, 1999, p. 90). Furthermore, blacks, Hispanics, and Native Americans are more likely to support boycotts than whites or Asians (Gardberg & Newburry, 2009). Evidence suggests that individuals with more education and higher income levels are more likely to support boycotts than individuals with less education and lower income levels (Gardberg & Newburry, 2009). Additionally, Gardberg and Newburry (2009) found that boycott supporters tend to be upwardly mobile members of marginalized groups.

Perceived Egregiousness

Consumers are initially prompted to participate in boycotts due to believing a company or organization is engaging in conduct that is wrong and has negative or harmful consequences. The objectionable conduct is perceived to be an egregious act because it causes an initial trigger, invokes negative feelings, and inspires action for consumers (Albrecht et al., 2013, p. 184; John & Klein, 2003, p. 1198; Klein et al., 2004, p. 93; Yuksel, 2013, p. 205). Perceived egregious actions are powerful predictors of boycott participation. However, consumers do not boycott for the same reasons (John & Klein, 2003, p. 1198) and not all consumers who perceive an action to be egregious will participate in boycotts (Klein, Smith, & John, 2004, p. 105). Based on boycott literature, it is proposed that the more egregious a consumer perceives an action, the more likely the consumer is to boycott (John & Klein, 2003, p. 1201; Klein et al., 2004, p. 105).

Proximity

In analyzing the possible reasons for boycott participation, external motivations may influence the desire and intent to boycott. An external motivating factor is proximity. Jones (1991) defines an individual's proximity to moral issues as "the feeling of nearness (social, cultural, psychological, or physical) that the moral agent has for victims (beneficiaries) of the evil (beneficial) act in question" (p. 376). In narrowing the concept and applying it to boycott behavior, Hoffmann (2013) defines proximity as "the closeness of the relationship between a single consumer and those who suffer from the actions of a certain company or another institution that stimulates the boycott call" (p. 215). He considers three facets of proximity: being personally, socially, and spatially affected. Therefore, he posits that, collectively, the level of proximity of the individual to the boycott issues increases the desire to boycott (p. 216).

Additional studies allude to proximity as a link between individuals and the likelihood of boycotting. Albrecht et al. (2013) discuss how involvement implies that a boycott topic represents an exciting and therefore motivating issue for consumers. The authors assert that the higher a consumer's involvement with the cause of the boycott, the higher his or her intention to participate in a boycott (pp. 181-182). Additionally, individuals reported that lack of interest in the boycott topic and laziness toward making a difference are reasons not to boycott. Further, Yuksel (2013) explains that individuals often perceive boycotts to be "out of sight, out of mind," referring to the physical distance between the individual and the boycott (pp. 207-209). Therefore, it is suggested that if a boycott issue is viewed as distant, boycott participation decreases. Drawing from social identity theory (Tajfel & Turner, 1986), it can be said that the external factor of motivation for boycott participation is influenced by perceived personal, social, and spatial proximity.

THEORETICAL FRAMEWORK

In the context of this study, the preceding constructs are examined through the theoretical lens of social identity theory (Tajfel & Turner, 1986) and the new social movements paradigm (Buechler, 1995).

Social Identity

An individual's identity is comprised of personal identity and social identity. Personal identity includes unique individual attributes and characteristics while social identity includes social membership categories, such as cultural groups, race or ethnicity, social class, or social roles, to name a few. Both aspects of personal identity and group membership affect communication (Harwood, 2006; Tajfel & Turner, 1986). The combination of personal and social aspects of identity contribute to individuals' external motivations of behavior in everyday situations. Therefore, in examining why people are choosing to boycott the NFL, it is necessary to explore how social identity influences motivations for boycott participation.

New Social Movements

The new social movements paradigm analyzes how contemporary collective action differs from historic movements. Developed as a reaction to the perceived deficiencies of collective action theories exploring social movements from strictly economic and political perspectives, the new social movements paradigm explores other motivators of collective action rooted in ideology, politics, and culture (Buechler, 1995; Pichardo, 1997; Welton, 1993). New social movements consider a cultural dimension because of complex human rights issues and require multiple layers of examination (Buechler, 1995). Other aspects of identity like race and ethnicity, sex, political affiliation, class, and age contribute to collective action behaviors. Furthermore, due to the complexity of issues involved in the NFL Take-a-Knee movement, including social injustice, patriotism, and free speech, the new social movements paradigm is a theoretical framework worthy of exploration and application regarding NFL boycotts.

RESEARCH QUESTIONS AND HYPOTHESES

The primary objective of this research study is to explore why individuals who support the Take-a-Knee protests or who oppose the protests are boycotting the NFL. Based on the extant literature, the following research questions are proposed:

RQ1: What factors significantly contribute to NFL boycott behaviors?

RQ2: To what extent does sex impact NFL boycott behavior?

Additionally, based on the preceding literature, the following hypotheses are proposed:

H1: Individuals with higher education levels are more likely to support the NFL boycotts.

H2: Individuals with higher levels of income are more likely to support the NFL boycotts.

METHODOLOGY

The research questions and hypotheses were tested in an empirical study of actual ongoing boycotts against the NFL. As with similar research (Klein et al., 2004), an advantage of this approach is the ability to examine real-time reactions to the protests and corresponding boycotts in the social milieu in which they occurred.

Sample

The invitation to take an online survey was extended to participants though social networking sites (SNS), specifically Facebook and Twitter, as well as Amazon Mechanical Turk (MTurk). Whereas participants recruited through SNS were not compensated, respondents participating through MTurk received financial compensation in the nominal amount of twenty-five cents for survey completion.

Data were collected in the months following the close of the 2017–2018 football season, February and March 2018. A cross-sectional, snowball and recruited sample of 474 adults participated in the study ($N = 474$). While some respondents lived outside the continental United States (2 percent), most resided within the continental United States, in the Midwestern (45 percent), Southeastern (21 percent), Southwestern (16 percent), Northeastern (11 percent), and Northwestern (5 percent) geographic regions. With respect to sex and age, women constituted 56 percent of the sample and most participants (57 percent) were between twenty-five to forty-four years old. In terms of race, 70 percent of respondents were Caucasian, 10 percent were black/African American, and 7 percent reported being multi-ethnic. Six percent of the sample stated they were Asian, 4 percent were Hispanic/Latino, and 3 percent categorized themselves as Native American or "other." The sample was more educated than the national average (US Census, 2010), with many respondents holding a graduate or professional degree (37 percent), four-year degree (30 percent), or two-year degree (7 percent). Of the respondents without a degree, many attended some college (20 percent), held a high school diploma (4 percent), or attended some high school (<1 percent). In terms of income, most respondents (27 percent) reported earning between $50,000 to $100,000 per year. Respondents were split along the political spectrum: liberal (44 percent), moderate (36 percent), and conservative (20 percent). Likewise, participants' religious affiliations were varied, the largest demographics consisting of the following: no religious affiliation (33 percent), Catholic (19 percent), Protestant (16 percent), and non-denominational (16 percent). Finally, based on the nature of this research, participants' military and law enforcement affiliations were examined. It was found that 3 percent of respondents were members of the armed forces and 2 percent were law enforcement officers.

Measures

The online survey instrument, hosted by Qualtrics, contained thirty-eight items intended to measure demographic data as well as how the following constructs impact boycott participation: commitment to the NFL, response to perceived egregious acts, and social proximity. Whenever possible, modified versions of existing instruments were used, and, for the most part, the constructs were measured on 7-point Likert scales ranging from "strongly disagree" to "strongly agree." *Commitment to the NFL* was assessed through seven items which asked questions such as, "prior to the Take-a-Knee protests, how likely were you to watch NFL games?" and "after the Take-a-Knee protests began, how likely were you to watch NFL games?" Adapted from Klein et al. (2004), *response to egregious acts* was measured through eight items. These items asked participants to agree or disagree with statements such as, "I feel the protests are disrespectful to the military" and "I feel that Colin Kaepernick has been treated fairly following the protests." Finally, *social proximity* was gauged through ten items adapted from Hoffman's (2013) research. These questions asked participants to agree or disagree with statements such as "issues related to police brutality directly impact me," "issues related to racial injustice directly impact me," and "issues related to military sacrifice directly impact me." Other Likert-style questions were asked to garner information about respondents' decision to participate in the boycotts, or the lack thereof. Finally, several open-ended questions were incorporated to allow participants to further clarify their opinions related to the boycotts, perceived egregiousness, and social proximity.

Data Analysis

As previously outlined above, multiple questions were asked to better understand several important concepts relevant to this research. Accordingly, principal components factor analysis with Varimax rotation (Eigenvalue > 1) was used to explore support for the Take-a-Knee protests, lack of support for the protests, proximity to issues related to police brutality and racial injustice, and whether challenges to American values loaded on different factors. In doing so, four scales were created. To investigate the reliability of these scales, an internal consistency coefficient was calculated using Cronbach's alpha. In all cases, the scales were found to be highly reliable.

The first scale represents *support for the protests* (3 items, α = .87). The second scale represents *lack of support for the protests* (3 items, α = .96). The third scale represents *proximity to issues related to police brutality and racial injustice* (4 items, α = .86). Finally, the fourth scale represents *challenges to American values* (patriotism/pro-military; 3 items, α = .89). No substantial increases in alpha for any of the scales could have been achieved by eliminating any of the items. Thus, internal reliability was established for each of the four scales.

Next, several four-step hierarchical regressions were conducted, with boycotting as the dependent variable, to identify key variables likely to predict boycotting behaviors associated with the NFL Take-a-Knee controversy *(RQ1)*. In total, three hierarchical regressions were run, one for each type of boycotting behavior: boycotting via viewership, boycotting via ticket purchases, and boycotting via merchandise purchases. Boycotting data were recoded to place respondents into one of three distinct groups: "boycotters," "partial boycotters," or "non-boycotters."

In step one, six demographic variables were entered to explore some of the previously identified antecedents to boycotting: race, sex, age, education, income, and political affiliation. In step two, building on the idea that boycott calls can influence consumer behavior, data reflecting the influence of the National Association for the Advancement of Colored People (NAACP) and other minority groups calling for an NFL boycott were added to the model along with the *support for protests scale*. Likewise, in step three, data reflecting the influence of President Donald Trump and other politicians calling for an NFL boycott were added along with the *lack of support for protests scale*. Finally, noting that demographics, boycott calls, and one's support of the protests, or lack thereof, alone does an incomplete job addressing the motivation to boycott in such a nuanced situation, in step four, the *proximity to issues related to police brutality and racial injustice* and the *challenges to American values* scales were added to the regression.

Finally, to address research question two and hypotheses one and two, special attention was paid to how three demographic variables (sex, education, and income) impact the three boycotting behaviors (viewership, ticket purchases, and merchandise purchases).

RESULTS

As outlined above, three hierarchical regressions were conducted to examine which factors significantly contribute to NFL boycott behaviors (Table 16.1). The first hierarchical regression, using *boycotting via viewership* as the dependent variable, hereafter referred to as regression one, revealed that at step one, demographic variables contributed significantly to the regression model, F (6, 438) = 9.5, $p < .001$ and accounted for 11.6 percent of the variation for boycotting via viewership. The overall model is statistically significant with age ($\beta = -.12, p < .01$) and race ($\beta = -.16, p < .001$) emerging as statistically significant unique contributors to the overall model. Introducing the influence of boycott calls made by the NAACP and other minority groups, as well as the *support for protests scale* in step two increased the variance to 26.2 percent and this change in R^2 was significant F (2, 436) = 43.25, $p < .001$. Both the boycott calls ($\beta = -.17, p < .001$) and *support for protests* scale ($\beta = .18, p = .05$) were found to be statistically significant unique contributors to the overall model. Adding the influence of boycott calls made by Trump and other politicians, along with the *lack of support for protests scale* to the regression model in step three increased the variance explained to 29.3 percent and this change in R^2 was significant F (2, 434) = 9.5, $p < .001$. Only Trump's boycott calls were found to be a statistically significant unique contributor at step three in the overall model ($\beta = -.16, p < .001$). Finally, the addition of the *proximity to issues related to police brutality and racial injustice* and the *challenges to American values* scales in step four explained an increase to 30.5 percent of the variation for boycotting via viewership and this R^2 was also significant F (2, 432) = 3.7, $p < .05$. The *challenges to American values* scale was found to be a statistically significant unique contributor to the overall model ($\beta = -.26, p < .05$) but *proximity to issues of police brutality and racial injustice* was not. Each significant contributing factor remained significant at each step of regression one.

Table 16.1. Regression for Predictors of NFL Boycott Behaviors

	Standardized beta coefficients		
Independent variables	Boycotting Viewership	Boycotting Tickets	Boycotting Merchandise
Step 1: Demographics			
Race	-.16***	-.15***	-.13***
Sex	-.04	-.02	-.02
Age	-.12**	-.14***	-.11*
Education	-.049	-.04	-.07
Income	.01	-.04	-.05
Political affiliation	.05	.7	.12*
Step 2: Support for protests			
Boycott calls—NAACP/minority groups	-.17***	-.21***	-.20***
Support for protests scale	.18*	.06	.09
Step 3: Lack of support for protests			
Boycott calls—Donald Trump/politicians	-.16***	-.10*	-.08
Lack of support for protests scale	.005	-.03	-.00
Step 4: Proximity			
Issues related to police brutality/racial injustice	-.05	.06	-.05
Challenges to American values	-.26*	-.37***	-.33**
Model statistics			
Adjusted R^2	.285	.304	.279
R^2	.305	.323	.299

Note. N = 474; *p < .05, **p < .01, ***p ≤ .001.

The second hierarchical regression, using *boycotting via ticket purchases* as the dependent variable, hereafter referred to as regression two, revealed that at step one the demographic variables contributed significantly to the regression model, $F (6, 438) = 10.7, p < .001$ and accounted for 12.7 percent of the variation for boycotting via ticket purchases. As with regression one, of the demographic independent variables, only age ($\beta = -.14, p < .001$) and race ($\beta = -.15, p < .001$) emerged as statistically significant unique contributors to the overall model. Introducing the influence of boycott calls made by the NAACP and other minority groups, as well as the *support for protests scale* in step two increased the explained variance to 27.2 percent and this change in R^2 was significant $F (2, 436) = 43.5, p < .001$. Additionally, like regression one, the boycott calls ($\beta = -.21, p < .001$) were found to be a statistically significant unique contributor to the overall model. However, the *support for protests* scale was not statistically significant. Adding the influence of boycott calls made by Trump and other politicians, along with the *lack of support for protests scale* to the regression model in step three explained 30.1 percent of the variance and this change in R^2 was significant $F (2, 434) = 8.9, p < .001$. Of these, only Trump's boycott calls were found to be a statistically significant unique contributor to the overall model ($\beta = -.10, p < .05$). Finally, the addition of the *proximity to issues related to police brutality and racial injustice* and the *challenges to American values* scales in step four increased the variation for boycotting via viewership to 32.3 percent and this R^2 was also significant $F (2, 432) = 6.9, p < .001$. The *challenges to American values* scale was found to be a statistically significant unique contributor to the overall model ($\beta = -.37, p <.001$). Each significant contributing factor remained significant at each step of regression two.

The third hierarchical regression, using *boycotting via merchandise purchases* as the dependent variable, hereafter referred to as regression three, revealed that at step one the demographic variables entered contributed significantly to the regression model, $F (6, 436) = 11.8, p < .001$ and accounted for 14 percent of the variation for boycotting via merchandise purchases. Of the demographic independent variables, age ($\beta = -.11, p < .05$), race ($\beta = -.13, p < .01$), and political affiliation ($\beta = .12, p < .05$) emerged as statistically significant unique contributors to the overall model. Introducing the influence of boycott calls made by the NAACP and other minority groups, as well as the *support for protests scale* in step two explained an increase to 26.4 percent of the variance explained and this change in R^2 was significant $F (2, 434) = 36.5, p < .001$. Like regression two, only the boycott calls ($\beta = -.20, p < .001$) were found to be a statistically significant unique contributor to the overall model. Adding the influence of boycott calls made by Trump and other politicians, along with the *lack of support for protests scale* to the regression model in step three explained an increase to 28.2 percent of the variance and this change in R^2 was significant $F (2, 432) = 5.5, p < .01$. Neither of these was found to be a statistically significant unique contributor to the overall model. Finally, the addition of the *proximity to issues related to police brutality and racial injustice* and the *challenges to American values* scales in step four increased the explained variation for boycotting via viewership to 30 percent and this R^2 was also significant $F(2, 430) = 5.2, p < .01$. As with regressions one and two, the *challenges to American values* scale was found to be a statistically significant unique contributor to the overall model ($\beta = -.33, p < .01$). Each significant contributing factor remained significant at each step of regression three.

In examining research question two, the three hierarchical regressions were analyzed and these findings indicate that there is no significant impact due to the sex of an individual on boycotting behavior related to the NFL protests. Thus, the findings related to *RQ2* support the selections from previous literature that state sex does not influence the likelihood to boycott (Neilson, 2010). This contributes to the discussion about how sex influences the likelihood to boycott. This ongoing debate also includes literature indicating that women are more likely to boycott (Klein et al., 2004), and that women are less likely to boycott (Gardberg & Newburry, 2009; Sherkat & Blocker, 1994).

In examining the first hypothesis that individuals with higher levels of education are more likely to support boycotting the NFL, the three hierarchical regressions were analyzed and the findings indicate that there is no significant impact due to education level on boycotting behavior related to the NFL protests. Thus, *H1* is not supported. Finally, to test the second hypothesis that individuals with higher levels of income are more likely to support boycotting the NFL, the three hierarchical regressions were analyzed and the findings suggest that there is no significant impact due to income level on boycotting behavior related to the NFL protests. Thus, *H2* is not supported.

DISCUSSION

Given the consumer marketing literature on boycott behavior, we sought to identify those factors that significantly contribute to NFL boycott behaviors in response to the Take-a-Knee movement. This research was exploratory in nature with the intention of introducing the idea of examining boycott behavior through a communication lens. Drawing from social identity theory (Tajfel & Turner, 1986), a theory typically falling within the sociocultural tradition in communication scholarship, we initially focused on individuals' demographic information as predictors of boycott behaviors and then expanded to account for the impact of boycott calls, support for the protests, lack of support for the protests, proximity to police brutality and racial injustice, and challenges to American values.

Despite research indicating that sex (Gardberg & Newburry, 2009; Klein et al., 2004; Sherkat & Blocker, 1994), education, and income (Gardberg & Newburry, 2009) influence boycott behavior, these were insignificant predictors in this study. These data suggest that with respect to the issues surrounding the Take-a-Knee controversy, these specific social identities do not play a prominent role in one's decision to boycott the NFL, from either side of the debate. Conversely, our findings suggest that age and race are the strongest demographic predictors of an individual's likelihood to boycott under these circumstances. This supports research suggesting that race (Friedman, 1999; Gardberg & Newburry, 2009) is an important factor in the decision to boycott. However, it is noteworthy that our data also indicate that whites are more likely to boycott the NFL than their non-white counterparts. This contrasts with previous research suggesting that minorities are more likely to boycott than whites (Gardberg & Newburry, 2009). These data also further the discussion about the significance of age and boycotting behaviors. Whereas Copeland (2014) asserts that there are no statistically significant effects for age, our findings indicate that age is among the strongest boycotting predictors. In fact, our data suggest that, overall, younger individuals are more likely to boycott the NFL than their older counterparts. These findings are consistent across all three regressions, indicating that race and age are significant predictors of all three boycotting behaviors (viewership, ticket purchases, merchandise purchases). Interestingly, regression three reflects that in addition to race and age, political affiliation was also a significant predictor of boycott behavior. In other words, political affiliation was only a significant predictor of boycott behavior with respect to boycotting in the form of merchandise purchases and not with boycotting via viewership or ticket purchases. In this case, conservatives were less likely to boycott via merchandise. The NFL protests and subsequently the NFL boycotts have proven to be a polarizing issue. The contradictory nature of these data with respect to previous boycott literature indicate that it may be the nature of these specific boycotts that inspire an us versus them, in-group versus out-group (Tajfel & Turner, 1986) mentality with respect to social identities related to race and age and the decision to communicate their displeasure with the NFL through the act of boycotting.

In considering demographic variables, and the inconsistent research about sex and boycotting (Gardberg & Newburry, 2009; Klein et al., 2004; Neilson, 2010; Sherkat & Blocker, 1994), we deemed it important to isolate and explore specifically how sex impacts NFL boycott behaviors. Our findings support the literature which states that sex does not significantly influence boycott behaviors (Neilson, 2010). Likewise, we wanted to isolate education and income to see if, like previous research, higher education levels and higher income levels make an individual more inclined to boycott in this type of nuanced situation. Our findings suggest that neither education nor income make a strong impact on the decision to boycott in this nuanced situation.

As indicated by the boycott literature, individuals do not always boycott for the same reasons (John & Klein, 2003). Given the varied reactions to the NFL protests, this was evident with respect to the NFL boycotts as well. Accordingly, in addition to demographic variables, we wanted to explore if boycott calls (NAACP and minority groups / Donald Trump and politicians), perceived egregiousness (support for protests / lack of support for protests), and proximity (police brutality and racial injustice / challenges to the American values of patriotism/pro-military) could significantly predict boycott behaviors. Our findings suggest that the boycott calls made by the NAACP and other minority groups as well as challenges to American values are the strongest predictors of an individual's likelihood to boycott under these circumstances. These data were consistent among all three regressions, indicating that they are significant predictors of all three boycotting behaviors (viewership, ticket purchases, and merchandise purchases). Interestingly, regression one reflects that in addition to boycott calls made by the NAACP and other minority groups and challenges to American values, support for protests was also a significant predictor of boycott behavior. In other words, one's support for the Take-a-Knee protests was only a significant predictor of boycott behavior with respect to boycotting in the form of viewership. It did not make a significant impact on boycotting via ticket or merchandise purchases. Finally, our findings indicate that the boycott calls made by Trump and other politicians made a significant impact on an individual's decision to boycott the NFL in the form of viewership and ticket purchases. However, unlike the ones made by the NAACP and other minority groups, these calls did not have a significant impact on an individual's decision to boycott via merchandise purchases.

The present research provides evidence that individuals are boycotting the NFL from both sides of the Take-a-Knee debate. Further, it suggests that calls from both sides impact individuals' decisions to punish the league for their involvement in the controversy. Interestingly, the only side in which the issues in question were influencing boycott behavior beyond the calls was with respect to American values (patriotism/pro-military) being subverted or challenged. This raises the question, why were individuals with proximity to police brutality and racial injustice not more likely to boycott because of these issues? It can be argued that individuals whose social identities are closely tied to minority groups have more experience belonging to American out-groups and therefore feel less of a challenge to their self-concept and social identity than those individuals who have more traditionally belonged to American social in-groups. If an individual constantly experiences racial injustice in a setting where it is often not recognized as such, one more injustice may not compel that individual to act. Thus, the lower likelihood to boycott. However, if an individual's values are rarely, if ever, challenged in a specific setting and then seen to be subverted, that individual may feel compelled to act in a way which helps maintain their personal and social identities. Hence, the higher likelihood to boycott.

Consistent with the new social movements paradigm (Buechler, 1995), our results highlight the complex nature of boycott behavior in response to issues as socially charged as the NFL boycotts. As this framework postulates, these boycotts are unique in that they are focused on individuals' perceptions of culturally based human rights issues on both sides of the controversy. While the present study is exploratory in nature and does not specifically address how culture and identity impact this type of boycott behavior, the findings provide evidence that there are many underlying factors, like those highlighted, that influence individuals to communicate their opinions on such a complex issue through the act of boycotting. Likewise, it opens the door for future scholarship to specifically explore how identity relates to culture and ideology as these factors influence boycott behaviors. Additional directions for future research are discussed below.

LIMITATIONS AND FUTURE RESEARCH

As with any study, this research is subject to limitations. Although efforts to reduce any potential bias were employed, it is possible that the sample is not an accurate representation of the wider population. More representation from minority voices in our sample would have been desirable. Future research could explore a more in-depth examination of minority perspectives on this issue. Likewise, future researchers may wish to explore these constructs with a wider range of educational backgrounds. With respect to results, although empirical work can be objectively assessed through statistical tests, the underlying decisions made in establishing a model ultimately affect these tests. It is possible that an unexamined construct is missing from the model or that a better model exists. For these reasons, we encourage continued study of boycott behaviors as they relate to socially charged issues that are perceived differently by varying populations. Moreover, in continued effort to further the communication literature on boycotting, future research should examine the direct effects of boycott calls, as well as the channels through which those calls are made, on boycott motivation. Finally, examining the NFL boycotts through a qualitative lens would be beneficial to further our understanding of the motivating factors impacting these boycotts as well as to tell the rich stories associated with the individuals who are so moved to boycott.

CONCLUSION

The current research explores the factors that significantly contribute to NFL boycott behaviors. It highlights how controversial social issues can impact individuals' social identities and how potential challenges to those identities can motivate people to act in ways that further divide Americans on topics that have traditionally created communication barriers, such as race, age, and political affiliation. Despite the study's limitations, it is significant for several reasons. First, the topic itself is important. Though closely tied to sports, it brings attention to issues that stem far beyond the football field to illuminate social problems deeply rooted in American society. Further, these data provide thought-provoking insight into what influences boycott participation in relation to these issues and encourage deeper dialogue to further uncover the motivations behind these factors. Second, since most boycotts commence due to one or more agreed upon egregious corporate acts, little is known about boycott behaviors associated with corporations that are the target of boycotts by different populations, for very different reasons. While the present study just scratches the surface of this topic, it provides a starting point for meaningful research opportunities. Finally, through the rejected hypotheses, this research suggests that the factors influencing boycott behaviors associated with these types of social concerns may be notably different than predictors for other types of boycotts. This further supports the need to consider how identity relates to culture and ideology in new social movements and how those movements translate into consumer and political behaviors.

REFERENCES

Albrecht, C.-M., Campbell, C., Heinrich, D., & Lammel, M. (2013). Exploring why consumers engage in boycotts: Toward a unified model. *Journal of Public Affairs*, 13(2), 180–189.

Bieler, D. (2017). Pro-Kaepernick crowd protests at NFL HQ as NAACP requests meeting with Roger Goodell. Washington: WP Company LLC d/b/a The *Washington Post*. Retrieved from https://tinyurl.com/y9a5a62n.

Blake, A. (September 24, 2017). Trump's full-blown culture war with the NFL. *Washington Post – Blogs*. Retrieved from https://tinyurl.com/ycz4skon.

Buechler, S. M. (1995). New social movement theories. *The Sociological Quarterly*, 36(3), 441-464.

Copeland, L. (2014). Conceptualizing political consumerism: How citizenship norms differentiate boycotting from buycotting. *Political Studies*, 62(S1), 172-186.

Friedman, M. (1999). *Consumer boycotts: Effecting change through the marketplace and the media*. New York: Routledge.

Gardberg, N. A., & Newburry, W. (2009). Who boycotts whom? Marginalization, company knowledge, and strategic issues. *Business & Society*, 52(2), 318–357.

Harwood, J. (2006). Communication as social identity. In G. Shepherd, J. St. John, & T. Striphas (Eds.), *Communication as . . . : Perspectives on Theory*. Thousand Oaks, CA: Sage.

Hoffmann, S. (2013). Are boycott motives rationalizations? *Journal of Consumer Research*, *12*(3), 214–222.

John, A., & Klein, J. (2003). The boycott puzzle: Consumer motivations for purchase sacrifice. *Management Science*, *49*(9), 1196–1209.

Jones, T. M. (1991). Ethical decision-making by individuals in organizations: An issue-contingent model. *Academy of Management Review*, *16*(2), 366–395.

Klein, J. G., Smith, N. C., & John, A. (2004). Why we boycott: Consumer motivations for boycott participation. *Journal of Marketing*, *69*(3), 92–109.

Mediaite: Conservative media group calls for nationwide boycott of NFL (2017). Chatham: Newstex. Retrieved from https://www.mediaite.com/online/conservative-media-group-calls-for-nationwide-boycott-of-nfl.

Neilson, L. A. (2010). Boycott or buycott? Understanding political consumerism. *Journal of Consumer Behaviour*, *9*(3), 214–227.

Pichardo, N. A. (1997). New social movements: A critical review. *Annual Review of Sociology*, *23*, 411–430.

Ripple, Z. (2017). NAACP official says they will boycott NFL if Roger Goodell refuses meeting. *New York Daily News*. Retrieved from http://www.nydailynews.com/sports/football/naacp-official-goodell-boycott-threat-article-1.3439641

Sherkat, D. E., & Blocker, T. J. (1994). The political development of sixties' activists: Identifying the influence of class, gender and socialization on protest participation. *Social Forces*, *72*(3), 821–842.

Stolle, D., Hooghe, M., & Micheletti, M. (2005). Politics in the supermarket: Political consumerism as a form of political participation. *International Political Science Review*, *26*(3), 245–269.

Tajfel, H., & Turner, J. C. (1986). The social identity theory of intergroup behavior. In S. Worchel & W. G. Austin (Eds.), *Psychology of Intergroup Relations*, pp. 7-24. Chicago: Nelson-Hall.

Talking points memo: Ted Cruz urges boycott of 'rich spoiled' NFL players who protest nat'l anthem (2016). New York: Newstex. Retrieved from https://talkingpointsmemo.com/Livewire/ted-cruz-mad-national-anthem-protestors-nfl.

U.S. Census Bureau (2010). Quick facts United States. Retrieved from https://www.census.gov/quickfacts/fact/table/US#viewtop.

Welton, M. (1993). Social revolutionary learning: The new social movements as learning sites. *Adult Education Quarterly*, *43*(3), 152–264.

Yuksel, U. (2013). Non-participation in anti-consumption: Consumer reluctance to boycott. *Journal of Macromarketing*, *33*(3), 204–216.

SEVENTEEN
Female Athletes in Media

Participating in the Take-a-Knee Movement

Colleen Kappeler and Nancy Flory

Mass media has a powerful influence on our beliefs. Most spectators view sports through media, rather than live; in Koivula's study of spectators, it was found that 63 percent of the viewers watched sports through media (p. 590). It is important to look at the gender representation in the media. The coverage of women tends to differ from men both in quantity and types of coverage (Koivula, 1999, p. 589). Sports reporting and media coverage of sporting events has historically been different for men and women. In fact, until the mid-1980s, sports historians did not include women in their studies (Williams, 1994, p. 45). When women began being included in sports history studies it was more as a compensatory history ("notable" women) or contributory history (Williams, 1994, p. 45), and this is even more so the case for black female athletes (Williams, 1994, p. 60). This lack of coverage, or lack of equal kind of coverage, contributes to women athletes not being taken as seriously by the public.

WOMEN ATHLETES IN SPORTS COVERAGE

Misogyny within the sports reporting world is still "alive and well" (O'Neill & Mulready, 2015, p. 665). Men tend to get more coverage than women in reporting of sporting events (Jones, 2013, p. 252; Kian, Mondello, & Vincent, 2009, p. 491; O'Neill & Mulready, 2015, p. 657; Whiteside & Rightler-McDaniels, 2013, p. 821). Even in reporting of high school students, boys receive more coverage than girls (Whiteside & Rightler-McDaniels, 2013, p. 821).

The terminology used by sports reporters is also quite different between men and women. Men are framed in terms of physical size, masculinity, commitment, and athleticism (Aull & Brown, 2013, p. 27; Billings et al., 2014, p. 151; Kian et al., 2009, p. 491; Whiteside & Rightler-McDaniels, 2013, p. 818). Women are often framed in terms of their emotions, family, sexual appeal, and gender specific attributes (Aull & Brown, 2013, p. 29; Jones, 2013, pp. 255-256, 259). Finally, photographs of male and female athletes are framed differently. Men are more often photographed in action shots while women are photographed in passive poses (Jones, 2013; Jones, Murrell, & Jackson, 1999; McKay & Johnson, 2008).

Very often, sports reporting tends to "reinforce embedded hegemonic ideologies that thwart women's success in sports" (Crosby, 2016, p. 229). Part of this has to do with the sportscasters themselves. In Jones's study, she found that the majority of Olympic sportscasters were white males from the United States, in turn creating a hegemonic atmosphere that "shapes what audiences digest" (pp. 232-233). According to Aull and Brown, the tendency of sports to "celebrate and legitimize heteronormative masculinity" has long been recognized (2013, p. 27). Part of the way the media reinforces these stereotypes is through the amount of coverage of athletes, the terms used to describe them, and through framing of photographs.

In her study of the online coverage of the 2008 Olympic games, Jones (2013) found that women's sporting events were not covered as much as men's (p. 252). Jones looked at four public broadcasters—ABC, BBC, CBC, and TVNZ. She found that the majority of the games covered male athletes' contests (p. 252). Women received an average of 41 percent of stories. The worst coverage was TVNZ, where women only received about a third of the coverage their male counterparts received (p. 252). Jones believes that the reporting "confirms a historic pattern" with only one third of Olympics coverage being about female athletes (p. 252). O'Neill and Mulready also found that women received less press coverage in their study of the UK reporting of before and after the 2012 Olympic games. They found that women received only 5 percent of the total coverage for any given year (p. 657). They also discovered that women "only get prominent coverage when they are winners" (p. 659). Even Kian et al.'s 2009 study, which purported to challenge the hegemony normally seen in reporting of male and female athletes, conceded that ESPN's internet outlets "upheld hegemonic masculinity in sport media content by devoting the overwhelming majority of their college basketball articles to the men's tournament" (p. 491).

Jones found that TVNZ made many more references to women's appearances than they did of men. This included sexually suggestive and irrelevant commentary. In addition, on CBC and TVNZ, women's relationships were reported twice as many times as men's (p. 255). Women were described in ways that stressed emotional weakness or dependency (p. 255). Some sites reported that a female athlete "burst into tears" or "fled in tears." Male athletes' flaws were less likely to be reported as faults. Men were described in ways that appeared to be more in control, such as "devastated" or "furious" (p. 256). Jones found that "stories exhibited bias by attributing men's failures to a lack of athletic skill, while women's failures were put down to a lack of commitment, a lack of courage or poor judgment" (p. 256).

Whiteside and Rightler-McDaniels's 2013 study shows the same tendencies in sports reporting. Stories on men included more references to physical size and height as compared to women (p. 818). Almost twice as much female athletes' coverage referenced emotions than males' (p. 819). And much media focusing on women in sports took a more "pornographic" approach, reporting on the women's bodies and outfits rather than on their skills or performance (McKay & Johnson, 2008).

Billings et al. found in their 2014 study of NBC's broadcast of the 2012 Olympics that male athletes were more likely than female athletes to have successes attributed to superior strength and female athletes were more likely than male athletes to have failures characterized as a lack of composure (p. 148). Female athletes were also more likely to receive comments about their attractiveness and emotions (p. 149). For instance, male swimmers received success comments about their commitment while women beach volleyball players received success comments about their appearance (p. 151).

Photographs also displayed hegemonic tendencies through the number of photographs of athletes and framing. Jones found in her study that there were 1.6 times as many photographs of men as women and twice as many photographs of men than women that were paired with lead stories (p. 253). TVNZ had the worst record for publishing just three photographs of women athletes on three different days, while the same days totals of male athletes were 18, 24, and 29 photographs (p. 253). Women's photographs were also found to be in less prominent places than men's (p. 254). In addition, Jones found that photographic framing showed hegemonic tendencies. In her study, one prominent female athlete was photographed crying, "framing her as a vulnerable woman unable to keep her composure" (p. 256). Further, more female athletes were photographed in passive or posed shots, while more men had active shots that showcased their achievements (p. 258). These types of discrepancies tend to trivialize women's athleticism (p. 258).

THEORY

In general, feminist theory looks at gender and whether both male and female (and now non-binary) individuals are being fairly represented in media and communication studies. Feminist theories are often fluid, building upon knowledge and understanding that has come before and reflecting on changes in society and communication in regard to gender (Scranton & Flinthoff, 2013). "Women's quest for equality in society has had its counterpart in the sports world" (Messner, 1988, p. 197). After the 1972 passage of Title IX, women gained a legal basis from which to fight for equality in high school and college sports. By the 1980s, feminist theory began to be applied in a broader scope, reaching beyond academics and into mainstream media (Cuklanz, 2016). "Beginning with the baseline of vast underrepresentation in mass media caused by women's lack of power and influence in media culture" media representations and theories have continued to develop over time (Cuklanz, 2016, p. 1).

As can be seen in the literature review, feminist theory often focuses on "gendered content in news coverage and other mainstream media products" discovering "gendered patterns of representation" and looking at the power that underlies these representations (Cuklanz, 2016, p. 2). This representation of gender can include women being presented with sexual descriptions, racial descriptions, or as emotional creatures in comparison with their strong male gender counterparts. According to Cuklanz (2016), researchers have found elements of "gendered mediation" showing that news coverage differs "based on the gender of the subject" and often brings in elements of gender gratuitously and unnecessarily (p. 3). "In other words, where women are found in news coverage, they also receive a different type of coverage than do men in the same type of story" (Cuklanz, 2016, p. 3). Because of these patterns, women's roles and contributions have been diminished within media representations that continue to value women "more for their bodies than for their ideas or real contributions to their sport" (Cuklanz, 2016, p. 4). This creates a basis for dominant theology and the exclusion, diminishment, or dismissing of women's power.

The liberal feminist concerns of the 1970s and 1980s have shifted but remain an issue. Female athletes may be moving into an era where we are seeing the results of the fight for legitimacy in sports and where "media marginalization and trivialization of female athletes appear transparently unfair and prejudicial" (Messner, 1988, p. 205). However, we have a sports media that still provides limited coverage of women's sports (Scranton & Flinthoff, 2013). "Since sport has been a primary arena of ideological legitimation for male superiority, it is crucial to examine the frameworks of meaning that the sports media employed to portray the emergence of female athletes" (Messner, 1988, p. 205). And within that framework, it is important to consider how the media presents female athletes and their social platform gained through sports as compared to male athletes.

METHOD

For this study, an analysis was done on articles that focused on female athletes who took a knee in solidarity with the movement begun by Kaepernick. The articles were purposefully chosen through Google searches on "female athletes who took a knee" in order to allow the sample to not focus on one particular news organization, but instead focus on the general way media discussed these athletes. There were approximately fifty articles on female athletes who knelt in solidarity with this movement, however many focused on the same women. Therefore, a purposive sample that selected twenty-five from the group of fifty possible, with attention to including articles representing each of the women and a wide sampling of media sources, was chosen. Attention was placed on seeing how the media described the women in terms of their actions in the movement as well as their descriptions by media sources that might suggest sexual emphasis. According to previous research, as shown earlier, female athletes have most often been described by the media in sexual terms, with a focus on body image and an absence in attention to strength in comparison to male athletes—both in physical and emotional terms.

The authors used a deductive qualitative content analysis with a focus on reproducibility based on previous research on media commentary when it came to female athletes and femininity, race, and personal strength. A qualitative content analysis was done on the media's presentation of the female athletes, especially comparing this coverage to that of previous studies that have shown a focus on sexuality and sexual characteristics, more than anything, when looking at women.

OVERVIEW OF MEDIA COVERAGE

Within weeks of San Francisco 49ers' Colin Kaepernick taking a knee at games to protest racial inequality and recent shootings, female athletes were kneeling too. Although it wasn't widely reported, women—from soccer players to cheerleaders—were taking a knee during the national anthem in solidarity with Kaepernick. Kaepernick sat in protest when the national anthem was played during an August preseason game in 2016. In September of that year, soccer star and Seattle Reign's midfielder Megan Rapinoe knelt during the national anthem as a "little nod to Kaepernick and everything he's standing for right now" she told American Soccer Now (McKirdy, 2016). Rapinoe said that she understood where Kaepernick was coming from since she dealt with discrimination as a gay American. "Being a gay American, I know what it means to look at the flag and not have it protect all of your liberties." She said that she hoped her actions would "Keep the conversation going."

Rapinoe isn't the only one who knelt in 2016. At the WNBA playoffs that year, the entire Indiana Fever team took a knee (Kahn, 2017). And that same month, WNBA Mercury's Kelsey Bone kneeled during the national anthem as well (Cancio & Wisniewski, 2016). The twenty-four-year-old center said, "This is an injustice that's happening. I think we're just quiet about it right now and that's something we have to change." Six weeks after Kaepernick first knelt in protest, Georgia Tech cheerleader Raianna Brown knelt during the national anthem at a game in Atlanta (Kahn, 2017). She tweeted about her decision. "Proudest & scariest moment as a yellow-jacket happened at the same time. Thank you @Kaepernick7 for inspiring to #TakeAKnee to take a stand."

Protests during the national anthem continued the next year. Four of Georgia's Kennesaw State cheerleaders took a knee during the national anthem at a 2017 game (AP, 2017). The next week, their school changed pregame ceremonies to keep the cheerleaders off the field (Roll, 2017). However, the next month KSU president Sam Olens announced that he would allow the cheerleaders to kneel in the tunnel during the national anthem (Stirgus, 2017).

In Washington, D.C., Howard University cheerleaders knelt during the national anthem just two miles from the White House (Tracy, 2017). "I think about the national anthem and what it stands for," said Sydney Stallworth, a captain of the cheering squad. "I think about liberty and justice for all, and how it's not being executed in our country right now. . . . Injustice is continuing. So we're going to kneel until we see a change."

Buena Vista University cheerleaders knelt during the national anthem at their homecoming football game. "We agreed kneeling was a peaceful way to protest against the social injustices black men and women face every day in the U.S.," said cheerleader Alyssa Parker (Minutaglio, 2017). Their coaches were supportive. However, a week later their university president, in response to a public backlash, forbid the cheerleaders from kneeling for the national anthem again. Parker chose to quit the cheer squad rather than back down. "I miss cheer every minute of every day," she said. "But I know in my heart that I did the right thing. . . . Resigning from my Buena Vista cheer team may be a small gesture, but I know it can make a difference."

Even high schoolers began to protest. Cheerleaders at James Logan High School in Union City, California, took a knee at their games (Armbrester, 2017). "I think us taking a knee came as a surprise to people, because a lot of people in the school think of cheerleaders as airheads," said Sasha Armbrester. "They think we're oblivious to what's going on in the world. But they're wrong."

Virtually all of the female athletes who took a knee said they did it because they had a platform. "When I protested, I joined countless other athletes and artists who have used their platforms to encourage America to become its best self," said Brown (Girlboss, 2017). "[I]t would be a disservice for me not to use my platform, no matter how big or small, to oppose unjust treatment."

Stallworth said, "I think about the national anthem and what it stands for. . . . And I think about how lucky I am to go to the greatest historically black university in the country . . . and so lucky to have this platform" (Tracy, 2017).

Indiana Fever's guard-forward Marissa Coleman talked about the team's decision to protest. "It was unanimous that we were going to do it together," she said (Schilken, 2016). We have a platform, and I think it's a disservice if we don't use it. This was bigger than basketball. As important as this game was, there are other things going on in this world. It's just to get conversations started."

As much as the athletes wanted to get a conversation started, it wasn't easy. Women hardly received the media attention that male athletes received. Women are at the forefront of political activism, but it is often overlooked (de la Cretaz, 2017). "For instance, Megan Rapinoe was the first white professional athlete to kneel for the anthem, but the Cleveland Browns' Seth DeValve often gets the credit" (i.d.). Even though women have been protesting since 2016, cheerleaders and WNBA players believe that the men will get the credit for the movement (Kahn, 2017). "I feel that this is definitely one of those cases where the men tend to get more of the attention," said Brown. "But it's important to know that it's not a one-sided issue." Coleman said essentially the same thing. "It's true that we don't make as much money and we don't get as much attention as our male counterparts," she said (Kahn, 2017). "[B]ut we'd be doing a disservice if we didn't use the platform that we do have and the voices that we do have to try to spark change."

After comparing the articles above with previous research, this study does not generally support earlier findings. Two articles described cheerleaders in gendered terms. "'I think about the national anthem and what it stands for,' said one of the captains of the squad, Sydney Stallworth, a junior from Odessa, Fla., *as she applied foundation to her face before the game*" (Tracy, 2017, p. 2). Rather than describe the cheerleader as an athlete, this article describes her in terms of her makeup application.

Raianna Brown was a black Georgia Tech cheerleader who knelt during the national anthem. Someone took a picture and the image went viral on Twitter in 2017. In an article about Brown, the author describes Brown as "*Clad in a resplendent yellow uniform.*" The description was gendered and irrelevant.

In contrast to earlier studies, we did not find female athletes described in emotional or sexual terms. None of the articles mentioned the cheerleaders' families or relationships they had. While the articles did not discuss an athlete's failures, they also did not describe the women as having a "lack of commitment, a lack of courage or poor judgment" (Jones, 2013, p. 256). On the contrary, at least one article gave the women credit for taking a leadership role and "blazing trails" (de la Cretaz, 2017, p. 1).

ANALYSIS AND FINDINGS

Overall, the articles were written in a straightforward manner. They did not exhibit noticeable bias against women or put the women in an unfavorable light. Print media of female athletes has tended to focus on performance and reinforces stereotypes of gender (Jones, Murrell, & Jackson, 1999, p.190). However, as we look at the media coverage of female athletes who knelt, very little was found in terms of the media using discriminatory language or sexually defining characteristics. Is that because the female athletes' participation in this movement was not considered big news, or are we seeing an uptrend in media where that type of description is no longer welcome?

There were not enough published pieces discussing the female athletes who knelt to make a conclusive argument on that. Though dozens of female athletes participated in the Take-a-Knee movement, they, as women, received very little attention for their participation. "We have a sports media that still provides limited coverage of women's sport" (Scranton & Flinthoff, 2013, p. 106). As Williams (1994) notes, women in sports have been written about more as compensatory history ("notable" women and their accomplishments) or as contributory history (women's contributions but focusing on their status in society) (p. 46). It seems that trend continues on today. In the articles found on female athletes who knelt, many included the story of the males' protest with women as a side note. The articles that focused only on female athletes were found in online magazines like *Elle* and *Girl Boss*, magazines that typically have a female audience.

In 1999, Koivula did a study of televised sports and how much news coverage there was for female athletes. His studies found that "less than 10% of the total examined news covered female athletes" (p. 602). Out of the 25 articles chosen here, only seven were published in national publications like *USA Today* or *CNN*. The female athlete who got the most attention was Megan Rapinoe, a national soccer player; secondly, attention was given to the WNBA players; and finally, some attention was given to cheerleaders in both professional and collegiate sports. One's platform certainly depends on the audience one has; however, it is still evident, just by the lack of stories in general, that female athletes did not receive the media focus that males did. The clearest example of this is

Cleveland Browns' Seth DeValve being named by the media as the first white athlete to join the protest when in fact Rapinoe, a white woman, had knelt earlier. This shows not only that female athletes are still undervalued for what they do, but that their voices may still be second to men in social movements. It is also part of a vicious circle, as underreporting of Rapinoe's kneeling may have led to fewer people knowing that she was the first white athlete to kneel resulting in more reporting that DeValve was first. Female athletes, especially black female athletes, do not always receive "equal or fair representation in media platforms, especially in broadcast news" (Brock, 2012, p. 529).

The #TakeAKnee movement, arguably, was started by a male athlete, and a football player at that. It could be argued that this automatically focuses the attention on male athletes, particularly football players, though Kaepernick's protest was started during pre-season games and at first received no media attention. However, since football gets more media coverage than most sports in America, the attention of the media stayed there rather than showcasing the inclusiveness of the movement by including all genders and races who chose to participate.

CONCLUSION AND FURTHER RESEARCH

Language used by the media to define female athletes may be improving, but the coverage of them is still sorely lacking. The athletes who spoke out in the movement did so because they have a platform to speak from as professional athletes. However, of what consequence is their platform when no one is watching? And in what ways would the Take-a-Knee movement have been different if the media had focused on all genders and races choosing to be involved rather than focusing their primary attention on black male athletes?

Future research into female athletes' participation in the movement would include a quantitative study of how many people even knew that women were participating. Given the low media coverage, it is likely that many American viewers do not know that female athletes knelt too. However, a survey of avid sports audiences would showcase the actual understanding in America of women's participation.

Hegemonic influences are still persisting in media coverage of sports. And even the athletes know it. Money, or discrepancies in payment, diminishes the platform female athletes have to speak from. And media coverage of the female athlete voices continues to silence them on their platform. Audiences know and see only what is put forth by the media, and without adequate representation, they are not getting the full picture of the movement.

REFERENCES

AP (2017). Kennesaw State cheerleaders take a knee to continue protest. *USA Today*. Retrieved from: https://www.usatoday.com/story/sports/ncaaf/2017/10/21/kennesaw-state-cheerleaders-take-a-knee-to-continue-protest/106897690/

Armbrester, S. (2017). Opinion: I'm a cheerleader, here's why I take a knee. *Youth Radio*. Retrieved from: https://youthradio.org/journalism/sports/im-a-cheerleader-heres-why-i-take-a-knee/

Aull, L. & Brown, D.W. (2013). Fighting words: a corpus analysis of gender representations in sports reportage. *Corpora, 8*(1), 27-52.

Billings, A.C., Angelini, J.R., MacArthur, P.J., Bissell, K., Smith, L.R., & Brown, N.A. (2014). Where the gender differences *really* reside: the "big five" sports featured in NBC's 2012 London primetime Olympic broadcast. *Communication Research Reports, 31*(2), 141-153.

Brock A (2012) From the blackhand side: Twitter as a cultural conversation. *Journal of Broadcasting & Electronic Media, 56*(4), 529–549.

Cancio, G. & Wisniewski, L. (2016). Mercury's Kelsey Bone to take anthem protests into WNBA playoffs. *Cronkite News*. Retrieved from: https://www.azcentral.com/story/sports/wnba/mercury/2016/09/16/mercurys-kelsey-bone-take-anthem-protests-into-wnba-playoffs/90522428/

Crosby, E.D. (2016). Chased by the double bind: intersectionality and the disciplining of Lolo Jones. *Women's Studies in Communication, 39*(2), 228-248.

Cuklanz, L. (2016). Feminist theory in communication. In K. B. Jensen & R.T. Craig (Eds.), (pp. 1-11). Hoboken, NJ: John Wiley & Sons.

De la Cretaz, B. (2017). All of the work, none of the credit: don't drop the ball on the WNBA's activism. *Bitchmedia*. Retrieved from: https://www.bitchmedia.org/article/wnba-players-on-the-frontlines

Girlboss. (2017). These are the female athletes that joined #TakeAKnee protests. *Girlboss*. Retrieved from: https://www.girlboss.com/girlboss/women-take-a-knee-nfl-protest

Jones, D. (2013). Online coverage of the 2008 Olympic Games on the ABC, BBC, CBC and TVNZ. *Pacific Journalism Review, 19*(1), 244-263.

Jones, R., Murrell, A.J., & Jackson, J. (1999). Pretty versus powerful in the sports pages: print media coverage of U.S. women's Olympic gold medal winning teams. *Sage Journals, 23*(2), pp. 183-192).

Kahn, M. (2017). Women athletes have been protesting for over a year. They're here to remind you this is bigger than Trump. *Elle*. Retrieved from: https://www.elle.com/culture/a12656426/women-athletes-protest-take-a-knee-trump-wnba/

Kasana, M. (2017). Who is Raianna Brown? The Georgia Tech dancer took a knee last year, too. *Bustle*. Retrieved from: https://www.bustle.com/p/who-is-raianna-brown-the-georgia-tech-dancer-took-a-knee-last-year-too-2446542

Kian, E.M., Mondello, M., & Vincent, J. (2009). ESPN—The women's sports network? A content analysis of internet coverage of March madness. *Journal of Broadcasting & Electronic Media, 53*(3), 477-495.

Koivula, N. (1999). Gender stereotyping in televised media sport coverage. *Sex Roles, 41*(7), 589-604.

McKay, J. & Johnson, H. (2008). Pornographic eroticism and sexual grotesquerie in representations of African American sportswomen. *Social Identities, 14*(4), 491-504.

McKirdy, E. (2016). USWNT star Megan Rapinoe takes knee in solidarity with Kaepernick. *CNN*. Retrieved from: https://www.cnn.com/2016/09/05/sport/megan-rapinoe-colin-kaepernick-anthem-kneel/index.html

Messner, M.A. (1988). Sports and male domination: the female athlete as contested ideological terrain. *Sociology of Sport Journal , 5*, 197-211.

Minutaglio, R. (2017). I quit cheer after my university told me I couldn't take a knee. *Cosmopolitan*. Retrieved from: https://www.cosmopolitan.com/politics/a13786879/cheerleader-take-a-knee-protest-alyssa-parker-interview/

Nylund, D. (2004). When in Rome: heterosexism, homophobia, and sports talk radio. *Journal of Sport and Social Issues, 28*(2), 136-168.

O'Neill, D. & Mulready, M. (2015). The invisible woman? A comparative study of women's sports coverage in the UK national press before and after the 2012 Olympic Games. *Journalism Practice, 9*(5), 651-668.

Roll, N. (2017). Retaliation for taking a knee? *Inside Higher Ed.* Retrieved from: https://www.insidehighered.com/news/2017/10/12/cheerleaders-knelt-during-anthem-were-removed-field-next-week

Schilken, C. (2016). WNBA's Indiana Fever players kneel together during national anthem before playoff game. *LA Times.* Retrieved from: http://www.latimes.com/sports/sportsnow/la-sp-wnba-anthem-protest-20160922-snap-story.html

Scranton, S. & Flinthoff, A. (2013). Gender, feminist theory, and sport. In D.L. Andrews & B. Carrington (Eds.), (pp. 96-111). *A companion to sport.* Malden, MA: Blackwell Publishing.

Stirgus, E. (2017). KSU cheerleaders resume kneeling for national anthem. *The Atlanta Journal-Constitution.* Retrieved from: http://www.myajc.com/news/ksu-cheerleader-resume-kneeling-for-national-anthem/kk2IVpzubApALSPqlCvMAK/

Tracy, M. (2017). Howard cheerleaders add voices to the anthem debate by taking a knee. *The New York Times.* Retrieved from: https://www.nytimes.com/2017/10/13/sports/ncaafootball/anthem-protests-howard-.html

Whiteside, E. & Rightler-McDaniels, J.L. (2013). Moving toward parity? Dominant gender ideology versus community journalism in high school basketball coverage. *Mass Communication and Society, 16,* 808-828.

Williams, L.D. (1994). Sports history from an Afro-American perspective. In *Women, Media and Sports,* Pamela Creedon (Ed.). Thousand Oaks, CA: Sage Publications, 45–66.

EIGHTEEN
Sitting to Take a Stand

Take-a-Knee and Student Protesting

Michelle Tabbanor

Throughout the history of communication studies, communication scholars have examined how the general public has responded to notable controversies. Many studies have identified differences in public opinion on topics such as student rights to equality and the ways in which opinions have shaped culture (Lovell, 2016; Rury & Hill, 2013; Watson & Rivera-McCutchen, 2016). Specifically, during times of controversy, social movements and protests have emerged, leading specific groups to advocate for a particular position (Meyer & Gamson, 1995; Lovell, 2016; Rury & Hill, 2013). The response to the Take-a-Knee controversy has been no exception to this, inciting debates between individuals, groups, political officials, and even sports teams based on attitudes toward player decisions to protest the national anthem, closely linked to the Black Lives Matter movement (Zaru, 2018). This chapter intends to address the impact that this debate has had on student attitudes toward current social movements, student rights, and national symbols, specifically dealing with the Take-a-Knee protests. In order to best understand the context for student response to the present discussion of the Take-a-Knee controversy, it is necessary to provide a review of previous literature regarding student protesting in the United States, student response to the Pledge of Allegiance, and the influence of celebrities like football players on fan involvement. It is also necessary to understand relevant theoretical perspectives including spiral of silence theory and parasocial relationships.

LITERATURE REVIEW

Student Protesting

Activists, including students, try to create change. As a result, students in the United States have protested to speak out on their positions and exercise their First Amendment rights to free speech. Though there has been debate about the validity of students exercising rights as minors, argument has been made for student rights superseding parental or institutional interference in student protesting ("Parents, students, and," 2011). Controversial student protesting has even been the subject of the 1969 Supreme Court case, *Tinker v. Des Moines*. This case was based on the silent protests of high school students in Des Moines who wore arm bands in school to protest the Vietnam War. The case was ruled in favor of the students on the basis that "students don't shed their constitutional rights at the school house gates" (Tinker v. Des Moines Podcast).

Students have been involved in protests to promote racial equality, like the civil rights protesting in the 1960s and 1970s, as well as more recent protests like the #BlackLivesMatter movement (Rury & Hill, 2013; Watson & Rivera-McCutchen, 2016). Their protests have also surrounded issues like gender equality, supporting feminist ideals, and challenging traditional gender roles (Graham, 2006; Lovell, 2016). In response to Colin Kaepernick's example, two private high school football players from Texas were expelled from their team after kneeling for the national anthem at a game (Coleman, 2017). In fact, before the controversy was enhanced by Donald Trump's involvement expressing disapproval of the players "disrespect" for the nation (Zaru, 2018), Gibbs (2017) reported that over 68 high schools witnessed protesting behavior revolving around the Take-a-Knee controversy. It seems likely that number increased after Trump's comments.

One of the most recent student protests was in response to the Marjory Stoneman Douglas High School shooting on February 14, 2018, in Parkland, Florida (Chavez, 2018). In response to the shooting, students across the country protested by walking out of school for seventeen minutes to lobby for stricter gun regulation. Though this is certainly not an exhaustive list of student protesting campaigns, these examples of the types of issues that students have rallied behind provide a context for the present discussion.

Spiral of Silence Theory

Student response to controversy can often be muted based on expected peer response. The spiral of silence theory helps explain the extent of student participation in protesting. The theory asserts that individuals will be more likely to express controversial morally loaded opinions if they perceive their opinion has majority support or is trending toward majority support and will be more likely to withhold their opinion if they feel that they will be isolated by expressing it due to that opinion trending toward the minority side (Noelle-Neumann, 1977; Perry & Gonzenbach, 2000). There are four basic assumptions of this theory: (1) that humans are social beings and fear isolation; (2) that people constantly observe their environments to avoid losing popularity and esteem; (3) people are able to distinguish between fields and opinions that are static and those that are changing; and (4) a spiral process occurs through which individuals perceive changes in group opinion and adopt a prominent opinion, while an alternative opinion is "pushed back" and those who support the alternative opinion ultimately still "stick to" the majority opinion (Noelle-Neumann, 1977, p. 144). Clemente & Roulet (2015) discussed the role of interpersonal relationships in an individual's sensitivity to public opinion, arguing that social actors are commonly influenced by friends and family and are greatly influenced by those with whom they frequently interact. Especially when studying young people, it is important to consider the role of peers and the influence that they can have on expression of opinion. Further, Ho, Chen, & Sim (2013) stated that spiral of silence "assumes that for morally loaded issues, fear of isolation propels people to gauge the opinion climates around them using the mass media to evaluate their social environment." This can be valuable for understanding student response to morally loaded situations, like protesting. One of the goals of this research is to better understand whether or not students withhold personal opinions about the Take-a-Knee controversy based on the opinions of those around them.

Parasocial Relationships

Another goal of the present research is to understand the role that celebrity plays in student protesting behavior. Significant research exists to support the idea that celebrities can have great influence on audience opinion (Meyer & Gamson, 1995; Wen & Cui, 2014; Singhal & Rogers, 1999). Even celebrity involvement in political and social activism can influence public opinion to an extent, often having a more indirect impact (Wen & Cui, 2014). This can be attributed, in part, to the parasocial relationships that audiences form with media personae.

Parasocial relationships are defined as the perceived "interpersonal relationships which can develop between a viewer and a mass media personality" (Singhal et al., 2004, p. 366). These interactions create a connection between audiences and media personae that exists from the perspective of audience members yet creates perceived bonds that impact how the audience members understand the media (Brown, 2015; Singhal & Rogers, 1999; Brown & de Matviuk, 2010; Earnheardt & Haridakis, 2009). Sports fans, specifically, can develop parasocial relationships through various media, like televised sports, movies, talk show interviews, sports memorabilia, and commercials featuring sports celebrities. When endorsing a particular product or idea, they have a sort of "star power" that creates an "emotional tie between the consumer and the star athlete so as to increase both product awareness and purchase intentions among target consumers" (Sun & Wu, 2014, p. 136).

Further, fans often experience intense emotions, as if they were similarly invested in the game like the players. This may partly stem from the glare of publicity on celebrities' private lives, which makes audiences feel as if they personally know the celebrities. With the rise in celebrity culture in the late twentieth century, media personae have been given a "privileged position of social influence that can shape, reinforce, and inculcate values and beliefs and promote specific social practices within diverse audiences" (Brown, 2015, p. 259). An audience member may relate to their favorite sports athlete by attempting to have conversations on social media, finding ways to meet the athlete, and believing that they are "a part of the athlete's world" (Earnheardt & Haridakis, 2009, p. 34; Rubin et al., 1985, p. 156). Of the three types of parasocial relationships discussed by Singhal et al. (2004), affectively oriented relationships would most closely relate to the connection a fan may feel with members of a sports team, as it refers to the audience's belief that his or her interests are "joined" with those of a media persona (p. 367). When fans follow a game or team closely, they may feel as though the team's wins and losses are their wins and losses. In the present research, adopting a particular athlete or sports team's perspective and ideals regarding the Take-a-Knee controversy could influence students' decisions about whether or not to participate in the protest.

METHODOLOGY

For the purpose of understanding the impact of the Take-a-Knee controversy on student protesting behavior, the following research questions have been presented:

> RQ1: How has the Take-a-Knee debate influenced student attitudes toward the Pledge of Allegiance?
>
> RQ2: What is the influence of celebrity on student attitudes about the Take-a-Knee debate?
>
> RQ3: What factors influenced student decisions to participate or not participate in protests against the Pledge of Allegiance?

In order to better interpret student response to the protests and the impact that they have had in schools, qualitative interviews were conducted featuring open-ended questions to allow interviewees to freely discuss the decision to participate or not participate in protests against the Pledge of Allegiance (see Patton, 2015). These interviews will assess the importance and witnessed behavioral outcomes that the viral controversy had on the students and school systems through both student and instructional perspectives. This should provide rich perspectives on the impact of the present debate and suggest implications for future debates of a similar nature.

Through face-to-face, semi-structured interviews, this research gathered perspectives from eleven current high school students and four high school instructional faculty members. Participants from this study were recruited from high schools in eastern Virginia, based on their current status as students or faculty members. Parental consent was provided for student participants under the age of eighteen, in compliance with Institutional Review Board standards. Through a series of questions and prompts, participants shared experiences and opinions related to student protesting, student rights, potential influences for protesting behavior, and their knowledge of and participation in the Take-a-Knee debate. Interview questions for students were focused more specifically on opinions regarding what would influence students to engage or not engage in protesting activities in school. Faculty interview questions focused more on whether or not they felt these protesting behaviors should be allowed in schools. In order to best understand the context for student response to the present discussion of the Take-a-Knee controversy, it is necessary to analyze and attempt to understand the perspectives of those who interact directly within school settings.

The list below provides organized information on the interview participants:

ANALYSIS AND DISCUSSION

All interview participants had general knowledge of the debate about Kaepernick's decision to not stand for the national anthem, allowing them to provide informed perspectives. It is also notable that another prominent national protest was occurring during the research period. A National School Walkout in public high schools followed the Marjory Stoneman Douglas High School shooting in Parkland, Florida (Karimi & Yan, 2018). All participants made reference to the shooting context in their responses to school protesting experiences.

The Debate

Before discussing the research questions, it is helpful to understand attitudes about the Take-a-Knee debate itself. Most of the participants

Table 18.1. Table 18.1 – List of Interview Participants and Their Demographic Makeup

Name	Role	Demographics
Sage	Student	Female/Biracial (Black & White)
Brianna	Student	Female/African American
Jalkah	Student	Female/Hispanic
Susan	Student	Female/White
Malkia	Student	Female/Indian
Connor	Student	Male/White
Leon	Student	Male/African American
Joshua	Student	Male/African American
Jarome	Student	Male/African American
Grayson	Student	Male/African American
Micah	Student	Male/African American
Nikolas	Teacher/Coach	Male/White
Randy	Teacher/Coach	Male/White
Arthur	Assistant Teacher	Male/African American
John	Teacher	Male/African American

simply shared their knowledge of how and why the protest began, while some also shared their opinions about Kaepernick's decision to kneel during the national anthem. Many participants agreed with Kaepernick's decision, supporting the idea that he was exercising his American right to express his beliefs through protesting. For example, Connor stated that Kaepernick began the Take-a-Knee movement as a way to "protest things that were going on in America that he did not agree with." He continued on to say that he believed that Kaepernick "has the right to do so, and that he should be allowed to express anything that he would like to." Although Connor agreed with Kaepernick exercising his right to protest, he also disagreed with his treatment of the flag stating, "I believe that [protesters] could have chosen other ways to express this . . . kneeling to the anthem is slightly disrespectful to the people who have gone and risked their lives to make sure that we have the right to protest."

Other participants agreed that kneeling for the flag can be viewed as disrespectful, including Joshua, who admitted that he can "see why they said it came off as disrespectful" to those who fight for the nation. Susan argued that everyone should stand for the anthem because "when a player kneels, the protest seems to be against the country instead of specifically targeted at black deaths by police forces." A similar viewpoint opposing Kaepernick's decision to kneel during the national anthem was shared by Grayson, who stated that it is "unpatriotic" to protest the flag itself. While he did hold this viewpoint, he also argued that it would be unpatriotic not to protest for what he believed in, since it is an American right to do so. Similarly, Sage argued that she did not agree with the "form of protest; however, I do support the cause." Sage disagreed with the idea of kneeling for the anthem because she did not feel that the Take-a-Knee protests "really do much to offer a solution to these issues; they merely draw attention to the increasing intolerance of American citizens."

In contrast, Brianna stated that she viewed Kaepernick's kneeling as "honorable" and argued that it "shouldn't be considered disrespectful" if people are able to understand the intention behind the action. Malkia concurred with this, arguing that taking a knee is "completely justified" by every citizen's constitutional rights. These differing opinions give an idea of the dichotomy of this debate from the student perspective. The following sections will discuss some of the reasons why the Take-a-Knee protest warrants examination of its impact on students.

Student Protesting and the Pledge of Allegiance

To better understand how student attitudes were influenced by these protests, the interviews were first analyzed according to attitudes regarding students' right to protest. As earlier discussed, students have historically been involved in protesting behavior based on a legal right to protest. The nature of this study merits discussion of perspectives of students' right to protest as well. The student participants all agreed that students should have the right to protest, providing personal perspectives as rationale for this belief. Connor stated his belief that, as American citizens, "everybody should have the right to protest and not protest." This sentiment was echoed by all but one faculty member interviewee. The majority of the faculty agreed that students should have the right to "express themselves just like adults do," as stated by Arthur. He argued that "I think just because young people are young, that doesn't mean that they don't have the right to say something that's presently affecting them." John also agreed with this point saying that students "have free will to do so."

Randy argued that it is "imperative" for students to become "active members of society, and what better way" than to protest. He further argued his belief that protesting should be a "cornerstone of what we do in these buildings, for kids to stand up for what they truly believe in." He commented on the challenges faculty members face attempting to help students exercise their right to protest, citing anti-protesting "directives" from the school system as obstacles that contribute to "suppressing our ability to maybe affect some change in the kids' attitudes." However, he identified himself as a "firm believer in speaking your mind, whether you're 15 years old or 58 years old or 90 years old," and he stated that, if done for the right reasons, "not standing for the pledge is a very distinct way of protesting." Brianna and Susan also noted that school administrations sometimes prohibit protesting activities, claiming at least that it is for safety reasons. Despite this fact, Brianna shared her belief that student protesting "gives us an advantage for protesting when we are older . . . it's sort of like practice, but it's a real issue."

The only teacher to argue against students' right to protest did so on the basis of lack of maturity. Nikolas stated that students "don't have principles at fourteen to fifteen. You're too young to have legitimate principles and be that strong in your convictions." While giving his argument, he acknowledged the fact that students have been endowed with "unalienable rights," but that they are "not mature enough to form informed opinions." He also expressed financial criteria saying, "If you don't pay taxes, you have no rights."

An element of the discussion of student rights regarding protesting is students' right to freedom of speech. Most interview participants included freedom of speech as a foundation for their argument regarding students' right to protest. Jalkah stated that she believed "protesting is definitely a way to exercise our freedom of speech," asserting that people often misunderstand the purpose of freedom of speech. She stated that "a lot of people don't realize that the freedom of speech is a right against our government. In case our government steps out of line, its people can rise up against something and be like, 'hey, like, you messed up [*laughs*] we don't like that.'" Faculty members also expressed their opinions of the role of freedom of speech, including Arthur's statement that students "have the right to stand up and give their freedom of speech."

In addition to opinions about the right to free speech as a valid support for student protesting, participants also gave their views on how and why freedom of speech should be respected. For example, Sage argued that freedom of speech should be used to promote positive issues by stating, "The right to protest definitely exercises free speech; however, I don't think that every aspect of free speech should be exercised just because it is legal. I think protesters should strongly consider acknowledging and appreciating the freedom that they have to protest and voice their beliefs, and if there is anything they do like about America, it should be that."

Sage also urged citizens to remember that in many other nations, "people are killed for protesting." Connor echoed this sentiment by stating, "Free speech is something that we need to hold dear and exercise because there are countries that don't have the right to free speech. . . . I think that we need to, as American citizens, need to express that as much as possible."

Grayson argued that since "teenagers don't really have a big voice right now . . . being able to exercise their free speech is important now more than ever."

On the contrary, much like his argument for student rights overall, Nikolas stated, "I don't care about the students' rights to freedom of speech as far as protesting against the pledge of allegiance." He argued that students do not have the maturity to make such decisions, and that students "don't deserve to protest against a country that affords them so many rights, because they were born with these rights, but men hundreds of years ago died for these rights." These perspectives help explain why students may participate in school protesting, specifically whether or not they think it is valid.

Student Response to the Pledge of Allegiance

In addition to kneeling, students might choose sitting for the school's Pledge of Allegiance time as a form of protest. With respect to the Take-a-Knee protests in school, interviewees described protest actions as either sitting or kneeling during the pledge. Most participants for this study agreed that because students are not required to stand for the pledge in Virginia, students were seen sitting prior to the Take-a-Knee protests. However, some participants had not experienced these protests. Sage stated that she had been "informed of people not standing for the pledge outside of my classes specifically," however those within the International Baccalaureate program she is a member of are "not particularly aware or concerned with these issues." Similarly, Jalkah stated that she had never witnessed her peers sitting during the pledge as a form of protest but has "seen people sit down because they just simply don't care, which is pretty sad." She also recalled an instance from the previous year, when her teacher acknowledged the lack of requirement to stand for the pledge. Jalkah shared a sentiment that she believed to be common, that "even though it's a right, it still makes the room uncomfortable when you see that one kid sitting down."

Conversely, two student participants claimed to have witnessed and participated in protesting the Pledge of Allegiance. Joshua stated that initially he sat during the pledge because he was "lazy," but the Take-a-Knee protests "gave me a reason not to stand for the pledge" in light of police brutality. Brianna also expressed that there were "quite a few students who did not stand for the pledge of allegiance," and that it "definitely started after people started doing Take-a-Knee." She described witnessing students getting out of their seats and kneeling in class, which she stated "was pretty cool . . . it was a big thing, at least for my graduating class." She went on to say that some students in her classes still choose to sit in protest.

Faculty observation of student response varied. Nikolas and John both witnessed students sitting for the pledge; however, Nikolas stated that he "always made it a point" to encourage his students to stand, while John expressed that he has at times wanted to tell his students, "Man, y'all need to stand up," but has kept in mind that it is not required. John further recounted a situation where a student said to him, "I don't respect this country." In the same vein, Arthur shared about the diversity of his students and that many lack identification with what the flag represents. He stated, "We have a diverse population here. . . . So, some of them feel like 'this does not represent me, because where I come from, I feel like my rights are being infringed upon.' . . . That has led to a great deal of our young people not standing for the flag, our girls included." Furthermore, Randy shared similar experiences with students regarding why they choose to sit during the Pledge of Allegiance. Randy spoke about his criteria for allowing students to protest the Pledge of Allegiance. He stated, "Usually I have them write me a little paragraph . . . if they have some legitimate concerns as to why they don't want to stand up and things then we can have a discussion about differences of opinion. . . . It's the black-on-black crime, it's the proliferation of officers and African American males [in conflict], it's basically those kinds of things." He argued that it is the students' prerogative to choose not to stand, but if they so decide "then you have to have some reasons." Since he has witnessed this type of behavior since before the Take-a-Knee protests began, he does not believe that students are sitting as a result of the protests. However, he did admit that popular events, such as popular protesting and national tragedies, do change the dynamics of student behavior.

Influencers of Protesting Behavior

Influence of Celebrity

As discussed in previous literature, audiences who follow media figures have the potential to form parasocial connection with them to the extent that they adopt the celebrity's values as their own. Therefore, interview participants were asked what influence they thought celebrities had on audience decision making. Most of the participants agreed that audiences tend to look up to celebrities as role models, specifically sports celebrities. Sage stated, "Considering how much Americans love sports, anything that a professional team does immediately attracts attention and starts trends." She continued on to say that, "Many fans may not even have an opinion on certain issues, and simply hop on the bandwagon when their favorite team protests. It becomes more about the actions of the athlete than the cause of the protest." Jalkah said that audiences "hear things on the news but they don't really pay attention to it . . . people watch the Super Bowl more than they watch the news." She also said, "When you look up to someone, as many people look up to their favorite NFL players, I feel like whatever they like you tend to begin to like too . . . people who look up to players who are participating in this protest, I feel like they are more likely of supporting the protest as well." Brianna's comments agreed. She said that audiences may "feel close" to celebrities and feel "pushed to do or think a specific way" as a result. She argued that this "connection" may even influence audiences to "protect" a favorite celebrity's point of view.

Connor held a slightly different perspective, arguing that audience attachment to an athlete often "depends on how much you are interested in that athlete." He said that for people who are diehard fans, "If the athlete does something that is aside from sports or aside from what they are there to do, then they're gonna wanna know about it. Whereas, if you take the person who just watches it for the fun of it, he's not necessarily gonna care" what the athlete says.

Similarly, Leon stated that the impact of sports celebrities is "humongous," and their true fans are "gonna be ride-or-die. . . . So, their fan base is gonna tell other people, and when that happens, it starts a movement." Grayson also argued that audience response will depend on the celebrity and how deep a connection exists between celebrity and fan, while Micah implied that audience dedication could be situational.

Faculty response was congruent with the perspective that celebrity opinions have an immense impact on audiences. Randy stated that celebrity influence is "huge," and that "athletes [and] artists have an incredible influence on young minds." He also said there are "a lot of people who are disgruntled with a lot of things that are happening in this country now, and they're looking for things. So, when someone comes out against something, it's almost like a badge of honor or kind of cool to go against whatever." Arthur resonated with this idea as well, stating that since his school has a history of producing National Football League (NFL) draft-worthy athletes, "when football players speak, or they say something, a lot of our kids listen because that's a big thing here . . . [Kaepernick] made an impact because of what sport he represented, but also that he took a stand for something that a lot of our kids can relate to daily." Nikolas agreed that athletes are "in a position of influences . . . so they can do so for the good or the bad," however, in the case of Kaepernick's protest, he believed that he did "more harm than good. . . . I think it was more divisive."

Celebrity Exposure

In addition to the consensus about the influence of athletes, a common theme expressed in the interviews was the idea that celebrity exposure is a factor that contributes to the popularity of certain social movements. Leon believed that celebrities use their platforms to elevate topics and make sure they garner attention saying, "people listen to people with clout." Similarly, though he does not agree with celebrities overutilizing their platforms for personal agendas, Connor said that celebrities "appeal to the people who are upper class . . . people see the higher ups doing it or agreeing with it, they're going to want to do it . . . it starts a chain reaction," much like the "cool kids" in high school would. Micah agreed that celebrities "have a bigger voice . . . they have a bigger audience." Similarly, Brianna said, "whenever [celebrities] say something the media covers it, and when the media covers it, it gets to people." Further, John accentuated that media has made public controversy "wide open for people to see now. . . . They show it on TV, they show it on the news. They definitely show it on social media." He continued on, while snapping his fingers in emphasis, stating that teenagers "have access to this stuff like [*snaps*] this . . . the different deaths of certain African Americans, which many people felt were unjustified."

Interview participants were asked further to identify things that they believed influenced students' decisions whether or not to participate in the Take-a-Knee protests. A common response was the influence of friends and peers. This response was given by both student and faculty participants. Jalkah said this but admitted that "parents are the ones who bring us up and they're the ones who laid down our basic beliefs and foundations and things in our lives," the pivotal point becomes "As soon as we start to grow up we're like, 'I'm mature and I can start to really figure out exactly what I believe in and stuff.' And I feel like if I were to see my friends, who are talking about a certain subject and they're starting to voice their opinions and they all agree basically about the same thing, then it kind of pushes me to want to fit in, like 'hey, I agree too.'"

Brianna described this as an "implied pressure" from peers that "definitely does persuade what you do." Connor added the stipulation that he would have to agree with a peer's rationale to be influenced. He stated, "If I hear them talk about why they're walking out, why they decide to either stay or walk out, that would appeal to me more instead of just some guy who said, 'I'm gonna do the walkout because I can or because it gets me out of school.'"

Nikolas agreed that students were conforming to their peers, but he also disclosed that on the football team that he coaches, "they all stand together . . . we are afforded the rights that we do have because of what people have done for us, and the least we can do is stand for the country that protects us." Therefore, in a way, the team can be understood as uninfluenced by peers, while at the same time, conforming to the team culture of unity. Malkia stated that she becomes "inspired" when she witnesses other students protesting and is "proud to be a part of a generation [of young people] who is not scared to voice their opinion."

Spiral of Silence

In this same vein, conformity can sometimes be seen as a way to conceal one's own feelings to avoid derision. In this case, spiral of silence could be an explanation for why students may choose to suppress their opinions and conform. Interview responses congruent with this perspective were given by both student and faculty participants. Connor stated that some people "just don't pay attention because they don't want to be accused of anything either way," but he, of course, said he would do research to decide whether to protest.

Similarly, Nikolas gave an example that suggests a spiral of silence occurs regarding the role of race in people's decisions to withhold their opinions. He said:

> If you're exercising your right to take a knee during the protest, you're exercising a certain level of "blackness," if you will. And if you're not protesting it, you're not exercising that right . . . are you doing so to follow your friends and maintain a certain level of blackness? Or if you are a white man on a predominantly black team, are you doing so to be in solidarity with your brothers that you play with . . . or are you doing it out of the feeling that you almost feel obligated to do so because you don't want to show any anti-blackness?

The contention between team unity and perceived racial obligation could certainly be enough to influence a player to omit expressing their own opinion and to conform instead.

A related indicator for influence would be a student's commitment to certain values. For example, Sage, Jalkah, and Leon all stated that they would be influenced to protest if their beliefs were attacked or degraded. Jalkah specifically expressed that she would take action if authorities in her school demeaned her beliefs. She stated that she would "feel a little violated, I guess. . . . I feel like something like that would really make me wanna say something." Micah also mentioned that he would be motivated to protest if the school was not providing good education, arguing that he would not protest if he were alone but would talk about it with others and "hopefully could get them involved." Similarly, Joshua stated that he would protest school authority figures who stereotyped students.

Arthur also asserted that morality influences student action, specifically when students witness violence. He said that students would speak out if they saw something that they didn't like. Joshua identified racial hatred as a problem that would convince students to protest, and Jarome admitted that to be true for him commenting that an African American Parkland High School shooter would have been shot instead of just being arrested, leading him to protest.

Desire for Inclusion

Another common theme amongst participants was student desire to be included in social movements ignited by current events. Faculty participants described this desire for inclusion as a form of "bandwagoning." Susan stated that some young people "just go along with the crowd and don't even know why they are protesting." Grayson and Jarome both admitted that they would follow a "bandwagon" if it revolved around a topic that intrigued them. Most of the faculty participants cited current events and movements as influencers, as well as arguing that students participate in movements "just to be a part of something," as stated by Nikolas. John saw Take-a-Knee protests similarly, stating, "You realize that it's not only [Kaepernick] that feels that way. If they're African Americans, they're gonna feel that way too. They're gonna say, 'oh wait a minute, this is going on' . . . the reality of it hits them . . . they're like 'this affects us too.'"

The perceived efficacy of protesting also affects participation. Randy said, "as an individual student they probably don't think they're affecting change much, but collectively, as a large group . . . they felt like they were doing something good, they felt like they were making a difference and that kind of a thing." He continued, "Now if change happens . . . then they can see that there's a light at the end of the tunnel. They can affect change. But if nothing happens and nothing is happening, then it's like, why bother? It's unfortunate." Sage echoed this opinion, most of his friends who don't participate think protests "are a waste of time and do not usually change anything. Many of the people I know turn to praying and loving one another as a more effective way to spark change."

Individual interview participants gave some other notable potential influencers prompting student involvement in protesting. These themes included the influence of social media, obligation to authority, and respect for the flag as motivators. Further, student participants expressed additional perspectives including admiration and desire for more peaceful protesting methods, as well as a focus on addressing the roots of problems rather than perpetuating them.

CONCLUSION

This study examined the protesting experiences in schools regarding the Take-a-Knee protests. Themes emerged based on student understanding of and attitudes toward the protests, experiences with school protests, attitudes toward student rights, and factors that may influence students to participate. This study first intended to discover how the Take-a-Knee protests influenced attitudes toward the Pledge of Allegiance. Through the interviews, participants expressed their experiences witnessing students sitting during the pledge, two of whom participated themselves. Participants identified some of the rationale behind these attitudes, including not wanting to pledge to a nation in which they feel disenfranchised, giving indication that some change in response to the Pledge of Allegiance has occurred since the beginning of the Take-a-Knee protests.

The research also aimed to understand the role that celebrity has played in influencing attitudes and protesting behavior. The consensus amongst participants was that celebrities have a major impact on audience opinion and often even behavior. Many of the participant responses described a sort of parasocial relationship with sports athletes that may influence audiences to rally behind the athlete in support of their cause.

Finally, this study intended to understand other factors that would potentially influence students to protest, many of which were identified by both student and faculty participants. Students clearly cited peer influence as a major protest participation factor. This described how the decision of whether or not to protest may be attributed to a spiral of silence effect. Another common influence identified was violated values, over which students would take a stand for or against a position.

Understanding these responses to the Take-a-Knee protests can provide insight on current student attitudes toward protesting and future protesting behavior. Current events and social movements have the potential to impact student impulse to protest, and the perspective of student rights is a determining factor that may also contribute to how students choose to express that impulse. Future research could aim to further identify influencers for student protesting behavior, specifically as new movements and events take place.

REFERENCES

Brown, W.J. (2015). Examining four processes of audience involvement with media personae: Transportation, parasocial interaction, identification, and worship. *Communication Theory* (10503293), *25(3)*, 259-283. doi: 10.1111/comt.12053

Brown, W.J., & de Matviuk, M.C. (2010). Sports celebrities and public health: Diego Maradona's influence on drug use prevention. *Journal of Health Communication*, *15(4)*, 358-373. doi: 10.1080/10810730903460575

Chavez, N. (2018, February 17). These are the heroes of the Florida school shooting. *CNN*. Retrieved from https://www.cnn.com/2018/02/17/us/florida-school-shooting-heroes/index.html

Clemente, M., & Roulet, T.J. (2015). Public opinion as a source of deinstitutionalization: A "spiral of silence" approach. *Academy Of Management Review, 40(1)*, 96-114. doi:10.5465/amr.2013.0279

Coleman, A. (2017, September 30). Local high school football players kicked off team after protest during anthem. *Houston Chronicle*. Retrieved from https://www.chron.com/sports/highschool/article/High-school-football-kicked-off-team-anthem-kneel-12242713.php

Earnheardt, A.C., & Haridakis, P.M. (2009). An examination of fan-athlete interaction: Fandom, parasocial interaction, and identification. *Ohio Communication Journal*, *47*, 27-53.

Gibbs, L. (2017). One man started a movement: Tracking the Kaepernick effect. ThinkProgress. Retrieved from https://thinkprogress.org/kaepernick-effect-database-b2f50ca7277f/

Graham, G. (2006). *Young activists: American high school students in the age of protest*. DeKalb, IL: Northern Illinois University Press.

Ho, S.S., Chen, V.H., & Sim, C.C. (2013). The spiral of silence: Examining how cultural predispositions, news attention, and opinion congruency relate to opinion expression. *Asian Journal of Communication, 23(2)*, 113-134.

Karimi, F., & Yan, H. (2018, April 20). 'We won't stop': Students across US renew demand for gun safety in second walkout. *CNN*. Retrieved from https://www.cnn.com/2018/04/20/us/national-school-walkout/index.html

Lovell, K. (2016). Girls are equal too: Education, body politics, and the making of teenage feminism. *Gender Issues, 33(2)*, 71. doi:10.1007/s12147-016-9155-8.pdf

Meyer, D.S., & Gamson, J. (1995). The challenge of cultural elites: Celebrities and social movements. *Sociological Inquiry, 65(2)*, 181-206.

Noelle-Neumann, E. (1977). Turbulences in the climate of opinion: Methodological applications of the spiral of silence theory. *Public Opinion Quarterly, 41(2)*, 143-158.

"Parents, students, and the pledge of allegiance: Why courts must protect the marketplace of student ideas." (2011). *Boston College Law Review, 52(1)*, 375-410.

Patton, M.Q. (2015). *Qualitative research & evaluation methods* (4th ed). Thousand Oaks, CA: Sage.

Perry, S.D. & Gonzenbach, W.J. (2000). Inhibiting speech through disproportionate exemplar distribution: Can we predict a spiral of silence? *Journal of Broadcasting and Electronic Media, 44(2)*, 268-281.

Rubin, A.M., Perse, E.M., & Powell, R.A. (1985). Loneliness, parasocial interaction, and local television viewing. *Human Communication Research, 12*, 155–180. doi-10.1111-j.1468- 2958.1985.tb00071.x.

Rury, J.L., & Hill, S. (2013). An end of innocence: African-American high school protest in the 1960s and 1970s. *History of Education, 42(4)*, 486-508. doi/10.1080/0046760X.2013.819126

Singhal, A., Cody, M.J., Rogers, E.M., Sabido, M. (2004*). Entertainment-education and social change: History, research, and practice*. New York: Routledge.

Singhal, A., & Rogers, E.M. (1999). *Entertainment-education: A communication strategy for social change*. New York: Routledge.

"Student and Faculty Protest." (2006). *Radical Teacher, 76*, p. 43.

Sun, T., & Wu, G. (2012). Influence of personality traits on parasocial relationship with sports celebrities: A hierarchical approach. *Journal of Consumer Behaviour, 11(2)*, 136-146. doi:10.1002/cb.1378

Tinker v. Des Moines Podcast. (n.d.). Retrieved from http://www.uscourts.gov/about-federal-courts/educational-resources/supreme-court-landmarks/tinker-v-des-moines-podcast

Watson, T.N., & Rivera-McCutchen, R.L. (2016). #BlackLivesMatter. *Journal of Cases in Educational Leadership, 19(2)*, 3-11. doi: 10.1177/1555458915626759.pdf

Wen, N., & Cui, D. (2014). Effects of celebrity involvement on young people's political and civic engagement. *Chinese Journal of Communication, 7(4)*, 409-428. doi:10.1080/17544750.2014.953964

Zaru, D. (2018, February 5). Donald Trump's unrelenting war with the NFL. *CNN*. Retrieved from https://www.cnn.com/2018/02/03/politics/trump-super-bowl-tom-brady-football-colin-kaepernick/index.html

NINETEEN

Solutions to the Fallout

Invitational Rhetoric and Differing Viewpoint Political Conversations

Katie Clarke and Chris Connelly

Engaging in divergent perspective conversations with relational partners can offer opportunities to further our understanding of the issue we are discussing, our relational partner, and ourselves. This can strengthen our relationships. Self-expansion model posits that relationships expose individuals to new ideas and perspectives thus meeting humans' fundamental need for continuous personal growth (Aron & Aron, 1996). As people develop relationships, "they gain access to the resources, perspectives, and identities of their relational partners which can expand their knowledge and increase their efficacy for interacting with this world" (Sheets, 2014, p. 960). Within relationships, people are happiest when learning from each other as newfound knowledge contributes to a growing sense of self (Aron et. al., 2000; Tsapelas, Aron, & Orbuch, 2009). Fulfilling the drive for self-expansion within relationships means continued opportunities to learn more about ourselves and each other through new experiences and new ideas (Aron et al., 2000).

Research confirms that divergent conversations fuel relationship satisfaction, but only in a limited capacity (Fredrickson, 2013). Tests confirm Losada's (1999) ratio, which suggests that productive groups and dyads have a negative to positive interaction ratio between one negative interaction to every 2.9 positive interactions on the low end and one negative interaction to every 11 positive interactions on the high end. One disagreeing communication interaction to every six to eight agreeing communication interactions is ideal as this spectrum correlates with the most high-performing groups and most satisfying relationships. These findings indicate that both constant conflict, and the relative absence of it, are symptomatic of a dysfunctional relationship. Absence of conflict can indicate lack of authenticity, or boredom, which is predictive of relational dissolution (Tsapelas, Aron, & Orbuch, 2009).

INVITATIONAL RHETORIC

Within conflict communication, some communication approaches are more successful than others in generating greater understanding, growth, and social connection. Foss and Griffin (1995) suggest invitational rhetoric as a way to "enter into a dialogue in order to share perspectives and positions, to see the complexity of an issue about which neither party agrees, and to increase understanding" (Bone, Griffin, & Scholz, 2008, p. 436). Invitational rhetoric is different from traditional rhetoric in that it abandons the aim of engaging in conversation in an effort to change, control, and devalue another's opinion through debate, argument, or persuasion. Instead, the goal in invitational rhetoric is singular: to create greater understanding. This is achieved as conversational partners are invited to "present their vision of the world" (Foss & Griffin, 1995, p. 7) and offer audiences the opportunity to see the world the way the rhetor does. Invitational rhetoric interactions allow for growth but changing others' opinions is "neither the ultimate goal nor the criterion for success in the interaction" (Bone, Griffin, & Scholz, 2008, p. 436).

Equality, immanent value, and self-determination are three tenants that invitational rhetoric rests upon in order to create conditions that can lead to generating greater understanding. Foss and Griffin (1995) also champion the use of "re-sourcement" in invitational rhetoric. Re-sourcement involves "disengaging from the framework, system, or principles from the precipitating message with a creative response so the issue is framed differently" (p. 9).

Challenges to Achieving Invitational Rhetoric

Existing communication research speaks to practices that contribute to, and detract from, communicator's abilities to achieve the conditions conducive to practicing invitational rhetoric. Levenson, Carstensen, and Gottman (1994) identified conversational elements that communicate a lack of value between participants thus leading to stunted conversations and relationships. Their findings indicate that conversational partners who communicate contempt, criticism, defensiveness, or stonewalling within interpersonal exchanges experience relationship deterioration.

Research Questions

By utilizing invitational rhetoric in interfaith conversations, people of different faiths were able to discuss their religious beliefs in a way that effectively created an empathic environment and cultivated bonding relationships between conversational partners (Sharier, 2015). The same may be true amongst people with differing political views. Through in-depth interviews with people who participated in Take-a-Knee conversations with friends or family members who held divergent perspectives on the matter, this study seeks to advance understanding of the use of invitation rhetoric in contributing to productive opposing viewpoint conversations about political issues within existing relationships. This study seeks to find answers to the following questions:

RQ1: Can conversations where relational partners express differing perspectives about a political issue be productive?

RQ2: What communication practices are present in productive conversations?

RQ3: What communication practices are present in unproductive conversations?

Within this research a productive conversation will be defined as a conversation that drives social connection between conversational partners and contributes to participants' better understanding of themselves, their conversation partners, perspectives on an issue, or the issue at hand. Conversely, an unproductive conversation will be defined as a conversation that drives social distance between conversational partners and does not contribute to furthering participants' understanding.

METHODOLOGY

The purpose of this study was to generate a list of directive communication strategies, grounded in data that can be used to help differing viewpoint conversational partners drive social connection and greater understanding. The Take-a-Knee movement is a multi-layered issue of a divisive nature, capable of serving as a source of conflict within stable, mature relationships crossing a myriad of socio-economic backgrounds and political beliefs. The issue itself is nebulous in nature, with some individuals positioned on similar sides of the issue but for very different reasons. It is this rich variety of dichotomous thinking that led to the exploration of conversations about this issue by utilizing a qualitative phenomenological approach.

Design

In an effort to focus directly on the inward experiences of the rhetor's understanding related to the polarizing conversations, the phenomenological approach adopts Van Manen's (1990) aim at a "deeper understanding of the nature and meaning of everyday experiences." Using this descriptive approach, a phenomenological strategy allows us to "explicate the meanings as we live them in our everyday existence" (Van Manen, 1990, p. 9). Through in-depth interviews, the goal was to understand the experiences of the participants while applying these experiences to what is currently known about invitational rhetoric theory.

Participants

Theoretical sampling, a process where the researcher simultaneously collects, codes, and analyzes data by using emerging data to guide what data to collect next, guided participant selection (Glaser, 1978). Over a dozen in-depth interviews were conducted with individuals who indicated that they had participated in a Take-a-Knee opposing viewpoint conversation within a close, existing relationship. Purposeful sampling was used to a limited extent as half of participants represented cases where relationships have been improved or sustained:

- Austin, age 29, and his parents (Interviewed 2/23/18)
- Dan, age 50, and community members he has led for 15 years (Interviewed 3/16/18)
- JB, age 38, and a colleague and good friend of 12 years (Interviewed 2/22/18)
- Joan, age 55, and her boyfriend (Interviewed 2/20/18)
- Shane, age 33, and his college buddy and good friend of 15 years (interviewed 2/8/18)
- Sam, age 30, and his friends of 10 years (interviewed 2/5/18)
- Ty, age 22, and his father (interviewed 3/5/18).

The other half of interview participants represented cases where relationships have been damaged as a result of these conversations:

- Andrea, age 48, and her cousin (interviewed 3/4/18)
- Colleen, age 25, and her brother (interviewed 3/16/18)
- Jessie, age 43, and her mother (interviewed 2/22/18)
- Brynn, age 18, in relation to her mom Joan's boyfriend of 2 years (interviewed 2/20/18)
- Julia, age 44, and her best friend of 25 years (interviewed 2/26/18)
- Patrick, age 50, and his business clients spanning 20 years (interviewed 2/26/18)
- Melissa, age 55, and her best friend of 35 years (interviewed 2/19/18).

In an effort to be representative, participants consisted of seven males and seven females, ranging in age from eighteen to fifty-five. However, this study's focus on relational impacts related to how individuals navigated divergent political perspective conversations was not incumbent on identity data. Participants were granted anonymity, allowing them to speak freely, so the names given above and throughout the paper are pseudonyms. The interview processes were conducted over a two-month time span with interviews conducted in homes, offices, cafeterias, and other locations.

Procedure

Interview times ranged from thirty minutes to one and a half hours, with an average interview time of approximately sixty minutes. While an interview guide was constructed, the interviews were more conversational in nature because conversational interviewing is regarded as one of the most effective data generating approaches (Brown, 2006). Participants were asked to share their conversational experiences with relational partners who held a differing perspective on the Take-a-Knee issue. The nature and longevity of the relationship, the conversational goal, the conversational subject matters and tone, and the outcome of the conversation were all explored through the eyes of the interview participant. Interviews were transcribed and the authors found common elements in productive and unproductive conversations through coding of the data.

ANALYSIS

Differing Political Perspective Conversations Can be Productive or Unproductive

An exploration of the outcomes and practices within relational partners' differing political-issue-perspective conversational experiences revealed consistent patterns. The first research question was answered as it was discovered that conversations between relational partners discussing their differing perspectives on a political issue can be productive. Several interview participants reported that engaging in divergent perspective conversations with friends and family members was a boon to their relationship and a practice they valued. These participants embraced these conversations as an opportunity to grow. They felt these conversations offered them a greater understanding of the issue, their relational partner, themselves, and a broader sense of the world.

Shane and his college buddy Eric have been engaging in divergent political issue conversations since they met fifteen years ago. Shane says, "Why hang out with people who think exactly as you do? That doesn't expand your thinking at all." Shane describes Eric as one of his best friends and says one thing he values most about Eric is that he has differing political perspectives and is willing to talk about them. Shane says, "It's more fun to talk about issues with Eric because he has a different perspective than I do, and we actually get to have intelligent conversations. I like exploring issues from different angles."

Democratic Party organizer Joan and her boyfriend Kevin, who is a former oil and gas lobbyist, are of different mindsets on many political issues. The two engage in political issue conversations on a regular basis. Joan says, "I have grown so much (from having these kinds of conversations). I am a better person because I'm learning a lot about these issues we discuss. But I'm also learning about how to have these conversations." Joan smiled and added, "And they make us closer because we understand more about each other and how our opinions have formed and what informs them. I think we gain more appreciation for each other."

JB has been working in real estate with her colleague and mentor Scott for twelve years. The two share an office, listings, and a lot of laughs and history. They also both boycotted the National Football League (NFL) this year but for different reasons. JB says, "We're not all carbon copies of each other. Thank God. Thank God we don't have to live surrounded by a million versions of ourselves." She laughs and then adds, "Instead we reach out and try to understand each other, and what is going on in our society, by trying to understand each other's perspectives. And it makes us all better people when we connect and practice compassion. That getting along, I think it's what we all want to see."

While these participants embraced and valued these types of conversations as drivers of greater understanding and relational bonding, they also acknowledged that these conversations are challenging. Joan appreciates that these conversations with Kevin make her feel closer to him and expand her understanding of the issue, but she adds, "It does give me some agitation. It isn't comfortable. I want to continue to have these conversations because it feels important so that we can understand, figure these things out, and keep moving forward." Shane's remarks echo Joan's as he says, "It's mentally challenging to have these kinds of conversations. And I enjoy the intellectual challenge, but it's not something I'd want to do all the time." He adds, "I enjoy it because life isn't supposed to be easy. We grow and we learn when we are challenged and stretched." Again, JB is on the same page as she acknowledged, "It's hard. But it's important. If we just walk around in our spiral shells, we never grow or get anything done."

Because some participants find these conversations rewarding, they feel the conversations are worth the challenge. However, findings revealed not all opposing viewpoint conversations within relationships are as fruitful. Some are relationally damaging. While some participants value learning about a different perspective, others find a different perspective feels challenging and elevates their own personal conviction and passion for their position. Although these participants do value learning, their convictions drive them to prioritize persuasion, often turning discussions into debate.

Andrea and her cousin Michael share differing opinions on the protests. The polarity of their positions led to the dissolution of their relationship. After Andrea posted an article opposing the protest, Michael defriended her from Facebook and suggested they no longer converse save for a civil greeting at family events. Noting they had "nothing in common," Michael added "you're really not part of my life." Although saddened by the rift, Andrea does not regret standing up for her beliefs despite the costs.

Invitational Rhetoric's Role in Productive and Unproductive Conversations

Once we had established that productive divergent perspective conversations are possible, but not always the case within existing relationships, we sought to find the common elements of productive and unproductive conversations. Findings indicated that those who were successful in strengthening their understandings and their relationships in divergent political conversations utilized invitational rhetoric. Those who did not use invitational rhetoric in differing perspective political conversations were unsuccessful in achieving increased social connection and greater understanding. The next part of the analysis shows how conversations with positive outcomes utilized, and conversations with negative outcomes failed to utilize, each of the tenants of invitational rhetoric including: communicating with the singular goal of increased understanding versus persuasion; subscribing to the ideas of equality, immanent worth, and self-determination; and employing the strategy of re-sourcement.

Invitational Rhetoric and the Goal of Understanding

Participants who reported productive opposing viewpoint conversations about "Take-a-Knee," and other polarizing political topics, engaged in these conversations with the singular goal of increasing understanding. They explicitly stated they weren't engaging in these conversations with the mission to persuade or change their conversational partner's position. In her conversations with her boyfriend Kevin, Joan says, "We aren't trying to change each other's opinions. We aren't even aiming to agree. We usually end with some new ideas to think about within our own understanding and agree to disagree." Shane's outlook is similar, saying, "I'm never going to change Eric's opinion. I don't even want to. . . . We are challenging each other to think through our perspectives . . . this makes both of us think more critically." When talking about their Take-a-Knee discussion, Shane says, "It's not even like a disagreement at all really. It's just a conversation, more of an inquiry. I guess my goal was just to learn *why* he felt the way he did."

Sam learned the hard way that trying to change someone's opinion can ruin a relationship. He says:

> You can't change people. Trying to do so only destroys the relationship. Choosing to be in a relationship is like choosing to buy a classic car. You get what you get, as is. The beauty of it is not its potential to be something else. The beauty of it is that it's a classic. So you can appreciate it for what it is, or move on. Because, you know, a new paint job is only going to depreciate the value.

Sam's insight, that trying to change people destroys relationships, was confirmed by interview subjects who damaged relationships with their family members and friends by engaging in divergent political conversations in the hopes of "exposing their (relational partner's) hypocrisies to them" or "opening their eyes." Conversational partners who aimed to change others experienced much frustration and relational strain. Julia is heartbroken that her 35-year friendship with her best friend Julie has been permanently damaged by recent political issue conversations where Julia attempted to "hold Julie accountable" and "get her to realize what she is doing and recognize her role in it." Recalling a conversation between Joan's liberal daughter and Joan's conservative boyfriend, Joan says, "It was bad. Insults were being hurled, neither listening to the other. It wasn't a goal of maintaining a relationship or establishing understanding. It was a goal of winning the argument at all costs." She adds that the cost was the relationship, "They won't ever speak again."

While findings show that communicating to win the argument or change the other's perspectives did not yield positive outcomes in divergent perspective conversations, it was also found that not talking about the issue in an attempt to keep the peace also negatively influenced relationships. Participants reported that "biting their tongue" or having "off the table" topics felt disingenuous and gave the relationship an air of artifice.

Confirming Foss and Griffin's (1995) invitational rhetoric theory, successful ability to achieve increased understanding in divergent perspective conversations did rest upon participants subscribing to invitational rhetoric's tenants of equality, immanent value, and self-determination.

Invitational Rhetoric and the Principle of Equality

An invitational rhetor's ability to welcome and achieve the ability to understand another's perspective rests upon their assent to the idea that their perspective is not superior to others (Foss & Griffin, 1995). This principle of equality points to the conception that all opinions have value. Many interview participants who had productive divergent viewpoint conversations explicitly mentioned that they valued and welcomed divergent perspectives. Some mentioned that the ability to have, and express, divergent opinions is a fundamental aspect of democracy. Dan is a high school principal who got caught in the crosshairs of high school parents making public comments on Facebook about high school students who did, and did not, participate in protests. In an attempt to get parents to take disparaging comments about students off of social media, Dan mediated successful conversations between these parents. He says communicating that he valued each parent's opinion equally played a critical role in mitigating the situation. He stated to the parents, "We are fortunate that in our country we can have beliefs that differ from each other's and we can have beliefs that differ from the ruling powers." Dan said the parents acknowledged that the ability to have and express different opinions is a foundational aspect in a free society, but that did not mean they needed to lash out at one another. He also hopes the lesson was to take these conversations offline as they had a more respectful tone when they were held in person.

The opposite of valuing divergent opinions is what Julia described as "my own incensed self-righteousness" and Melissa called an attitude of "I'm right, you're wrong. So sit down and shut up." Manson (2016) calls it "moral superiority" and goes on to say that, "being outraged and even offended by those who don't agree with you is highly addictive because it feels *good*" (p. 112). Participant interviews confirm it can "feel good" to view one's opinion as morally superior. However, the data also indicated that this tendency is relationship poison. No matter what interview participants called it, those who experienced either their relational partner or themselves offering communication that conveyed the belief that their position was superior to those who held a diverging perspective were unable to maintain the relationship.

Lifelong family relationships and forty-year-old friendships were ruined by Facebook posts that labeled the divergent perspectives their family members or friends held as "idiotic," "crazy," and "nuts." Many wish they had quit Facebook before becoming aware of their relational partner's publicly shared opinion about the inferiority of the opinion they hold. Participants broadly indicated there was no recovering from any of these instances.

Invitational Rhetoric and the Principle of Immanent Value

In addition to valuing divergent perspectives, the success of invitational rhetoric also rests on the rhetor's ability to acknowledge and value their conversational partner's inherent worth as something independent of their opinions. Foss and Griffin (1995) maintain that an individual's worth need not be earned nor can it be taken away by our thoughts or deeds. Immanent value implies all living beings have value just by nature of their existence. Holding the idea that an individual's value as a person, and as a relational partner, is unrelated to their political opinions was a common denominator amongst those who relayed successful divergent perspective conversation experiences. For example, Shane considers Eric one of his best friends and maintains that while he values Eric's divergent opinions, the two would be friends no matter what Eric thought about a political issue. Joan says that when it comes to her long term romantic relationship partner, "I'm looking for a companion, not someone to go campaigning with." JB, who adores her work mentor and values his relationship as one of the most central in her life says, "We have to be able to recognize that having a different perspective does not make someone an enemy." Julia, who regrets losing her friendship over a divergent political conversation gone wrong laments, "You can't make a new old friend. I did not have my priorities right. I made her feel like her political opinions made her a bad person. And that breaks my heart. Because she's not a bad person at all."

Conversations that resulted in positive outcomes effectively separated differing opinions from the individuals involved. Prioritization of the person and the relationship over differing perspectives allowed for actual listening, the asking of inquisitive questions genuinely aimed at understanding, and communication that conveyed that the person and their perspectives were valued.

Findings also suggested that maintaining shared experiences and conversations outside of the divergent political conversations aided in sustaining these relationships. Successful divergent conversation subjects took part in activities that did not revolve around discussing political issues but instead provided a landscape of shared joy and connection on a regular basis.

Another method for conveying immanent value within successful divergent discussions was avoiding generalizations. Joan says that she and Kevin have a policy to only talk about issues, never people. So, while they may discuss Colin Kaepernick's position on "Take a Knee," Kevin would never say anything derogatory about Kaepernick or his supporters. Likewise, while Joan openly articulates her disappointment in President Donald Trump's tweets about his position on the NFL's response, she refrains from saying anything negative to Kevin about Trump or his supporters.

In analyzing damaging divergent discussions, the opposite was at play. The use of generalizations was prevalent and the practice of interchanging individuals and people groups with the issues was frequent. Many participants who reported experiencing relational fallout with a partner who had differing opinions were referred to by their partner as a liberal or conservative "as if it was a bad word," said Melissa. She notes her friend Lisa "Just hates liberals. And she posts ugly stuff about liberals on Facebook. And I'm a liberal!"

Those who were able to separate the worth of their relationship partner from their positions on issues had more positive conversational outcomes.

Invitational Rhetoric and the Principle of Self-Determination

The third principal invitational rhetoric is founded upon is the concept of self-determination. Foss and Griffin (1995) explain that for invitational rhetoric to be achieved individuals must be granted authority in determining their own positions and must be "unconditionally accepted as the expert in their own life" (Johnson, 1992, p. 162). Our data indicated that refraining from efforts to change an opinion is critical in granting relational partner's agency over their own perspectives. Those who gave their conversational partners agency, and credit, for forming their own opinions often found that negative stereotypes they'd held about those who supported that position were defied. This strengthened understanding and relationships. Conversely, suggesting that a relational partner's opinion was the product of persuasion from an outside entity negated the person's agency in forming and holding their opinion. This behavior stunted conversations and relationships.

A February 18, 2018, episode of *60 Minutes* explored aspects of participating in multiple perspective political discussions. An individual from the discussion group shared that one of the most valuable insights he had garnered from participating in the multiple perspective conversations was that he had become aware that often political party spokespeople fail to adequately represent the thoughts of those within the party. He suggested:

> Those of us that are on the right side of the equation, don't always want to be defined by Mitch McConnell and Paul Ryan. And the folks on the left, they don't always want to be necessarily defined by Chuck Schumer and Nancy Pelosi. Because there are positions that those groups hold that aren't real congruent with what a lot of us think sometimes. And you know, maybe that's our fault for letting the parties go the way they have and the platforms that have been created. But ultimately it's gonna be up to us if we want to fix it or not. (Simon, Messick, Laguerre-Wilkinson, & Weingart, 2018)

By engaging in discussions where we allow our conversational partner credit and agency in defining their own position we learn that not "all liberals" or "all conservatives" think or behave in stereotypical, negative ways. In fact, in chapter 12 in this volume it is reported that Democrats and Republicans at the grassroots level had little rationale in common with the statements of the political leaders of their parties (Rhett & Weiss, 2019).

Invitational Rhetoric and the Strategy of Re-sourcement

Finally, invitational rhetoric encourages re-sourcement, which involves reframing the conversation to create more holistic understandings (Foss & Griffin, 1995). This strategy was commonly employed by those who had productive conversations through the use of statements designed to enhance increased understanding and relational bonding. For example, JB and Scott will often say, "Ultimately we both want the same thing." Case in point, while they both boycotted the NFL for different reasons, they realized both were boycotting because they value and want justice and respect for lives.

In heated conversations with others Joan says she will often re-source, or reframe the conversation by stating, "I love that you care just as much about the future of our country as I do." She laughs and adds that the good thing about people having such strong opinions is, "At least we aren't struggling with apathy!" This reframe technique was not present in the discussions that ended poorly, suggesting that continued engagement in a binary framework leads to elevation of the issue transcending harmony within a relationship.

CONCLUSION AND FUTURE STUDY

Finding that differing political issue perspective conversations within existing relationships can be productive and lead to a sense of personal growth and deeper connection confirms Aron's and Aron's (1996) self-expansion model. Employment of invitational rhetoric within productive divergent political issue conversations, and the absence of it within polarizing political conversations that damaged relationships, confirms the utility of Foss and Griffin's (1995) invitational rhetoric's approach, tenets, and strategies. These findings also verify Losada's (1999) ratio confirming that while relationship partners that offer different perspectives do provide the opportunity to learn and grow, divergent conversations are challenging and can detract from relational satisfaction if they become the dominant form of interaction.

In observing the current challenges of polarization which permeate American society, the issues discussed in this study are highly relevant. There is ample room for elaboration of these findings. For example, data indicates the presence of mediated effects and findings also indicated different re-sourcement strategies show varying degrees of efficacy in reframing bilateral conversations toward productive solution-finding orientations. Thirteenth century poet Rumi writes, "Out beyond the ideas/ Of wrongdoing and rightdoing, / There is a field. / I'll meet you there" (quoted in Barks, 1995, p. 16). Invitational rhetoric provides a way for relational partners who hold divergent political perspectives to meet out in the field, past polarization, as they find their way to greater understandings, potential solutions, and each other.

REFERENCES

Aron, E. N., & Aron, A. (1996). Love and expansion of the self: The state of the model. *Personal Relationships*, 3(1), 45-58.

Aron, A., Norman, C. C., Aron, E. N., McKenna, C., & Heyman, R. E. (2000). Couples' shared participation in novel and arousing activities and experienced relationship quality. *Journal of Personality and Social Psychology*, 78(2), 273.

Barks, C. (1995). *The essential Rumi-reissue: New expanded edition*. New York: Harper Collins.

Bone, J. E., Griffin, C. L., & Scholz, T. M. L. (2008). Beyond traditional conceptualizations of rhetoric: Invitational rhetoric and a move toward civility. *Western Journal of Communication*, 72(4), 434-462. doi:10.1080/10570310802446098

Brown, B. (2006). Shame resilience theory: A grounded theory study on women and shame. *Families in Society: The Journal of Contemporary Social Services*, 87(1), 43-52.

Doherty, C., Kiley, J., & Jameson, B. (2016). Partisanship and political animosity in 2016. Washington, DC: Pew Research Center.

Foss, S. K., & Griffin, C. L. (1995). Beyond persuasion: A proposal for an invitational rhetoric. *Communication Monographs*,62(1), 2-18. doi:10.1080/03637759509376345

Fredrickson, B. L. (2013). Updated thinking on positivity ratios. *The American Psychologist*, 68(9), 814-822. doi:10.1037/a0033584.

Gramlich, J. (2016). America's political divisions in 5 charts. Washington, DC: Pew Research Center.

Holt-Lunstad, J., Smith, T. B., & Layton, J. B. (2010). Social relationships and mortality risk: A meta-analytic review: E1000316. *PLoS Medicine*, 7(7) doi:10.1371/journal.pmed.1000316

Johnson, S. (1992). The ship that sailed into the living room: Sex and intimacy reconsidered.

Levenson, R. W., Carstensen, L. L., & Gottman, J. M. (1994). Influence of age and gender on affect, physiology, and their interrelations: A study of long-term marriages. *Journal of Personality and Social Psychology*, 67(1), 56.

Losada, M. (1999). The complex dynamics of high performance teams. *Mathematical and Computer Modelling*, 30(9-10), 179-192.

Luo, Y., Hawkley, L. C., Waite, L. J., & Cacioppo, J. T. (2012). Loneliness, health, and mortality in old age: A national longitudinal study. *Social Science & Medicine*, 74(6), 907-914.

Manson, M. (2016). *The Subtle Art of Not Giving a F* ck: A Counterintuitive Approach to Living a Good Life*. Macmillan Publishers Aus, p. 112.

Rhett, M. & Weiss, J. (2019) Rights and respect: How politicians and their followers view anthem protests. In S. D. Perry (Ed.), *Pro football and the proliferation of protest: Anthem posture in a divided America*. Lanham, MD: Lexington.

Sharier, J. A. (2015). Redefining interfaith discourse: Applying invitational rhetoric to religion. *Young Scholars in Writing*, 9, 87-97.

Sheets, V. L. (2014). Passion for life: Self-expansion and passionate love across the life span. *Journal of Social and Personal Relationships*, 31(7), 958-974.

Simon, T., Messick, G., Laguerre-Wilkinson, Weingart. J. (Producers) (February 18, 2018). *60 minutes*. [Television series]. New York, New York: CBS.

Tsapelas, I., Aron, A., & Orbuch, T. (2009). Marital boredom now, predicts less satisfaction nine years later. *Psychological Science*, 20, 543-545.

Van Manen, M. (1990). *Researching lived experience: Human science for an action sensitive pedagogy*. Albany: State University of New York Press.

TWENTY
Reflections in Overtime

Stephen D. Perry and Shreya Shukla

An expression, a high-visibility platform, and a symbol—these are the three elements at the center of disagreement in the Take-a-Knee/Stand-for-the-Anthem story. What contributes depth of hermeneutical ignorance based on one's position in the conflict are the symbolic status of the American flag, one's expectations toward the separation of sport and politics, and the interpretation of kneeling during the national anthem. The interaction of faith and patriotism can further cement someone's opposition or support (Mattson & Phillips, 2019). Is kneeling an expression of disrespect? Is it a "gesture of pain and distress" (Siegel, 2017)? Or is it both, an expression of protest and a show of respect for the military? Society seems deadlocked on the answers, but as yet, no one is shaking hands to acknowledge the end of the game.

This book has explored various facets of communication's importance in the Anthem-Kneeling controversy. A few things are clear. First, people on both sides of the issue are prejudiced toward their own perspective, they are emotionally invested in their viewpoint, and as a result they prefer to maintain the stance of listening avoidance. Yes, they may hear the other side, but they don't listen with empathy to what the other side is saying.

But contributing to the lack of listening is the failure of primary voices to carry the pathos and even the full ethos needed to attract the ears, hearts, and minds of the opposition. Kaepernick's position as a person in whom the audience would emotionally invest struggled because of his privilege as a well-paid athlete who hadn't clearly been invested in the cause before taking a seat and then a knee. His believability was further damaged by at least a single prominent statement reflecting disgust toward America and being photographically captured wearing socks symbolically demeaning police generally.

His foil in this debate eventually became the president of the United States. President Trump, however, used a derogatory term toward athletes who were engaged in the peaceful kneeling protest by calling them "sons of bitches." Such distasteful rhetoric damaged his ability to be seen sympathetically. Further, Trump's own history of conflict with the NFL allowed opponents to attribute other ulterior motives to his attacks on the league for allowing the kneeling. These factors, then, contribute to the maintenance of hermeneutical ignorance by people on both sides of the issue who use the spokesperson on the other side as justification for staunchly maintaining their perspective and allowing that to play out through mimicking the protests, participating in social networked advocacy, boycotting various aspects of the NFL, and even refusing to continue previously important interpersonal relationships.

Pro Football and the Proliferation of Protest: Anthem Posture in a Divided America has analyzed the game plans, planted new turf, and illuminated the scoreboard on both sides of this complex debate. It has examined the movement's historic, racial, gender-based, and demographic angles, to provide more clarity on issues of national importance—unity in diversity, empathy, and respect.

THE PROTEST

"We don't get to eat at home, so we're going to eat on this field" ("Hutchins Center," 2018, para 4). According to Kaepernick, this comment from a member of Castlemont High School's football team, which took a knee after Kaepernick first knelt in protest, is imprinted in his memory. "And I feel like it's not only my responsibility, but all our responsibilities—as people that are in positions of privilege, in positions of power—to continue to fight for them, and uplift them, empower them," he said in his remarks during the W. E. B. Du Bois Medal Ceremony where he was recognized by the Hutchins Center for African & African American Research at Harvard University ("Hutchins Center," 2018, para 5; "Eight to be," 2018). Kaepernick took a knee to protest against racial injustice and police brutality, starting a movement and debate that still continued as of this writing. While this book does not seek to end the movement or debate, it does attempt to shed light on points at which audience perceptions on both sides may not equate with reality. Hopefully the pictures in our heads can be more aligned with reality than rhetoric.

While Kaepernick began his protest by sitting on the bench during the national anthem in the first preseason game of the San Francisco 49ers (Taylor, Brand, & Amiri, 2018), he later knelt in protest. In chapter 7, Cosby highlights the role of Nate Boyer, a former NFL player and United

States Army Green Beret, in this change (2019a). A face-to-face meeting between the two eventually led to Kaepernick making the decision to kneel during the anthem instead of sit, with Boyer's support. To Boyer, kneeling represented respect. "Soldiers take a knee in front of a fallen brother's grave, you know, to show respect. When we're on a patrol, you know, and we go into a security halt, we take a knee, and we pull security" (Cosby, 2019a). This is one of the major takeaways from the book. To Boyer, as passed on to Kaepernick, "the idea of *taking a knee* presented an opportunity to respectfully engage in a call for awareness or action," (Cosby, 2019a). It shows that there was a development in Kaepernick's stance, one that involved a show of respect for the military.

As Perry notes in chapter 1, Kaepernick stated that his protest did not indicate an anti-American attitude; instead, he was fighting to make a country he loved better (2019). The details of what was referred to earlier, however, included the existence of photos of him wearing socks with illustrations of pigs in police hats. He also stated that he wouldn't stand up or show pride in the American flag. These together raised questions about whether he really was working to help a country he loved (Witz, 2016). It added another layer to the debate. If his actions and statements had been consistently pro-American there could have been more respect for kneeling and kneeling might have been seen as a sign of respect.

THE PERCEPTION

The platform that Kaepernick used played a major role in the perception of his protest because of the high visibility it commanded. The historic lens provided by chapter 2 showed the similarity between Kaepernick's protest and that of John Carlos and Tommie Smith during the 1968 Summer Olympics in Mexico City (Nyamandi & Bolin, 2019). As in the case of the Olympics, some view using the distinctly American, National Football League platform as a very visible form of embarrassment for the country. The phrase "untypical exhibitionism," used for the 1968 Olympic protest (Hurschmann, 1968) reflects this idea. Moreover, as the students' and teachers' reactions in chapter 18 show, the protests evoked responses on either side because of this high-profile platform (Tabbanor, 2019). Protesting the United States' Anthem during one distinctly American sport, however, stands in stark contrast to the unbridled patriotism displayed in the American motorsport series of NASCAR as noted in chapter 14 (Bullock, 2019). This contrast both suggests the NFL could have been proactive had they wanted to promote patriotism, and points to the diverse makeup of the NFL and the extreme lack of diversity in the high profile positions of NASCAR, which help explain that difference.

Take-a-Knee supporters could argue that using a platform such as the NFL is the very reason the protest gained attention. However, because of the emotional weight attached to the national anthem, the protest drew more attention to the act of kneeling being disrespectful than to the issue of racial injustice. Such attention, initially promoted through social media by several celebrities, was magnified when echoed by President Donald Trump's tweets on the issue (Moore, 2019; Kemp, 2019).

Surprisingly, chapter 12 revealed that support of and opposition to the protest existed among the grassroots participants in both parties. But it also showed that for most people of both parties, only Trump's comments were able to be recalled (Rhett & Weiss, 2019). While politician statements stuck close to the party line, grass roots voices overlapped with some Democrats opposing Kaepernick and some Republicans supporting his kneeling. Members of both parties emphasized the importance of free speech but neither party's adherents thought the other party understood the voices of their own. In fact, relatively few politicians were willing to speak out on the issue at all.

THE MEDIA

While politicians spoke infrequently on the issue, talk radio spent hours on it. It may be that partisan perceptions come through the voices that are seen as representing certain parties who railed for or against Kaepernick's position or Trump's position. So next, we'll break down what we discovered about the media—both traditional and social media.

The use of tweets and hashtags in the protest were much more active early in the 2017 NFL season, but the hashtags had yet to coalesce around agreed upon versions (Duckett & Sacra, 2019). Chapter 12 showed that tweeters tended to use not only the hashtags favoring their individual point of view and that of groups with which they sought to align, but also typically used anti-sentiment hashtags in order to draw an audience of others in the Twitter community with differing points of view. Ultimately, scholars found that semantic communities tended to converge around (1) discussion of the national anthem and the NFL; (2) Trump and political conservatism; or (3) racial injustice and political liberalism, as individuals identified shared interests in particular ideas.

Among those steering the conversation on Twitter as well as other social media platforms were celebrities. Chapter 10 showed how tweets from celebrities of both races both supported and opposed Kaepernick's kneeling in response to the anthem (Moore, 2019). The difference appears to be that African Americans who spoke out against it tended to recant their statements and remove such posts to protect their image and brand among current and potential fans. Still, it is clear that celebrities were the first to oppose kneeling during the anthem in respect for the military—something that has generally been credited to Trump. It seems Trump may have been siding with other celebrity posts, but his posts carried the weight to change the conversation from emphasizing excessive use of force by police to one of disrespecting the military and the sacrifice of those who died protecting the flag (Kemp, 2019).

Another layer that this book explored was the effect of racial implications on digital discourse. In chapter 11, Cosby proposed that "the identification of race as associated with a movement had a direct association with the way the movement itself was perceived, as well as users' attitudes toward the movement and its participants" (2019b). Race and the perception of a movement were inextricably interwoven for many on both sides of the movement. "Admittedly, many activists intentionally include racial language and/or artifacts in their discourse in an effort to secure the relationship with race as the impetus for the movement," says Cosby (2019b).

As for mainstream media, Feld, Sacra, and Butler mentioned in chapter 6 that "the conservative news outlet, Fox News, published over twice as many articles as CNN and four times as many articles as the *Wall Street Journal* during the same time frame" (2019) in relation to the Take-a-Knee movement. This higher frequency made it appear that Fox News found it important to present the story more than the other news outlets, "with a negative slant in almost half of the articles" (Feld, Sacra, & Butler, 2019). Conservative talk radio similarly were antagonistic toward Kaepernick (King & Frederick, 2019). On the other hand, almost no negative presentations of Kaepernick were found in the combined minority targeted media that was analyzed (Feld, Sacra, & Butler, 2019).

The media also seemed to have a partial blind spot about women athletes taking a knee. Chapter 17 showed how Meagan Rapinoe is rarely, if ever, reported as being the first athlete to kneel in solidarity with Kaepernick (Kappeler & Flory, 2019). Instead, that distinction has regularly been attributed to the second *male* athlete without using the modifier of his sex. And though many other women have used their sport venues to kneel, little coverage has emphasized their participation. Interestingly, the researchers also found that the language discussing women who chose to kneel failed to exhibit features of misogyny that have been identified in other types of reporting about female athletes. Yet the evidence was clear that the power of the female athlete to exert influence on social change was deemed much less newsworthy than that of men who kneeled.

A CONVERSATION

This book seeks to promote listening and conversation. Chapter 1 refers to the investigation of police-civilian interactions by communication scholars, which revealed that the dearth of communication accommodation played a role in stigmatization, uncertainty, and disputes (Dixon,

Schell, Giles, & Drogos, 2008). As chapter 19 highlighted, the perception of equality is the fulcrum of relationships—refusal to consider the other person as an equal while considering opinions can negatively impact a relationship (Clarke & Connelly, 2019). Invitational rhetoric can help in the successful navigation of relationships between people who subscribe to differing opinions, as its aim is to see the layers of complexity in an issue and create greater understanding (Clarke & Connelly, 2019). Its approach, tenets, and strategies can serve as tools to help partners navigate the emotional waters of deeply held opposing positions such as those held by people on opposite sides of the Take-a-Knee/Stand-for-the-Anthem debate.

Chapter 5 presented an instance of a demonstrated understanding of both sides with the Cowboys organization kneeling to pray before standing for the national anthem as a team (King & Frederick, 2019). Developments since then have seen the Dallas Cowboys' executive vice president Stephen Jones reportedly insinuating that "any Cowboys player protesting during the national anthem would be released from the team" (Breech, 2018). But the NFL, which had proposed a policy prohibiting kneeling, put that conduct policy on hold to avoid bringing the issue back to the forefront in the middle of the 2018 season (Robinson, 2018). The initial stance of the Dallas Cowboys provides an example of how support and respect for diverse opinions can be presented. Even seemingly opposing sides of the conversation share parallel values of patriotism, American unity, the right to free speech, and an interest in separating entertainment from politics (King & Frederick, 2019; Rhett & Weiss, 2019).

There are other ways forward as well. The South African experience of modifying the post-apartheid anthem to include elements of the anthem that had been a symbol of South Africa under white rule might suggest a way to bring unity to the American anthem. The perspectives of the southern interviewees in chapter 4, backed by the writings of other scholars, clearly indicate that some do not find the anthem in its current form represents them (Andrea & Hayes, 2019). Thus, it invokes pride in some and represents racism for others. Perhaps by choosing to modify some words of the later verses of the "Star-Spangled Banner" to incorporate elements of "Lift Every Voice and Sing" or a similar song that positively represents the African-American heritage, we could both maintain the iconic symbolism in the song's familiar first verse and eradicate the lingering vestiges of racism, replacing them with elements that celebrate the unity of all Americans.

It is unclear whether anthem-related protests over excessive force used by police officers could be mollified by a change in the anthem, but such a change would be meaningful. Providing an anthem that is fully embraced by more Americans would help create an atmosphere in which we can embrace unity while solving differences. A lot of elements define the United States of America; liberty, democracy, freedom, and prosperity, to name a few. To all these, let respect, empathy, and neighborliness be added as the ones that all sides strive most to attain. May we "discover a new language, a language which helps [people] to understand one another, in spite of publicity, a language which permits men to abandon their despairing solitude, and avoids both rational sterility and subjective emotionalism" (Ellul, 1989, p. 105; Mattson & Phillips, 2019), and in so doing, may we overcome our hermeneutical ignorance before it is too late and the final whistle blows.

REFERENCES

Andrea, P. A. & Hayes, E. S. (2019). America's greatness compromised: The "Star-Spangled Banner" as a symbol of nationalism, identity, and division. In S. D. Perry (Ed.), *Pro football and the proliferation of protest: Anthem posture in a divided America*. Lanham, MD: Lexington.

Breech, J. (2018, July 27). Cowboys strongly hint that anyone who protests during national anthem will be cut from team. *CBSSports.com*. Retrieved from https://www.cbssports.com/nfl/news/cowboys-strongly-hint-that-anyone-who-protests-during-national-anthem-will-be-cut-from-team/

Bullock, C. (2019). A great American race: Visual rhetoric in NASCAR's national anthem ceremonies. In S.D. Perry (Ed), *Pro-football and the proliferation of protest: Anthem posture in a divided America*. Lanham, MD: Lexington.

Clarke, K. & Connelly, C. (2019). Solutions to the fallout: Invitational rhetoric and differing viewpoint political conversations. In S. D. Perry (Ed.), *Pro football and the proliferation of protest: Anthem posture in a divided America*. Lanham, MD: Lexington.

Cosby, N.B. (2019a). How social media activists and their hashtags have encouraged and informed their followers on the Take-a-Knee movement. In S. D. Perry (Ed.), *Pro football and the proliferation of protest: Anthem posture in a divided America*. Lanham, MD: Lexington.

Cosby, N.B. (2019b). The role of race in the perceptions of and response to the protests. In S.D. Perry (Ed.), *Pro football and the proliferation of protest: Anthem posture in a divided America*. Lanham, MD: Lexington.

Dixon, T. L., Schell, T. L., Giles, H., & Drogos, K. L. (2008). The influence of race in police-civilian interactions: A content analysis of videotaped interactions taken during Cincinnati police traffic stops. *Journal of Communication*, 58(3), 530–549. https://doi.org/10.1111/j.1460-2466.2008.00398.x

Duckett, J. & Sacra, D. (2019). Together we tweet: A cloud protest exploratory study examining the evolution of #TakeAKnee. In S. D. Perry (Ed.), *Pro football and the proliferation of protest: Anthem posture in a divided America*. Lanham, MD: Lexington.

"Eight to be honored as W. E. B. Du Bois medalists." (2018, September 20). *The Harvard Gazette*. Retrieved from https://news.harvard.edu/gazette/story/2018/09/kaepernick-and-chappelle-among-eight-du-bois-medalists-at-harvard/

Ellul, J. (1989). *The presence of the kingdom* (2nd ed.). (O. Wyon, Trans.) Colorado Springs, CO: Helmers & Howard.

Feld, K., Sacra, D. & Butler, S. A. Kaepernick portrayals: A content analysis of six media outlets. In S.D. Perry (Ed.), *Pro football and the proliferation of protest: Anthem posture in a divided America*. Lanham, MD: Lexington.

Hurschmann, B. (1968, October 21). Smith, Carlos ousted from Olympic Games. *Spartan Daily*, p. 1.

"Hutchins Center Honors Presents the W. E. B. Du Bois Medal Ceremony." (2018, October 11). Hutchins Center for African & African American Research. Retrieved from https://hutchinscenter.fas.harvard.edu/event/hutchins-center-honors-presents-w-e-b-du-bois-medal-ceremony

Kappeler, C. & Flory, N. (2019). Female athletes in media: Participating in the Take-a-Knee movement. In S.D. Perry (Ed.), *Pro football and the proliferation of protest: Anthem posture in a divided America*. Lanham, MD: Lexington.

Kemp, K. (2019). NFL national anthem protests: A cluster analysis of President Trump's tweets. In S. D. Perry (Ed.), *Pro football and the proliferation of protest: Anthem posture in a divided America*. Lanham, MD: Lexington.

King, K. & Frederick, E. (2019). Influencing America: Sports and conservative radio. In S. D. Perry, (Ed.), *Pro football and the proliferation of protest: Anthem posture in a divided America*. Lanham, MD: Lexington.

Mattson, B. & Phillips, A. (2019). Articulating Christianity and patriotism: Identifying a hermeneutical impasse through emerging meanings. In S. D. Perry (Ed.), *Pro football and the proliferation of protest: Anthem posture in a divided America*. Lanham, MD: Lexington.

Moore, C. (2019). Celebrity response to Take-a-Knee, Kaepernick and NFL protests. In S. D. Perry, (Ed.), *Pro football and the proliferation of protest: Anthem posture in a divided America*. Lanham, MD: Lexington.

Nyamandi, V. & Bolin, A. (2019). The more things change. . . . A history of national anthem protests. In S. D. Perry (Ed.), *Pro football and the proliferation of protest: Anthem posture in a divided America*. Lanham, MD: Lexington.

Perry, S. D. (2019). Division and hermeneutical ignorance in America: Reasons to examine the anthem kneeling controversy. In S. D. Perry (Ed.), *Pro football and the proliferation of protest: Anthem posture in a divided America*. Lanham, MD: Lexington.

Rhett, M. & Weiss, J. (2019). Rights and respect: How politicians and their followers view anthem protests. In S. D. Perry (Ed.), *Pro football and the proliferation of protest: Anthem posture in a divided America*. Lanham, MD: Lexington.

Robinson, C. (2018, October 15). Silence on NFL's anthem issue will speak volumes at fall owners meetings. Yahoo Sports. Retrieved from https://sports.yahoo.com/silence-nfls-anthem-issue-will-speak-volumes-fall-owners-meetings-034409942.html

Siegel, L. (2017, September 25). Why Kaepernick takes the knee. *The New York Times*. Retrieved from https://www.nytimes.com/2017/09/25/opinion/nfl-football-kaepernick-take-knee.html

Tabbanor, M. (2019). Sitting to take a stand: Take-a-Knee and student protesting. In S. D. Perry (Ed.), *Pro football and the proliferation of protest: Anthem posture in a divided America*. Lanham, MD: Lexington.

Taylor, J., Brand, A., & Amiri, F. (2018, September 4). 'Take a knee': A complete guide to the NFL anthem controversy, starting with Kaepernick's first protest. NBC News. Retrieved from https://www.nbcnews.com/news/sports/take-knee-complete-guide-nfl-anthem-controversy-starting-kaepernick-s-n906241

Witz, B. (2016, September 1). This time Colin Kaepernick takes a stand by kneeling. *The New York Times*. Accessed March 16, 2018, at https://www.nytimes.com/2016/09/02/sports/football/colin-kaepernick-kneels-national-anthem-protest.html.

Index

#BlackLivesMatter (#BLM), 7, 90, 93, 131, 143, 176, 179, 180, 182, 183, 184, 187, 191, 254, 268
#BoycottNFL, 88–91, 179, 180, 182, 183, 187
#KneelNFL, 6, 7, 88, 89
#MAGA, 134, 176, 179, 180, 181, 182, 183, 184, 187
#MeToo, 1, 182, 183, 184
#Resist, 179, 180, 182, 183, 184, 187
#TakeAKnee, 6, 7, 88–92, 138, 153, 155, 157, 176–189, 246, 249

700 Club, 217
82nd Airborne division, 200, 202, 203

Abdul-Jabbar, Kareem, 5
Abdul-Rauf, Mahmoud, 6, 117
abolitionists, 48, 286
activist ideology, 209, 213, 214, 216, 217, 218, 220, 222
actors, 134, 135–136, 139, 140; political, 186; social, 186–188, 255
actress, 129, 134, 135, 138, 140
advocacy, 86, 141, 148, 284
advocates, 19, 50, 137, 138, 139, 140, 141, 213
affordances, 175, 177, 186, 188, 189
African National Congress, 20, 21
agency, 279
Alcindor, Lew, 5
America the Beautiful, 56
American flag. *See* United States flag
American sacramentalism, 209, 213, 216, 217, 219
anti-American, 3, 4, 167, 285
anti-military, 4, 137, 167
apartheid, 20, 23, 288
articulation theory, 209, 211
Ashe, Arthur, 5

athletes, 3, 5, 6, 65, 69, 74, 90, 91, 94, 116, 117, 118, 120, 121, 123, 124, 129, 130, 133, 137, 139, 151–152, 193, 195, 196, 218, 225, 242, 247, 249, 263, 284; African-American / black, 5, 17–18, 74, 117, 131, 140, 151, 249; female, 9, 25, 241, 242–243, 244–245, 247, 247–249, 249, 287; male, 242–243, 245, 247, 249. *See* National Football League athletes
Atlanta Journal-Constitution, 35, 36, 37, 38, 39
Australian Rugby Union, 21, 22, 23

"Battle of the Sexes," 5
Beyoncé, 129, 140
black lives matter, 1, 2, 91, 151, 160, 181, 211, 253
black power, 18–19, 20, 140, 150; black power movement, 18
blogs, 59, 119, 212, 216, 217, 218; bloggers, 25, 76, 125; microblog, 115, 125, 176
Booker, Cory, 162, 163, 164, 165, 166
Bormann, Ernest, 61, 161
Boston Tea Party, 163
boycott, 5, 7, 8–9, 17–18, 19, 66, 68, 88, 89, 90, 91, 93, 96, 122, 124, 130, 135, 179, 179–180, 180, 181, 182, 183–184, 187, 194, 225, 226–228, 228, 229, 230, 231–235, 232–234, 235–239, 274, 280, 284
brand, 9, 130, 193, 196–197, 197, 198, 202, 286
Brown, Michael, 5
Burke, Kenneth, 35, 118–119, 122, 130, 132, 210
Bush, George W., 25, 74, 130, 160, 161
buycott, 9, 226

Carey, James, 15, 16
Carlos, John, 6, 17, 18, 19, 20, 27–28, 74, 116
cars, 151, 195. *See also* racing cars
celebrity, 4, 10, 59, 93, 106, 107, 129–130, 130–141, 253, 255, 256, 263, 267, 286; exposure, 263; influence, 130, 262, 263
ceremonial, 209, 213, 216, 220, 222
Charleston Gazette, 23
Cheney, Dick, 161
Chicago Defender, 19
chi-square analysis, 218
Christian, 4, 8, 49, 75, 109, 209, 210, 211, 212, 213, 214, 215, 216, 217–218, 219–223
Christian anarchy, 210, 219–220, 221
Christianity, 8, 109–110, 134, 209, 210, 211–212, 212, 213, 214, 216, 218, 219, 220, 221, 222
civil religion, 210, 213, 219
civil rights, 7, 8, 17, 64, 65, 135, 160, 163, 164; movement, 1, 19, 33, 140, 160, 254
Civil War, 1, 32, 164
clothing, 64, 131, 141
cloud protest theory, 175, 176, 177, 185, 188, 189
cluster analysis, 34, 34–35, 40, 119, 120, 125
CNN, 66, 68, 73, 77, 79, 80, 81, 92, 120, 129, 155, 160, 166, 248, 287
coaches, 4, 24, 51, 66, 246, 258, 259–260, 264
collective action, 175–176, 177, 186, 188, 228
collective identity, 131, 132, 195, 203, 204
Congressional Black Caucus, 162, 165
connectedness, 47, 50
constitution, 1, 89, 151, 162, 164, 210
constitutional rights, 75, 125, 133, 254, 259
Cornyn, John, 162, 163, 166
criminal justice, 165
Cruz, Ted, 162, 163, 169
cultural studies, 26
Cup Series (NASCAR), 197, 205

Daytona 500, 194, 196, 197, 197–198, 199, 200, 201, 202, 203, 204–205
Daytona Beach, Florida, 194
Daytona international speedway, 200, 201, 202
de Klerk, Frederick, 21
degree centrality, 176, 178, 179, 180, 182, 183, 184
Democrat, 1, 2, 37, 78, 159, 160, 161, 161–162, 162, 163, 164, 165, 166, 167, 168–169, 170, 184, 215, 274, 279, 286
Denver Post, 35, 38, 39, 41
Die Stem, 20–21, 22, 22–23, 23
discrimination, 18, 63, 148, 157, 161, 167, 182, 245
divergent perspectives conversations, 269, 271, 273, 275, 276, 277–278, 280
diversity, 16, 57, 64, 92, 137, 196, 198, 203, 204, 218, 262, 284, 285
division, 1, 3, 35, 40, 47, 50, 56, 60, 65, 69, 116, 121, 124, 126, 130, 132, 134, 222, 225
drivers. *See* racing drivers
Duffy, Sean, 160

Eagleton affair, 161
Eagleton, Thomas, 161
Ellul, Jacques, 210, 219, 221, 222, 223
entertainer, 67, 129–130, 131
equality, 67, 69, 81, 88–89, 90, 118, 123, 124, 132, 139, 150, 165, 169, 244, 253, 254, 270, 275, 276, 288
ethnic identity, 45
Evangelical, 110, 134, 170, 214, 215, 216, 217, 218, 219
Evangelicalism, 211–219

Facebook, 85, 87, 88, 90, 91, 91–92, 93, 133, 135, 137, 152, 153–155, 217, 229, 275, 277, 278
factor analysis, 231
fantasy theme, 61, 62, 70, 159, 161, 167, 170
Farr-Jones, Nick, 22
feminism, 25, 32, 244, 254
Ferguson, Missouri, 5
First Amendment, 117, 125, 137, 140, 163, 164, 254
flag, American. *See* United States flag

Flood, Curt, 5
football players, 3, 3–4, 4–5, 9, 39, 40, 42, 57, 62, 63, 65–66, 66–67, 68, 69, 73, 74, 75, 81, 82, 85–86, 89, 90, 91, 94–95, 106, 107, 108, 111, 115, 116, 117–118, 120, 121–122, 123, 123–124, 124, 129, 130, 133, 134, 134–135, 139, 140, 148, 151, 152, 153, 155, 162, 164, 165, 168, 177, 180, 182, 189, 194, 216, 217, 225, 249, 253, 254, 256, 258, 263, 265, 284, 288
Fox and Friends, 135, 216
Fox News, 77, 79, 80, 81, 82, 134, 161, 218, 287
framing, 7, 28, 32, 33, 34, 40, 40–41, 41, 42, 70, 74, 75, 76, 77, 78, 79, 80, 80–82, 111, 112, 119, 131, 148, 175, 176, 177, 180, 185, 186, 188, 189, 209, 210, 211, 212, 213, 214, 215, 242, 243, 270, 280
France, Bill, 194
Franco, Francisco, 5
free will, 46, 259
freedom of association, 163
freedom of religion, 163
freedom of speech, 74, 76, 89, 151, 167, 168, 169, 260, 261

Gardner, Cory, 162, 165, 170
Gephi, 178, 179
God Bless America, 5
Goldwater, Barry, 160
Goodell, Roger, 62, 120, 163
grassroots, 159, 166, 169, 170, 286
The Great American race, 194, 197, 205. *See also* Daytona 500
group consciousness, 161

Hail Columbia, 54
Harris, Kamala, 162
hashtag, 6, 6–7, 88, 89–91, 93, 96–98, 104, 119, 120, 121, 124, 131, 132, 134–135, 138, 139, 141, 151, 153, 157, 175, 176, 177, 178, 179, 179–180, 181, 182, 183, 184, 185, 186–187, 188, 189, 286; co-occurrence, 176–177, 178, 179, 180, 181, 185, 186, 187–188, 189
healthcare, 165, 165–166
The Herald, 23

hermeneutical ignorance, 3, 8, 283, 284, 289
hermeneutical impasse, 2, 210, 220, 222, 223
hero, 65–66, 67, 70, 74, 76, 82, 109, 139, 210
Hitler, Adolph, 6

identification, 6, 45, 47, 50, 53, 65, 69, 86, 118, 119, 123, 124, 126, 130–132, 134, 136, 138, 141, 155, 157, 159, 162, 176, 195, 198, 199, 262, 287
identity, 9, 45, 46–47, 47, 50, 55, 70, 130, 131–132, 139, 175, 186, 189, 194, 195, 196, 197, 198, 203–204, 204, 205, 210, 226, 228, 237–238, 239, 273. *See also* social identity theory
ideology, 60, 89, 92, 98, 110, 116, 123, 131, 134, 137, 148, 159, 162, 185, 209, 213, 214, 216, 217, 218, 220, 222, 228, 238, 239
immigration, 1, 25, 26
inequality, 6, 22, 27, 41, 46, 49, 52, 64, 73, 90, 117, 123, 125, 126, 145, 155, 245
influence, 2, 16, 17, 20, 31, 33, 41, 57, 67, 69, 76, 77, 86, 87, 88, 96, 98, 99, 101, 106, 130–131, 139, 141, 145, 147, 155, 157, 159, 160, 170, 176, 186, 198, 199, 211, 219, 226, 227, 228, 231, 232–235, 236, 238, 239, 241, 244, 249, 253, 255, 256, 257, 259, 262–263, 263, 263–265, 265–266, 266, 266–267, 276, 287
Instagram, 133, 134, 137, 138, 140
instrumental involvement, 47
interfaith conversations, 271
interviews, 17, 51, 52–53, 53, 54–55, 55, 56, 57, 62, 68, 88, 92, 96, 98, 98–99, 112, 133, 135, 136, 137, 146, 147–148, 149, 153, 155, 156, 161–162, 165, 167, 168, 212, 212–213, 213, 214, 215, 216, 256–257, 258, 259, 260, 261, 262, 263–264, 265, 266, 267, 271, 272–273, 273, 276, 276–277, 288
invitational rhetoric. *See* rhetoric, invitational

Jackson Lee, Sheila, 4, 117
Jakes, T.D., 216

Jeffress, Robert, 216
Jersey, 68, 93, 96, 117, 137, 139, 217
Johnson, Lyndon B., 160

Kaepernick, Colin, 39, 46, 48, 51, 53, 54, 56, 57, 63, 64, 73–74, 75, 76, 77, 78, 79, 80–82, 82, 85, 88, 89, 90, 91, 92, 93, 94–95, 105, 106, 107, 108–110, 110, 111, 112, 115, 116, 117–118, 120, 123, 129–130, 132, 133, 134, 135, 136, 137, 139–141, 141, 150–151, 153–155, 155, 163, 167, 169, 179, 180, 181, 183, 187, 189, 193–194, 199, 209, 216, 217, 225, 230, 245, 245–246, 249, 254, 257, 258–259, 263, 266, 278, 283, 284–285, 286, 287
Kennedy, John F., 160
Key, Francis Scott, 48–49, 52, 56, 68, 140
King, Billie Jean, 5
King, Martin Luther, Jr., 184
kneeling. *See* United States National Anthem, kneeling during
Kouandjio, Cyrus, 216

Latino, 136, 140, 229
legendary, 5, 136, 138, 194
liberty, 46, 90, 155, 216, 246, 247, 289
Lift Every Voice and Sing, 52, 288
Lincoln, Abraham, 160
Los Angeles Times, 19, 35, 38, 79
Losada's ratio, 269, 280

Mainline Protestant, 212, 214, 215, 218, 219
Major League Baseball (MLB), 5, 50, 51, 75, 133
Mandela, Nelson, 22, 23
Marjory Stoneman Douglas High School, 254, 257
McCaskill, Claire, 168
McConnell, Mitch, 168, 279
McGovern, George, 161
meaning-negotiation phase, 186, 188
media, 1, 2, 6, 7, 9, 10, 15, 16, 19–22, 22–23, 24, 25, 26, 27, 28, 31, 32, 33, 34, 35, 37, 38, 39–41, 42, 60, 63, 66, 67, 74, 75–76, 76, 77, 78, 79, 79–81, 80, 82, 85, 86, 87, 103, 108, 116, 119, 120, 121, 124, 130, 130–131, 131, 132, 133, 136, 137, 151, 161, 175, 176, 182, 194, 195, 196, 204, 210, 211, 212, 218, 241, 242, 243, 244–245, 248–249, 255–256, 262, 263, 266, 286, 287. *See also* newspapers; social media; radio
melting pot, 53
Mexico City, Mexico, 17, 18, 285
micro-blogging, 115, 125, 176
military. *See* United States Military
MLB. *See* Major League Baseball
modularity, 176, 178, 179, 180, 181, 182, 183, 184, 185, 185–186
moral obligation, 209, 213, 216, 216–217, 219, 220, 222
moral superiority, 277
movement, 1, 6–7, 9, 18, 19, 24, 31, 32, 34, 35, 36, 37, 38, 39, 40, 41, 48, 86, 86–99, 88, 96–98, 119, 121, 124, 131, 140, 145–146, 146, 147, 148, 149, 150, 153, 155, 160, 175–176, 176, 177, 185, 186, 188, 189, 190, 193, 204, 211, 221, 228, 238, 239, 249, 253, 254, 263, 266, 267, 287. *See also* Take-a-knee
Mundine, Anthony, 26
music, 25, 45–46, 47, 48, 49, 51, 54, 55, 56, 61, 135, 140

NAACP (National Association for the Advancement of Colored People), 163, 231, 232–234, 237
National Association for Stock Car Auto Racing. *See* NASCAR
National Association for the Advancement of Colored People. *See* NAACP
NASCAR (National Association for Stock Car Auto Racing), 9, 121, 124, 194–196, 197, 198, 202, 203, 203–205, 285. *See also* The Great American race; racing
national anthem, United States, 9, 56, 184, 286, 288; as symbol, 2, 7, 20, 27, 45–46, 47, 49, 50–51, 52, 53, 54–55, 56, 57, 107, 108, 132, 194, 201, 204, 210, 216, 217, 219, 246, 247; ceremony, 4, 5, 10, 50, 55, 57, 73, 111, 194, 198, 199, 200, 200–201, 202–203, 204–205; controversy, 6, 10, 57, 65, 67–68, 115, 179, 212, 225, 257, 283,

288; history of, 48–49, 54, 57, 140; kneeling during, 2, 3, 6, 8, 39, 61, 73, 91, 96, 106, 108, 118, 122, 124, 129, 132, 134, 135, 137, 163, 165, 180, 193, 216, 225, 245–246, 247, 254, 258–259, 283, 284, 286; NFL policy regarding, 4, 75, 82, 106, 123, 124, 125, 288; perceptions of, 10, 56–57; protest of, 3, 4, 6, 9, 15, 16, 18–19, 19, 24–25, 25, 27, 27–28, 42, 51, 56, 62, 65, 70, 78, 81, 86, 88, 94–95, 105, 108, 111, 115–117, 117, 122, 123, 124, 125, 126, 130, 135, 136, 137, 152, 153, 155, 175, 176, 177, 189, 194, 195, 199, 204, 209, 221–222, 245, 246, 253, 284, 285, 288; reactions to, 53, 54, 55, 57, 90, 92, 110, 188, 286; respect for, 121, 122, 124, 155, 167, 187, 204, 213, 216, 217; Spanish version, 25, 27; standing during, 3, 4, 8, 9, 46, 54, 64, 73, 75, 107, 121, 122, 124, 134, 155, 163, 164, 182, 194, 213, 258, 288

National Basketball Association (NBA), 5, 6, 74, 117, 124, 133, 135, 139

National Football League (NFL), 3–4, 4, 9, 39, 40, 53, 62, 62–63, 63, 64, 65, 66, 68, 69, 73, 74, 75, 78, 82, 88, 91, 93, 94, 96, 105, 106, 108, 110, 115, 116, 117, 118, 120, 121–122, 123, 124, 125, 132, 133, 134, 134–135, 136, 137, 138, 140, 151, 153, 155, 163, 168, 179, 180, 182, 188, 189, 190, 193, 230, 263, 278, 284, 285, 286; boycotts, 8–9, 66, 68, 88, 89, 90, 91, 93, 96, 122, 124, 130, 135, 166, 179, 179–180, 180, 181, 182, 183, 184, 187, 194, 225, 228, 229, 230, 231, 232–234, 235, 235–239, 274, 280, 284; protests. *See* protest. *See also* Football players

National Hockey League (NHL), 39

national identity, 9, 45, 47, 55, 198, 210

national school walkout, 257, 264

nationalism, 8, 57, 64, 107, 109, 110, 112, 221, 231, 237

nationhood, 50, 194, 195, 197, 198, 201, 202, 203–204

Navy, United States, 50, 152, 200, 201, 203

NBA. *See* National Basketball Association

Negro spiritual, 52

neighborliness, 210, 221, 221–222, 223, 289

new social movements paradigm, 228, 238

New York Times, 3, 19, 32, 35, 36, 37, 38, 39, 166

newspapers, 17, 19, 21, 28, 32, 33, 34, 35, 36, 37, 38, 39, 40, 41, 63, 102

NFL. *See* National Football League

NHL. *See* National Hockey League

Nixon, Richard, 116, 121, 161

Nkosi Sikelel' iAfrika, 20, 21, 23–24

Obama, Barack, 39, 116, 160, 161

Occupy Wall street, 31, 33, 35, 38, 40, 41, 145, 176

Olympics, 5, 15, 16, 17, 17–18, 19–21, 22, 25, 27–28, 74, 94, 116–117, 242, 243, 285

O'Neal, Shaquille, 133, 135, 136

online news, 77, 79–80

opposing viewpoint conversations, 112, 271, 272, 274, 275

opposition, 4, 6, 9, 18, 28, 31, 40, 68, 69, 70, 92, 98, 106, 107, 119, 130, 132, 133, 135, 136, 141, 145, 204, 225, 226, 283, 286

oppression, 52, 88, 91, 108–109, 117, 129, 136, 137, 141, 147, 196

Owens, Jesse, 6

parasocial relationships, 131, 141, 253, 255–256, 262, 267

Parkland, Florida, 202, 254, 257, 266

Party identification, 78, 159, 160, 161, 162, 166

pastors, 212, 216, 218, 219

patriotic gesture, 46, 219

patriotism, 4, 8, 45–46, 47, 51, 52, 53, 54, 55, 56, 57, 63, 64, 69, 70, 73–74, 76, 81, 88–89, 90, 91, 107, 108, 110, 117, 141, 155, 163, 164, 169, 187, 193, 195, 198, 203, 209, 210, 211–212, 213, 214, 216, 218, 219, 220, 221, 222, 225, 228, 283, 285, 288

Paul, Rand, 162, 163–164

peer influence, 254–255, 264–265, 267
Pelosi, Nancy, 162, 163, 164, 165, 279
Pence, Mike, 118, 180, 187
perceived egregiousness, 227, 230, 237
Petty, Richard, 194, 197, 199
phenomenological, 271, 272
Pledge of Allegiance, 10, 90, 155, 163, 253, 257, 260, 261, 261–262, 267
police, 2, 3, 4, 5, 7, 10, 33, 73, 74, 81, 85, 105, 106, 109, 111, 115, 121, 129, 132, 136, 140, 141, 151, 157, 159, 160, 165, 166, 167, 186–187, 189, 230, 231, 232–234, 235, 237, 258, 261, 284, 285, 287, 288
political, 1, 5–6, 6, 7, 9, 10, 15, 20, 21, 22, 23, 24, 26, 27, 27–28, 32, 36, 37, 38, 40, 40–41, 42, 47, 48, 53, 59, 64–65, 65, 73, 74–75, 76, 79, 80, 80–81, 82, 85, 86, 88, 95–96, 101–102, 103, 104, 106, 107, 112, 116, 119, 126, 130, 131, 139, 145, 159, 161, 162, 166, 167, 168, 169, 177, 183, 184, 186, 193, 195, 197, 204–205, 211, 213, 228, 230, 231, 232–234, 234, 236, 239, 247, 255, 271, 273, 273–274, 275, 276, 278, 279, 280; conservatism, 59–60, 60, 61, 62, 63, 64, 66, 67, 68, 68–69, 69–70, 74, 76, 77, 78, 79, 80, 81, 82, 107, 168, 179, 181, 187, 188, 193, 194, 211, 213, 215, 230, 236, 276, 278, 279, 286, 287; consumerism, 9, 226; correctness, 46, 49–50; ideology, 77, 112, 134, 159, 162; liberalism, 60, 63, 66, 69, 70, 74, 76, 77, 78, 79, 80, 81, 146, 182, 187–188, 213, 215, 230, 244, 276, 278, 286; progressivism, 63–64, 70; symbolism, 46, 47
politicians, 1, 10, 23, 24, 32, 38, 106, 107, 116, 119, 126, 145, 159, 161–162, 164, 166, 168, 170, 197, 218, 231, 232, 232–234, 234, 237, 253, 279, 286
politics, 20, 21, 36, 60, 61, 69, 70, 75, 102, 120, 145, 149, 160, 211, 226, 228, 283, 288
politics of visibility, 177, 186, 187, 188, 189
prayer, 8, 64, 109, 110, 134, 201, 202, 204, 216, 220, 221, 266, 288
prejudice, 2–3, 18, 169, 283

president. *See* United States, president. *See also* Bush, George W.; Obama, Barack; Trump, Donald
pride, 19, 28, 45, 46, 47, 53, 55, 73, 88–89, 90, 105, 107, 108, 115, 122, 132, 155, 198, 203, 204, 285, 288
propaganda, 167, 168
protest, 1, 5, 6, 7, 9, 10, 15, 16, 17, 20–21, 22, 23, 24, 26, 27–28, 31, 32, 32–33, 33, 34, 35, 36, 37, 38, 40, 40–42, 46, 65, 74, 116–117, 131, 136, 138, 140, 145, 151, 155, 164, 165, 175, 176, 177, 185, 188, 189, 193, 204, 253, 254–255, 256, 257, 259–260, 261, 261–262, 262, 265, 265–267, 277, 283, 285. *See also* Protest of United States national anthem; Take-a-knee
protesters, 7, 16, 20–21, 25, 26, 31, 32, 33, 35, 37, 38, 40, 41, 42, 61, 110, 120, 123, 137, 140, 165, 166, 169, 258, 260
proximity, 182, 227–228, 230, 231, 232, 232–234, 234, 235, 237
public relations, 120

race, 1, 2–3, 6, 8, 9, 26, 27, 36, 45, 48, 51, 53, 61, 69, 88–89, 90, 91, 92, 96, 104, 108, 111, 115, 117, 120–121, 123, 124, 125, 131, 137, 140, 141, 145–149, 153–155, 155–156, 157, 161, 166, 226, 228, 229, 231, 232–234, 236, 239, 245, 249, 265, 286–287. *See also* racism
racial inequality, 6, 46, 49, 52, 73, 117, 123, 125, 126, 155, 245
racial injustice, 3, 4, 8, 46, 51, 54, 56, 81, 121, 129, 163, 165, 176, 230, 231, 232, 232–234, 234, 235, 237, 284, 286
racial minorities, 161
racial symbolism, 166
racing, 194, 195, 196, 197, 199, 200, 205; cars, 195, 196, 201, 202, 203; drivers, 194, 195, 196, 197, 201, 202, 203, 204; tracks, 196, 200, 201, 202. *See also* Olympics; NASCAR
racism, 8, 18, 52, 63, 90, 99, 109, 117, 123, 137, 146, 151, 152, 156, 157, 169, 180, 210, 217, 221, 288
radio, 6, 7, 25, 59–60, 60, 61, 62, 63, 64, 65, 66, 66–67, 67–68, 68, 69–70, 133, 139, 148, 193, 286, 287

Rapinoe, Megan, 9, 140, 245, 247, 248
Reid, Eric, 3
relational bonding, 274, 280
relational dissolution, 270
relational partners, 269, 271, 273, 280
relationship preservation, 49
repatriation, 48, 49
Republican, 1, 2, 115, 117, 159, 160, 161, 161–162, 163, 163–164, 164, 165, 166, 167, 168, 168–169, 169, 170, 184, 215, 279, 286
rhetoric, 2, 7, 34, 35, 61, 70, 73, 88–89, 89–90, 90–91, 92, 94, 104, 116, 118, 119, 122, 122–123, 124–126, 130, 131, 132, 137, 141, 148, 153–155, 157, 161, 163, 170, 193, 194, 196, 197, 204, 210, 270, 284; invitational, 10, 222, 270–271, 272, 275, 276, 277, 279, 280, 288; vision, 62, 69–70; visual, 194, 197, 198, 199, 202, 203, 204, 205
Richmond, Cedric, 162
Riggs, Bobby, 5
Robertson, Pat, 216, 217
Roman Catholic, 212, 214, 215, 216, 218, 219, 230
Roosevelt, Theodore, 160
Ryan, Paul, 162, 163, 168, 279

sacrifice. *See* United States Military sacrifice
Sanders, Bernie, 162
San Francisco 49ers, 2, 3, 73, 75, 108, 116, 129, 136, 137, 139, 245, 284
San Francisco Chronicle, 19
school shooting, 202, 204, 254, 257
Scott, Tim, 162, 164
self-determination, 270, 275, 276, 279
self-expansion model, 105, 269
self-righteousness, 277
Semantic community, 176, 177, 178, 179, 180, 181, 182, 183–184, 185–187, 286
sense of community, 45, 47
SIT. *See* Social identity theory
slavery, 8, 9, 46, 48, 49, 51, 52–53, 56
Smith, Tommie, 6, 17, 18, 74, 116, 285
soccer, 5, 9, 140, 245, 248
social activism, 46, 95–96, 215, 221, 255
social connection, 262, 270, 271, 275

social identity, 197, 198, 203, 204, 237
social identity theory (SIT), 159, 160–161, 162, 198, 227, 228, 235
social inequality, 145–146
social media, 6, 6–7, 33, 74, 76, 85–86, 87, 88, 90, 91, 92–95, 96–99, 101, 104, 105, 110, 116, 120, 131–132, 133, 136, 139, 146, 147, 148, 148–149, 150, 151, 153, 155, 156, 157, 166, 175, 177, 179, 184, 185, 186, 189, 193, 222, 256, 263, 266, 277, 286. *See also* Facebook; Instagram; Twitter
social proximity, 230
social reality, 41, 62, 161
societal deviance, 49
solidarity. *See* unity
South, The. *See* Southern culture
South Africa, 5, 15, 17, 20–22, 22–23, 24, 27, 288
Southern culture, 1, 51, 55, 56, 57, 65, 194, 196, 288
spiral of silence, 253, 254–255, 265, 267
Springboks (South African rugby team), 20, 23, 23–24
sports, 5–6, 7, 9, 15–16, 22, 24, 26, 27, 49, 50, 52, 53, 55, 59–60, 60, 61, 62, 62–63, 64, 65, 66–67, 68, 69, 70, 74–75, 91, 106, 110, 117, 121, 124, 129, 130, 136, 148, 151, 152, 155, 166, 170, 194, 195, 196, 198, 199, 204, 205, 210, 216, 239, 241–242, 243, 244, 244–245, 248–249, 249, 253, 255–256, 262–263, 267. *See also* football players; Major League Baseball; National Basketball Association; National Football League; Olympics; soccer
Star-Spangled Banner. *See* National anthem
students, 4, 6, 18, 38, 93, 157, 202, 215, 254, 256, 256–257, 259–260, 261–262, 264, 265, 265–266, 266–267, 277, 285
student rights, 253, 254, 257, 260, 261, 266, 267
suffrage, 31, 32, 35, 35–37, 40, 41, 163
Sydney Morning Herald, 21–22, 23

Take-a-knee, 2, 9, 15, 16, 27, 28, 31, 35, 39, 40, 41, 42, 46, 53, 56, 62, 85, 87,

88, 89, 90, 91, 92, 92–93, 94, 96, 98, 102, 103, 104, 105, 106, 107, 109, 110, 111, 112, 130, 132, 133, 134, 135, 136–137, 138, 139, 140, 141, 147, 148, 148–149, 150–151, 153, 155, 159, 161, 162, 167, 193, 195, 203, 204, 210, 211, 219, 220, 223, 225, 228, 229, 230, 231, 235–236, 237, 248, 249, 253, 254, 255, 256, 257, 257–259, 261–262, 264, 266, 266–267, 267, 271, 272, 273, 275–276, 283, 285, 287, 288

talk radio, 6, 7, 59, 60, 61, 63, 64, 70, 286, 287

TCAT. *See* Twitter content and analysis toolkit

teacher, 17, 51, 258, 259–260, 261, 285

Tebow, Tim, 109, 210

television, 25, 60, 62, 66, 77, 79, 96, 133, 134, 135, 139, 140, 211, 212, 217, 218

terministic screen, 118, 123, 124, 126, 130, 132, 133, 134, 135, 137, 138, 139, 141

theory of identification, 35, 45, 118, 119, 130, 132

Thurmond, Strom, 160

Tinker v. Des Moines, 254

Trump, Donald, 3, 4, 5, 39, 41, 62, 64–65, 66, 67, 69, 70, 74, 75, 81, 86, 88, 91, 94, 106–107, 109, 115–116, 117, 118, 119–126, 133, 134–135, 137–138, 138–139, 140, 141, 155, 160, 164, 165, 165–166, 166, 168, 169, 170, 179–180, 180, 181, 182, 183, 184, 187, 188, 194, 199, 219, 231, 232, 232–234, 234, 237, 254, 278, 284, 286

Twitter, 85, 87, 88, 92, 93, 103, 106, 111, 116, 118, 119–121, 123–124, 125–126, 133, 134, 135, 136, 137, 138, 152, 153, 175, 176–177, 177, 178, 179, 180, 184, 187, 188, 189, 229, 247, 286

Twitter content and analysis toolkit (TCAT), 178, 179

United Kingdom, 21, 49

United States, 9, 15, 16, 17, 31, 32, 37, 48, 49, 60, 62, 63, 64, 65, 67, 69, 70, 77, 78, 104, 145, 146, 147, 148, 151, 156, 164, 166, 170, 177, 194, 195, 209, 214, 217, 220, 225, 229, 242, 253, 254, 289; armed forces. *See* United States military; flag, 65, 200, 202; Olympic team, 5, 17, 18, 19; president, 64, 125, 284

United States military, 39, 51, 75, 76, 89, 90, 107, 108, 109, 122, 125, 133, 152, 200, 202, 203, 204, 210, 220, 230; negative responses to, 4, 75, 76, 91, 94, 95, 112, 133, 137, 155, 159, 163, 165, 166, 167, 169, 230, 287; positive responses to, 53, 73, 116, 132, 141, 169, 182, 204, 213, 231, 237, 283, 285, 286; sacrifice, 107, 108, 109, 132, 141, 166, 167, 217, 230, 287; uniform, 108, 134, 155, 200

unity, 10, 35, 50, 52, 54, 55, 66, 67, 68, 88, 89, 90, 123, 126, 134, 138, 141, 145, 164, 165, 166, 168, 265, 284, 288

veterans, 4, 7, 24, 73, 90, 94, 108, 132, 133, 134, 139, 151, 152, 155, 182, 217; day, 64, 182

Vietnam, 41; protest, 37, 38, 40, 167

villain, 65, 69, 70, 74, 76, 82, 135, 138, 149

Villanueva, Alejandro, 4, 66, 134

war, 9, 49, 56, 214; of 1812, 47, 48, 49, 54; Civil, 1, 32, 164; Cold, 37, 38; Vietnam, 1, 31, 32, 34, 35, 37, 38, 41, 116, 254; World I, 36, 50

Washington Post, 5, 22, 35, 36, 38, 39, 75, 81, 109, 166

Waters, Maxine, 168

white supremacist, 140, 166

white supremacy, 52, 63, 146

women's movement, 32, 34, 41

Women's March, 1

World Series, 5, 50. *See also* baseball

Yankee Doodle, 54

YouTube, 133, 199

About the Editor

Stephen D. Perry earned his PhD from the University of Alabama in 1995. He is the director of graduate programs in communication and the interim dean of the Robertson School of Government at Regent University. He previously taught at Illinois State University and Stillman College. His prior books include *Olympics, Media, and Society* and *Communication Theories for Everyday Life*. He is the former editor of the journal *Mass Communication and Society* and has published more than two dozen peer reviewed journal articles in outlets such as *Journalism and Mass Communication Quarterly, Journal of Communication, Journal of Applied Communication Research, Journal of Radio and Audio Media,* and *Journal of Broadcasting and Electronic Media*. Perry has been a sports broadcaster and journalist, has held local elected office, and served as a Fulbright Scholar in journalism in the Republic of Mauritius.

About the Contributors

Pauline A. Andrea currently serves as public relations manager for DeKalb County Government, Georgia, and has extensive experience as a communications professional and brand strategist. She earned her master of arts in strategic communication from Liberty University, and is currently a doctoral candidate in communication at Regent University.

Nadine Barnett Cosby earned her PhD in communication at Regent University. She has over twenty years of experience in radio, television, and film, working in several capacities at notable media outlets including Fox 5, Lifetime Television Networks, and Disney/ABC. She teaches at Iona College and has won the Hugh F. McCabe award for social justice.

Andrew Bolin currently serves as the program chair and assistant professor of broadcasting at Vincennes University, Indiana. He earned his master of arts degree from the University of Southern Indiana, and has presented his research at academic conferences.

Christina Bullock is a managing editor for the CarMax Digital and Technology Innovation Center and previously served as a senior marketing and communications professional for the National Automobile Dealers Association. She has an MA from Georgetown University in communication, culture, and technology, and is a doctoral candidate in communication at Regent University.

Steve Butler is a manager and program analyst in the FBI's national security branch who earned his master's degree from the University of Oklahoma. From acting as the director of public affairs for the U.S. Marine Corps to his current role in the FBI, Steve has diverse communication experiences.

Katie Clarke serves on the Whitefish School District Board of Trustees in Montana. She completed her master of arts degree from the University of Denver, taught at institutions in Alaska and Hawaii, and has presented at several conferences. She is a doctoral candidate in communication at Regent University.

About the Contributors

Chris Connelly is the chief of staff for Congresswoman Vicky Hartzler. He completed master's degrees from the United States Naval War College and Regent University. Chris has taught at Liberty University and has a lengthy career serving in various political communication roles. He is a doctoral candidate in communication at Regent University.

Jana Duckett earned her master's degree from Regent University and acts as the associate director of digital marketing and communication for the Catholic University of America. She has taught undergraduate and graduate courses and presented papers at various conferences. She is a doctoral candidate in communication at Regent University.

Brooke Dunbar has presented her research at several conferences. She earned her master's degree from Northwestern State University of Louisiana. She teaches at Messiah College and served as a graduate editorial assistant for this volume. She is a doctoral candidate in communication at Regent University.

Kimberly Feld received her master's degree from Arizona State University. She is a residential faculty member at Glendale Community College. Kimberly has extensive international experience as an educator serving in locations from Hungary to Kabul, Afghanistan.

Nancy Flory writes for James Robison's online publication The Stream. She received a master's degree in journalism from the University of North Texas and has taught at the university level. She is a member of Kappa Tau Alpha, an honorary society for excellence in communication and journalism.

Eric Frederick teaches at Pace University, New York, York College, and Academy of Art University, California. His experience ranges from being a television reporter to serving in Christian ministries. Eric earned his master's degree at Westminster Theological Seminary.

Haley Higgs teaches at Georgia Southern University and has presented at various academic conferences. She has public relations experience, and earned her master's degree from Kent State University. She is a doctoral candidate in communication at Regent University.

Colleen Kappeler is visiting professor of communication and digital media at Carthage College, Wisconsin. She earned her master's degree from Union Institute and University, Ohio. Her research has been presented at national conferences, including winning top paper honors at the AEJMC conference in 2017.

Kalah Kemp received her master's degree from Missouri State University. She serves as an assistant professor at College of the Ozarks. Kalah has also taught at American University in Dubai, UAE, and Missouri State University—Liaoning Normal University, China. She has research interests in social media effects and mass communication.

Kelvin King teaches at Lawson State Community College, Alabama. He earned his master's degree from Miami University, Ohio, has presented his research on sports and communication at multiple conferences and has published a novel. He is a doctoral candidate in communication at Regent University.

Brian Mattson earned his master's degree from Grand Rapids Theological Seminary, Michigan. He teaches at Grace Bible College, writes, and creates content for graduate courses. Brian has extensive experience in Christian ministry.

Candace Moore has presented her research on intercultural communication, minorities, and visual representations at academic conferences. She is currently senior communications director at Grace Fellowship Church in the Baltimore, Maryland, area. Candace completed her master's degree at Ball State University, Indiana.

Varaidzo Nyamandi earned her master's degree from Dallas Baptist University. She teaches at Collin College, Tarrant County College, and Richland College, Texas. Varaidzo also attended the Zimbabwe Open University and has worked for nonprofit organizations in Zimbabwe and Southern Africa.

Andrew Phillips serves as the preaching minister for the Graymere Church of Christ in Columbia, Tennessee, and he also teaches for Freed-Hardeman University in Dickson, Tennessee. He earned two master's degrees at Harding School of Theology in Memphis, Tennessee. He is a doctoral candidate at Regent University and has presented his research at academic conferences.

Dara Phillips has taught at Warner University, Florida, and earned her master's degree from Liberty University, Virginia. She has also served in administrative roles in higher education.

Michael Rhett received his master's degree from Montclair State University, New Jersey. He has presented his research at conferences, and currently teaches at Pillar College, New Jersey.

About the Contributors

Deborah Sacra earned her master's degree from East Tennessee State University. She has extensive experience working in Liberia, Africa, as an educator, with radio, and in a medical mission organization.

Jennifer Saint Louis teaches and assists students at Broward College, Florida. She completed her master's degree at Florida International University and has presented at conferences located in Peru, Texas, Florida, and North Carolina. She is a doctoral candidate in communication at Regent University.

Elizabeth Sheffield-Hayes earned her master's degree from Savannah College of Art and Design. She has published magazine articles and maintains a blog. Elizabeth currently teaches at Albany State University, Georgia.

Shreya Shukla was a journalist for *The Telegraph*, India, hosted a children's broadcast in India, and later applied her skills in instructional design and marketing. She completed a second master's degree, in communication, at Regent University.

Michelle Tabbanor earned her master's degree from Regent University. She teaches at Tidewater Community College, Virginia, and is a Doctoral Fellow at Regent University. Michelle has presented her research at the BEA conference and published in the *Journal of Radio and Audio Media*.

Joshua Weiss received his master's degree from Regent University. He teaches at Southwestern Assemblies of God University in Waxahachie, Texas. He is co-founder and chief marketing officer for ARK Mediacom, Inc. He also serves as the general manager for the International Broadcasting Network.

Megan Westhoff teaches at Pittsburg State University, Kansas. She earned her master's degree at Pittsburg State. Megan's research has been presented at several regional and national conferences. She is a doctoral candidate in communication at Regent University.

www.ingramcontent.com/pod-product-compliance
Lightning Source LLC
Chambersburg PA
CBHW032032300426
44117CB00009B/1032